MOSAICS

THIRD EDITION

MOSAICS

FOCUSING ON PARAGRAPHS IN CONTEXT

KIM FLACHMANN

PEARSON
Prentice
Hall

Upper Saddle River, New Jersey 07458

Library of Congress Cataloging-in-Publication Data

Flachmann, Kim.
   Mosaics, focusing on paragraphs in context / Kim Flachmann.—3rd ed.
      p. cm. — (Mosaics)
   Includes index.
      ISBN 0-13-189348-3 (student ed.) — ISBN 0-13-189349-1 (annotated instructor's ed.)
      1. English language—Paragraphs—Problems, exercises, etc.   2. English
   language—Rhetoric—Problems, exercises, etc. I. Title: Focusing on paragraphs in context.
   II. Title. III. Mosaics (Upper Saddle River, N.J.)

   PE1439.F58 2005
   808'.042—dc22

                                                              2003066031

Editorial Director: *Leah Jewell*
Senior Acquisitions Editor: *Craig Campanella*
Editorial Assistant: *Joan Polk*
Developmental Editor-in-Chief: *Rochelle Diogenes*
Development Editor: *Marta Tomins*
Media Project Manager: *Christy Schaack*
Marketing Director: *Beth Mejia*
VP/Director of Production and Manufacturing: *Barbara Kittle*
Production Editor: *Maureen Benicasa*
Production Assistant: *Marlene Gassler*
Copyeditor: *Krystyna Budd*
Permissions Coordinator: *Ron Fox*
Text Permission Specialist: *Jane Scelta*
Prepress & Manufacturing Manager: *Nick Sklitsis*

Prepress & Manufacturing Buyer: *Ben Smith*
Creative Design Director: *Leslie Osher*
Interior & Cover Designer: *Carmen DiBartolomeo, C2K, Inc.*
Director, Image Resource Center: *Melinda Reo*
Manager, Rights and Permissions: *Zina Arabia*
Manager, Visual Research: *Beth Brenzel*
Image Permission Coordinator: *Charles Morris*
Cover Art: *Jellybeans, Omni-Photo Communications, Inc*
Composition: *Interactive Composition Corporation*
Printer/Binder: *Qubecor World Book Services*
Cover Printer: *Phoenix Color Corporation*

This book was set in 11/13 Goudy.

Credits and acknowledgments borrowed from other sources and reproduced, with permission, in this textbook appear on appropriate page within text (or on pages 699–700).

Pearson Education LTD, London
Pearson Education Australia PTY, Limited
Pearson Education Singapore, Pte. Ltd
Pearson Education North Asia Ltd
Pearson Education, Canada, Ltd
Pearson Educación de Mexico, S. A. de C.V.
Pearson Education–Japan
Pearson Education Malaysia, Pte. Ltd
Pearson Education, Upper Saddle River, New Jersey

For
Christopher

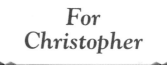

PEARSON
Prentice
Hall

10 9 8 7 6 5 4 3 2 1
ISBN 0-13-189348-3

BRIEF CONTENTS

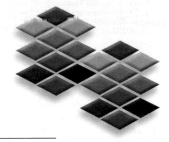

CONTENTS

CHAPTER **13**   **Analyzing Causes and Effects 189**

CHAPTER **14**   **Arguing 206**

PREFACE

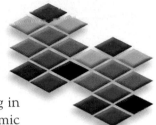

Experience tells us that students have the best chance of succeeding in college if they learn how to respond productively to the varying academic demands made on them throughout the curriculum. One extremely important part of this process is being able to analyze ideas and think critically about issues in many different subject areas. *Mosaics: Focusing on Paragraphs in Context* is the second in a series of three books that teach the basic skills essential to all good academic writing. This series illustrates how the companion skills of reading and writing are parts of a larger, interrelated process that moves back and forth through the tasks of prereading and reading, prewriting and writing, and revising and editing. In other words, the *Mosaics* series shows how these skills are integrated at every stage of the writing process.

THE *MOSAICS* SERIES

This third edition of the *Mosaics* series consists of three books, each with a different emphasis: *Focusing on Sentences in Context*, *Focusing on Paragraphs in Context*, and *Focusing on Essays*. The first book highlights sentence structure, the second book paragraph development, and the third the composition of essays. Each book introduces the writing process as a unified whole and asks students to begin writing in the very first chapter. Each volume also moves from personal to more academic writing. The books differ in the length and level of their reading selections, the complexity of their writing assignments, the degree of difficulty of their revising and editing strategies, and the length and level of their student writing samples.

This entire three-book series is based on the following fundamental assumptions:

- Students build confidence in their ability to read and write by reading and writing.
- Students learn best from discovery and experimentation rather than from instruction and abstract discussions.
- Students need to discover their personal writing process.
- Students learn both individually and collaboratively.

- Students profit from studying both professional and student writing.
- Students benefit most from assignments that actually integrate thinking, reading, and writing.
- Students learn how to revise by following clear guidelines.
- Students learn grammar and usage rules by editing their own writing.
- Students must be able to transfer their writing skills to all their college courses.
- Students must think critically and analytically to succeed in college.

HOW THIS BOOK WORKS

Mosaics: Focusing on Paragraphs in Context teaches students how to write effective paragraphs. For flexibility and easy reference, this book is divided into five parts:

Part I: The Writing Process
Part II: Writing Effective Paragraphs
Part III: Essays: Paragraphs in Context
Part IV: From Reading to Writing
Part V: Handbook

Part I: The Writing Process   All five chapters in Part I demonstrate the cyclical nature of the writing process. They begin with the logistics of getting ready to write and then move systematically through the interlocking stages of the process by following a student essay from prewriting to revising and editing. Part I ends with a quiz that students can take to identify their "Editing Quotient"—their strengths and weaknesses in grammar and mechanics.

Part II: Writing Effective Paragraphs   Part II, the heart of the instruction in this text, teaches students how to write paragraphs by introducing the rhetorical modes as patterns of development. It moves from personal writing to more academic types of writing: describing, narrating, illustrating, analyzing a process, comparing and contrasting, dividing and classifying, defining, analyzing causes and effects, and arguing. Within each chapter, students write their own paragraphs, read professional paragraphs, study the paragraphs of other students, and finally revise and edit the paragraph they wrote earlier in the chapter. By following specific guidelines, students learn how to produce a successful paragraph using each rhetorical mode.

Part III: Essays: Paragraphs in Context   The next section of this text helps students move from writing effective paragraphs to writing effective essays. It systematically illustrates the relationship between a paragraph and an essay. Then it explains the essay through both professional and student examples. Part III ends with a series of writing assignments and workshops designed to encourage students to write, revise, and edit an essay and then reflect on their own writing process.

Part IV: From Reading to Writing   Part IV of this text is a collection of readings arranged by rhetorical mode. Multiple rhetorical strategies are at work in most of these essays, but each is classified according to its primary rhetorical purpose. As a result, students can refer to particular essays in this part that demonstrate a rhetorical mode they are studying in Part II. In this way, students can actually see the features of each rhetorical mode at work in an extended piece of writing. Each professional essay is preceded by pre-reading activities that will help students focus on the topic at hand and then is followed by 10 questions that move students from literal to analytical thinking as they consider the essay's content, purpose, audience, and paragraph structure.

Part V: Handbook   Part V is a complete handbook, including exercises, that covers eight main categories: Sentences, Verbs, Pronouns, Modifiers, Punctuation, Mechanics, Effective Sentences, and Choosing the Right Word. These categories are coordinated with the Editing Checklist that appears periodically throughout this text. Each chapter starts with five self-test questions so that students can determine their strengths and weaknesses in a specific area. The chapters provide at least three types of practice after each grammar concept, moving the students systematically from identifying grammar concepts to writing their own sentences. Each unit ends with a practical "Editing Workshop" that asks students to use the skills they just learned as they work with another student to edit their own writing. Unit Tests—including practice with single sentences and paragraphs—complete each unit.

APPENDIXES

The appendixes will help students keep track of their progress in the various skills they are learning in this text. References to these appendixes are interspersed throughout the book so that students know when to use them as they study the concepts in each chapter:

Appendix 1: Critical Thinking Log
Appendix 2: Revising and Editing Peer Evaluation Forms
Appendix 3: Revising and Editing Peer Evaluation Forms for an Essay

OVERALL GOAL

Ultimately, each book in the *Mosaics* series portrays writing as a way of thinking and processing information. One by one, these books encourage students to discover how the "mosaics" of their own writing process work together to form a coherent whole. By demonstrating the interrelationship among thinking, reading, and writing on progressively more difficult levels, these books promise to help prepare students for success in college throughout the curriculum.

UNIQUE FEATURES

Several unique and exciting features separate this book from other basic writing texts:

- It moves students systematically from personal to academic writing.
- It uses both student writing and professional writing as models.
- It demonstrates all aspects of the writing process through student writing.
- It integrates reading and writing throughout the text.
- It teaches revising and editing through student writing.
- It features culturally diverse reading selections that are of high interest to students.
- It teaches rhetorical modes as patterns of thought.
- It helps students discover their own writing process.
- It includes a complete handbook with exercises.
- It offers worksheets for students to chart their progress in reading and writing.

ACKNOWLEDGMENTS

I want to acknowledge the support, encouragement, and sound advice of several people who have helped me through the development of the *Mosaics* series. First, Prentice Hall has provided guidance and inspiration for this project through the wisdom of Craig Campanella, senior acquisitions editor; the insights and vision of Marta Tomins and Harriett Prentiss, development editors; the diligence and clairvoyance of Maureen Benicasa, production editor; the foresight and prudence of Leah Jewell, editorial director; the boundless creative inspiration of Rachel Falk, former marketing manager; the resourceful oversight of Rochelle Diogenes, editor-in-chief, development; the brilliant leadership of Yolanda de Rooy, President of Humanities and Social Sciences; the hard work and patience of Jane Scelta, permissions editor; the guidance and fortitude of Krystyna Budd, copyeditor; and the common sense and organization of Joan Polk, editorial assistant for developmental English. Also, this book would not be a reality without the insightful persistence of Phil Miller, publisher for Modern Languages.

I want to give very special thanks to Cheryl Smith, my constant source of inspiration in her role as consultant and adviser for the duration of this project. She was also the author of the margin annotations and the coordinator of the *Mosaics Instructor's Resource Manuals*. I am also grateful to Rebecca Hewett, Valerie Turner, and Li'i Pearl for their discipline and hard work on the *Instructor's Resource Manuals* for each of the books in the series. And I want to thank Brooke King, Crystal Huddleston, Zandree Stidham, and Anne Elrod for their expertise and assistance.

In addition, I am especially grateful to the following reviewers who have guided me through the development and revision of this book: Lisa Berman, Miami-Dade Community College; Patrick Haas, Glendale Community College; Jeanne Campanelli, American River College; Dianne Gregory, Cape Cod Community College; Clara Wilson-Cook, Southern University at New Orleans; Thomas Beery, Lima Technical College; Jean Petrolle, Columbia College; David Cratty, Cuyahoga Community College; Allison Travis, Butte State College; Suellen Meyer, Meramec Community College; Jill Lahnstein, Cape Fear Community College; Stanley Coberly, West Virginia State University at Parkersville; Jamie Moore, Scottsdale Community College; Nancy Hellner, Mesa Community College; Ruth Hatcher, Washtenaw Community College; Thurmond Whatley, Aiken Technical College; W. David Hall, Columbus State Community College; Marilyn Coffee, Fort Hays State University; Richard Pepp, Massasoit Community College; Harvey Rubinstein, Hudson County Community College; T. Allen Culpepper, Manatee Community College; Elizabeth Marsh, Bergen Community College; Bonnie Ronson, Hillsborough Community College; Ann Hamblin, Amarillo College; JoAnn Foriest, Prairie State College; and Ann A. Engeler, Northwest Arkansas Community College.

I also want to express my gratitude to my students, from whom I have learned so much about the writing process, about teaching, and about life itself, and to Cheryl Smith's classes, who tested various sections of the books and gave me good ideas for revising them over the past three years. Thanks finally to the students who contributed paragraphs and essays to this series: Josh Ellis, Jolene Christie, Mary Minor, Michael Tiede, and numerous others.

Finally, I owe a tremendous personal debt to the people who have lived with this project for the last two years; they are my closest companions and my best advisors: Michael, Christopher, and Laura Flachmann. To Michael, I owe additional thanks for the valuable support and feedback he has given me through the entire process of creating and revising this series.

Kim Flachmann

I

THE WRITING PROCESS

What student's mind—what writer's mind—has not begun to write
without knowing really where it will go, only to learn at the end
where it meant to start?

—Victor Kantor Burg

Part I of *Mosaics* is designed to build your confidence as a writer. In
these five chapters, you will learn more about the writing process so that
you can understand and take control of the unique way you write. As you
mold the writing process into a series of stages and activities that will work
for you, you will become more aware of your own strengths and weaknesses
as a writer. You can then use this information throughout the text to establish your identity in the community of writers.

1 GETTING STARTED

The simple act of using the written word to communicate makes a person a writer. Whether you use writing to make a grocery list, e–mail a friend, do your history assignment, or write a report for your manager, you are part of a community of writers. In fact, you *are* a writer.

Any piece of writing more formal than a grocery list, however, is usually the result of a sequence of activities. On the surface, these activities may seem to have very little to do with the act of writing itself. But they make up what is called the *writing process*, and learning to use this process to help you communicate your ideas is what this book is all about.

YOUR PERSONAL WRITING RITUAL

Though all writers are different, some general principles apply to everyone—students and professional writers alike. Before you can begin the writing process, you need to set aside a time and place for your task, gather supplies, and think of yourself as a writer.

1. *Set aside a special time for writing, and plan to do nothing else during that time.* The dog's bath can wait until tomorrow, the kitchen appliances don't have to be scrubbed today, drawers can be cleaned and organized some other time, and the dirt on the car won't turn to concrete overnight. When you first get a writing task, a little procrastination is good because it gives your mind time to plan your approach to the assignment. The trick is to know when to quit procrastinating and get down to work.

2. *Find a comfortable place with few distractions.* In her famous essay *A Room of One's Own*, Virginia Woolf claims that all writers have a basic need for space, privacy, and time. You need to set up a place of your own that suits your needs as a writer, and it should be a place where you are not distracted or interrupted. Some people work best sitting in a straight chair at a desk, while others write in a big armchair or on a bed.

The particular place doesn't matter, as long as you feel comfortable writing there.

Even if you are lucky enough to have a private study area, you may find that you still need to make some adjustments. For example, you might want to turn off the ringer on your phone during the time you spend on your writing assignments. Or you may discover that tuning your radio to a jazz station helps you shut out noise from other parts of the house but doesn't distract you in the way that talk shows or rock music might. One student may write sitting in bed with her legs crossed, wearing jeans and a T-shirt; another may prefer sprawling on the floor in pajamas. The point is this: Whatever your choices, you need to set up a working environment that is comfortable for you.

3. *Gather your supplies before you begin to write.* Who knows what great idea might escape while you search for a pen that works or a for-matted disk! Some writers use a legal pad and a pencil to get started on a writing task, while others go straight to their computers. One of the main advantages of working on a computer is that once you type in your ideas, changing them or moving them around is easy. As a result, you are more likely to revise when you work on a computer and, there-fore, you will probably turn in a better paper. Whatever equipment you choose, make sure it is ready at the time you have set aside to write.

4. *Think of yourself as a writer.* Once you have a time and place for writ-ing and all the supplies you need, you are ready to discover your own writing process. Understanding your unique habits and rituals is ex-tremely important to your growth as a writer. So in the course of recog-nizing yourself as a writer, take a moment now to record some of your own preferences when you write.

P r a c t i c e 1 Explain the rituals you instinctively follow as you pre-pare to write. Where do you write? At what time of day do you produce your best work? Do you like noise? Quiet? What other details describe your writ-ing environment? What equipment do you use to write?

KEEPING A JOURNAL

The word *journal* means "a place for daily writing." Your journal is a place for you to record ideas, snatches of conversation, dreams, descriptions of people, pictures of places or objects—whatever catches your attention.

If you use a notebook for your journal, take some time to pick a size and color that you really like. Some people choose spiral-bound notebooks;

others prefer cloth-bound books or loose-leaf binders. You might even want a notebook divided into sections so that different types of entries can have their own location. The choice is yours—unless your instructor specifies a particular journal. Just remember that a journal should be a notebook you enjoy writing in and carrying with you.

Your journal might even be electronic. However, unless you have a laptop or hand-held computer, you won't have your electronic journal with you all the time. So you need to schedule time to write at your computer every day. If you use a hand-held computer, remember to download your entries to your main computer on a regular basis. Also be sure to back up computer journal entries on a disk and save your work fairly often so you don't lose anything in a power failure. You may also want to print hard copies of your journal entries to take with you to class.

To help improve your life as a writer, you will find a personal journal extremely valuable. As with any skill, the more you practice, the more you will improve. In addition, your journal is a collection of thoughts and topics for your writing assignments. In other words, your journal is a place to both generate and retrieve your ideas. Finally, writing can help you solve problems. Writing in your journal can help you discover what you think and feel about specific issues and lets you think through important choices you have to make.

You can use this textbook to help you establish the habit of journal writing. For example, in your journal you might answer the questions that accompany the instruction in Parts II and III of this text, the readings in Part IV, and the writing exercises in the handbook (Part V). You might also want to use your journal for prewriting or generating ideas on a specific topic. Keeping track of your journal is much easier than tracking down assorted scraps of paper when you need them.

Making at least one section of your journal private is also a good idea. Sometimes when you think on paper or let your imagination loose, you don't want to share the results with anyone, but those notes can be very important in finding a subject to write about or in developing a topic.

Everyone's journal entries will be different and will often depend on the instructor's objectives in a particular course. But some basic advice applies to all entries, whether you keep your journal on paper or on a computer.

1. Date your entries. (Jotting down the time is also useful so you can see when your best ideas occur.)

2. Record anything that comes to your mind, and follow your thoughts wherever they take you (unless your instructor gives you different directions).

3. Download or tape anything into your journal that stimulates your thinking or writing—cartoons, magazine ads, poems, pictures, advice columns, and pages from the Internet.

4. Think of your journal as someone to talk to—a friend who will keep your cherished ideas safe and sound and won't talk back or argue with you.

◆ *P r a c t i c e   2*   Begin your own journal.

1. Buy a notebook that you like, and write in it.
2. Make at least two journal entries on your computer.
3. Which type of journal do you prefer—paper or electronic? Write an entry explaining your preference.

THE WRITING PROCESS

The writing process begins the minute you get a writing assignment. It involves all the activities you do, from choosing a topic to turning in a final draft. During this time, you will be thinking about your topic on both a subconscious and conscious level. Whether you are washing your car, reading in the library, preparing a meal, or writing a draft of your paper, you are going through your writing process. The main parts of the process are outlined here.

Prewriting

Prewriting refers to all activities that help you explore a subject, generate ideas about it, settle on a specific topic, establish a purpose, and analyze the audience for your essay. In Chapter 2, you will learn different strategies for accomplishing these goals before you actually begin to write a draft of your paragraph or essay. Your mission at this stage is to stimulate your thinking before and during the act of writing. Every time you think of a new idea at any time during the writing process, you are prewriting.

Writing

When you have lots of ideas to work with, you are ready to start writing. Writing involves expanding some of your best ideas, organizing your thoughts to reflect your purpose, and writing a first draft. To start on your draft, you may want to spread out your class notes, your journal entries, or various other prewriting notes so that you can start to string your ideas together into coherent sentences. This is the time to keep your thoughts flowing without worrying too much about grammar, punctuation, or spelling.

Revising

As you may already suspect, the process of writing is not finished with your first draft. You should always revise your work to make it stronger and better. Revising involves rethinking your content and organization so that your writing says exactly what you want it to. (Editing, the last step, focuses on correcting grammar and spelling.) Your main goal in revising is to make sure that the purpose of your essay is clear to your audience and that your main ideas are supported with details and examples. In addition, you should check that your organization is logical.

Editing

The final step in the writing process is editing. In this stage, you should read your paragraph or essay slowly and carefully to make sure no errors in grammar, punctuation, mechanics, or spelling have slipped into your draft. Such errors can distract your reader from the message you are trying to communicate or can cause communication to break down altogether. Editing gives you the chance to clean up your draft so that your writing is clear and precise.

Writing as a Cycle

Even though we talk about the stages of writing, writing is actually a cyclical process, which means that at any point you may loop in and out of other stages. The diagram on the next page shows how the stages of the writing process can overlap.

Once you start on a writing project, the stages of writing do not occur in any specific order. You may change a word (revise) in the very first sentence that you write and then think of another detail (prewrite) that you can add to your opening sentence and next cross out and rewrite a misspelled word (edit)—all in the first two minutes of your writing task. Although you may approach every writing project in a different way, we hope that as you move through Part I, you will establish a framework for your personal writing process and start to get comfortable as a writer working within that framework.

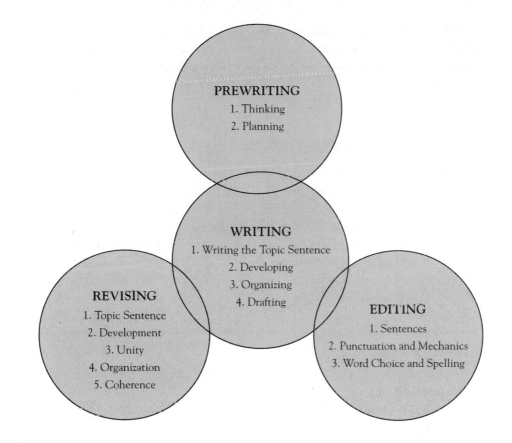

PREWRITING
1. Thinking
2. Planning

WRITING
1. Writing the Topic Sentence
2. Developing
3. Organizing
4. Drafting

REVISING
1. Topic Sentence
2. Development
3. Unity
4. Organization
5. Coherence

EDITING
1. Sentences
2. Punctuation and Mechanics
3. Word Choice and Spelling

◆ *Practice 3*

1. Explain prewriting in your own words.

   _____

   _____

2. Describe your writing environment.

   _____

   _____

3. What does "writing" consist of?

   _____

   _____

4. What is the difference between revising and editing?

_____

_____

WRITING ASSIGNMENT

This first writing assignment is much like the writing tasks you will be responding to throughout this book. You'll be working on this assignment yourself over the next four chapters as you apply what you are learning about the writing process. At the same time, we will follow the work of a student named Travis Morehouse so you can see how he approaches and completes the same assignment. By the end of Chapter 5, you will have a feel for the entire writing process, which is essential to strengthening your identity as a writer.

WRITE YOUR OWN PARAGRAPH

Think about a favorite place that you visit frequently. It could be somewhere that is peaceful, beautiful, or busy. It could be a restaurant, a park, or a place of employment or worship. Then describe this location for someone who has never been there. Explain to your readers the sights, sounds, tastes, smells, and textures that attract you to this spot.

PREWRITING

Many students are surprised that a number of steps in the writing process occur before the actual act of putting words on paper. These steps fall into the general category of **prewriting.** Prewriting activities help us do the following tasks:

- Explore a subject
- Generate ideas about the subject
- Settle on a specific topic
- Establish a purpose
- Analyze our audience

Let's begin this chapter by looking at activities that many writers use to stimulate their thinking as they approach a writing assignment. You will get a chance to try each one. Consider keeping your responses to these activities in a journal that you can refer to throughout the course.

THINKING

Thinking is always the initial stage of any writing project. It's a time to explore your topic and let your mind run free over the material you have to work with. We'll explore six activities that promise to stimulate your best thoughts: reading, freewriting, brainstorming, clustering, questioning, and discussing. You will see how Travis Morehouse uses each strategy and then have a chance to try out the strategy yourself.

Reading

Sometimes a good way to jump-start your thinking and your writing process is to surf the 'Net or read an article on your topic. If you take notes on sources as you read, you may find yourself spinning off into your own thoughts on the subject.

Travis's Reading Travis read the following paragraph from an essay titled "Micanopy" by Bailey White. It stimulated his thoughts about his own favorite place, so he jotted several notes to himself in the margins.

Wow! She   But the reason I drive the two hundred miles year
must   after year is the bookstore. The building is tall, a
really   beautiful pink brick. The sign says,
like this
place!
                                O. Brisky
                                 Books
                              Old Used Rare
                             Bought and Sold
                          Out of Print Search Service   *What is*
                                                                     this?

I can   Even before you go inside, you can smell the old,
always   used, and rare books. On sunny days, Mr. Brisky
smell old   arranges a collection of books on a table on the side-
books.   walk. There are books in the windows and stacks of
                     books on the floor just inside the entrance. From an
Name of   open back door the misty green light of Micanopy
town?   shines into the dust. Tendrils of wisteria have crept in *Plants?*
                     through the doorway and are stealthily making their
                     way toward the religion and philosophy section.

Later, Travis made this entry in his journal.

> I really liked Bailey White's description of the bookstore. The first sentence shows how much she likes this place. She gives so many examples about why she drives two hundred miles just to go to this bookstore. I don't really have a place that I would drive that far to see. I wish I did! I wouldn't say a bookstore or library is my favorite place. I get too bored looking at so many books, but I do like feeling alone in such a big place. I guess my favorite place would just be out of the house. Far, far away where no one can find me. I love to be by myself, even though most of my friends don't understand this.

Your Reading Read the following paragraph from "Magpies," an essay by Amy Tan (pages 256–260), and take notes in the margins as you read. Then, in your journal, write down any thoughts this paragraph stimulates.

Sitting in this bed, I admired everything as if I were a princess. This room had a glass door that led to a balcony. In front of the window door was a round table of the same wood as the bed. It too sat on carved lion's legs and was surrounded by four chairs. A servant had already put tea and sweet cakes on the table and was now lighting the houlu, a small stove for burning coal.

Freewriting

Writing about anything that comes to your mind is freewriting. You should write without stopping for five to ten minutes. Do not worry about grammar or spelling. If you get stuck, repeat an idea or start rhyming words. The mere act of writing makes writers think of other ideas. So just keep writing.

Travis's Freewriting   Travis had trouble freewriting, but he followed directions and just started in.

Here I am in English class, and we're supposed to be freewriting. But I don't know what to write about—my mind is a complete blank. Blank blank blankety blank. I could write about my car. It's been burning oil like crazy. Wherever I drive, there's a trail of blue smoke. I have to put in a quart of oil every week or two! But I don't want to take it in because I don't have the money to get it fixed. The rest of my tuition payment is due. I need money coming in, not going out. But if I don't get my car fixed, I'm not going to be able to get to school. That would not be good. School ends up being an escape for me—from my family, from my friends, from my teachers. It's where my dreams are. I don't know what these dreams are yet, but I think they're at school. For the first time in my life I actually like school. Who would have thought?

Focused freewriting is the same procedure focused on a specific topic—either one your instructor gives you or one you choose. It is a systematic way of turning thoughts and impressions into words.

Travis's Focused Freewriting   Travis produced the following focused freewriting in his journal. He is trying to get his mind ready to write about his favorite place.

> I don't know what I consider to be my favorite place.
> I usually just get in my car and drive when I want to
> get away from things. I guess I can consider that ridge
> I sometimes go to as my favorite place. I do end up
> driving there when I just feel like I want to leave
> everything behind. I like how I can see the city and
> the river from up high. I especially like to be there
> during sunsets because it is always so beautiful. I feel
> a peace that I can't seem to describe. Although no one
> would really understand anyway.

Your Freewriting   To start preparing for your own paragraph, try a focused freewriting assignment by writing in your journal about some of your favorite places.

Brainstorming

Like freewriting, brainstorming draws on free association—one thought naturally leads to another. But brainstorming is usually done in list form. You can brainstorm by yourself, with a friend, or with a group. Regardless of the method, list whatever comes into your mind on a topic—ideas, thoughts, examples, facts. As with freewriting, don't worry about grammar or spelling.

Travis's Brainstorming   Here is Travis's brainstorming on his favorite place:

> the ridge—high above the city
> can see the city
> the river—always has boats
> sometimes I can see cars
> the sunsets are really beautiful
> the city lights always look cool when it gets dark
> sometimes it can get really cold at night
> it's peaceful
> I can be alone
> I can think out my problems

Your Brainstorming   Brainstorm in your journal about a favorite place or several favorite places.

Clustering

Clustering is like brainstorming, but it has the advantage of showing how your thoughts are related. To cluster, take a sheet of blank paper, write a key word or phrase in the center of the page, and draw a circle around it. Next, write down and circle any related ideas that come to mind. As you add ideas, draw lines to the thoughts they are related to. Try to keep going for two or three minutes. When you finish, you'll have a map of your ideas that can help you find your way to a good paragraph.

Travis's Cluster   Here is Travis's cluster:

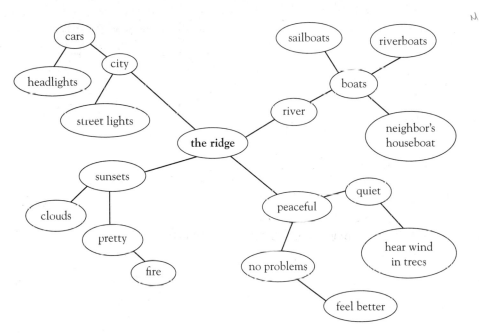

Your Cluster   Write "favorite place" in the middle of a piece of paper, circle it, and draw a cluster of your own personal associations with these words.

Questioning

Journalists use the questions known as the "five *W*s and one *H*"—Who? What? When? Where? Why? and How?—to check that they've included all the important information in a news story. You can use these same questions to generate ideas on a writing topic.

Travis's Questions   Here is how Travis used questioning to generate ideas on his topic:

Who?	I most enjoy being by myself up here, but I sometimes bring my friend Carlos because he thinks it's cool too.
What?	My favorite place that is really quiet and peaceful, the ridge that sits high above the city.
When?	My absolute favorite time to be here is when the sun goes down. The sun looks like it's on fire before it finally sets.
Where?	The ridge that's high above the city.
Why?	I can think up here. The beautiful sunset and the city and river help me clear my mind so I can solve problems.
How?	Just watching the boats and looking at the view make me feel better.

Your Questions   In your journal, answer these six questions about your favorite place: Who? What? When? Where? Why? How?

Discussing

Run your ideas by friends, classmates, and tutors. Often they'll have a perspective on your topic that will give you some entirely new ideas. Make sure you record your notes from these conversations so you don't lose the ideas.

Travis's Discussion   Here are Travis's notes from a conversation he had with his roommate about his favorite place:

> Because I have never spent much time thinking about the ridge, I am now trying to figure out why I enjoy this spot so much. When discussing the ridge with my roommate, Ralph, I remember that it's during sunsets when I feel most at peace. We discussed my love for the river and how the beauty of the place makes my problems disappear and how city lights shine after the sun goes down. I realize that this spot means more to me than I first thought. I want to tell my classmates about this place without sounding sentimental; I'm afraid that people will think I am too sensitive.

Your Discussion   Discuss your favorite place with someone, and record notes from your conversation in your journal.

◆ *Practice 1A*   Now that you have been introduced to several prewriting strategies, which is your favorite? Why do you like it best?

◆ *Practice 1B*   Using two prewriting strategies on one assignment is often a good idea. What is your second favorite prewriting strategy? Why do you like this strategy?

PLANNING

In this course, you'll be writing paragraphs—single paragraphs at first and paragraphs in essays later. A paragraph is a group of sentences on a single topic. The first line of each paragraph is indented to show that a new topic or subtopic is starting. Although paragraphs vary in length, typical paragraphs in student themes usually range from 50 to 250 words, averaging about 100 words.

Writing a paragraph takes planning. You need to make certain decisions about your subject, your purpose for writing, and your audience before you actually write, so that the task of writing is as smooth and stress-free as possible.

- **What is your subject (person, event, object, idea, etc.)?** A paragraph focuses on a single topic and includes related thoughts and details. Your first decision, therefore, is about your *subject:* What are you going to write about? Sometimes your topic is given to you—for example, when your sociology instructor assigns a paper on drug abuse among teenagers. But at other times, you choose your own topic. In such cases, choosing a subject that interests you is the best strategy. You will have more to say, and you will enjoy writing much more if you find your topic appealing.

- **What is your purpose?** Your *purpose* is your reason for writing a paragraph. Your purpose could be to explore your feelings on a topic (*to do personal writing*), to tell a friend about something funny that happened to you (*to entertain*), to explain something or share information (*to inform*), or to convince others of your position on a controversial issue (*to persuade*). Whatever your purpose, deciding on it in advance makes writing your paragraph much easier.

1.

- *Who is your audience?* Your *audience* consists of the people for whom your message is intended. The more you know about your audience, the more likely you are to accomplish your purpose. The audience for your writing in college is usually your instructor, who represents what is called a "general audience"—people with an average amount of knowledge on most subjects. A general audience is the group to aim for in all your writing unless you are given other directions.

Practice 2 Identify the subject, purpose, and audience of each of the following paragraphs.

1. At the heart of *America's Promise* are five basic promises made to every child in America. To point kids in the right direction, to help them grow up strong and ready to take their place as successful adults, these five promises must be fulfilled for all youth: (1) an ongoing relationship with a caring adult—parent, mentor, tutor, or coach; (2) a safe place with structured activities during non-school hours; (3) a healthy start; (4) a marketable skill through effective education; and (5) a chance to give back through community service. (COLIN POWELL, "A Promise to Our Youth")

   Subject: _America's promise to the youth_

   Purpose: _to point Adults in the right direc_

   Audience: _Parents and children_

2. My best friend just got arrested for rioting. Until yesterday, she was a great student with an unblemished record, and now she will be spending school time in court trying to keep out of jail. I don't know why she did it; she says she got caught up in the energy of the crowd. That just sounds like an excuse to me. She knew she was doing something wrong, she knew she was hurting business owners, and she did it anyway. I know she'll be punished for what she did and that will be humiliating enough, but I don't think she realizes her parents, friends, and teachers will now see her as someone who has the potential for getting into trouble.

   Subject: _trouble with law_

   Purpose: _to informe_

   Audience: _Younger Adults_

3. If you're a man, at some point a woman will ask you how she looks. "How do I look?" she'll ask. You must be careful how you answer this question. The best technique is to form an honest yet sensitive opinion, then collapse on the floor with some kind of fatal seizure. Trust me. This is the easiest way out, because you will never come up with the right answer. (DAVE BARRY, "The Ugly Truth About Beauty")

Subject: _Womens Appearance_

Purpose: _informe or entertain et_

Audience: _Men_

4. The press is about finding the truth and telling it to the people. In pursuit of that, I am making a case for the broadest possible freedom of the press. However, with that great gift comes great responsibility. The press—print and electronic—has the power to inform, but that implies the power to distort. The press can lead our society toward a more mature and discriminating understanding of the process by which we choose our leaders, make our rules, and construct our values, or it can encourage people to despise our systems and avoid participating in them. The press can teach our children a taste for violence, encourage a fascination with perversity and inflicted pain, or it can show them a beauty they have not known. The press can make us wiser, fuller, surer, and sweeter than we are. (MARIO CUOMO, "Freedom of the Press Must Be Unlimited")

Subject: _Freedom of press_

Purpose: _To informe or convince_

Audience: _Any body_

5. My friends say that when I get in my car, I become blind to my surroundings. I have driven next to friends and not seen them, have been waiting at stop lights next to friends and not noticed them, and have passed friends on a small two-lane road and not known it. I tell them it's because I am very engrossed in my driving; I take driving a vehicle very seriously. Actually, though, I am usually daydreaming about where I wish I could be going.

Subject: _Driving Alertness_

Purpose: *Informe*

Audience: *general*

Travis's Plans   Travis made the following decisions before beginning to write about his favorite place:

Subject: the peacefulness of the ridge

Purpose: personal—to reflect on the characteristics of my favorite place

Audience: general—I want people who read this to imagine a similar place where they can think about their problems

Your Plans   Identify the subject, purpose, and audience of the paragraph you will write on your favorite place.

Subject: _____

Purpose: _____

Audience: _____

WRITING

Writing is made up of several steps that lead you to your first draft. At this point, you have been given a topic (a favorite place) and worked through various prewriting techniques with that subject. You have also generated a number of ideas that you can use in a paragraph and decided on a subject, purpose, and audience. In this chapter, you will learn first how to write a topic sentence. Next, you will add some specific, concrete details to your notes from prewriting activities and choose a method of organization for your paragraph. Finally, you will write the first draft of your paragraph, which you will then revise and edit in Chapters 4 and 5. Again, you will be writing alongside Travis as he goes through the writing process with you.

WRITING THE TOPIC SENTENCE

The decisions you made in Chapter 2 about subject, purpose, and audience will lead you to your topic sentence. The **topic sentence** of a paragraph is its controlling idea. A typical paragraph consists of a topic sentence and details that expand on the topic sentence. Although a topic sentence can appear as the first or last sentence of its paragraph, it functions best as the first sentence. Beginning a paragraph with the topic sentence gives direction to the paragraph and provides a kind of road map for the reader.

A topic sentence has two parts—a topic and a statement about that topic. The topic should be limited enough that it can be developed in the space of a paragraph.

Topic	Limited Topic	Statement
Writing	In-class writing	is difficult but is good practice for a job.
Voting	Voting in the United States	is a right of citizenship.

Sports	Participation in sports	makes people well rounded.
Anger	Road rage	seems to me like a waste of energy.

◆ **P r a c t i c e   1 A**   Limit the following topics. Then develop them into statements that could be topic sentences.

Topic	Limited Topic	Statement
1. Weekends	_____	_____
2. Work	_____	_____
3. Restaurants	_____	_____
4. Reading	_____	_____
5. Winter	_____	_____

◆ **P r a c t i c e   1 B**   Complete the following topic sentences. Make sure they are general enough to be developed into a paragraph but not too broad.

1. Automobile accidents _____.

2. _____ is my favorite movie.

3. Smoking _____.

4. Teen pregnancies _____.

5. _____ must be brought under control in the United States.

◆ **P r a c t i c e   1 C**   Write topic sentences for the following paragraphs.

1. _____

When I come home from school, Rusty is always the first one to greet me. He usually jumps on me and knocks me down, but I am used to this. After we wrestle on the ground, he follows me to my room and sits by my feet while I do homework. Every once in a while he'll nudge my hand so I will pet him. When I go to bed, Rusty always sleeps with me at night, which is nice because I can snuggle up to his fur and know that I am safe.

2. _____

First, you must undergo an intensive scuba diving class that includes a lot of reading and calculating. Next, you must practice scuba skills in a pool so you can learn how to react if, for instance, your breathing regulator comes out of your mouth underwater. Then you have four checkout dives in the ocean. Finally, after six weeks of preparation, you'll be a certified scuba diver.

3. _____

It will be two stories and will be painted blue. Inside it will have at least four bedrooms and an office for me to work. It will have a grand kitchen and enough room to entertain all my friends and co-workers. A pool would be nice, with a lush backyard for my dogs to get lost in. And I hope that it will be close to my mom and dad's house.

Travis's Topic Sentence   Travis writes a topic sentence that he thinks represents his whole paragraph. It introduces a ridge in his hometown.

Limited Topic	**Statement**
A high, wooded ridge	overlooks my hometown.

Your Topic Sentence   Write a topic sentence here that can serve as the controlling idea for your paragraph.

Limited Topic   **Statement**

_____   _____

DEVELOPING

After you have written a topic sentence, you are ready to develop the specific details that will make up the bulk of your paragraph. Later in this text, you will learn about different methods of developing your ideas, such as describing, using examples, comparing and contrasting, and defining. For now, we are simply going to practice generating concrete supporting details and examples that are directly related to a specific topic. Concrete words refer to anything you can see, hear, touch, smell, or taste, like *trees, boats, water, friends, fire alarm,* and *fresh bread.* They make writing come alive because they help us picture what the writer is discussing.

◆ **P r a c t i c e   2** For each of the following topic sentences, list five details and/or examples to develop them.

1. If I win the lottery, I will be the envy of all my friends.

   _____

   _____

   _____

   _____

   _____

2. People can't always count on their relatives.

   _____

   _____

   _____

   _____

   _____

3. My favorite pastime is fun as well as challenging.

   _____

   _____

   _____

   _____

   _____

4. Palm readers must lead interesting lives.

   _____

   _____

   _____

_____

_____

5. People living in big cities need never get bored.

_____

_____

_____

_____

Travis's Development   To come up with concrete details and examples that would support his topic sentence, Travis goes back to the questions he used during his planning stage (five *W*'s and one *H*) and adds these details.

Who?	I like to be by myself
What?	rowboats, sailboats, motorboats, freight liners
	I like the sailboats best because I love to sail
	car lights outlining the streets in the distance
When?	sunset—pink and purple
	light at dusk; moonlight
	headlights streaming through the darkness
Where?	outside the city
	above the city
	people in the city don't know I am watching
Why?	the scent of honeysuckle on a hot summer day
	the smell of the earth
	birds building nests, scolding other birds to keep them away
	traffic noises, wind, rain, thunder, lightning
	problems fade away
How?	peaceful, quiet
	I can think out my problems

Your Development   Choose one of the prewriting activities you learned in Chapter 2, and use it to generate more specific details and examples about your topic sentence.

ORGANIZING

At this point, you are moving along quite well in the writing process. You were given a topic for your paragraph (a favorite place). You have determined your subject, purpose, and audience, and you have written your topic sentence. You have also thought of details, examples, and facts to develop your topic sentence. Now you are ready to organize your ideas. What should come first? What next? Would one way of organizing your ideas accomplish your purpose better than another?

Most paragraphs are organized in one of five ways:

1. General to particular
2. Particular to general
3. Chronologically (by time)
4. Spatially (by physical arrangement)
5. One extreme to another

Let's look at these methods of organization one by one.

General to Particular

The most common method of organizing details in a paragraph is to begin with a general statement and then offer particular details to prove or explain that topic sentence. The general-to-particular paragraph looks like this, although the number of details will vary:

Topic Sentence
  Detail
  Detail
  Detail

Here is a paragraph organized from general to particular:

Over the last two years, I have become an adventurous person be-cause of my friend Taylor. When I met Taylor, she had just signed up for a rock-climbing class, and it sounded so interesting that I joined too. We loved climbing the amazingly tall rocks so much that we decided to try skydiving. We both jumped out of a plane attached to a qualified instructor; it was incredible. In fact, we've been back four times. Now we are trying our hands at exploring the ocean and are in the middle of scuba-diving lessons. By the time we are certified, we'll be off on a two-week vacation to South America, where we can participate in all three exciting sports.

P r a c t i c e   3 A   Turn to the essay "What Is Poverty?" on page 325, and find two paragraphs organized from general to particular.

P r a c t i c e   3 B   Write a paragraph organized from general to particular that begins with this sentence: "Several people I know have broken bad habits."

Particular to General

Occasionally, the reverse order of particular to general is the most effective way to organize a paragraph. In this case, examples or details start the paragraph and lead up to the topic sentence, which appears at the end of the paragraph. This type of organization is particularly effective if you suspect that your reader might not agree with the final point you are going to make or you need to lead your reader to your opinion slowly and carefully. A particular-to-general paragraph looks like this, although the number of details may vary:

> Detail
> Detail
> Detail
> Topic Sentence

Here is an example of particular-to-general organization:

Two sunny-side-up eggs, the whites rimmed with ruffled edges, lay in the middle of the plate. Specks of red pimento and green pepper peeked out of a heap of perfectly diced hash brown potatoes. Alongside lay strips of crispy, crinkly, maple-flavored bacon. A tall glass of ice-cold orange juice stood to my left. A big mug of steaming coffee was at my right. Then the biggest blueberry muffin in the universe was delivered straight from the oven, its aroma curling up to my nose. I broke it open and spread it with real butter. Nobody makes breakfast like my mom!

Practice 4A   Turn to the essay "Eleven" on page 265, and find one paragraph in the first half of the essay that demonstrates particular-to-general organization.

Practice 4B   Write a paragraph organized from particular to general that ends with this sentence: "Some people put their free time to good use."

Chronological Order

When you organize details chronologically in a paragraph, you are arranging them according to the passage of time—in other words, in the order in which they occurred. Most of the time when you tell a story or explain how to do something, you use chronological order. Paragraphs organized chronologically use such signal words as *first, then, next,* and *finally.*

Topic Sentence
  First
  Then
  Next
  Finally

Here is an example of a paragraph organized in chronological order:

Paper training is an easy way to housebreak a puppy. First, locate a box that is low enough for the puppy to climb in and out of easily. Then, line the box with newspapers and place it in an area that is always available to the puppy. Next, place the puppy in the box at regular intervals. As soon as the puppy begins to understand what is required, scold him or her for making mistakes. Finally, praise the puppy when he or she uses the box properly, and you will soon have a well-trained puppy.

Practice 5A   Turn to the essay "Shedding the Weight of My Dad's Obsession" on page 331, and find two paragraphs that are organized chronologically.

Practice 5B   Write a topic sentence for the following group of sentences. Then organize the sentences into a paragraph using chronological order. Add words, phrases, or sentences as necessary to smooth out the paragraph.

Topic Sentence: _____

Add the color of your choice to the melted wax.

Drop a wick in the melted wax.

First, melt some paraffin in a saucepan.

Put the mold in the refrigerator overnight. (This way, the wax will contract and will be easy to get out of the mold the next day.)

Finally, take the candle out of the mold and admire your creation.

Pour the melted wax in a candle mold of any shape.

Spatial Order

Another method of arranging details is by their relationship to each other in space. You might describe someone's outfit, for example, *from head to toe* or recount your summer travels across the country *from the east coast to the west coast*. Beginning at one point and moving detail by detail around a specific area is the simplest way of organizing by space. This method uses signal words such as *here*, *there*, *next*, *across*, and *beyond* to help the reader move through the paragraph smoothly and efficiently.

Topic Sentence
  Here
  There
  Next
  Across
  Beyond

Here is an example of a paragraph that uses spatial organization:

The prison was ringing with angry men wanting attention. In the first cell was a small prickly man who was yelling the loudest. He was banging a cup on the bars to signal that he needed something to drink. The next cell held two men who were trying to get their energy up to yell but couldn't seem to make their vocal chords work. The guard was grateful for this small favor. Across the room, a ferocious-looking man waving a newspaper was in the third cell. He was citing a passage from the paper and demanding his rights. Opposite the first cell was a generally quiet man who was reciting the names of people. All the prisoners in this particular block were gearing up for quite a day.

◆ *P r a c t i c e   6 A*   Turn to the essay "Homeless Woman Living in a Car" on page 275, and find one paragraph in the first half of the essay that uses spatial organization.

◆ *P r a c t i c e   6 B*   Write a topic sentence for the following group of sentences. Then write a paragraph putting the sentences in spatial order. Add words, phrases, or sentences as necessary to smooth out the paragraph.

Topic Sentence: _____

> Actually, the plant should separate the bed from the door.
>
> I'll begin by putting my bed against the west wall in the north corner of the room.
>
> I would like my floor plant to be next to the head of my bed.
>
> My bureau fits perfectly in the southeast corner of the room.
>
> The desk will be best in the southwest corner of the room where the window is.
>
> The entire east wall is covered with closets.
>
> My bookcase will go between the bed and the desk (on the west wall).

One Extreme to Another

Sometimes the best way to organize a paragraph is from one extreme to another: from most important to least important, from most troublesome to least troublesome, from most serious to least serious, from most humorous to least humorous, and so on. (Of course, you can also move from least to most.) Use whatever extremes make sense for your topic. For example, you might describe the courses you are taking this term from most important to least important in terms of a career. On returning from a trip, you might talk about the places you visited from least interesting to most interesting. Arranging your ideas from one extreme to another has one distinct advantage over the other four approaches—it is the most flexible. When no other method of organization works, you can always organize details from one extreme to the other. Words such as *most, next most, somewhat,* and *least* signal transitions in this type of paragraph.

> Topic Sentence
> > Most
> > Next most

Somewhat

Least

Here is an example of organization that moves from one extreme to the other:

I like some of my extracurricular activities better than others. My <u>favorite</u> is dance. I take classes in jazz, tap, and ballet, and I'm anxious to get home on the days I go to the dance studio. My <u>next favorite</u> activity is track. During track season, my schedule is tight, but I really look forward to working out every day. Although no one would believe it, my <u>next favorite</u> activity is shopping for school supplies. I love going to the big office supply stores and getting lost for 30 minutes or so. It is really like going into another world. When I emerge, I have some supplies that will make my life as a student easier. My <u>least favorite</u> activity is work. I work part time delivering food for a restaurant at night. No matter when I deliver the food, it is too late or too cold or too hot. No one is satisfied. That is why this is my <u>least favorite</u> task.

Practice 7A Turn to the essay "A Fable for Tomorrow" on page 303, and find two paragraphs that are organized from one extreme to the other.

Practice 7B Write a topic sentence for the following group of sentences. Then write a paragraph arranging the sentences from one extreme to another. Add words, phrases, and sentences as necessary to smooth out the paragraph. Also, label your system of classification: from most _____ to least _____ or from least _____ to most _____.

Topic Sentence: _____

I am failing math.
I still do not understand when to use semicolons in my writing.
My English instructor says my style of writing is loose.
I am barely passing music theory.

I have cut my philosophy class twice.
My tennis coach is mad at me.
I have not talked to my family in two weeks.
I have more homework than I could do in my lifetime.
I hardly ever have time to sleep.

Travis's Organization   Travis decides to organize his paragraph from one extreme to another—from his most favorite view to his least favorite view from the ridge. He first wants to introduce the ridge that sits over his hometown. Then he plans to describe his favorite views from this isolated place (the river with its boats, the beautiful sunset, and finally the city at night). He thinks the following order might work. He lists as many concrete details as he can under each view.

General: A high, wooded ridge is in my hometown.

Most Favorite View:	I love the river.
Specific Details:	I like the sailboats because I love to sail.
	I like to see different kinds of boats—rowboats, sailboats, motorboats, freight liners
Next Favorite View:	sunset—beautiful
Specific Details:	at dusk; moonlight
	clouds from pink to purple to red
	sun like fire
Third Favorite View:	I like seeing the whole city.
Specific Details:	headlights streaming through the darkness
	lighting the streets
	traffic noises, wind, rain, thunder, lightning
Concluding Thoughts:	I like to be by myself.
Specific Details:	peaceful, quiet
	I can think out my problems.
	problems fade away

Does the method of organization that Travis has chosen suit his topic? Would any other method of organization work as well?

Your Organization   What method of organization will work best for your ideas about your favorite place? Why do you think this method will be best?

DRAFTING

Drafting is putting your thoughts on paper. Having completed lots of prewriting activities, you're ready to write a working draft of your paragraph in complete sentences—no more lists and circles. The prewriting phase of this process has helped you generate lots of ideas, observations, and details for your paragraph. If you let these notes lead you to related ideas, you will have plenty of material to work with. At this stage, don't worry too much about grammar or spelling; you'll deal with those particulars when you edit your writing.

Travis's First Draft   Here is Travis's first draft, the result of his thinking, planning, developing, and organizing. (We'll look at editing errors at the next stage.)

> A high, wooded ridge overlooks my hometown. I can sit up there and see the river, the sunset, and the city. The sun shines like fire, and then the sun is gone behind the ridge. I love the river best, I can always see the river. I watch different kinds of boats on the river. I see rowboats, sailboats, motorboats, and freight liners. I have always liked to sail. My next favorite view is the sunset. Some nights the sunset is really beautiful. There are huge clouds when the sun goes down behind them. When it gets dark. I can see the headlights of the cars moving through the city streets. I bet people don't realize they're being watched. The headlights follow the street lights. When I am up high above the city, I get lost in my dreams. All my troubles melt away. I just look around this place, think about this place's beauty, and feel good—automatically.

Your First Draft   Write a draft of your thoughts on your favorite place.

_____

_____

_____

_____

_____

_____

_____

_____

_____

_____

_____

REVISING

As you know, the writing process does not end with your first draft. **Revising** means "seeing again," and that is exactly what you should try to do when you revise—see your writing again from as many different angles as possible.

More specifically, revising your writing means working with it so that it says exactly what you mean in the most effective way. Revision involves both *content* (what you are trying to say) and *form* (how you deliver your message). Having a friend or tutor read your paper before you revise it is a good idea so that you can see if you are communicating clearly.

Revising content means working with your words until they express your ideas as accurately and completely as possible. Revising form consists of working with the organization of your writing. When you revise, you should look closely at five basic elements of your paragraph, listed in the following checklist.

REVISING CHECKLIST ✔

TOPIC SENTENCE
- ✔ Does the topic sentence convey the paragraph's controlling idea?
- ✔ Does the topic sentence appear as the first or last sentence of the paragraph?

DEVELOPMENT
- ✔ Does the paragraph contain *specific* details that support the topic sentence?
- ✔ Does the paragraph include *enough* details to explain the topic sentence fully?

UNITY
- ✔ Do all the sentences in the paragraph support the topic sentence?

> **ORGANIZATION**
> ✔ Is the paragraph organized logically?
>
> **COHERENCE**
> ✔ Do the sentences move smoothly and logically from one to the next?

Let's look at these revision strategies one by one.

Topic Sentence

> ✔ Does the topic sentence convey the paragraph's controlling idea?
> ✔ Does the topic sentence appear as the first or last sentence of the paragraph?

As you learned in Chapter 3, every paragraph has a topic sentence that states its controlling idea. This sentence gives direction to the rest of the paragraph. It consists of both a limited topic and a statement about that topic. Generally, the topic sentence is the first sentence in a paragraph, but occasionally it is the last sentence, as in particular-to-general order.

 Practice 1A   Revise the underlined topic sentences so that they introduce all the details and ideas in their paragraphs.

1. <u>I have many friends.</u> I know that if I talk to Sean about a problem, he won't repeat it to anyone. He's also great to talk to because he never really tells me what I should do. Instead, he gives me what he thinks are all of my options and then helps me decide what to do. Karen, on the other hand, is a wonderful person, and I love to spend time with her. But I know she has trouble keeping a secret. She is great to talk to about small problems (things I don't care if anyone else knows about), but not the big problems. These friends mean a lot to me.

   Revised Topic Sentence: _____

   _____

2. I really enjoy watching suspense films because I am constantly afraid of what may happen next. Then I like the action movies. These are great because they move so fast and they usually have the best special effects. I hate it when they throw in love stories, though. This just

takes away from the real action. My least favorite are the romantic love stories. I can't stand to watch people for over two hours going through near-misses or traumatic problems. I know they are going to end up together in the end, so spare me the time to get there! <u>Overall, going to movies is a lot of fun.</u>

Revised Topic Sentence: _____

_____

3. <u>Buying a car is not an enjoyable experience.</u> First, the buyers have to decide on whether they want a new car or a used car. Some people want a new car because they know they won't have to worry about it breaking down for a while and they would have a longer warranty. Others want the price break a used car brings, but they don't know the people selling the cars, and they are afraid of getting ripped off. A good compromise might be to buy a used car from a reputable car dealership. This way the buyer gets the best of both worlds.

Revised Topic Sentence: _____

_____

◈ *Practice 1B* Write a topic sentence for each of the following paragraphs.

1. _____

I always have to put my sweats on and tie back my hair. I then sit on the couch and watch TV, all the while looking at my study guide and feeling guilty that I'm not putting more energy into it. After about a half hour, I realize I am going to get a bad grade on my test if I keep up this behavior, so I turn the TV off, get comfortable, and start studying hard. If I go through this routine, then I know I will have a good study session and will get a good grade on a test.

2. _____

Yet she goes with us every year. She complains about sleeping in a tent, cooking over an open fire, and not having a clean bathroom for a week. Aunt Rita always ends up having fun, but she hates to do so much extra work. We love to joke with her and tease her about being a "city slicker." Every year she says she will never go camping again, but we always make sure she comes along. I guess this has turned into a family ritual, and I'm glad. I always enjoy her company—especially when she complains.

3. _____

Even though my roommate has her own room, she leaves clothes all over the place. I've found jeans on the couch, sweaters in the kitchen, and underwear in the bathroom. I once peeked into her room, which was so cluttered I couldn't even see her carpet. When she cooks, she leaves pots, pans, and dishes (all dirty and caked with food) all over the place.

Travis's Revision   When Travis looks back at his topic sentence in Chapter 2, he realizes it does not accurately introduce what he talks about in his paragraph. His topic sentence only tells readers that a ridge overlooks his hometown, not that this ridge is his favorite place:

Topic Sentence: A high, wooded ridge overlooks my hometown.

He decides to expand his topic sentence so that it more accurately introduces the details that will follow in his paragraph:

Revised Topic Sentence: A high, wooded ridge **that** overlooks my hometown **is my favorite place.**

He feels that this topic sentence introduces his favorite place and will let him talk about the river, the sunset, and the city.

Your Revision   With these guidelines in mind, revise your topic sentence.

Your Topic Sentence: _____

Your Revised Topic Sentence: _____

_____

Development

> ✔ Does the paragraph contain *specific* details that support the topic sentence?
> ✔ Does the paragraph include *enough* details to explain the topic sentence fully?

Details are the building blocks that you combine to construct a paragraph. The details in your paragraph should be as specific as possible, and you need to provide enough details to support your topic sentence. If you keep both of these guidelines in mind, you will develop your paragraphs specifically and adequately.

Can you recognize details that are more specific than other details? This is a major part of development. Look at the following details, and see how they move from general to specific and from abstract to concrete. As you learned in Chapter 3, concrete words refer to items you can see, hear, touch, smell, or taste—as opposed to abstract words that refer to ideas and concepts, like *hunger* and *happiness*.

transportation (general, abstract)
   vehicle
         car
              Dodge
                    Dodge Durango
                          red Dodge Durango
                          red Dodge Durango
                          with four-wheel drive
                          and black interior
                          (specific, concrete)

nutrition (general, abstract)
   food
         meat
              beef
                  tri-tip
                        tri-tip marinated in sauce
                          tri-tip marinated in
                          Aunt Bertha's homemade
                          barbecue sauce
                          (specific, concrete)

◆ *P r a c t i c e* *2A*   Underline the most specific word or phrase in each group.

1. street, small road, Westwind Avenue, city, neighborhood
2. household, chores, weekend, rag, employment
3. grade point average, science major, Chemistry, sulfuric acid, science lab

4. landscaping, address, plant, garden, city planning
5. mountains, California, ski resort, Dave's Run, a ski resort in Mammoth

◆ *P r a c t i c e   2 B*   Fill in the blanks so that each sequence moves from the general and abstract to the specific and concrete.

1. homework

   _____

   _____

   _____

2. _____

   dog

   _____

   _____

3. trouble

   _____

   _____

   _____

4. _____

   _____

   _____

   state championship

5. _____

   _____

   piano

   _____

Travis's Revision   When Travis looks at his first draft, he realizes that he can make his details much more specific and concrete. Here are three sentences that he revises (with concrete details in bold type).

Revised: I can sit up there and see the river **with its many ripples,** the **colorful** sunset, and the city **with lots of tall buildings.**

Revised: There are huge clouds **that change from pink to purple to red** when the sun goes down behind them.

Revised: ~~All my troubles~~ **Homework and family problems** melt away.

In addition to providing specific, concrete details, you need to furnish enough details to support the main idea of each paragraph. Without enough details, the main idea of a paragraph will not be adequately developed and may be misunderstood.

Practice   3A   List three details that could support each of the following sentences.

1. Some people have funny hobbies.

   _____

   _____

   _____

2. The campus health center is a friendly place.

   _____

   _____

   _____

3. My favorite food is Italian.

   _____

   _____

   _____

4. My paycheck never lasts as long as it should.

_____

_____

_____

5. Exercising is important for people of all ages.

_____

_____

_____

◆ *P r a c t i c e **3 B*** Develop the following topic sentences with enough specific details.

1. Advertising surrounds us every day all day long.

_____

_____

_____

2. The cost of living affects salaries.

_____

_____

_____

3. Severe mood changes are a sign of depression.

_____

_____

_____

4. Most people use their sense of right and wrong to make major decisions.

____

____

____

5. College life can be frustrating.

____

____

____

Travis's Revision Travis's paragraph needs *more* details and *more specific* details to help it communicate its message. Travis accomplishes this by adding more details about the river, the sunset, the city, and his feelings. He talks about how the street lights guide the cars, he explains how the boats look like toys, he compares the colors in the clouds to a kaleidoscope and a color wheel, and he talks about time stopping when he is on the ridge.

General statement

A high, wooded ridge **that** overlooks my hometown **is my favorite place.** I can sit up there and see the river **with its many ripples,** the **colorful** sunset, and the city **with lots of tall buildings.** The sun shines like fire, and then the sun is gone behind the ridge. I love the river best, I can always see the river. I watch different kinds of boats on the river. I see rowboats, sailboats, motorboats, and freight liners. **The boats look like toys because I am up so high.** I have always liked to sail. My next favorite view is the sunset. Some nights the sunset is really beautiful. There are huge clouds **that change from pink to purple to red** when the sun goes down behind them. **Sometimes I think of a kaleidoscope, and other times I think of a color wheel that spins in slow motion.** When it gets dark. I can see the headlights of the cars moving through the city streets. I bet people don't realize they're being watched. The **bright** headlights

Specific details

Specific comparison

Specific details

Concrete details

More
details

follow the street lights **as if the street lights are
showing the cars where to go.** When I am up high
above the city, I get lost in my dreams, **and time
doesn't exist. Homework and family problems** melt
away. I just look around this place, think about this
place's beauty, and feel good—automatically.

*Specific
comparison*

*Concrete
details*

Your Revision   Add more details to your paragraph, making your explanations and descriptions as concrete and specific as possible.

Unity

✔ Do all the sentences in the paragraph support the topic sentence?

A paragraph has unity when it discusses the one idea that is introduced in the topic sentence. All other sentences in a paragraph expand on this controlling idea and relate to it in some way. Information that is not about the main idea is considered irrelevant and does not belong in the paragraph.

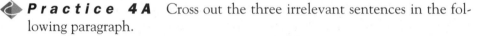 ***Practice 4A***   Cross out the three irrelevant sentences in the following paragraph.

Reading helps bring back memories from our own lives. I never liked to read until I had Ms. Fischer. If we are reading about the thrill of McGwire's record in home runs, we might remember a great sports event in our lives. I never liked sports, but my mom made me play soccer. If we are reading about Jules Verne traveling around the world, memories of our favorite trips might come to the surface of our minds. I liked Europe, but all I wanted to do was go home. I was also missing my girlfriend. Reading is a wonderful way to lose ourselves in the lives of others while reliving some important moments in our own lives.

Practice 4B   Cross out the three irrelevant sentences in the following paragraph.

Your body has a three-stage reaction to stress: (1) alarm, (2) resistance, and (3) exhaustion. In the alarm stage, your body recognizes the presence of stress and, through a release of hormones from the endocrine glands, prepares for fight or flight. I've been there; I have felt the fight feeling before. In the resistance stage, your body repairs any damage caused by the stress. Repairing must be difficult for the body, but it has to be done. If the stress does not go away, however, the body cannot repair the damage and must remain alert. This plunges you into the third stage—exhaustion. If this state continues long enough, you may develop one of the diseases of stress. I'll bet these diseases are diffcult to diagnose and cure, but I don't know for sure. The best idea would be to learn how to deal with stress of all kinds and use it to your benefit.

Travis's Revision   Travis sees now that some of his sentences do not fit into his paragraph. In his case, the comments about his love for sailing and about people not knowing they are being watched do not support his topic sentence, the first sentence in his paragraph. If these details were dropped, the revised paragraph would look like this:

> A high, wooded ridge that overlooks my hometown is my favorite place. I can sit up there and see the river with its many ripples, the colorful sunset, and the city with lots of tall buildings. The sun shines like fire, and then the sun is gone behind the ridge. I love the river best, I can always see the river. I watch different kinds of boats on the river. I see rowboats, sailboats, motorboats, and freight liners. The boats look like toys because I am up so high. ~~I have always liked to sail.~~ My next favorite view is the sunset. Some nights the sunset is really beautiful. There are huge clouds that change from pink to purple to red when the sun goes down behind them. Sometimes I think of a kaleidoscope, and other times I think of a color wheel that spins in slow motion. When it gets dark. I can see the headlights of the cars moving through the city streets. ~~I bet people don't realize they're being watched.~~ The bright headlights follow the street lights as if the street lights are showing the cars where to go. When I am up high above the city, I get lost in my dreams, and time doesn't exist. Homework and family problems melt away. I just look around this place, think about this place's beauty, and feel good—automatically.

Your Revision   Read your paragraph carefully, and cross out any irrelevant sentences or ideas.

Organization

> ✔ Is the paragraph organized logically?

In Chapter 3, you learned five ways to organize your paragraphs:

1. General to particular
2. Particular to general
3. Chronologically (by time)
4. Spatially (by physical arrangement)
5. One extreme to another

You might want to review pages 24–31 for an explanation of each of these methods.

The method that you choose depends to a great extent on your topic and your purpose. What are you trying to accomplish? What order will help you deliver your message as effectively and efficiently as possible?

P r a c t i c e   5 A   Reorganize the following sentences so that they are in a logical order. Then identify your method of organization.

This is convenient because it's at the beginning of the Riverwalk.

Hours later, I walk back to my car and think of the day I can return.

I always eat at my favorite Mexican restaurant first.

Whenever I visit San Antonio, my hometown, I always go to the Riverwalk.

I usually end my journey near a road that will lead me to the Alamo.

I always park at the end with the newest hotels and mall.

I then walk down the paths, stopping in all of the unique shops.

I always stop here because it is a wonderful historical monument.

This way I can spend hours just walking along the beautiful paths and stopping in my favorite places.

Method of Organization: _____

P r a c t i c e   5 B   Reorganize the sentences in the following paragraph so that they are in a logical order. Then label your method of organization.

I know that I have about three feet when I get out of bed before I run into the dresser. It is especially bad at night, when I don't have my contacts in and I have to get from my bed to the bathroom. My sight is so bad that I can't even see three feet in front of me without my contacts. From the doorway, I then go left and walk three steps to the bathroom. From the dresser, if I turn right, I have to walk five steps to get to the doorway of my room. If I reverse my steps and count backward, I can usually make it to and from the bathroom without breaking a toe or crashing into a wall.

Method of Organization: _____

Travis's Revision   In Chapter 3, Travis decided that the best way to organize his paragraph was from most favorite to least favorite. But now he needs to make sure that every detail is in the right place. He notices a sentence about the sunset that is out of order, so he moves the sentence to the part of the paragraph that focuses on the sunset.

> A high, wooded ridge that overlooks my hometown is my favorite place. I can sit up there and see the river with its many ripples, the colorful sunset, and the city with lots of tall buildings. ~~The sun shines like fire, and then the sun is gone behind the ridge.~~ I love the river best, I can always see the river. I watch different kinds of boats on the river. I see rowboats, sailboats, motorboats, and freight liners. The boats look like toys because I am up so high. My next favorite view is the sunset. Some nights the sunset is really beautiful. There are huge clouds that change from pink to purple to red when the sun goes down behind them. Sometimes I think of a kaleidoscope, and other times I think of a color wheel that spins in slow motion. **The sun shines like fire, and then the sun is gone behind the ridge.** When it gets dark. I can see the headlights of the cars moving through the city streets. The bright headlights follow the street lights as if the street lights are showing the cars where to go. When I am up high above the city, I get lost in my dreams, and time doesn't exist. Homework and family problems melt away. I just look around this place, think about this place's beauty, and feel good—automatically.

Your Revision   Double-check the method of organization you chose in Chapter 3, and make sure each of your details is in its proper place.

Coherence

> ✔ Do the sentences in the paragraph move smoothly and logically from one to the next?

A well-written paragraph is coherent—that is, its parts *cohere*, or stick together. The paragraph is smooth, not choppy, and readers move logically from one thought to the next, seeing a clear relationship between the ideas. Here are four different strategies that writers use to help readers follow their train of thought: *transitions*, *repeated words*, *synonyms*, and *pronouns*.

Transitions

Transitional words and phrases are like bridges or links between thoughts. They show your readers how one idea is related to another or when you are moving to a new point. Good use of transitions makes your writing smooth rather than choppy.

Choppy: I watch different kinds of boats on the river. I see rowboats, sailboats, motorboats, and freight liners.

Smooth: I watch different kinds of boats on the river. **For instance,** I see rowboats, sailboats, motorboats, and freight liners.

Transitions have very specific meanings, so you should take care to use the most logical one.

Confusing: I watch different kinds of boats on the water. **Besides,** I see rowboats, sailboats, motorboats, and freight liners.

Here is a list of some common transitional words and phrases that will make your writing more coherent. They are classified by meaning.

Some Common Transitions

Addition:	*moreover, further, furthermore, besides, and, and then, likewise, also, nor, too, again, in addition, next, first, second, third, finally, last*
Comparison:	*similarly, likewise, in like manner*
Contrast:	*but, yet, and yet, however, still, nevertheless, on the other hand, on the contrary, after all, in contrast, at the same time, otherwise*

Emphasis:	*in fact, indeed, to tell the truth, in any event, after all, actually, of course*
Example:	*for example, for instance, in this case*
Place:	*here, there, beyond, nearby, opposite, adjacent to, near*
Purpose:	*to this end, for this purpose, with this objective*
Result:	*hence, therefore, accordingly, consequently, thus, as a result, then, so*
Summary:	*to conclude, to sum up, to summarize, in brief, on the whole, in sum, in short, as I have said, in other words, that is*
Time:	*meanwhile, at length, immediately, soon, after a few days, now, in the meantime, afterward, later, then, sometimes, (at) other times, still*

See pages 372–374 in the Handbook (Part V) for more information on transitions.

Practice 6A   Fill in the blanks in the following paragraph with logical transitions.

People should spay or neuter their animals so that we don't end up with kittens and puppies that no one wants. _____, a family might have a male cat that they let roam the neighborhood, and this cat might get a female cat pregnant. _____ who will care for the new kittens? Some people give them away or take them to a neighborhood SPCA. Some people, _____, just let the kittens roam free, hoping someone will take care of them. This irresponsible action causes more problems, _____.

Practice 6B   Rewrite the following paragraph, adding at least three transitions to make it more coherent.

Growing up, my brother, sister, and I always looked forward to the summer Saturdays that our dad took us water-skiing. We often prepared the night before for our outing the next day. We would get our day-bags packed and our clothes ready to put on. We would pack a lunch big enough for all of us. We would make sure we had plenty of sodas for the entire day. We loved spending the whole day with him.

We hated that time went so fast. When he would drop us back at home, we would anxiously wait for the next Saturday to come.

Repeated Words

Repeating key words also helps bind the sentences of a paragraph together and guide readers through its ideas. At the same time, too much repetition becomes boring.

> Effective Repetition: Sometimes **I think of** a kaleidoscope, and other times **I think of** a color wheel that spins in slow motion.

Practice 7A   Underline the four effective repeated words in the following paragraph.

> I worked in a law firm during my first summer break from college because I wanted to discover if a legal career was really for me. The law firm I worked in was very large, and many of the lawyers specialized in criminal law. I learned quite a lot about tricky defense strategies at this law firm, and I decided that if I did pursue a law degree, I would become a prosecutor, not a defender. Actually working in a law firm was a great way to learn more about the legal profession.

Practice 7B   Add five repeated words where appropriate to clarify and smooth out the following paragraph.

> My friend Manuel is a TV addict. He watches it for over 10 hours every day, and he never gets his homework finished. He doesn't understand that his instructors won't let him turn in his work late, so he watches it whenever he's home. The shows he watches on it are usually pretty boring; they don't require thought when he watches them. But he loves to sit there and watch it anyway. I hope he'll learn soon that watching it instead of doing other things can only lead to nowhere.

Synonyms

Next, using *synonyms* can link your sentences and help you avoid needless repetition. Synonyms are words that have identical or similar meanings. They can add variety and interest to your writing. A thesaurus, or book of synonyms, can help you locate the best replacements for specific words.

In the following example from Travis's paragraph, Travis uses *town* in place of one of his references to *city*.

Original Reference: When I am up high above the **city,** I get lost in my dreams, and time doesn't exist.

Synonym: When I am up high above the **town,** I get lost in my dreams, and time doesn't exist.

Practice 8A   Underline at least four synonyms that refer to cooking in the following paragraph.

> I have loved to cook since I was 12 years old. My mother taught me everything I know. I especially love to cook for my dad because he is what we call "cooking challenged." When he cooks, he thinks microwaving is the only way to go, and even then he overcooks or burns the food. He kids me for cooking from scratch and using traditional methods because he firmly believes there's only one way to cook. I broil; he microwaves. I roast; he microwaves. I barbecue; he microwaves. But he always praises me for my culinary ability because in the end, he knows I will someday be a famous chef.

Practice 8B   Replace two references to *professor* with synonyms in the following paragraph.

> I have discovered that one key to making good grades is to get a good professor. A good professor can encourage me to do my best and can make learning fun. I find that I do better for professors who don't just lecture the entire time but let us interact with one another in some way. Professors with a sense of humor also encourage me to perform better. They actually make me look forward to coming to their classes. The good professors simply help me earn a good grade.

Pronouns

The final way to link your sentences is with *pronouns*. When appropriate, you can replace specific words with pronouns. Not only do pronouns link your ideas, but they also keep your writing moving at a fairly fast pace.

Travis uses a pronoun to get rid of a repetition of the word *boats*.

Repetition: I watch different kinds of boats on the river. For instance, I see rowboats, sailboats, motorboats, and freight liners. **The boats** look like toys because I am up so high.

Pronoun: I watch different kinds of boats on the river. For instance, I see rowboats, sailboats, motorboats, and freight liners. ~~The boats~~ **They** look like toys because I am up so high.

For more information on pronouns, see pages 364–367 in the Handbook (Part V).

 P r a c t i c e   9 A   Underline the 14 pronouns in the following paragraph.

When I was preparing for my wedding, I relied a lot on my best friend, Tanya. She helped me pick out my dress, decide on the flowers, and book the banquet hall. They all were the perfect choices for me. Tanya worked in a craft store, so she was able to help me decorate the hall for a reasonably cheap price. Throwing a wedding is a huge event, and Tanya was a great friend throughout the process. I couldn't have done it without her.

 P r a c t i c e   9 B   Add five pronouns where appropriate in the following paragraph.

Tom, Sandy, and I have been friends for life. Tom, Sandy, and I met in third grade when we all tried to survive the neighborhood bully on our walks home. Tom, Sandy, and I went through high school together and are now attending the same college. Tom, Sandy, and my college is two hours from our hometown. So, Tom, Sandy, and I share an apartment. Our apartment is very nice, and our apartment is always clean. I hope that Tom, Sandy, and I will always remain good friends.

Travis's Revision   When Travis checks his paragraph for coherence, he decides his writing can use some improvement. So he makes the following revisions that help bind his sentences together and show the relationships between his ideas.

Here is Travis's paragraph with transitions, repeated words, synonyms, and pronouns highlighted.

repetition

A high, wooded ridge that overlooks my hometown is my favorite place. I can sit up ~~there~~ **on the ridge** and see the river with its many ripples, the colorful sunset, and the city with lots of tall buildings.

pronoun I love the river best, I can always see ~~the river~~ **it** from the ridge. I watch different kinds of boats on the ~~river~~ **water**. For instance, I see rowboats, sailboats, motorboats, and freight liners. ~~The boats~~ **They** look like toys because I am up so high. My next favorite view is **the sunset**. Some nights **the sunset** is really beautiful. There are huge clouds that change from pink to purple to red when the sun goes down behind them. **Sometimes I think of** a kaleidoscope, and **other times I think of** a color wheel that spins in slow motion. The sun shines like fire, and then ~~the sun~~ **it** is gone behind the ridge. **Finally,** when it gets dark. I can see the headlights of the cars moving through the city streets. The bright headlights follow the street lights as if the street lights are showing the cars where to go. When I am up ~~high~~ **on the ridge** above the ~~city~~ **town**, I get lost in my dreams, and time doesn't exist. **On the whole,** homework and family problems melt away. I just look around this place, think about ~~this place's~~ **its** beauty, and feel good—automatically.

repetition

synonym

repetition

transition
repetition

transition

repetition

transition

repetition

transition
pronoun

transition

pronoun

synonym

pronoun

Transitions   In addition to *for instance*, *sometimes*, and *other times*, Travis added two more transitions to his paragraph. What are they?

_____

List the meaning of all five transitions in Travis's paragraph:

1. Transition: _____   Meaning: _____

2. Transition: _____   Meaning: _____

3. Transition: _____   Meaning: _____

4. Transition: _____   Meaning: _____

5. Transition: _____   Meaning: _____

Repeated Words   When Travis checked his paragraph for repeated key words, he thought he needed to refer directly to the ridge more often. So he revised some of his sentences. How many new references to the ridge did he add?

_____

Synonyms   When Travis looked at his paragraph again, he found another opportunity to use a synonym to link his ideas more clearly. Besides the addition of *town* for *city*, what other synonym does Travis use in his revision?

_____ for _____

Pronouns   Finally, in addition to substituting *they* for *boats*, Travis found three more places to use pronouns to bind his paragraph together. Where are these places in his paragraph?

_____ for _____

_____ for _____

_____ for _____

Your Revision   Now it's time to make your essay more coherent.

Transitions   Check the transitions in your paragraph. Do you use enough transitions so that your paragraph moves smoothly and logically from one idea to the next? Do you use your transitions correctly?

Repeated Words   Look at your paragraph to see when you might want to repeat a key word. Then revise your paragraph accordingly.

Synonyms   Look for places in your paragraph where you might add synonyms to link your sentences. Use a thesaurus in book form or on your computer if you need help.

Pronouns   Check your paragraph for opportunities to use pronouns. Add appropriate pronouns.

Travis's Revised Paragraph   After revising his topic sentence, his development, his unity, his organization, and his coherence, Travis produced the following revised paragraph. All of his revisions are in bold type.

A high, wooded ridge **that** overlooks my hometown **is my favorite place.** I can sit up ~~there~~ **on the ridge** and see the river **with its many ripples,** the **colorful** sunset, and the city **with lots of tall buildings.** ~~The sun shines like fire, and then the sun is gone behind the ridge.~~ I love the river best, I can always see ~~the river~~ it from **the ridge.** I watch different kinds of boats on the **river water. For instance,** I see rowboats, sailboats, motorboats, and freight liners. ~~The boats~~ **They** look like toys because I am up so high. ~~I have always liked to sail.~~ My next favorite view is the sunset. Some nights the sunset is really beautiful. There are huge clouds **that change from pink to purple to red** when the sun goes down behind them. **Sometimes I think of a kaleidoscope, and other times I think of a color wheel that spins in slow motion. The sun shines like fire, and then** ~~the sun~~ **it is gone behind the ridge. Finally,** when it gets dark. I can see the headlights of the cars moving through the city streets. ~~I bet people don't realize they're being watched.~~ The **bright** headlights follow the street lights **as if the street lights are showing the cars where to go.** When I am up ~~high~~ on the ridge above the ~~city~~ **town,** I get lost in my dreams, **and time doesn't exist. On the whole,** ~~All my troubles~~ **homework and family problems** melt away. I just look around this place, think about ~~this place's~~ **its** beauty, and feel good—automatically.

Your Revised Paragraph   Now that you have applied all the revision strategies to your own writing, write your revised paragraph here.

_____

_____

_____

_____

_____

_____

_____

_____

_____

_____

_____

_____

_____

_____

_____

_____

EDITING

After you have revised your paragraph, you are ready to edit it. **Editing** involves checking your grammar, punctuation, mechanics, and spelling to be sure that your writing is free of errors. Grammar, punctuation, mechanics, and spelling are as important to communicating clearly as well-chosen words. They help your reader navigate through your writing. Nothing confuses readers more than editing errors. These errors attract the readers' attention and can distract them from what you are saying.

For easy reference, we have divided the editing strategies into three large categories in the following checklist: sentences, punctuation and mechanics, and word choice and spelling. This checklist doesn't cover all the grammar and usage problems you may find in your writing, but it focuses on some of the main mistakes college students frequently make.

EDITING CHECKLIST ✔

SENTENCES
✔ Does each sentence have a main subject and verb?

✔ Do all subjects and verbs agree?

✔ Do all pronouns agree with their nouns?

✔ Are modifiers as close as possible to the words they modify?

PUNCTUATION AND MECHANICS
✔ Are sentences punctuated correctly?

✔ Are words capitalized properly?

WORD CHOICE AND SPELLING
✔ Are words used correctly?

✔ Are words spelled correctly?

YOUR EQ (EDITING QUOTIENT)

You might want to start the editing stage by finding your EQ (editing quotient). Knowing this information will help you look for specific errors in your writing and make your editing more efficient.

To determine your EQ, read the paragraphs in Practice 1, identifying each error you find from the following list. Then score your answers in Practice 2, and see if your errors form any pattern by charting them in Appendix 5.

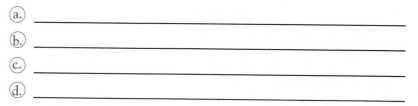 ***Practice 1***   **EQ Test** In the following paragraphs, underline the errors you find, and label them a, b, c, and so on. Then list them on the lines below the paragraph. The number of lines corresponds to the number of errors in the paragraph.

The possible errors are listed here:

abbreviation	end punctuation	pronoun agreement
capitalization	fragment	run-together sentences
comma	modifier	spelling
confused word	number	subject-verb agreement
		verb form

1. A lot of teenage girls are influenced by what they see in the movies and on TV. Some of the actresses are so thin that rumors begin about their various eating disorders. Which they all deny. Sometimes actresses don't get roles because they are "too heavy." Even though these actresses are at their ideal weight. The message Hollywood sends is that ultra-thin is best young girls take this message to heart. Hollywood provides physical role models for all of society these role models are not always good to follow.

    (a.) _____

    (b.) _____

    (c.) _____

    (d.) _____

2. Bilingual education is a problem in California. The people have passed propositions that eliminate such programs, much of the population believe bilingual programs must be present in schools. In order for second-language learners to learn. Surely a happy medium

exist somewhere between the nonfunctioning programs and total elimination. Perhaps the solution lies in finding a program. To accommodate both students and taxpayers.

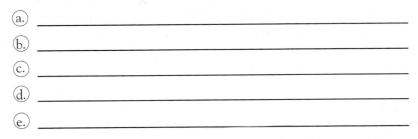

3. Pesticide use on fruits and vegetables has ran into trouble because it is often misunderstood. The government places strict regulations on chemical use in fields, each chemical must be tested and approved for each crop it is used for. Often pesticides degrade within twenty–four hours when exposed to sunlight. Strict rules apply to the application of a chemical, the reentry time for workers, and the time that must lapse before harvesting the fruits and vegetables. Hefty fines imposed on violators of proper pesticide use. People who have swore off nonorganic foods need to become better informed about the rules and regulations regarding pesticides.

4. Political campaigns have become difficult to watch because of the constant intrusion into candidates' personal lives. What starts out as a clean campaign quickly turns dirty. When one candidate exposes a secret about their opponent's past. From that point on, a candidate is explaining and apologizing for their past, and quite often they launch an attack of their own. Just once a clean political campaign would be nice to see the American public would not know what to do.

(a.) _____

(b.) _____

c. _____

d. _____

e. _____

f. _____

5. Many people do not understand how severely allergies can affect someone. Most people think that a runny nose and a little sneezing are no big deal allergies can cause severe headaches, asthma, rashes, and sometimes death. Suffering from severe allergies, days can really be miserable. Sometimes people must take daily medications so they can live a normal life, which may include steroids. But people with bad allergies live in constant fear that they'll eat, be stung by, or be prescribed something that might kill them, allergies can be very hard on people.

a. _____

b. _____

c. _____

d. _____

6. Violence on television is influencing America's youth. Teenagers whose daily lives involve watching violent tv shows have killed people. Parents need to monitor what their children watch. In order to guarantee the children don't see, and become desensitized by too much violence. Censoring violent television shows will not help those children who are unsupervised, parents must take control of what their children watch?

a. _____

b. _____

c. _____

d. _____

e. _____

7. 17 college students were needlessly killed last Friday night because they ignored the law. A group of students held a party in an

abandoned warehouse that had "CONDEMNED" signs all over the place the students ignored the warnings. At about 1:00 a.m., a fire broke out, because most of the exits were blocked off, some students did not get out alive. Sergeant Mary Thomas of the local fire department said that it was a horrible tragedy. Maybe now people will understand. The seriousness of the signs.

(a.) _____

(b.) _____

(c.) _____

(d.) _____

(e.) _____

8. Genetic research has made some great, although scary, advances in the past decade. Agriculture is bennefitting from genetically altered crops. That are comprised of insect-resistant and disese-resistant plants. Yet now genetic research is capable of cloning an animal, it is probably capable of cloning human life. At what point does science go to far?

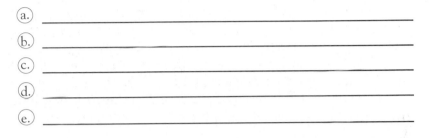

(a.) _____

(b.) _____

(c.) _____

(d.) _____

(e.) _____

9. Studies have proved that children who listen to Classical music when they are young are more likely to be better students later in life. Beethoven and Mozart can stimulate young brains and open there minds for further learning, classical music has been proved to produce students who yearn for more knowledge. Researchers have even stated that listening to classical music while studying create an environment for retaining more information. Than an environment with no music. If children are brought up with classical music in their lives it could become a lifelong, beneficial habit.

(a.) _____

(b.) _____

(c.) _____

(d.) _____

(e.) _____

(f.) _____

10. People who are thinking about owning a dog need to understand all that is involved in the care. First of all. Dogs must be taken to the vet for a series of shots the animal should also be spayed or neutered. Proper food and medicines must be purchased. As well as toys and treats. People must also invest alot of their time in the animal. A dog is perceptive, and responds to the way they are treated. Anything less than full health care and quality time is simply unfair to the dog.

(a.) _____

(b.) _____

(c.) _____

(d.) _____

(e.) _____

(f.) _____

 Practice 2 **EQ Answers** Score your answers in Practice 1 using the following answer key. Then chart your errors in Appendix 5.

1. A lot of teenage girls are influenced by what they see in the movies and on TV. Some of the actresses are so thin that rumors begin about their various eating disorders. [a]Which they all deny. Sometimes actresses don't get roles because they are "too heavy."[b]Even though these actresses are at their ideal weight.[c]The message Hollywood sends is that ultra-thin is best young girls take this message to heart.[d]Hollywood provides physical role models for all of society these role models are not always good to follow.

(a.)   *fragment*

(b.)   *fragment*

(c.)   *run-together sentences or end punctuation*

(d.)   *run-together sentences or end punctuation*

2. Bilingual education is a problem in California. [ⓐ]<u>The people have passed propositions that eliminate such programs,</u> [ⓑ]<u>much</u> of the population <u>believe</u> bilingual programs must be present in schools. [ⓒ]<u>In order for second-language learners to learn.</u> Surely a happy [ⓓ]<u>medium exist</u> somewhere between the nonfunctioning programs and total elimination. Perhaps the solution lies in finding a program. [ⓔ]<u>To accommodate both students and taxpayers.</u>

   (a.)   *run-together sentences or end punctuation*

   (b.)   *subject-verb agreement*

   (c.)   *fragment*

   (d.)   *subject-verb agreement*

   (e.)   *fragment*

3. Pesticide use on fruits and vegetables [ⓐ]<u>has ran</u> into trouble because it is often misunderstood. [ⓑ]<u>The government places strict regulations on chemical use in fields, each chemical must be tested and approved for each crop it is used for.</u> Often pesticides degrade within [ⓒ]<u>twenty–four</u> hours when exposed to sunlight. Strict rules apply to the application of a chemical, the reentry time for workers, and the time that must lapse before harvesting the fruits and vegetables. [ⓓ]<u>Hefty fines imposed on violators of proper pesticide use.</u> People who [ⓔ]<u>have swore</u> off nonorganic foods need to become better informed about the rules and regulations regarding pesticides.

   (a.)   *verb form*

   (b.)   *run-together sentences or end punctuation*

   (c.)   *number*

   (d.)   *fragment*

   (e.)   *verb form*

4. Political campaigns have become difficult to watch because of the constant intrusion into candidates' personal lives. What starts out as a clean campaign quickly turns dirty. [ⓐ]<u>When one candidate exposes a secret about</u> [ⓑ]<u>their</u> opponent's past. From that point on, a candidate is explaining and apologizing for [ⓒ]<u>their</u> past, and quite often [ⓓ]<u>they</u> launch an attack of [ⓔ]<u>their</u> own. [ⓕ]<u>Just once a clean</u>

political campaign would be nice to see the American public would not know what to do.

(a.) _____ fragment _____

(b.) _____ pronoun agreement _____

(c.) _____ pronoun agreement _____

(d.) _____ pronoun agreement _____

(e.) _____ pronoun agreement _____

(f.) _____ run-together sentences or end punctuation _____

5. Many people do not understand how severely allergies can affect someone. ⓐMost people think that a runny nose and a little sneezing are no big deal allergies can cause severe headaches, asthma, rashes, and sometimes death. ⓑSuffering from severe allergies, days can really be miserable. Sometimes people must take daily medications so they can live a normal life, ©which may include steroids. ⓓBut people with bad allergies live in constant fear that they'll eat, be stung by, or be prescribed something that might kill them, allergies can be very hard on people.

(a.) _____ run-together sentences or end punctuation _____

(b.) _____ modifier _____

(c.) _____ modifier _____

(d.) _____ run-together sentences or end punctuation _____

6. Violence on television is influencing America's youth. Teenagers whose daily lives involve watching violent ⓐtv shows have killed people. Parents need to monitor what their children watch. ⓑIn order to guarantee the children don't see,©and become desensitized by too much violence. ⓓCensoring violent television shows will not help those children who are unsupervised, parents must take control of what their children watch?©

(a.) _____ capitalization _____

(b.) _____ fragment _____

(c.) _____ comma _____

(d.)   *run-together sentences or end punctuation* _____

(e.)   *end punctuation* _____

7.   (a)17 college students were needlessly killed last Friday night because they ignored the law. (b)A group of students held a party in an abandoned warehouse that had "CONDEMNED" signs all over the place the students ignored the warnings. (c)At about 1:00 a.m., a fire broke out, because most of the exits were blocked off, some students did not get out alive. (d)Sergeant Mary Thomas of the local fire department said that it was a horrible tragedy. Maybe now people will understand. (e)The seriousness of the signs.

(a.)   *number* _____

(b.)   *run-together sentences or end punctuation* _____

(c.)   *run-together sentences or end punctuation* _____

(d.)   *abbreviation* _____

(e.)   *fragment* _____

8.   Genetic research has made some great, although scary, advances in the past decade. Agriculture is(a)bennefitting from genetically altered crops. (b)That are comprised of insect-resistant and(c)disese-resistant plants. (d)Yet now genetic research is capable of cloning an animal, it is probably capable of cloning human life. At what point does science go(e)to far?

(a.)   *spelling* _____

(b.)   *fragment* _____

(c.)   *spelling* _____

(d.)   *run-together sentences or end punctuation* _____

(e.)   *confused word* _____

9.   Studies have proved that children who listen to(a)Classical music when they are young are more likely to be better students later in life. (b)Beethoven and Mozart can stimulate young brains and open (c)there minds for further learning, classical music has been proved to produce students who yearn for more knowledge. Researchers

have even stated that [d]<u>listening</u> to classical music while studying <u>create</u> an environment for retaining more information. [c]<u>Than an environment with no music.</u> If children are brought up with classical music in their lives[f] it could become a lifelong, beneficial habit.

a. _capitalization_

b. _run-together sentences or end punctuation_

c. _confused word_

d. _subject-verb agreement_

e. _fragment_

f. _comma_

10. People who are thinking about owning a dog need to understand all that is involved in the care. [a]<u>First of all.</u> [b]<u>Dogs must be taken to the vet for a series of shots the animal should also be spayed or neutered.</u> Proper food and medicines must be purchased. [c]<u>As well as toys and treats.</u> People must also invest [d]<u>alot</u> of their time in the animal. A dog is perceptive,[e] and responds to the way [f]<u>they</u> are treated. Anything less than full health care and quality time is simply unfair to the dog.

a. _fragment_

b. _run-together sentences or end punctuation_

c. _fragment_

d. _spelling_

e. _comma_

f. _pronoun agreement_

◆ *P r a c t i c e   3*   **Finding Your EQ** Turn to Appendix 5, and chart the errors you didn't identify in Practice 1. Then place your errors on the second EQ chart, and see what pattern they form.

HOW TO EDIT

Editing is a two-part job: First, you must locate the errors. Then you must know how to correct them.

Finding Your Errors

Since you can't correct errors until you find them, a major part of editing is proofreading. *Proofreading* is reading to catch grammar, punctuation, mechanics, and spelling errors. If you do not proofread carefully, you will not be able to make the changes that will improve your writing.

One good idea is to read your paragraphs backward, starting with the last sentence first, so you can concentrate on your sentences. Another technique is to keep an error log, in which you list the mistakes you commonly make. An Error Log is provided for you in Appendix 6. To use this log in proofreading, read your paper for one type of error at a time. For example, if you often write fragments, you should read your paper once just to catch fragments. Then read it again to find a second type of error. Asking a friend or tutor to read your writing is always a good idea because you might be missing some errors in your writing that another reader will see. When others read your writing, they might want to use the editing symbols on the inside back cover to label your errors. Then the page references on this chart will guide you to corrections for your errors. You can also use the grammar or spell check on your computer, which will point out possible grammar or spelling errors and make suggestions for correcting them.

Correcting Your Errors

After you find your errors, you need to correct them. To guide you through this phase, a handbook appears in Part V of this text, along with a list of correction symbols (inside back cover) that your instructor might use on your papers.

As you proofread, you should record in your Error Log the corrections you make in your writing. This log can then help you get control of these errors. If you record your corrections each time you find errors, you will eventually learn the grammar concepts that are confusing to you.

Finally, you should use the Editing Checklist at the beginning of this chapter to help you edit your writing. As you attempt to answer each one of the questions on this checklist, look up the grammar items in Part V and make your corrections.

◆ *P r a c t i c e 4* **Using the Handbook** Using the Handbook in Part V, list the page number where you can learn to correct each error you found in Practice 1. This will help you start to use the Handbook as a reference guide.

abbreviation   page _____

capitalization   page _____

comma   page _____

confused word   page _____

end punctuation   page _____

fragment   page _____

modifier   page _____

number   page _____

pronoun agreement   page _____

run-together sentences   page _____

spelling   page _____

subject-verb agreement   page _____

verb form   page _____

 Practice 5   **Using the Error Log and the Spelling Log** Turn to Appendixes 6 and 7, and start an Error Log and a Spelling Log of your own with the errors you didn't identify in Practice 1. For each error, write out the mistake, the Handbook reference, and your correction.

 Practice 6   **Using the Editing Checklist** Use the Editing Checklist at the beginning of this chapter to edit two of the paragraphs from Practice 1. Rewrite the entire paragraphs.

Travis's Editing   When Travis proofreads his paper for grammar, punctuation, mechanics, and spelling, he finds two errors that he looks up in Part V and corrects. The first error is a run-together sentence:

Run-Together: I love the river best, I can always see it from the ridge.

Travis realizes that this sentence has too many subjects and verbs without any linking words or end punctuation between them. He looks up "run-together" on page 408 of Part V and corrects the error by putting a comma and a coordinating conjunction (*and*) between the two sentences.

Correction: I love the river best, **and** I can always see it from the ridge.

He also finds a sentence that doesn't sound complete—it is not a sentence but a fragment:

Fragment: Finally, when it gets dark.

When he looks up the problem in Part V (page 392), he learns that a fragment is easily corrected by connecting it to another sentence.

Correction: Finally, when it gets dark**/,** I can see the headlights of the cars below me moving through the city streets.

Travis's Edited Draft   Both of these errors are corrected here in Travis's edited draft.

    A high, wooded ridge that overlooks my hometown is my favorite place. I can sit up on the ridge and see the river with its many ripples, the colorful sunset, and the city with lots of tall buildings. I love the river best, **and I** can always see it from the ridge. I watch different kinds of boats on the water. For instance, I see rowboats, sailboats, motorboats, and freight liners. They look like toys because I am up so high. My next favorite view is the sunset. Some nights the sunset is really beautiful. There are huge clouds that change from pink to purple to red when the sun goes down behind them. Sometimes I think of a kaleidoscope, and other times I think of a color wheel that spins in slow motion. The sun shines like fire, and then it is gone behind the ridge. Finally, when it gets dark**/,** I can see the headlights of the cars moving through the city streets. The bright headlights follow the street lights as if the street lights are showing the cars where to go. When I am up on the ridge above the town, I get lost in my dreams, and time doesn't exist. On the whole, homework and family problems melt away. I just look around this place, think about its beauty, and feel good— automatically.

Your Editing   Proofread your paragraph carefully to find errors. Then use at least two of the methods from this chapter to help you correct any errors you made in your paragraph. Record your errors and their corrections here.

_____

_____

_____

_____

_____

_____

_____

_____

Your Edited Draft   Now write out a corrected draft of your paragraph.

_____

_____

_____

_____

_____

_____

_____

_____

_____

_____

_____

_____

Review of the Writing Process

Cluoo for Review

- The **writing process** is a series of cyclical tasks that involves prewriting, writing, revising, and editing.
- **Prewriting** consists of generating ideas and planning your paragraph.
  Thinking: Reading, freewriting, brainstorming, clustering, questioning, discussing
  Planning: Deciding on a subject, purpose, and audience
- **Writing** includes writing a topic sentence, developing your ideas, organizing your paragraph, and writing a draft.
  Writing a topic sentence: A limited topic and a statement about that topic
  Developing: Making details more specific; adding details and examples
  Organizing: General to particular, particular to general, chronological, spatial, one extreme to another
  Drafting: Writing a first draft
- **Revising** means "seeing again" and working with organization and development.
- **Editing** involves proofreading and correcting your grammar, punctuation, mechanics, and spelling errors.

◆ *Review Practice 1*

1. What are the four main parts of the writing process?

   _____

2. What is your favorite prewriting activity? Why is it your favorite?

   _____

3. What individual activities do you find yourself doing to start on a writing project?

   _____

4. Where do you usually do your academic writing? Do you write your first draft on a computer? What time of day do you do your best writing?

_____

5. Do you usually let a tutor or friend look at your draft before you revise it?

_____

6. What is the difference between revising and editing?

_____

_____

7. What are the three main categories of editing?

_____

_____

8. Explain editing.

_____

9. What are the two main phases of editing?

_____

10. Do you try to get someone to read your writing before you turn it in? Explain your answer.

_____

_____

 Review Practice 2 Develop each of the following topics into topic sentences, limiting them as much as possible. Then, by following the guidelines furnished in Part I, develop one topic sentence into a paragraph.

1. My English class
2. National politics

3. My favorite pastime
4. Families
5. On the way to school
6. When students relax
7. My dream job
8. The best stereo system
9. What supervisors should never do
10. The clothes I wear to school

Review Practice 3 Revise the paragraph you wrote for Review Practice 2, using the checklist on pages 33–34.

Review Practice 4 Edit the paragraph you wrote for Review Practice 2, using the checklist on page 55.

P
A
R
T

II

WRITING EFFECTIVE PARAGRAPHS

Writing, like life itself, is a voyage of discovery.

—HENRY MILLER

Part II of *Mosaics* will help you write effective paragraphs. These nine chapters will teach you how to use each rhetorical mode to bring out your best writing. First, each chapter provides you with specific guidelines to follow for writing in a particular mode. Then the chapter shows you how to apply those guidelines to three paragraphs—two written by professional writers and one by a student writer. Finally, the chapter takes you through the stages of revising and editing, showing you how to systematically improve your drafts with each of these strategies.

6

DESCRIBING

You can observe a lot just by watching.

—YOGI BERRA

We all use description every day of our lives when we tell others about

The noisy home we grew up in
The worn-leather smell of our favorite baseball glove
The sour taste of a lemon
The smoothness of a snake's skin
The beauty of a special sunset
A sudden clap of thunder in the middle of a quiet night

Whatever you do, description is a large part of your daily thought and language. Your friends might ask what kind of CD player you just bought for your car; your parents may want to know what your duties will be in your new job; your supervisor might need a description of the project you just completed. You really can't communicate effectively without being able to describe people, places, objects, and activities for different audiences.

Description paints a picture in words to help a reader visualize something you have seen or heard or done. Writing about some early memories, Mike Rose describes "a peculiar mix" of elements in his life. What memories do you have of your younger years? Do they form any distinct pattern?

I have many particular memories of this time, but in general these early years seem a peculiar mix of physical warmth and barrenness: a gnarled lemon tree, thin rugs, a dirt alley, concrete in the sun. My uncles visited a few times, and we went to the beach or to orange groves. The return home, however, left the waves and spray, the thick leaves, and split pulp far in the distance. I was aware of my parents watching their money and got the sense from their conversations that things could quickly take a turn for the worse. I started taping pennies to the bottom of a shelf in the kitchen.

Before continuing in this chapter, take a moment to record some of your own memories. Save your work because you will use it later in the chapter.

> **✎ WRITE YOUR OWN DESCRIPTION**
>
> What are some of your most vivid memories from childhood? Do any of them form a single impression when you think about them? Write a paragraph describing your clearest recollection.

HOW TO WRITE A DESCRIPTION PARAGRAPH

Describing is a very natural process that we all do simply and freely without any complex directions. But have you noticed that some people seem to describe events and objects more clearly than other people do? When they tell you what they saw or did, you feel as though you were there too. You can improve your description skills by following a few simple guidelines:

1. *Decide on a dominant impression—the feeling or mood you are trying to communicate.* Do you want your reader to feel sorry for you, to sense the excitement of an amazing fireworks display, or to share your disappointment in a bad restaurant? Choosing a dominant impression will give your description focus and unity. You can't possibly write down everything you observe about a person, place, incident, or object. The result would be a long, confusing, and probably boring list. But if you first decide on a dominant impression for your description, you can then choose which details will best convey that impression.

    The dominant impression Rose conveys about his childhood is its strange mix of "warmth and barrenness [emptiness]." This dominant impression gives his paragraph focus and helps him choose the details that will communicate this feeling most effectively.

2. *Draw on your five senses to write a good description.* If you use all your senses, your readers will be able to see, hear, smell, taste, or touch what you are describing as if they were there with you having the same experience. The more senses you draw on, the more interesting your description will be.

    Look again at Rose's description. He uses his sense of touch when he talks about "physical warmth and barrenness" and refers to "concrete in the sun." He draws on sight when he mentions "a gnarled lemon tree, thin rugs, a dirt alley." "The waves and spray, the thick leaves, and split pulp" draw on our senses of touch and sight. His paragraph is vivid because of all the specific sensory details he furnishes.

3. **When you describe, try to show *rather than* tell *your readers what you want them to know.*** You can tell someone you bought a "great new car." But if you say you bought a "sleek, new black Blazer with four-wheel drive, a tan interior, custom wheels, and an awesome stereo," you're *showing* your readers why you are so excited about your purchase.

   If Rose had simply stopped after stating his dominant impression (that he felt a combination of physical warmth and barrenness in his early childhood), he would be *telling* his readers how he felt. Instead, he *shows* them: The sensory details he cites demonstrate his main point, and the statement "I started taping pennies to the bottom of a shelf in the kitchen" shows us that the feeling of "barrenness" had even seeped into the family finances.

4. ***Organize your description so that your readers can easily follow it.*** Most descriptions are organized from general to particular (from main idea to details), from particular to general (from details to main idea), or spatially (from top to bottom, left to right, inside to outside, and so on). These patterns are all easy for readers to follow.

   Mike Rose organizes his paragraph from general to particular. He starts with the main idea that his childhood was a mixture of "physical warmth and barrenness" and then explains this idea with specific details of both the love and good times (warmth) along with the poverty and insecurity (barrenness) he experienced. In his paragraph, the idea of "warmth" is represented by references to "concrete in the sun," his uncle's visits, trips to the beach, outings to the orange groves, and home. He characterizes the barrenness of his childhood with such details as "a gnarled lemon tree, thin rugs, a dirty alley"; "parents watching their money"; and "pennies under the kitchen counter." The choice and order of these details make Rose's topic sentence come alive.

DISCOVERING HOW DESCRIPTION WORKS

Let's look at two other descriptions. In an autobiographical essay, Joseph Bruchac talks about growing up as a mixture of Native American, Slovak, and French. Accepting his ethnic heritage was a big step he had to take in order to be at peace with himself as a person. As you read this paragraph, ask yourself what dominant impression Bruchac is trying to communicate to his readers.

What do I look like? The features of my face are big: a beaked nose, lips that are too sensitive, and sand-brown eyes and dark eyebrows that lift one at a time like the wings of a bird, a low forehead that looks higher because of receding brown hair, an Adam's apple like a broken bone, two ears that were normal before wrestling flattened one of them. Unlike my grandfather's, my skin is not brown throughout the seasons but sallow in the winter months, though it tans dark and quickly when the sun's warmth returns. It is, as you might gather, a face I did not used to love. Today I look at it in the mirror and say, *Bruchac, you're ugly and I like you*. The face nods back at me, and we laugh together.

1. The entire paragraph creates a certain mood. What is this dominant impression that Bruchac communicates?

   _____

2. In this particular passage, Bruchac describes his face predominantly through the sense of seeing, with a few references to touching and hearing. List at least one example of each of these senses in this paragraph.

   Seeing: _____

   _____

   _____

   Touching: _____

   Hearing: _____

3. Bruchac works hard in this paragraph to *show* rather than *tell* us what he looks like. He tells us that the features of his face are "big." What three details go beyond telling to *show* us his face is "big"?

   _____

   _____

   _____

4. What does Bruchac compare to the wings of a bird? To a broken bone? These comparisons are called *similes* (comparisons between two unlike items using *like* or *as*). How do they *show* rather than *tell*?

   _____

   _____

   _____

5. How does Bruchac organize the details in his paragraph? List some of his details in the order they appear. Then identify his method of organization: general to particular, particular to general, or spatial.

_____   _____

_____   _____

_____   _____

_____   _____

Method of organization: _____

In the next example, an excerpt from "American Horse," author Louise Erdrich describes the house where a poor family lived. See if you can picture this place as she describes it.

They could see the house was empty at first glance. It was only one rectangular room with whitewashed walls and a little gas stove in the middle. They had already come through the cooking lean-to with the other stove and washstand potatoes and a package of turkey necks. Vicki Koob noted that in her perfect-bound notebook. The beds along the walls of the big room were covered with quilts that Albertine's mother, Sophie, had made from bits of old wool coats and pants that the Sisters sold in bundles at the mission. There was no one hiding beneath the beds. No one was under the little aluminum dinette table covered with a green oilcloth or the soft brown wood chairs tucked up to it. One wall of the big room was filled with neatly stacked crates of things—old tools and springs and small half-dismantled appliances. Five or six television sets were stacked against the wall. Their control panels spewed colored wires, and at least one was cracked all the way across. Only the topmost set, with coat-hanger antenna angled sensitively to catch the bounding signals around Little Shell, looked like it could possibly work.

1. What dominant impression do you think Erdrich creates in this paragraph?

_____

2. Erdrich describes the house she is visiting mainly through the sense of seeing, with one reference to touching. Record at least one example of each of these senses from this paragraph.

Seeing: _____

_____

Touching: _____

3. Like Bruchac, Erdrich *shows* rather than *tells* us what this house looks like. List three details that go beyond telling to *showing*.

_____

_____

_____

4. How does Erdrich organize the details in her paragraph? List some of her details in the order they appear. Then identify her method of organization: general to particular, particular to general, or spatial.

_____   _____

_____   _____

_____   _____

_____   _____

_____   _____

_____   _____

Method of organization: _____

REVISING AND EDITING A STUDENT PARAGRAPH

Here is a descriptive paragraph written by Joe Simmons, a college student. As you read it, figure out what dominant impression Joe is trying to communicate, and think of ways he might convey this impression more fully.

[1]I started college. [2]I decided to redecorate my room. [3]It is now one of my favorite places in the world. [4]But it used to remind me of a damp cave with no light. [5]The room had no personality at all.

[6]Now the walls is loaded with posters of my favorite mottoes. [7]And musical groups. [8]The bed came from Goodwill Industries and is made of black wrought iron. [9]The space at an angle to my bed is a window covered by some wild curtains of blue, green, silver, and lavender that my grandma made. [10]My antique desk with a roll-top is against the wall opposite my bed the top of it is always buried with everything but school work. [11]Some incense sits on a small table next to my door. [12]My door is usually closed so I can get some peace and quiet. [13]I love the silent times behind my door. [14]When no one can get to me.

This paragraph is Joe's first draft, which now needs to be revised and edited. First, apply the Revising Checklist below to the content of Joe's draft. When you are satisfied that his ideas are fully developed and well organized, use the Editing Checklist on pages 82–83 to correct his grammar and mechanics errors. Answer the questions after each checklist. Then write your suggested changes directly on Joe's draft.

REVISING CHECKLIST ✔

TOPIC SENTENCE
✔ Does the topic sentence convey the paragraph's controlling idea?
✔ Does the topic sentence appear as the first or last sentence of the paragraph?

DEVELOPMENT
✔ Does the paragraph contain *specific* details that support the topic sentence?
✔ Does the paragraph include *enough* details to explain the topic sentence fully?

UNITY
✔ Do all the sentences in the paragraph support the topic sentence?

ORGANIZATION
✔ Is the paragraph organized logically?

COHERENCE
✔ Do the sentences move smoothly and logically from one to the next?

Topic Sentence

1. What dominant impression does Joe communicate in his paragraph?

_____

2. Put brackets around Joe's topic sentence. Does it convey Joe's dominant impression?

_____

3. Rewrite it if necessary to introduce all the ideas in Joe's paragraph.

_____

Development

1. Does the paragraph draw on all five senses? Record three details from
   Joe's paragraph that come from three different senses. Label each example with the sense related to it.

Sense	Detail
_____	_____
_____	_____
_____	_____

2. Does Joe's paragraph *show* rather than *tell* readers what they need to
   know?

_____

Give three examples.

_____

_____

_____

3. Add another detail to Joe's paragraph.
4. Add one simile to Joe's paragraph. (Reminder: A simile is a comparison between two unlike items using *like* or *as*.)

Unity

1. Read each of Joe's sentences with his topic sentence (revised, if necessary) in mind.
2. Drop or rewrite any of his sentences that are not directly related to his topic sentence.

Organization

1. Read Joe's paragraph again to see if all the sentences are arranged logically.
2. List some of his details in the order they appear. Then identify his method of organization: general to particular, particular to general, or spatial.

_____   _____

_____   _____

_____   _____

Method of organization: _____

Coherence

For a list of transitions, see pages 46–47.

1. Circle three transitions Joe uses.
2. Explain how one of these makes Joe's paragraph easier to read.

_____

Now rewrite Joe's paragraph with your revisions.

EDITING CHECKLIST ✔

SENTENCES

✔ Does each sentence have a main subject and verb?

✔ Do all subjects and verbs agree?

✔ Do all pronouns agree with their nouns?

✔ Are modifiers as close as possible to the words they modify?

PUNCTUATION AND MECHANICS

✔ Are sentences punctuated correctly?

✔ Are words capitalized properly?

WORD CHOICE AND SPELLING
✔ Are words used correctly?
✔ Are words spelled correctly?

Sentences

Subjects and Verbs

1. Underline the subjects once and verbs twice in your revision of Joe's paragraph. Remember that sentences can have more than one subject-verb set.

2. Does each of the sentences have at least one subject and verb that can stand alone?

For help with subjects and verbs, see Chapter 30.

3. Did you find and correct Joe's two fragments? If not, find and correct them now.

For help with fragments, see Chapter 31.

4. Did you find and correct Joe's run-together sentence? If not, find and correct it now.

For help with run-togethers, see Chapter 32.

Subject-Verb Agreement

1. Read aloud the subjects and verbs you underlined in your revision of Joe's paragraph.

For help with subject-verb agreement, see Chapter 35.

2. Did you find and correct the subject and verb that do not agree? If not, find and correct them now.

Pronoun Agreement

1. Find any pronouns in your revision of Joe's paragraph that do not agree with their nouns.

For help with pronoun agreement, see Chapter 39.

2. Correct any pronouns that do not agree with their nouns.

Modifier Errors

1. Find any modifiers in your revision of Joe's paragraph that are not as close as possible to the words they modify.

For help with modifier errors, see Chapter 42.

2. Rewrite sentences if necessary so that modifiers are as close as possible to the words they modify.

Punctuation and Mechanics

Punctuation

For help with punctuation, see Chapters 43–47.

1. Read your revision of Joe's paragraph for any errors in punctuation.

2. Find the two fragments and one run-together sentence you revised, and make sure they are punctuated correctly.

Mechanics

For help with capitalization, see Chapter 48.

1. Read your revision of Joe's paragraph for any errors in capitalization.

2. Be sure to check Joe's capitalization in the fragments and run-together sentence you revised.

Word Choice and Spelling

Word Choice

For help with confused words, see Chapter 54.

1. Find any words used incorrectly in your revision of Joe's paragraph.

2. Correct any errors you find.

Spelling

For help with spelling, see Chapter 55.

1. Use spell-check and a dictionary to check the spelling in your revision of Joe's paragraph.

2. Correct any misspelled words.

Now rewrite Joe's paragraph again with your editing corrections.

REVISING AND EDITING YOUR OWN PARAGRAPH

Returning to the description paragraph you wrote earlier in this chapter, revise and edit your own writing. The checklists will help you apply what you have learned to your own paragraph.

REVISING CHECKLIST ✓

TOPIC SENTENCE
- ☐ Does the topic sentence convey the paragraph's controlling idea?
- ☐ Does the topic sentence appear as the first or last sentence of the paragraph?

DEVELOPMENT
- ☐ Does the paragraph contain *specific* details that support the topic sentence?

□ Does the paragraph include *enough* details to explain the topic sentence fully?

UNITY

□ Do all the sentences in the paragraph support the topic sentence?

ORGANIZATION

□ Is the paragraph organized logically?

COHERENCE

□ Do the sentences move smoothly and logically from one to the next?

Topic Sentence

1. What dominant impression are you trying to communicate in your paragraph?

_____

2. Put brackets around your topic sentence. Does it convey your dominant impression?

_____

3. How can you change your topic sentence if necessary to introduce all the ideas in your paragraph?

_____

Development

1. Does your paragraph draw on all five senses? Record three details from your paragraph that draw on three different senses. Label each example with the sense it draws on.

Sense	Detail

2. Does your paragraph *show* rather than *tell* readers what they need to know? Give three examples.

_____

_____

_____

3. Add another detail to your paragraph.
4. Add one comparison or simile to your paragraph. (Reminder: A simile is a comparison between two unlike items using *like* or *as*.)

Unity

1. Read each of your sentences with your topic sentence in mind.
2. Drop or rewrite any sentences not directly related to your topic sentence.

Organization

1. Read your paragraph again to see if all the sentences are arranged logically.
2. List some of your details in the order they appear. Then identify your method of organization: general to particular, particular to general, or spatial.

_____

_____

_____

_____

_____

Method of organization: _____

Coherence

1. Circle three transitions you used.

2. Explain how one of these makes your paragraph easier to read.

For a list of transitions, see pages 46–47.

Now rewrite your paragraph with your revisions.

EDITING CHECKLIST ✔

SENTENCES
- ✔ Does each sentence have a main subject and verb?
- ✔ Do all subjects and verbs agree?
- ✔ Do all pronouns agree with their nouns?
- ✔ Are modifiers as close as possible to the words they modify?

PUNCTUATION AND MECHANICS
- ✔ Are sentences punctuated correctly?
- ✔ Are words capitalized properly?

WORD CHOICE AND SPELLING
- ✔ Are words used correctly?
- ✔ Are words spelled correctly?

Sentences

Subjects and Verbs

1. Underline the subjects once and verbs twice in your revised paragraph. Remember that sentences can have more than one subject-verb set.

2. Does each of your sentences have at least one subject and verb that can stand alone?

For help with subjects and verbs, see Chapter 30.

For help with fragments, see Chapter 31.

3. Correct any fragments you have written.

4. Correct any run-together sentences you have written.

For help with run-togethers, see Chapter 32.

Subject-Verb Agreement

For help with subject-verb agreement, see Chapter 35.

1. Read aloud the subjects and verbs you underlined in your revised paragraph.
2. Correct any subjects and verbs that do not agree.

Pronoun Agreement

For help with pronoun agreement, see Chapter 39.

1. Find any pronouns in your revised paragraph that do not agree with their nouns.
2. Correct any pronouns that do not agree with their nouns.

Modifier Errors

For help with modifier errors, see Chapter 42.

1. Find any modifiers in your revised paragraph that are not as close as possible to the words they modify.
2. Rewrite sentences if necessary so that your modifiers are as close as possible to the words they modify.

Punctuation and Mechanics
Punctuation

For help with punctuation, see Chapters 43–47.

1. Read your revised paragraph for any errors in punctuation.
2. Make sure any fragments and run-together sentences you revised are punctuated properly.

Mechanics

For help with capitalization, see Chapter 48.

1. Read your revised paragraph for any errors in capitalization.
2. Be sure to check your capitalization in any fragments or run-together sentences you revised.

Word Choice and Spelling
Word Choice

For help with confused words, see Chapter 54.

1. Find any words used incorrectly in your revised paragraph.
2. Correct any errors you find.

Spelling

For help with spelling, see Chapter 55.

1. Use spell-check and a dictionary to check your spelling.
2. Correct any misspelled words.

Now rewrite your paragraph again with your editing corrections.

PRACTICING DESCRIPTION

Reading Suggestions

In Chapter 21, you will find two essays that follow the guidelines for writing description that you studied in this chapter: "Magpies" by Amy Tan and "Longing to Die of Old Age" by Alice Walker. You might want to read these selections before writing another description. As you read, notice how the writers pull you into each experience through sensory details.

Writing Workshop

Guidelines for Writing a Description Paragraph

1. Decide on a dominant impression—the feeling or mood you are trying to communicate.
2. Draw on your five senses to write a good description.
3. When you describe, try to *show* rather than *tell* your readers what you want them to know.
4. Organize your description so that your readers can easily follow it.

1. Place yourself in this scene, and describe it in as much detail as possible. Imagine that you can see, hear, smell, taste, and touch everything in this picture. What are your sensations? How do you feel? Before you

begin to write, be sure you decide what dominant impression you want to convey. Then choose your details carefully.

2. Starting college is an important decision for students and everyone associated with them—parents, children, friends, relatives, even the household pets. Describe a person who was helpful with your decision to go to college. Be sure you decide on a dominant impression before you begin to write.

3. You have been asked to write a short statement for your psychology class on the study environment that is best for you. Describe this environment. Where do you study? What sounds do you hear? What do you eat or drink as you study? What do you wear? Help your readers picture your study environment so that they feel they are actually there. Be sure you decide on a dominant impression before you begin to write.

4. Create your own description assignment (with the help of your instructor), and write a response to it.

Revising Workshop

Small Group Activity (5–10 minutes per writer)   Working in groups of three or four, each person should read his or her description paragraph to the other members of the group. Those listening should record their reactions on a copy of the Peer Evaluation Form in Appendix 2A. After your group goes through this process, give your evaluation forms to the appropriate writers so that each writer has two or three peer comment sheets for revising.

Paired Activity (5 minutes per writer)   Using the completed Peer Evaluation Forms, work in pairs to decide what you should revise in your paragraphs. If time allows, rewrite some of your sentences, and have your partner check them.

Individual Activity   Rewrite your paper, using the revising feedback you received from other students.

Editing Workshop

Paired Activity (5–10 minutes per writer)   Swap papers with a classmate, and use the editing portion of your Peer Evaluation Form to identify as many grammar, punctuation, mechanics, and spelling errors as you can. If time allows, correct some of your errors, and have your partner check them.

Record your grammar, punctuation, and mechanics errors in the Error Log (Appendix 6) and your spelling errors in the Spelling Log (Appendix 7).

Individual Activity   Rewrite your paper again, using the editing feedback you received from other students.

Reflecting on Your Writing

When you have completed your own paragraph, answer these five questions:

1. What was most difficult about this assignment?
2. What was easiest?
3. What did you learn about description by completing this assignment?
4. What do you think are the strengths of your description? What are its weaknesses?
5. What did you learn from this assignment about your own writing process—about preparing to write, about writing the first draft, about revising, and about editing?

7

NARRATING

> One writes out of one thing only—one's own experience. Everything depends on how relentlessly one forces from this experience the last drop, sweet or bitter, it can possibly give.

—JAMES BALDWIN

Although you may not realize it, you are already very good at narrating. Think of the times you told someone about something that happened to you:

> The traffic jam on the way to school today
> The conversation you had at the gym last night
> The funny experience at the mall
> Your favorite vacation as a child

Narrating is storytelling. Whenever you tell someone about something that happened to you—your senior prom, a job interview, an argument with your spouse, a terrific (or terrible) date—you are narrating. We probably rely more on narration than on any other rhetorical mode. Even jokes depend on our ability to tell a story.

Narration is a powerful way of focusing other people's attention on the thoughts you want to share with them. Because narration is often based on personal experience, it also teaches us about life. Russell Baker, a newspaper writer and the author of an award-winning autobiography titled *Growing Up*, recalls the "sweet times" in his house when he was a young child. Can you think of an event that taught you something important about life? What was the event? What did you learn?

> The summer I was four years old my mother bought me my first book and started to teach me to read. One night at bedtime she and my father

stretched out on the blanket for sleep, but before dousing the lamp my father wanted to see how I was progressing with the written word.

They placed me between them with the open book. I knew a few words, but under pressure to perform forgot everything. It was beginner material: "cat," "rat," "boy," "girl," "the." I didn't recognize a word.

My mother was disappointed that I could do nothing but stare stupidly at the printed page. My father saved my pride. "Have a little patience with him," he said. Taking the book in hand, he moved me close against him and rubbed his cheek against mine. "Now," he said, pointing to a word, "you know that word, don't you?"

I did indeed. "The," I said.

"You're a smart boy. I bet you know this one too."

"Boy," I said.

When I read most of the sentence without too much help, he said to my mother, "You're doing good with him. Maybe we ought to send him to college." Pleased, my mother reached across me and kissed him on the cheek. Smiling down at me, he said, "You want to go to college?" They both laughed a little at this. Maybe he liked the extravagance of the idea as much as she did. Then he turned off the kerosene lamp. That night they let me sleep between them.

Before continuing in this chapter, take a moment to record a story of your own. Save your work because you will use it later in the chapter.

✎ WRITE YOUR OWN NARRATION

What are some events in your life that have taught you important lessons? Does one event stand out in your mind? What lesson did it teach you? Write a paragraph telling the students in your class about this event.

HOW TO WRITE A NARRATION PARAGRAPH

To write a narration paragraph, you simply tell a story with a point to it. It doesn't have to be a heart-stopping adventure or a romantic episode with a happy ending. Just draw on what you know, as the quotation that opened this chapter suggests. Choose an event that matters to you, and give your readers a sense of that event's significance. Here are some guidelines to help you make your narrative interesting.

1. ***Make sure your story has a point.*** Before you begin to write, decide what the main point of your story is. What is your purpose for writing

the narrative? We have all heard stories that seem to go on forever with no apparent point. Such unfocused narratives become boring very quickly.

In the excerpt you just read, Russell Baker captures the pride he and his parents felt as he showed off his new reading skills. All the details in the story build up to this main point.

2. *Use the five W's and one H to construct your story.* The five W's and one H are the questions *Who? What? When? Where? Why?* and *How?* These are the questions journalists use to make sure they cover all the basic information in a news story. Though you may not be a journalist, these questions can help you come up with details and ideas for a well-developed narrative paragraph.

   When you review Baker's story, you can see that he might have used the reporter's questions to guide his writing: Who is present? What is each person doing? When is this scene taking place? Where are they? Why is Baker proud of himself? How do we know this was a memorable event for Baker? Baker covers the answers to all these questions in this brief narrative.

3. *Use vivid descriptive details to develop your story.* The more specific your details, the more vivid your story becomes because your readers will actually be able to picture the scenes. These descriptive details should fill in the ideas you generated with the six journalistic questions.

   Look again at Baker's story. From this narrative, we know that Baker is four years old; we know it is bedtime; we know Baker is between his parents in bed; we know he is reading his first book, which is full of words like "cat," "rat," "boy," "girl," and "the"; we know his father encouraged him by rubbing his cheek against Baker's; we know Baker finally read the words "the" and "boy"; we know his parents were pleased enough to let him sleep between them that night. These descriptive details help readers participate in Baker's narrative.

4. *Organize your narration so that your readers can easily follow it.* Most narratives are organized chronologically, according to a time sequence. Begin your paragraph with a topic sentence, and then arrange your details in the order they happened: First this happened, then that, and next something else. Help your reader follow your narrative by using good transitions—words like *first, second, then, next,* and *finally.* Good transitions also make your narrative smooth rather than choppy.

   Russell Baker organizes his narrative chronologically. It moves through time from one incident to the next. Baker begins by explaining that his mom was teaching him how to read when he was four years old, continues by relating how he was going to show his father his progress, and finishes by implying how happy he was that his parents were so proud of him. Because it follows a single time sequence and does not jump around, this paragraph is easy to follow.

DISCOVERING HOW NARRATION WORKS

Let's consider two more narration paragraphs. In the first example, Brent Staples, the author of the autobiography *Parallel Time: Growing Up in Black and White*, relates an event that happened in his English class. What do you think Staples's main point is?

> [Miss Riley] had a talent for reaching us. One day while reading to us, she came across the word "rhubarb" and was stunned to find that none of us had ever tasted it. Her eyes flashed in amazement; you could see a novel solution taking shape. Later that week, she came to class with a tray of rhubarb pielets, one for each of us. As the tray went around the room, she held aloft a stalk of rhubarb and talked about its origins. We bit into the pies in unison. "Taste how it's sweet and tangy at the same time," she said. She watched intently, as though tasting the pie through our mouths.

1. All the details in Staples's paragraph lead to one main point. What is that point?

   _____

2. Staples covers all the journalist's questions. Record at least one detail the author uses in response to each question.

   Who? _____

   What? _____

   When? _____

   Where? _____

   Why? _____

   How? _____

3. Staples uses vivid descriptive details to develop his brief story. In your opinion, which two details are most vivid? What makes them so vivid?

_____

_____

_____

4. How does Staples organize the details in this paragraph? List some of his details in the order they appear. Then identify his method of organization.

_____   _____

_____   _____

_____   _____

Method of organization: _____

The next paragraph is from a book titled *Deaf in America: Voices from a Culture*. It was written by Bernard Bragg, a deaf man. In it, Bragg recalls his thoughts and feelings as a young child left alone at a residential school for deaf students. Can you feel the fear in this paragraph?

> I asked again where we were going, but [my mother] gave no reply. For the first time, I began to feel a sense of fear and foreboding. I stole glances at her face, but it was immobile, and her eyes were fixed on an unseen place somewhere ahead. We rode for a long time, and then we stopped and found ourselves in front of an enormous building. We walked into the building, and once inside I was immediately struck by a medicinal, institutional smell. This did not look like a hospital or like any other building I had seen before. My mother bent down, turned me toward her, and said, "This is where you will get your education. You will live here for a while. Don't worry. I will see you again later." Then she couldn't seem to say any more. She hugged me quickly, gave me a kiss, and then, inexplicably, left.

1. The main point of this paragraph is not as obvious as the main point of the previous example; nevertheless, all the details support one main point. What is that point?

_____

2. Bragg covers all the journalist's questions. Record at least one detail he uses in response to each question.

Who? _____

What? _____

When? _____

Where? _____

Why? _____

How? _____

3. Bragg uses vivid descriptive details to develop his brief story. In your opinion, which two details are most vivid? Why are they vivid?

    _____

    _____

4. How does Bragg organize the details in this paragraph? List some of his details in the order they appear. Then identify his method of organization.

    _____   _____

    _____   _____

    _____   _____

    _____   _____

    _____   _____

    Method of organization: _____

REVISING AND EDITING A STUDENT PARAGRAPH

Following is a narrative paragraph written by a student named Robert Martinez. As you read his paragraph, try to figure out his main point.

¹We started our vacation early in the morning fishing for bass. ²We had gone to the lake so many times with our dads, and now we

were there all by ourselves. ³Boy, this was a great feeling? ⁴We settled back. ⁵And waited for those nibbles on my line. ⁶The first sign of trouble came when the conservation officer's boat started heading toward us. ⁷Suddenly, I remembered fishing licenses, a detail our dads always took care of for us. ⁸We were worried, but we didn't think that anything really bad would happen. ⁹Except for once when I got caught cheating on a science test, I had never been in trouble before. ¹⁰But we have several friends who get in trouble all the time. ¹¹The conservation officer looked serious. ¹²Can you imagine our surprise when he told us we really were in trouble. ¹³We were under arrest. ¹⁴Suddenly, we weren't so excited about being on our own.

This paragraph is Robert's first draft, which now needs to be revised and edited. First, apply the Revising Checklist below to the content of Robert's draft. When you are satisfied that his ideas are fully developed and well organized, use the Editing Checklist on page 100 to correct his grammar and mechanics errors. Answer the questions after each checklist. Then write your suggested changes directly on Robert's draft.

REVISING CHECKLIST ✔

TOPIC SENTENCE
✔ Does the topic sentence convey the paragraph's controlling idea?
✔ Does the topic sentence appear as the first or last sentence of the paragraph?

DEVELOPMENT
✔ Does the paragraph contain *specific* details that support the topic sentence?
✔ Does the paragraph include *enough* details to explain the topic sentence fully?

UNITY
✔ Do all the sentences in the paragraph support the topic sentence?

ORGANIZATION
✔ Is the paragraph organized logically?

COHERENCE
✔ Do the sentences move smoothly and logically from one to the next?

Topic Sentence

1. What is Robert's main point in his paragraph?

   _____

2. Put brackets around Robert's topic sentence. Does it convey Robert's
   main point?

   _____

3. Rewrite it if necessary to introduce all the ideas in his paragraph.

   _____

   _____

Development

1. Does the paragraph answer all the journalist's questions? Record at
   least one detail Robert uses in response to each question.

   Who? _____

   What? _____

   When? _____

   Where? _____

   Why? _____

   How? _____

2. Add two new details to Robert's paragraph that support his main idea.

Unity

1. Read each of Robert's sentences with his topic sentence (revised, if
   necessary) in mind.
2. Cross out the two sentences not directly related to Robert's topic
   sentence.

Organization

1. Read Robert's paragraph again to see if all the sentences are arranged
   logically.

2. List the word clues in Robert's paragraph that tell you how it is organized. Then identify his method of organization.

_____   _____

_____   _____

Method of organization: _____

Coherence

1. Circle two words or phrases Robert repeats.
2. Explain how one of these makes Robert's paragraph easier to read.

_____

Now rewrite Robert's paragraph with your revisions.

EDITING CHECKLIST ✔

SENTENCES
- ✔ Does each sentence have a main subject and verb?
- ✔ Do all subjects and verbs agree?
- ✔ Do all pronouns agree with their nouns?
- ✔ Are modifiers as close as possible to the words they modify?

PUNCTUATION AND MECHANICS
- ✔ Are sentences punctuated correctly?
- ✔ Are words capitalized properly?

WORD CHOICE AND SPELLING
- ✔ Are words used correctly?
- ✔ Are words spelled correctly?

Sentences

Subjects and Verbs

For help with subjects and verbs, see Chapter 30.

1. Underline the subjects once and verbs twice in your revision of Robert's paragraph. Remember that sentences can have more than one subject-verb set.

2. Does each of the sentences have at least one subject and verb that can stand alone?

_____

3. Did you find and correct Robert's fragment? If not, find and correct it now.

For help with fragments, see Chapter 31.

Subject-Verb Agreement

1. Read aloud the subjects and verbs you underlined in your revision of Robert's paragraph.

2. Correct any subjects and verbs that do not agree.

For help with subject-verb agreement, see Chapter 35.

Pronoun Agreement

1. Find any pronouns in your revision of Robert's paragraph that do not agree with their nouns.

2. Did you find and correct the two pronouns that do not agree with their nouns? If not, find and correct them now.

For help with pronoun agreement, see Chapter 39.

Modifier Errors

1. Find any modifiers in your revision of Robert's paragraph that are not as close as possible to the words they modify.

2. Rewrite sentences if necessary so that modifiers are as close as possible to the words they modify.

For help with modifier errors, see Chapter 42.

Punctuation and Mechanics

Punctuation

1. Read your revision of Robert's paragraph for any errors in punctuation.

2. Find the fragment you revised, and make sure it is punctuated correctly.

3. Did you find and correct his other two punctuation errors? If not, find and correct them now.

For help with punctuation, see Chapters 43–47.

Mechanics

1. Read your revision of Robert's paragraph for any errors in capitalization.

2. Be sure to check Robert's capitalization in the fragment you revised.

For help with capitalization, see Chapter 48.

Word Choice and Spelling

Word Choice

For help with confused words, see Chapter 54.

1. Find any words used incorrectly in your revision of Robert's paragraph.

2. Correct any errors you find.

Spelling

For help with spelling, see Chapter 55.

1. Use spell-check and a dictionary to check the spelling in your revision of Robert's paragraph.

2. Correct any misspelled words.

Now rewrite Robert's paragraph again with your editing corrections.

REVISING AND EDITING YOUR OWN PARAGRAPH

Returning to the narration paragraph you wrote earlier in this chapter, revise and edit your own writing. The checklists will help you apply what you have learned to your own paragraph.

REVISING CHECKLIST ✔

TOPIC SENTENCE
- ☐ Does the topic sentence convey the paragraph's controlling idea?
- ☐ Does the topic sentence appear as the first or last sentence of the paragraph?

DEVELOPMENT
- ☐ Does the paragraph contain *specific* details that support the topic sentence?
- ☐ Does the paragraph include *enough* details to explain the topic sentence fully?

UNITY
- ☐ Do all the sentences in the paragraph support the topic sentence?

ORGANIZATION
- ☐ Is the paragraph organized logically?

COHERENCE
- ☐ Do the sentences move smoothly and logically from one to the next?

Topic Sentence

1. What is the main point you are trying to make in your paragraph?

_____

2. Put brackets around your topic sentence. Does it convey your main idea?

_____

3. How can you change your topic sentence if necessary to introduce all the ideas in your paragraph?

_____

Development

1. Does your paragraph answer all the journalist's questions? Record at least one detail you use in response to each question.

Who? _____

What? _____

When? _____

Where? _____

Why? _____

How? _____

2. Add two new details to your paragraph that support your main idea.

Unity

1. Read each of your sentences with your topic sentence (revised, if necessary) in mind.
2. Drop or rewrite any sentences not directly related to your topic sentence.

Organization

1. Read your paragraph again to see if all the sentences are arranged logically.

2. List the word clues in your paragraph that tell you how it is organized. Then identify your method of organization.

_____

_____

Method of organization: _____

Coherence

1. Circle two words or phrases you repeat.
2. Explain how one of these makes your paragraph easier to read.

_____

_____

Now rewrite your paragraph with your revisions.

EDITING CHECKLIST ✔

SENTENCES

☐ Does each sentence have a main subject and verb?

☐ Do all subjects and verbs agree?

☐ Do all pronouns agree with their nouns?

☐ Are modifiers as close as possible to the words they modify?

PUNCTUATION AND MECHANICS

☐ Are sentences punctuated correctly?

☐ Are words capitalized properly?

WORD CHOICE AND SPELLING

☐ Are words used correctly?

☐ Are words spelled correctly?

Sentences

Subjects and Verbs

For help with subjects and verbs, see Chapter 30.

1. Underline the subjects once and verbs twice in your revised paragraph. Remember that sentences can have more than one subject-verb set.

2. Does each of your sentences have at least one subject and one verb that can stand alone?

---

3. Correct any fragments you have written.

4. Correct any run-together sentences you have written.

For help with fragments, see Chapter 31.

For help with run-togethers, see Chapter 32.

Subject-Verb Agreement

1. Read aloud the subjects and verbs you underlined in your revised paragraph.

2. Correct any subjects and verbs that do not agree.

For help with subject-verb agreement, see Chapter 35.

Pronoun Agreement

1. Find any pronouns in your revised paragraph that do not agree with their nouns.

2. Correct any pronouns that do not agree with their nouns.

For help with pronoun agreement, see Chapter 39.

Modifier Errors

1. Find any modifiers in your revised paragraph that are not as close as possible to the words they modify.

2. Rewrite sentences if necessary so that your modifiers are as close as possible to the words they modify.

For help with modifier errors, see Chapter 42.

Punctuation and Mechanics

Punctuation

1. Read your revised paragraph for any errors in punctuation.

2. Make sure any fragments and run-together sentences you revised are punctuated correctly.

For help with punctuation, see Chapters 43–47.

Mechanics

1. Read your revised paragraph for any errors in capitalization.

2. Be sure to check your capitalization in any fragments or run-together sentences you revised.

For help with capitalization, see Chapter 48.

Word Choice and Spelling

Word Choice

1. Find any words used incorrectly in your revised paragraph.

2. Correct any errors you find.

For help with confused words, see Chapter 54.

Spelling

For help with spelling, see Chapter 55.

1. Use spell-check and a dictionary to check the spelling in your revised paragraph.
2. Correct any misspelled words.

Now rewrite your paragraph again with your editing corrections.

PRACTICING NARRATION

Reading Suggestions

In Chapter 22, you will find two narrative essays that follow the guidelines you studied in this chapter: "Eleven" by Sandra Cisneros and "Choosing the Path with Honor" by Michael Arredondo. You might want to read these selections before writing another narration. As you read, notice how the writers cover the journalistic questions and use vivid descriptive details to pull you into their narratives, making the significance of the essays all the more meaningful.

Writing Workshop

Guidelines for Writing a Narration Paragraph

1. Make sure your story has a point.
2. Use the five *W*'s and one *H* to construct your story.
3. Use vivid descriptive details to develop your story.
4. Organize your narration so that your readers can easily follow it.

1. Place yourself in this scene, and write a narrative about what is happening. How did you get here? Why are you here? Where are you going? Be sure to decide on a main point before you begin to write.

2. We have all had experiences that began as carefree adventures and ended up as misadventures. Imagine that a national magazine is asking for honest stories about experiences that turned bad unexpectedly. The winning story will be published, and the author will win $200. You decide to enter the competition. The directions are to explain an experience in such a way that you reveal your feelings about this activity. Be sure to decide on a main point before you begin to write.

3. Your high school's alumni newsletter has asked you to explain an episode that influenced the values you hold today. Recall an event that influenced the kind of person you are today. First, identify one of your core values, such as honesty, hard work, a strong sense of responsibility, independence, or patience. Then think back to what happened to give you this particular value, and write a paragraph telling the story about that value. The purpose of this narrative is to give current high school students some sense of how values might form in their own lives. Where can they look? How do values develop? Be sure to decide on a main point before you begin to write.

4. Create your own narration assignment (with the help of your instructor), and write a response to it.

Revising Workshop

Small Group Activity (5–10 minutes per writer) Working in groups of three or four, each person should read his or her narrative paragraph to the other members of the group. Those listening should record their reactions on a copy of the Peer Evaluation Form in Appendix 2B. After your group goes through this process, give your evaluation forms to the appropriate writers so that each writer has two or three peer comment sheets for revising.

Paired Activity (5 minutes per writer) Using the completed Peer Evaluation Forms, work in pairs to decide what you should revise in your paragraphs. If time allows, rewrite some of your sentences, and have your partner check them.

Individual Activity Rewrite your paper, using the revising feedback you received from other students.

Editing Workshop

Paired Activity (5–10 minutes per writer) Swap papers with a classmate, and use the editing portion of your Peer Evaluation Form to identify as many grammar, punctuation, mechanics, and spelling errors as you can. If time allows, correct some of your errors, and have your partner check them. Record your grammar, punctuation, and mechanics errors in the Error Log (Appendix 6) and your spelling errors in the Spelling Log (Appendix 7).

Individual Activity Rewrite your paper again using the editing feedback you received from other students.

Reflecting on Your Writing

When you have completed your own essay, answer these five questions:

1. What was most difficult about this assignment?

2. What was easiest?

3. What did you learn about narration by completing this assignment?

4. What do you think are the strengths of your narration paragraph? What are its weaknesses?

5. What did you learn from this assignment about your own writing process—about preparing to write, about writing the first draft, about revising, and about editing?

ILLUSTRATING

CHAPTER 8

> As you go on writing and thinking, your ideas will
> arrange themselves. They will arrange themselves as
> sand strewn upon stretched parchment does—as I
> have read somewhere—in response to a musical note.
>
> —WILLIAM BUTLER YEATS

Think of the many times you have said to someone, "What do you mean? Can you give me an example?" We use examples every day to make a point.

Point:	We spend a lot of money on medical research in the United States.
Example:	Nationally, we spend over $1 billion a year on cancer research.
Point:	San Francisco is an exciting city.
Example:	Crossing the Golden Gate Bridge is a thrill, and the people and cable cars are always in motion.

Illustrating is simply giving examples to make a point. In other words, examples or "illustrations" are specific instances that explain a general statement. Examples come very naturally in daily conversation. You might say, for instance, that professional athletes train hard and long to maintain their skills and then give a couple of examples to prove your point: Andre Agassi trains six to eight hours a day all year long, Tiger Woods spends five hours a day at the driving range, and Shaquille O'Neal lifts weights for two hours a day, seven days a week.

You can draw examples from your experience, your observations, and your reading. Well-chosen examples supply concrete detail to support abstract ideas such as courage, embarrassment, understanding, love, and boredom. For example, you can *tell* your reader that you were bored ("I was bored"), or you can *show* how bored you were by giving an example ("I was so bored that I read the cereal box"). Similarly, you can make a generalization ("I like sweets") more interesting by furnishing specifics ("I love chocolate").

For his article "It's Such a Pleasure to Learn," Wallace Terry interviewed a 100-year-old man named John Morton-Finney. In his topic sentence, Terry uses the general term *special* to describe Morton-Finney. In the rest of the paragraph, he uses specific examples to support this statement. Who are some special people in your life?

> John Morton-Finney is a very special old man. Born the son of a former slave, he served in World War I, became fluent in six foreign languages, earned 11 degrees, taught school until he was 81, and still practices law. His thirst for learning has never abated. In his 60s, he started college all over again, earning his fourth bachelor's degree at 75. Today he attends law-school seminars with the wide-eyed eagerness of a freshman.

Before continuing in this chapter, take a moment to write your own paragraph using examples. Save your work because you will use it later in the chapter.

✎ WRITE YOUR OWN ILLUSTRATION

Who is a very special person in your life? Why is this person so special? Write a paragraph that starts with a general statement about your special person and includes specific examples to support your claim.

HOW TO WRITE AN ILLUSTRATION PARAGRAPH

To write an illustration paragraph, you use examples to support a point you want to make. Although good examples come in a variety of forms, they often draw on description. For example, if you say that someone is a good cook, you might give the following examples, all of which draw on description: His chicken pot pie has huge chunks of chicken and carrots and the flakiest crust ever; he makes a really crunchy cole slaw; and the sweet, nutty smell of his cinnamon rolls makes you want to eat breakfast three times a day. Furnishing examples usually just means following your instincts, but the guidelines here will help you write a paragraph that uses examples in clear and interesting ways.

1. ***State your main point in your first sentence.*** Before you begin to write, think about the main point you want to make. Then choose your words as carefully as possible to express that idea as the topic sentence of your paragraph. This should be your first sentence. In the rest of your paragraph, you will explain this main point through the examples you furnish.

   In the sample paragraph at the beginning of this chapter, Terry expresses his main point in his first sentence: *John Morton-Finney is a very special old man*. He introduces this idea as the focus of the paragraph and then sets out to expand on it.

2. ***Choose examples that focus on the point you want to make.*** The examples themselves serve as your explanation of the paragraph's main point. They help you prove that your main point is true, and they should all be directly related to your main point. As in a well-written descriptive paragraph, good examples *show* rather than *tell* the readers what the author is trying to say.

   In his paragraph, Terry provides examples from Morton-Finney's life that *show* why he is special. All of the examples in the paragraph focus on this single point: Morton-Finney's specialness. This clear focus makes this paragraph coherent and unified.

3. ***Use a sufficient number of examples to make your point.*** How many examples is enough? That depends on the point you are trying to make. Usually, two or three short examples are sufficient, although sometimes one extended example is the best choice.

   Wallace Terry offers eight examples to demonstrate how special Morton-Finney's life really was: son of a slave, World War I veteran, six foreign languages, 11 degrees, teacher until 81, law practice, fourth bachelor's degree at 75, law seminars. He wants to make sure his readers have no doubts whatsoever about the truth of his main point.

4. ***Organize your illustrations so that your readers can easily follow along.*** Most illustration paragraphs are organized from general to particular—in other words, a general statement is followed by examples. The examples should also be organized in some logical way—chronologically, spatially, or by extremes (most to least or least to most).

   Terry organizes his paragraph from general to particular and presents two different sets of examples chronologically. The first six examples name some extraordinary feats in Morton-Finney's life: son of a slave, World War I, six languages, 11 degrees, teaching until 81, practicing law at age 100. Two more chronological examples demonstrate his thirst for learning: his fourth bachelor's degree at age 75 and his law seminars. Terry's method of organizing these illustrations allows us to follow his train of thought easily.

DISCOVERING HOW ILLUSTRATION WORKS

Let's look at two more example paragraphs. The first is by Karl Taro Greenfeld from an essay called "Life on the Edge." In it, Greenfeld uses examples to support his topic sentence. How many examples does he provide?

More Americans than ever are injuring themselves while pushing their personal limits. In 1997, the U.S. Consumer Product Safety Commission reported that 48,000 Americans were admitted to hospital emergency rooms with skateboarding-related injuries. That's 33% more than the previous year. Snowboarding E.R. visits were up 31%, mountain climbing up 20%. By every statistical measure available, Americans are participating in and injuring themselves through adventure sports at an unprecedented rate.

1. What main idea do you think Greenfeld is trying to communicate in this paragraph?

   _____

2. How does each of Greenfeld's examples explain his main point? List the three main examples he furnishes, and explain how they are related to his topic sentence.

   Example 1: _____

   Example 2: _____

   Example 3: _____

3. Does Greenfeld include enough examples to make his point? Explain your answer.

   _____

   _____

4. How are the examples in Greenfeld's paragraph arranged? Look at your list of examples in response to question 2 to help you answer this question. Then identify Greenfeld's method of organization.

   Method of organization: _____

The next paragraph, from "A Century of Women" by Lynn Peters Alder, also uses examples to prove its point. As you read this paragraph, try to put Alder's main point in your own words.

What a century for women. In countries around the world, women have overturned several millennia's worth of second-class citizenship to participate at nearly all levels of society. We have won the right to vote, own property, make our own decisions about sexual orientation, marriage, motherhood, and custody of our children. Should we choose to marry, we can keep our own names and legal identities. We can pursue higher education, have our own credit, earn and control our own money. We have access to most jobs, are rapidly establishing our own businesses, and are being elected to political office in ever-increasing numbers. We have established our right to sexual pleasure and reproductive freedom.

1. What main idea do you think Alder is trying to communicate?

     _____

2. Alder groups her examples in five different sentences. How does each sentence illustrate her main idea?

     "won the right" _____

     "choose to marry" _____

     _____

     money _____

     _____

     jobs _____

     sexual freedom _____

3. Does Alder use enough examples to make her point? Explain your answer.

     _____

     _____

4. How does Alder organize her examples: chronologically or spatially? Do you think this method is the best choice? Why or why not?

_____

_____

REVISING AND EDITING A STUDENT PARAGRAPH

Following is a paragraph written by Amanda Bliss, a freshman in college. As you read her paragraph, try to figure out Amanda's main point.

[1]When I was growing up I never understood the holidays. [2]My mom always wanted everyone to get along all year long. [3]The tension begins about a week before Thanksgiving she starts bringing a ton of strange foods into the house. [4]We had evergreen wreaths on every door, evergreen candle holders, evergreen tablecloths with matching napkins, and evergreen baskets with pine cones. [5]At about the same time the strange foods come into the house, she decides that every room in the house needs decorations of some sort. [6]One year their was so much stuff that smelled like cinnamon in our house that I dreamed to often about working in a spice factory. [7]During another year, Mom decided that are entire house should smell like evergreen, and look like a pine forest. [8]Mom had finally gone off the deep end, who is usually a stable person.

This paragraph is Amanda's first draft, which now needs to be revised and edited. First, apply the Revising Checklist below to the content of Amanda's draft. When you are satisfied that her ideas are fully developed and well organized, use the Editing Checklist on page 117 to correct her grammar and mechanics errors. Answer the questions after each checklist. Then write your suggested changes directly on Amanda's draft.

REVISING CHECKLIST ✔

TOPIC SENTENCE
- ✔ Does the topic sentence convey the paragraph's controlling idea?
- ✔ Does the topic sentence appear as the first or last sentence of the paragraph?

DEVELOPMENT
- ✔ Does the paragraph contain *specific* details that support the topic sentence?
- ✔ Does the paragraph include *enough* details to explain the topic sentence fully?

UNITY
- ✔ Do all the sentences in the paragraph support the topic sentence?

ORGANIZATION
- ✔ Is the paragraph organized logically?

COHERENCE
- ✔ Do the sentences move smoothly and logically from one to the next?

Topic Sentence

1. What is Amanda's main idea in this paragraph?

   _____

2. Put brackets around Amanda's topic sentence. Does it convey Amanda's main idea?

   _____

3. Rewrite it if necessary to introduce all the ideas in her paragraph.

   _____

   _____

Development

1. Are Amanda's examples specific enough?

   _____

   Add another more specific detail to an example in her paragraph.

2. Does she give enough examples to make her point?

   _____

   Add at least one new example to Amanda's paragraph to strengthen her topic sentence.

Unity

1. Read each of Amanda's sentences with her topic sentence (revised, if necessary) in mind.

2. Cross out the one sentence that does not relate to Amanda's topic sentence.

Organization

1. Read Amanda's paragraph again to see if all the sentences are arranged logically.

2. List some of her examples in the order they appear. Then identify her method of organization.

_____

_____

_____

_____

_____

Method of organization: _____

3. Move the one sentence that is out of place in Amanda's paragraph.

Coherence

For a list of transitions, see pages 46–47.

1. Circle three transitions, repetitions, synonyms, or pronouns Amanda uses.

For a list of pronouns, see pages 364–365.

2. Explain how one of these makes Amanda's paragraph easier to read.

_____

_____

Now rewrite Amanda's paragraph with your revisions.

EDITING CHECKLIST ✔

SENTENCES
✔ Does each sentence have a main subject and verb?

✔ Do all subjects and verbs agree?

✔ Do all pronouns agree with their nouns?

✔ Are modifiers as close as possible to the words they modify?

PUNCTUATION AND MECHANICS
✔ Are sentences punctuated correctly?

✔ Are words capitalized properly?

WORD CHOICE AND SPELLING
✔ Are words used correctly?

✔ Are words spelled correctly?

Sentences

Subjects and Verbs

1. Underline the subjects once and verbs twice in your revision of Amanda's paragraph. Remember that sentences can have more than one subject-verb set.

2. Does each of the sentences have at least one subject and verb that can stand alone?

For help with subjects and verbs, see Chapter 30.

3. Did you find and correct Amanda's run-together sentence? If not, find and correct it now.

For help with run-togethers, see Chapter 32.

Subject-Verb Agreement

1. Read aloud the subjects and verbs you underlined in your revision of Amanda's paragraph.

2. Correct any subjects and verbs that do not agree.

For help with subject-verb agreement, see Chapter 35.

Pronoun Agreement

1. Find any pronouns in your revision of Amanda's paragraph that do not agree with their nouns.

2. Correct any pronouns that do not agree with their nouns.

For help with pronoun agreement, see Chapter 39.

Modifier Errors

For help with modifier errors, see Chapter 42.

1. Find any modifiers in your revision of Amanda's paragraph that are not as close as possible to the words they modify.

2. Did you find and correct her misplaced modifier? If not, find and correct it now.

Punctuation and Mechanics

Punctuation

For help with punctuation, see Chapters 43–47.

1. Read your revision of Amanda's paragraph for any errors in punctuation.

2. Find the run-together sentence you revised, and make sure it is punctuated correctly.

3. Did you find and correct her two comma errors? If not, find and correct them now.

Mechanics

For help with capitalization, see Chapter 48.

1. Read your revision of Amanda's paragraph for any errors in capitalization.

2. Be sure to check Amanda's capitalization in the run-together sentence you revised.

Word Choice and Spelling

Word Choice

For help with confused words, see Chapter 54.

1. Find any words used incorrectly in your revision of Amanda's paragraph.

2. Did you find and correct her three confused words? If not, find and correct them now.

Spelling

For help with spelling, see Chapter 55.

1. Use spell-check and a dictionary to check the spelling in your revision of Amanda's paragraph.

2. Correct any misspelled words.

Now rewrite Amanda's paragraph again with your editing corrections.

REVISING AND EDITING YOUR OWN PARAGRAPH

Returning to the illustration paragraph you wrote earlier in this chapter, revise and edit your own writing. The checklists will help you apply what you have learned to your own writing.

REVISING CHECKLIST ✓

TOPIC SENTENCE
☐ Does the topic sentence convey the paragraph's controlling idea?

☐ Does the topic sentence appear as the first or last sentence of the paragraph?

DEVELOPMENT
☐ Does the paragraph contain *specific* details that support the topic sentence?

☐ Does the paragraph include *enough* details to explain the topic sentence fully?

UNITY
☐ Do all the sentences in the paragraph support the topic sentence?

ORGANIZATION
☐ Is the paragraph organized logically?

COHERENCE
☐ Do the sentences move smoothly and logically from one to the next?

Topic Sentence

1. What is the main point you are trying to communicate in your paragraph?

_____

2. Put brackets around your topic sentence. Does it convey your main idea?

_____

3. How can you change your topic sentence if necessary to introduce all the ideas in your paragraph?

_____

Development

1. Are your examples specific enough?

_____

Add another more specific detail to an example in your paragraph.

2. Do you give enough examples to make your point?

_____

Add at least one new example to your paragraph to strengthen your topic sentence.

Unity

1. Read each of your sentences with your topic sentence in mind.
2. Drop or rewrite any sentences not directly related to your topic sentence.

Organization

1. Read your paragraph again to see if all the sentences are arranged logically.
2. List some of your examples in the order they appear. Then identify your method of organization.

_____

_____

_____

_____

Method of organization: _____

Coherence

1. Circle three transitions, repetitions, synonyms, or pronouns you use.

2. Explain how one of these makes your paragraph easier to read.

For a list of transitions, see pages 46–47.

For a list of pronouns, see pages 364–365.

_____

_____

Now rewrite your paragraph with your revisions.

EDITING CHECKLIST ✔

SENTENCES

☐ Does each sentence have a main subject and verb?

☐ Do all subjects and verbs agree?

☐ Do all pronouns agree with their nouns?

☐ Are modifiers as close as possible to the words they modify?

PUNCTUATION AND MECHANICS

☐ Are sentences punctuated correctly?

☐ Are words capitalized properly?

WORD CHOICE AND SPELLING

☐ Are words used correctly?

☐ Are words spelled correctly?

Sentences

Subjects and Verbs

1. Underline the subjects once and verbs twice in your revised paragraph. Remember that sentences can have more than one subject-verb set.

2. Does each of your sentences have at least one subject and verb that can stand alone?

For help with subjects and verbs, see Chapter 30.

_____

For help with fragments, see Chapter 31.

For help with run-togethers, see Chapter 32.

3. Correct any fragments you have written.

4. Correct any run-together sentences you have written.

Subject-Verb Agreement

For help with subject-verb agreement, see Chapter 35.

1. Read aloud the subjects and verbs you underlined in your revised paragraph.
2. Correct any subjects and verbs that do not agree.

Pronoun Agreement

For help with pronoun agreement, see Chapter 39.

1. Find any pronouns in your revised paragraph that do not agree with their nouns.
2. Correct any pronouns that do not agree with their nouns.

Modifier Errors

For help with modifier errors, see Chapter 42.

1. Find any modifiers in your revised paragraph that are not as close as possible to the words they modify.
2. Rewrite sentences if necessary so that your modifiers are as close as possible to the words they modify.

Punctuation and Mechanics

Punctuation

For help with punctuation, see Chapters 43–47.

1. Read your revised paragraph for any errors in punctuation.
2. Make sure any fragments and run-together sentences you revised are punctuated correctly.

Mechanics

For help with capitalization, see Chapter 48.

1. Read your revised paragraph for any errors in capitalization.
2. Be sure to check your capitalization in any fragments and run-together sentences you revised.

Word Choice and Spelling

Word Choice

For help with confused words, see Chapter 54.

1. Find any words used incorrectly in your revised paragraph.
2. Correct any errors you find.

Spelling

For help with spelling, see Chapter 55.

1. Use spell-check and a dictionary to check the spelling in your revised paragraph.
2. Correct any misspelled words.

Now rewrite your paragraph with your editing corrections.

PRACTICING ILLUSTRATION

Reading Suggestions

In Chapter 23, you will find two essays that use examples to make their point: "Homeless Woman Living in a Car" by "Diane" and "Walk on By" by Brent Staples. You might want to read these selections before writing another assignment using illustrations. As you read, notice how the writers use examples to support and advance their ideas.

Writing Workshop

> **Guidelines for Writing an Illustration Paragraph**
>
> 1. State your main point in your first sentence.
> 2. Choose examples that focus on the point you want to make.
> 3. Use a sufficient number of examples to make your point.
> 4. Organize your illustration so that your readers can easily follow along.

1. Identify one of the themes in this collage. Then explain what you think the collection of pictures says about this theme.
2. Share with your classmates one of your opinions about the United States government, and use examples to explain it.
3. Use examples or illustrations to explain your observations on the increased interest in fitness among Americans.
4. Create your own illustration assignment (with the help of your instructor), and write a response to it.

Revising Workshop

Small Group Activity (5–10 minutes per writer)   Working in groups of three or four, each person should read his or her illustration paragraph to the other members of the group. Those listening should record their reactions on a copy of the Peer Evaluation Form in Appendix 2C. After your group goes through this process, give your evaluation forms to the appropriate writers so that each writer has two or three peer comment sheets for revising.

Paired Activity (5 minutes per writer)   Using the completed Peer Evaluation Forms, work in pairs to decide what you should revise in your paragraphs. If time allows, rewrite some of your sentences, and have your partner check them.

Individual Activity   Rewrite your paper, using the revising feedback you received from other students.

Editing Workshop

Paired Activity (5–10 minutes per writer)   Swap papers with a classmate, and use the editing portion of your Peer Evaluation Form to identify as many grammar, punctuation, mechanics, and spelling errors as you can. If time allows, correct some of your errors, and have your partner check them. Record your grammar, punctuation, and mechanics errors in the Error Log (Appendix 6) and your spelling errors in the Spelling Log (Appendix 7).

Individual Activity   Rewrite your paper again, using the editing feedback you received from other students.

Reflecting on Your Writing

When you have completed your own essay, answer these five questions:
1. What was most difficult about this assignment?
2. What was easiest?
3. What did you learn about using illustrations by completing this assignment?
4. What do you think are the strengths of your illustration paragraph? What are its weaknesses?
5. What did you learn from this assignment about your own writing process—about preparing to write, about writing the first draft, about revising, and about editing?

ANALYZING A PROCESS

CHAPTER 9

In order to read properly what one has written, one
must think it again.

—JULES RENARD

Just visit any bookstore to find out how much we depend on process
analysis in our daily lives. Books with such titles as the following have been
on the best-seller lists for years.

How to Dress for Success
I Dare You! How to Stay Young Forever
How the West Was Won
Why We Love: The Nature and Chemistry of Romantic Love
How to Win Friends and Influence People
How to Make 1,000,000 in the Stock Market Automatically!

When we **analyze a process,** we explain how to do something or how something happened. Process analysis involves explaining an activity or event
according to what comes first, second, and so forth. Think about how often
you try to explain something. If you want to teach someone how to snow-
board, if someone wants to know what caused John F. Kennedy Jr.'s plane to
crash, if you're late for a class or for your job, if someone doesn't understand
how a car engine works, what is the first thing you say? "Let me explain."

In "Playing to Win: Do You Think like a Champ?" Coach Mike Shanahan
of Super Bowl fame explains how to be a winner—on the field and in life. In
other words, the author is analyzing a process. You have been reading how-to
process analysis all your life in the form of instruction manuals, recipes, and
directions for assembling products. In this paragraph, Shanahan provides an
excellent example of how-to analysis. What activities can you analyze? In
what areas can you give people advice?

It's easy to become a winner if you're simply willing to learn from those who have been winners themselves. Find out who has had the most success at what they do. Watch their technique. Observe their methods. Study their behavior. By finding the best people in your industry, you'll learn what their routines are, the mistakes they made along the way, and the various scenarios they're forced to confront on a day-to-day basis. Then not only can you imitate their habits, but you can also imitate their results. It can be that easy.

Before continuing in this chapter, take a moment to write your own process analysis. Save your work because you will use it later in this chapter.

✎ WRITE YOUR OWN PROCESS ANALYSIS

Think of an activity that you enjoy or that you do well. Consider all the steps involved in this activity. Then write directions for someone else to follow. (Some possible topics are how to change a tire, make a bed, get money from an ATM, keep a young child entertained, play pickup basketball, make chocolate chip cookies, change the oil in a car, relax after a stressful day, plan a surprise party, give a manicure, or cheer up a friend.)

HOW TO WRITE A PROCESS ANALYSIS PARAGRAPH

Most process analysis essays fall into one of two categories. The first type tells *how to do something,* such as change a tire, write an essay, or program a VCR. The second type clarifies *how something happened* or *how something works,* such as how the Civil War started, how Bill Gates became a billionaire, how glasnost changed the Soviet Union, how a cell phone functions, or how the heart pumps blood.

Explaining a process is often much easier in speech than in writing. Think about the last time you gave someone directions to get someplace. Your listener probably interrupted a couple of times to ask a question or clarify what you meant. ("If I pass Randall Road, have I gone too far?") Or perhaps you saw a confused look on the person's face, so you knew you had to reexplain or add information. ("Don't worry, you can count stoplights. Elm Street is the fifth stoplight.") In a conversation, you can rely not only on your words to communicate but also on the tone of your voice, the expression on your face, and the movements of your hands and body.

When you write, however, you don't have face-to-face contact, so your listener can't ask what you mean, and you don't have the chance to add information or clear up confusion along the way. You must therefore furnish all the steps in the exact order in which they must occur. Your job will be much easier if you follow the guidelines listed here.

1. *State in the topic sentence what the reader should be able to do or understand by the end of the paragraph.* The topic sentence should give your readers a road map for what's to follow. They need to know where they're headed from the beginning of the paragraph. For example, a person giving directions might start by saying, "It's easy to get to Jeff's house from here." That introduces the task. You also want to try to make your topic sentence as interesting as possible. Look at the difference in these topic sentences for a paragraph about making a cup of coffee:

   Topic Sentence 1: I am going to tell you how to make a really good cup of coffee.

   Topic Sentence 2: Everyone can make coffee, but I have a secret for making the best cup of coffee you will ever taste.

   Mike Shanahan's topic sentence says exactly what the readers will learn when they read his paragraph—how to become a winner. The rest of his paragraph explains how to achieve a winning edge.

2. *Explain the rest of the process in the remainder of the paragraph.* By the end of a "how-to" paragraph, your reader should be able to perform the activity you are analyzing. In the "how-something-works" paragraph, the reader should be able to operate the device being discussed. And in the "how-something-happened" paragraph, the readers should understand more about a particular event.

   The success of a process analysis paragraph depends to a great extent on how well you know your audience. Since you are giving them complete directions, you need to understand how much they already know about a process. Knowing your audience also helps you decide how much detail you need to include and which terms to define.

   Shanahan's paragraph tells us how to be a winner in four easy steps:

   a. Find out who has had the most success at what they do.
   b. Watch their technique.
   c. Observe their methods.
   d. Study their behavior.

He even tells us the results we can expect after following these steps.

3. ***Organize your material in chronological order.*** Your readers need to know what happens first, second, and so on in order to perform a task or understand a device or an event. This is why transitions such as *first*, *second*, and *then* are very common in process paragraphs. Most process analysis paragraphs are organized chronologically (according to a time sequence), with the explanation starting at one point and progressing step by step through the process, directions, or event.

Explaining every step of a process is very important. Suppose, for example, that you see these directions for preparing a frozen pizza:

> Preheat the oven to 425 degrees. If you like a crisp crust, put the pizza directly on the oven rack. If you prefer a soft crust, put the pizza on a cookie sheet. Bake for 20 minutes. Remove from the oven and enjoy.

Do you have all the information you need here to prepare a frozen pizza? What about the wrapping paper and the cardboard that just caught fire in the oven? The step after "Preheat the oven" should be "Remove all wrapping paper and cardboard from the pizza."

The guidelines in Shanahan's paragraph are in a loose chronological order. They move from identifying winners to studying their behavior. Shanahan uses no transitions with his guidelines. He simply writes them as commands. Near the end of his paragraph, he uses the word "then" to lead his readers into the final two sentences.

DISCOVERING HOW PROCESS ANALYSIS WORKS

Having examined the "how to do something" process analysis, we're now going to look at the second type of process analysis with a paragraph about how something works. The key to writing this form of process analysis is understanding your topic. If you're unclear about some part of the process, your reader will end up confused about it too. The first example here explains how a copying machine works. See if you can understand the details well enough to explain the process to someone else.

> Static electricity enables a photocopier to produce almost instant copies of documents. At the heart of the machine is a metal drum that is given a negative charge at the beginning of the copying cycle. The optical system then projects an image of the document on the drum. The electric charge disappears where light strikes the metal surface, so only dark parts of the image remain charged. Positively charged particles of toner powder are then applied to the drum. The charged parts of the drum attract the dark powder, which is then transferred to a piece of paper. A heater seals the powder to the paper, and a warm copy of the document emerges from the photocopier.

1. What process does this paragraph explain? Which sentence gives you this information?

   _____

2. Explain the process in your own words.

   _____

   _____

   _____

3. Is the information about this process in chronological order? What word clues tell you the author's method of organization?

   _____

The next example explains how something happened. This type of process analysis gives readers background information and details to help them understand an event or a current situation. As with other types of process analysis, this type is organized chronologically because it consists of many steps or events that occurred one after the other. The following paragraph, about Post-it Notes™, is a good example of this type of analysis. See if you can follow the steps in this analysis.

> Post-it Notes™ were spawned by an accidental discovery in a laboratory in St. Paul, Minnesota, where research was being conducted into extra-strong glue in 1968. One series of experiments produced an adhesive that was so lacking in sticking power that the company, 3M, dismissed it as useless. However, one of its employees, a chemist named Art Fry, sang in a choir and came up with the idea of using the new glue to make bookmarks for his hymnal that could be removed when they were no longer needed without damaging the page. Fry tried to persuade the firm that it was throwing away a discovery that could have worldwide uses. But it was an uphill battle. Finally, in 1980, 3M began selling pads of note tags with a strip of the weak adhesive along one edge for use in offices. Not only were they removable, but they could be restuck somewhere else. Today, it's hard to imagine life without them!

1. What is the purpose of this paragraph? State it in your own words.

   _____

   _____

2. Do you understand how Post-it Notes™ were discovered? Explain the main facts about this discovery.

_____

_____

_____

_____

3. If you didn't understand the process, what else do you need to know?

_____

_____

4. Are the details in the paragraph organized chronologically? Is this order effective for what the author is explaining? Why or why not?

_____

_____

_____

REVISING AND EDITING A STUDENT PARAGRAPH

Following is a process analysis paragraph written by Victor Cantanzaro, a student. As you read it, notice when his paragraph tells you what he is explaining.

[1]You will be surprised to find out how furniture goes from the store to your door. [2]First of all, most furniture stores hire independent trucking agencies to deliver their orders. [3]These delivery services have to schedule their days very tightly so they can get as much furniture delivered per day as possible. [4]Customers don't understand this idea. [5]They go on errands and make life very difficult for the delivery service. [6]Why can't they wait patiently for their furniture when they know it's coming? [7]Then the driver's deliver the furniture in the order set by the computer. [8]The drivers from the delivery service has to pick up the furniture at the furniture stores in reverse order so that the pieces of furniture they're going to deliver first is at the end of the truck. [9]The drivers always call the customers once the days schedule is set. [10]The weather outlook is a major part of packing the truck,

because the furniture has to be covered with plastic, foam, or paper. [11]Depending on the conditions outside. [12]The worst situation is customers who decide when the delivery truck arrives. [13]That they don't want the furniture after all.

This paragraph is Victor's first draft, which now needs to be revised and edited. First, apply the Revising Checklist below to the content of Victor's draft. When you are satisfied that his ideas are fully developed and well organized, use the Editing Checklist on page 133 to correct his grammar and mechanics errors. Answer the questions after each checklist. Then write your suggested changes directly on Victor's draft.

REVISING CHECKLIST ✔

TOPIC SENTENCE
✔ Does the topic sentence convey the paragraph's controlling idea?
✔ Does the topic sentence appear as the first or last sentence of the paragraph?

DEVELOPMENT
✔ Does the paragraph contain *specific* details that support the topic sentence?
✔ Does the paragraph include *enough* details to explain the topic sentence fully?

UNITY
✔ Do all the sentences in the paragraph support the topic sentence?

ORGANIZATION
✔ Is the paragraph organized logically?

COHERENCE
✔ Do the sentences move smoothly and logically from one to the next?

Topic Sentence

1. What is Victor's purpose in this paragraph?

_____

2. Put brackets around Victor's topic sentence. Does it state his purpose?

_____

3. Write an alternate topic sentence.

_____

_____

Development

1. Do Victor's details explain the process of delivering furniture step by step?

_____

2. Where do you need more information?

_____

3. What new details can you add to Victor's paragraph to make his steps clearer?

_____

Unity

1. Read each of Victor's sentences with his topic sentence (revised, if necessary) in mind.
2. Cross out the three sentences not directly related to Victor's topic sentence.

Organization

1. Read Victor's paragraph again to see if all the sentences are arranged logically.
2. List the general steps covered in this paragraph.

_____   _____

_____   _____

_____   _____

3. Circle in item 2 the one step that is out of order.
4. Renumber the sentences in chronological order.

Coherence

1. Circle three transitions Victor uses.

2. Explain how one of these makes Victor's paragraph easier to read.

For a list of transitions, see pages 46–47.

_____

Now rewrite Victor's paragraph with your revisions.

ⒺDITING CHECKLIST ✔

SENTENCES
  ✔ Does each sentence have a main subject and verb?
  ✔ Do all subjects and verbs agree?
  ✔ Do all pronouns agree with their nouns?
  ✔ Are modifiers as close as possible to the words they modify?

PUNCTUATION AND MECHANICS
  ✔ Are sentences punctuated correctly?
  ✔ Are words capitalized properly?

WORD CHOICE AND SPELLING
  ✔ Are words used correctly?
  ✔ Are words spelled correctly?

Sentences

Subjects and Verbs

1. Underline the subjects once and verbs twice in your revision of Victor's paragraph. Remember that sentences can have more than one subject-verb set.

2. Does each of Victor's sentences have at least one subject and verb that can stand alone?

For help with subjects and verbs, see Chapter 30.

_____

3. Did you find and correct the two fragments in Victor's first draft? If not, find and correct them now.

For help with fragments, see Chapter 31.

Subject-Verb Agreement

For help with subject-verb agreement, see Chapter 35.

1. Read aloud the subjects and verbs you underlined in your revision of Victor's paragraph.
2. Did you find and correct the two subjects and verbs that do not agree? If not, find and correct them now.

Pronoun Agreement

For help with pronoun agreement, see Chapter 39.

1. Find any pronouns in your revision of Victor's paragraph that do not agree with their nouns.
2. Correct any pronouns that do not agree with their nouns.

Modifier Errors

For help with modifier errors, see Chapter 42.

1. Find any modifiers in your revision of Victor's paragraph that are not as close as possible to the words they modify.
2. Rewrite sentences if necessary so that the modifiers are as close as possible to the words they modify.

Punctuation and Mechanics
Punctuation

For help with punctuation, see Chapters 43–47.

1. Read your revision of Victor's paragraph for any errors in punctuation.
2. Find the two fragments you revised, and make sure they are punctuated correctly.
3. Did you find and correct Victor's two apostrophe errors? If not, find and correct them now.

Mechanics

For help with capitalization, see Chapter 48.

1. Read your revision of Victor's paragraph for any errors in capitalization.
2. Be sure to check Victor's capitalization in the fragments you revised.

Word Choice and Spelling
Word Choice

For help with confused words, see Chapter 54.

1. Find any words used incorrectly in your revision of Victor's paragraph.
2. Correct any errors you find.

Spelling

1. Use spell-check and a dictionary to check the spelling in your revision of Victor's paragraph.

For help with spelling, see Chapter 55.

2. Correct any misspelled words.

Now rewrite Victor's paragraph again with your editing corrections.

REVISING AND EDITING YOUR OWN PARAGRAPH

Returning to the process analysis paragraph you wrote earlier in this chapter, revise and edit your own writing. The checklists will help you apply what you have learned to your own paragraph.

REVISING CHECKLIST ✓

TOPIC SENTENCE
- ☐ Does the topic sentence convey the paragraph's controlling idea?
- ☐ Does the topic sentence appear as the first or last sentence of the paragraph?

DEVELOPMENT
- ☐ Does the paragraph contain *specific* details that support the topic sentence?
- ☐ Does the paragraph include *enough* details to explain the topic sentence fully?

UNITY
- ☐ Do all the sentences in the paragraph support the topic sentence?

ORGANIZATION
- ☐ Is the paragraph organized logically?

COHERENCE
- ☐ Do the sentences move smoothly and logically from one to the next?

Topic Sentence

1. What is your purpose in this paragraph?

_____

2. Put brackets around your topic sentence. Does it state your purpose?

    _____

3. How can you change it if necessary to introduce all the stages of the activity you are analyzing?

    _____

Development

1. Do the details in your paragraph explain step by step the activity you are discussing?

    _____

2. Where do you need more information?

    _____

3. What details can you add to your paragraph to make your analysis clearer?

    _____

Unity

1. Read each of your sentences with your topic sentence in mind.
2. Drop or rewrite any sentences not directly related to your topic sentence.

Organization

1. Read your paragraph again to see if all the sentences are arranged in chronological order.
2. What word clues help your readers move logically through your paragraph?

    _____

Coherence

For a list of transitions, see pages 46–47.

1. Circle three transitions you used.
2. How do these transitions move your readers smoothly and logically from one sentence to the next?

_____

_____

3. Add another transition to your paragraph to make it read more smoothly.

Now rewrite your paragraph with your revisions.

EDITING CHECKLIST ✔

SENTENCES
- ☐ Does each sentence have a main subject and verb?
- ☐ Do all subjects and verbs agree?
- ☐ Do all pronouns agree with their nouns?
- ☐ Are modifiers as close as possible to the words they modify?

PUNCTUATION AND MECHANICS
- ☐ Are sentences punctuated correctly?
- ☐ Are words capitalized properly?

WORD CHOICE AND SPELLING
- ☐ Are words used correctly?
- ☐ Are words spelled correctly?

Sentences

Subjects and Verbs

1. Underline the subjects once and verbs twice in your revised paragraph. Remember that sentences can have more than one subject-verb set.

   For help with subjects and verbs, see Chapter 30.

2. Does each of your sentences have at least one subject and verb that can stand alone?

_____

   For help with fragments, see Chapter 31.

3. Correct any fragments you have written.
4. Correct any run-together sentences you have written.

   For help with run-togethers, see Chapter 32.

Subject-Verb Agreement

For help with subject-verb agreement, see Chapter 35.

1. Read aloud the subjects and verbs you underlined in your revised paragraph.
2. Correct any subjects and verbs that do not agree.

Pronoun Agreement

For help with pronoun agreement, see Chapter 39.

1. Find any pronouns in your revised paragraph that do not agree with their nouns.
2. Correct any pronouns that do not agree with their nouns.

Modifier Errors

For help with modifier errors, see Chapter 42.

1. Find any modifiers in your revised paragraph that are not as close as possible to the words they modify.
2. Rewrite sentences if necessary so that your modifiers are as close as possible to the words they modify.

Punctuation and Mechanics

Punctuation

For help with punctuation, see Chapters 43–47.

1. Read your revised paragraph for any errors in punctuation.
2. Make sure any fragments and run-together sentences you revised are punctuated correctly.

Mechanics

For help with capitalization, see Chapter 48.

1. Read your revised paragraph for any errors in capitalization.
2. Be sure to check your capitalization in any fragments or run-together sentences you revised.

Word Choice and Spelling

Word Choice

For help with confused words, see Chapter 54.

1. Find any words used incorrectly in your revised paragraph.
2. Correct the errors you find.

Spelling

For help with spelling, see Chapter 55.

1. Use spell-check and a dictionary to check the spelling in your revised paragraph.
2. Correct any misspelled words.

Now rewrite your paragraph again with your editing corrections.

PRACTICING PROCESS ANALYSIS

Reading Suggestions

In Chapter 24, you will find two essays that illustrate the guidelines you have studied in this chapter: "Getting Out of Debt (and Staying Out)" by Julia Bourland suggests effective ways to manage money and live debt-free, and "Coming Over" by Russell Freedman explains how immigrants got into the United States at the turn of the twentieth century. You might want to read these selections before writing another process analysis paper. As you read, notice how the writers explain every step of the process carefully and completely.

Writing Workshop

Guidelines for Writing a Process Analysis Paragraph

1. State in the topic sentence what the reader should be able to do or understand by the end of the paragraph.
2. Explain the rest of the process in the remainder of the paragraph.
3. Organize your material in chronological order.

1. Place yourself in the scene on the previous page, and write a process analysis paragraph explaining the background, an event leading up to the picture, or an activity in the photograph. Be sure your explanation covers all steps or stages of the process you are discussing. Be sure that your topic sentence tells what the reader should know by the end of the paragraph.

2. Tell your classmates about a sport or hobby that you enjoy. Include what it takes to get started in this activity and what the satisfactions are. For example, how would a person get started playing the guitar, collecting stamps, or snowboarding? And what could it lead to?

3. Your college newspaper is running a special edition on study habits, and the editor has asked you to write an article explaining how you manage all the demands on your time, including studying, socializing, working, and keeping family obligations. Prepare your explanation for the next edition of the paper.

4. Create your own process analysis assignment (with the help of your instructor), and write a response to it.

Revising Workshop

Small Group Activity (5–10 minutes per writer)   Working in groups of three or four, each person should read his or her process analysis to the other members of the group. Those listening should record their reactions on a copy of the Peer Evaluation Form in Appendix 2D. After your group goes through this process, give your evaluation forms to the appropriate writers so that each writer has two or three peer comment sheets for revising.

Paired Activity (5 minutes per writer)   Using the completed Peer Evaluation Forms as guides, work in pairs to decide what you should revise in your paragraphs. If time allows, rewrite some of your sentences, and have your partner check them.

Individual Activity   Rewrite your paper, using the revising feedback you received from other students.

Editing Workshop

Paired Activity (5–10 minutes per writer)   Swap papers with a classmate, and use the editing portion of your Peer Evaluation Forms to identify as many grammar, punctuation, mechanics, and spelling errors as you can. If time allows, correct some of your errors, and have your partner check them.

Record your grammar, punctuation, and mechanics errors in the Error Log (Appendix 6) and your spelling errors in the Spelling Log (Appendix 7).

Individual Activity Rewrite your paper again using the editing feedback you received from other students.

Reflecting on Your Writing

When you have completed your own essay, answer these five questions:

1. What was most difficult about this assignment?
2. What was easiest?
3. What did you learn about process analysis by completing this assignment?
4. What do you think are the strengths of your process analysis? What are its weaknesses?
5. What did you learn from this assignment about your own writing process—about preparing to write, about writing the first draft, about revising, and about editing?

CHAPTER 10

COMPARING AND CONTRASTING

All good writing is swimming under water and
holding your breath.

—F. SCOTT FITZGERALD

We rely on comparison and contrast to make many decisions—both big
and small—that affect our lives every day:

What to have for breakfast
Where to go on vacation
Which college to attend
Which person to marry

Actually, you are comparing and contrasting constantly. In fact, comparison
and contrast are at the heart of our competitive society. When we are children, we compare our toys with our friends' toys and what we wear with how
the in-group dresses. As we grow up, we learn that colleges award scholarships and coaches put together athletic teams by comparing our abilities
with other students' abilities. Even after college, comparison and contrast
are essential elements in our social and professional lives.

Comparison and contrast allow us to understand one subject by putting
it next to another. **Comparing** involves discovering similarities; **contrasting**
is based on finding differences. But comparison and contrast are generally
considered part of the same process. As a result, the word *compare* is often
used to refer to both techniques.

In the following paragraph, Shannon Brownlee uses humor to compare
and contrast the behavior of preteens and teenagers. As you read, see if you
can figure out Brownlee's purpose.

One day, your child is a beautiful, charming 12-year-old, a kid who pops
out of bed full of good cheer, clears the table without being asked, and brings

home good grades from school. The next day, your child bursts into tears when you ask for the salt and listens to electronic music at maximum volume for hours on end. Chores? Forget it. Homework? There's little time, after talking to friends on the phone for five hours every night. Mornings? Your bluebird of happiness is flown, replaced by a groaning lump that can scarcely be roused for school. In short, your home is now inhabited by a teenager.

Before continuing in this chapter, take a moment to write a comparison/contrast paragraph of your own. Save your work because you will use it later in this chapter.

WRITE YOUR OWN COMPARISON/CONTRAST

Think of two individuals you know, such as two friends, two dates, two grandmothers, or two coworkers. How are they similar? How are they different? Write a paragraph comparing or contrasting these two people.

HOW TO WRITE A COMPARISON/CONTRAST PARAGRAPH

To write a good comparison/contrast paragraph, you need to focus on items that will lead to a specific point. The following guidelines will help you write a comparison/contrast paragraph.

1. *State the point you want to make with your comparison in your topic sentence.* All good comparisons have a point. You might be using comparison and contrast to reveal a team's strengths and weaknesses. Or you might be trying to find the best stereo system or the most durable camera. Whatever your purpose, the items you are comparing or contrasting should be stated clearly in your topic sentence along with your main point.

   In Shannon Brownlee's paragraph, Brownlee explains the normal transition from preteen to teenager. She does this by comparing the pleasant preteen behavior with that of the difficult teenager. The author saves her main idea for the last sentence, which ties together the entire paragraph.

2. *Choose items to compare and contrast that will make your point most effectively.* To write a successful comparison, you need to choose items

from the same category. For example, you can compare two movies to make a point, but it would be difficult to compare a movie with a swimming pool and come to any sensible conclusion.

When you choose two items to compare, you might want to brainstorm a list of similarities and differences to see what patterns emerge. A common characteristic in this list will give your paragraph a focus. Brownlee's brainstorming might have looked something like the following:

Preteenager	**Teenager**
cheerful	sullen
communicates with parents	avoids parents, talks with friends
loves school	hates school, won't do homework
no emotional problems	bursts into tears without warning
responsible at home	avoids chores at home
looks forward to getting up	hates to get out of bed

3. ***Organize your paragraph either by topics or by points of comparison.*** When you are ready to write, you have to decide whether to organize your ideas by topics or by points of comparison. Both methods are effective.

Brownlee's paragraph is organized by topic—preteens and teens. First she talks about topic A, preteens; then she deals with topic B, teens. The result is a paragraph with the pattern AAAA, BBBB:

Topic by Topic

A	Preteen Emotions
A	Preteen Chores
A	Preteen Homework
A	Preteen Mornings
B	Teen Emotions
B	Teen Chores
B	Teen Homework
B	Teen Mornings

Brownlee could just as easily have organized her paragraph by points of comparison—emotions, chores, homework, and mornings. In this case, her outline would fall into the pattern AB, AB, AB, AB:

Point by Point

Emotions	A	Preteen Emotions
	B	Teen Emotions
Chores	A	Preteen Chores
	B	Teen Chores
Homework	A	Preteen Homework
	B	Teen Homework
Mornings	A	Preteen Mornings
	B	Teen Mornings

Notice that Brownlee discusses the same four qualities in both the topical pattern (AAAA, BBBB) and the point-by-point pattern (AB, AB, AB, AB). If you mention one topic for one group, you should mention it for the other group. Also, in both patterns, the qualities should always be discussed in the same order. If emotions are first for one topic, they should be first for the second topic as well. Following the same order makes your comparison easy for your reader to follow.

DISCOVERING HOW COMPARISON AND CONTRAST WORK

Looking at two more comparison/contrast examples will help you understand your options for developing this type of paragraph. First, Marie Winn compares reading and television. See if you can figure out her main points.

Children's feelings of power and competence are nourished by [a] feature of the reading experience that does not obtain for television: the nonmechanical, easily accessible, and easily transportable nature of reading matter. Children can always count on a book for pleasure, though the television set may break down at a crucial moment. They may take a book with them wherever they go, to their room, to the park, to their friend's house, to school to read under the desk: they can *control* their use of books and reading materials. The television set is stuck in a certain place; it cannot be moved easily. It certainly cannot be casually transported from place to place by a child. Children must not only watch television wherever the set is located, but they must watch certain programs at certain times and are powerless to change what comes out of the set and when it comes out.

1. What is Winn's main idea in this paragraph?

   _____

   _____

2. What exactly is Winn comparing or contrasting in this paragraph? List her main points under the topics below.

Books	**Television**
_____	_____
_____	_____
_____	_____

3. Does Winn organize her paragraph by topics or by points of comparison?

   _____

The next example, by Deborah Tannen, compares and contrasts the behavior of groups of boys and girls when they are young. What is the main idea the author is trying to convey in this comparison?

Anthropologists Daniel Maltz and Ruth Borker point out that boys and girls socialize differently. Little girls tend to play in small groups or, even more common, in pairs. Their social life usually centers around a best friend, and friendships are made, maintained, and broken by talk—especially "secrets." If a little girl tells her friend's secret to another little girl, she may find herself with a new best friend. The secrets themselves may or may not be important, but the fact of telling them is all-important. It's hard for new-comers to get into these tight groups, but anyone who is admitted is treated as an equal. Girls like to play cooperatively; if they can't cooperate, the group breaks up.

Little boys tend to play in larger groups, often outdoors, and they spend more time doing things than talking. It's easy for boys to get into the group, but not everyone is accepted as an equal. Once in the group, boys must jockey for their status in it. One of the most important ways they do this is through talk: verbal display such as telling stories and jokes, challenging and sidetracking the verbal displays of other boys, and withstanding other boys' challenges in order to maintain their own story—and status. Their talk is often competitive talk about who is best at what.

1. Although this excerpt is two paragraphs, they share a single topic sentence. What is their topic sentence?

   _____

2. What exactly is Tannen comparing or contrasting in this paragraph? List some of her main points under the topics below.

Girls	Boys
_____	_____
_____	_____
_____	_____
_____	_____

3. Does Tannen organize her paragraphs by topics or by points of comparison?

   _____

REVISING AND EDITING A STUDENT PARAGRAPH

Following is a comparison/contrast paragraph written by Nathalie Johnson, a college student. Her comparison identifies some real differences between two teachers. As you read, see if this comparison is clear to you.

> [1]Ms. Tramel, my art teacher, and Mr. Morgan, my physics teacher, have two different approaches to their students. [2]Students eventually find out that even though Mr. Morgan doesn't smile much, he cares more about the students than they initially think he does. [3]When a student first meets Ms. Tramel, they think she is an easy teacher because she is so friendly. [4]Ms. Tramel encourages students to work hard on their own Mr. Morgan helps students study by giving them study questions and working with them outside of class. [5]I couldn't believe I got an A from Mr. Morgan. [6]He always helped me outside of class. [7]They both like their students a lot; however, Mr. Morgan doesn't smile as much as Ms. Tramel. [8]A student learns very quickly that both of these teachers will be there for them no matter what; even though the teachers express themselves in different ways.

This paragraph is Nathalie's first draft, which now needs to be revised and edited. First, apply the Revising Checklist that follows to the content of

Nathalie's draft. When you are satisfied that her ideas are fully developed and well organized, use the Editing Checklist on page 150 to correct her grammar and mechanics errors. Answer the questions after each checklist; then write your suggested changes directly on Nathalie's draft.

REVISING CHECKLIST ✔

TOPIC SENTENCE

✔ Does the topic sentence convey the paragraph's controlling idea?

✔ Does the topic sentence appear as the first or last sentence of the paragraph?

DEVELOPMENT

✔ Does the paragraph contain *specific* details that support the topic sentence?

✔ Does the paragraph include *enough* details to explain the topic sentence fully?

UNITY

✔ Do all the sentences in the paragraph support the topic sentence?

ORGANIZATION

✔ Is the paragraph organized logically?

COHERENCE

✔ Do the sentences move smoothly and logically from one to the next?

Topic Sentence

1. What is the main point of Nathalie's paragraph?

   _____

2. Put brackets around Nathalie's topic sentence. Does it introduce her main point?

   _____

3. Write an alternate topic sentence.

   _____

   _____

Development

1. Does Nathalie compare the same qualities in both teachers?

   _____

2. Where do you need more information?

   _____

3. What specific details can you add to Nathalie's paragraph to make her comparison more effective?

   _____

   _____

Unity

1. Read each of Nathalie's sentences with her topic sentence (revised, if necessary) in mind.
2. Cross out the two sentences not directly related to Nathalie's topic sentence.

Organization

1. Read Natalie's paragraph again to see if all the sentences are arranged logically.
2. List some of the points Nathalie compares and contrasts in her paragraph in the order they appear.

Ms. Tramel	**Mr. Morgan**
_____	_____
_____	_____
_____	_____
_____	_____

3. Is the paragraph organized by topics or by points of comparison?

   _____

4. Move the one sentence that is out of order.

Coherence

1. Circle all of Nathalie's references to "teacher" or "teachers."

2. Change two of these words to synonyms.

    Now rewrite Nathalie's paragraph with your revisions.

EDITING CHECKLIST ✔

SENTENCES

✔ Does each sentence have a main subject and verb?

✔ Do all subjects and verbs agree?

✔ Do all pronouns agree with their nouns?

✔ Are modifiers as close as possible to the words they modify?

PUNCTUATION AND MECHANICS

✔ Are sentences punctuated correctly?

✔ Are words capitalized properly?

WORD CHOICE AND SPELLING

✔ Are words used correctly?

✔ Are words spelled correctly?

Sentences

Subjects and Verbs

For help with subjects and verbs, see Chapter 30.

1. Underline Nathalie's subjects once and verbs twice. Remember that sentences can have more than one subject-verb set.

2. Does each of Nathalie's sentences have at least one subject and verb that can stand alone?

For help with run-togethers, see Chapter 32.

3. Did you find and correct Nathalie's run-together sentence? If not, find and correct it now.

Subject-Verb Agreement

1. Read aloud the subjects and verbs you underlined in your revision of Nathalie's paragraph.

2. Correct any subjects and verbs that do not agree.

For help with subjects-verb agreement, see Chapter 35.

Pronoun Agreement

1. Find any pronouns in your revision of Nathalie's paragraph that do not agree with their nouns.

2. Did you find and correct the two pronouns that do not agree with their nouns? If not, find and correct them now.

For help with pronoun agreement, see Chapter 39.

Modifier Errors

1. Find any modifiers in your revision of Nathalie's paragraph that are not as close as possible to the words they modify.

2. Rewrite sentences if necessary so that modifiers are as close as possible to the words they modify.

For help with modifier errors, see Chapter 42.

Punctuation and Mechanics

Punctuation

1. Read your revision of Nathalie's paragraph for any errors in punctuation.

2. Find the run-together sentence you revised, and make sure it is punctuated correctly.

3. Did you find and correct Nathalie's semicolon error? If not, find and correct it now.

For help with punctuation, see Chapters 43–47.

Mechanics

1. Read your revision of Nathalie's paragraph for any errors in capitalization.

2. Be sure to check Nathalie's capitalization in the run-together sentence you revised.

For help with capitalization, see Chapter 48.

Word Choice and Spelling

Word Choice

1. Find any words used incorrectly in your revision of Nathalie's paragraph.

2. Correct any errors you find.

For help with confused words, see Chapter 54.

Spelling

For help with spelling, see Chapter 55.

1. Use spell-check and a dictionary to check the spelling in your revision of Nathalie's paragraph.

2. Correct any misspelled words.

Now rewrite Nathalie's paragraph again with your editing corrections.

REVISING AND EDITING YOUR OWN PARAGRAPH

Returning to the comparison/contrast paragraph you wrote earlier in this chapter, revise and edit your own writing. The checklists will help you apply what you have learned to your own paragraph.

REVISING CHECKLIST ✔

TOPIC SENTENCE

☐ Does the topic sentence convey the paragraph's controlling idea?

☐ Does the topic sentence appear as the first or last sentence of the paragraph?

DEVELOPMENT

☐ Does the paragraph contain *specific* details that support the topic sentence?

☐ Does the paragraph include *enough* details to explain the topic sentence fully?

UNITY

☐ Do all the sentences in the paragraph support the topic sentence?

ORGANIZATION

☐ Is the paragraph organized logically?

COHERENCE

☐ Do the sentences move smoothly and logically from one to the next?

Topic Sentence

1. What main point are you trying to make in your paragraph?

   _____

2. Put brackets around your topic sentence. Does it introduce your main point and your topics?

   _____

3. How can you change it if necessary to introduce your main point and your topics?

_____

Development

1. Do you cover the same characteristics of both topics?

_____

2. Where do you need more information?

_____

3. What specific details can you add to your paragraph to make your comparison more effective?

_____

_____

Unity

1. Read each of your sentences with your topic sentence in mind.
2. Drop or rewrite any sentences not directly related to your topic sentence.

Organization

1. Is your paragraph organized by topics or by points of comparison?

_____

2. Is the order you chose the most effective approach to your subject?

_____

Coherence

1. Circle any words you repeat.
2. Should any of them be replaced with pronouns or synonyms?

_____

Now rewrite your paragraph with your revisions.

EDITING CHECKLIST ✔

SENTENCES

☐ Does each sentence have a main subject and verb?

☐ Do all subjects and verbs agree?

☐ Do all pronouns agree with their nouns?

☐ Are modifiers as close as possible to the words they modify?

PUNCTUATION AND MECHANICS

☐ Are sentences punctuated correctly?

☐ Are words capitalized properly?

WORD CHOICE AND SPELLING

☐ Are words used correctly?

☐ Are words spelled correctly?

Sentences

Subjects and Verbs

For help with subjects and verbs, see Chapter 30.

1. Underline the subjects once and verbs twice in your revised paragraph. Remember that sentences can have more than one subject-verb set.

2. Does each of your sentences have at least one subject and verb that can stand alone?

For help with fragments, see Chapter 31.

For help with run-togethers, see Chapter 32.

3. Correct any fragments you have written.

4. Correct any run-together sentences you have written.

Subject-Verb Agreement

For help with subject-verb agreement, see Chapter 35.

1. Read aloud the subjects and verbs you underlined in your revised paragraph.

2. Correct any subjects and verbs that do not agree.

Pronoun Agreement

For help with pronoun agreement, see Chapter 39.

1. Find any pronouns in your revised paragraph that do not agree with their nouns.

2. Correct any pronouns that do not agree with their nouns.

Modifier Errors

1. Find any modifiers in your revised paragraph that are not as close as possible to the words they modify.
2. Rewrite sentences if necessary so that your modifiers are as close as possible to the words they modify.

For help with modifier errors, see Chapter 42.

Punctuation and Mechanics

Punctuation

1. Read your revised paragraph for any errors in punctuation.
2. Make sure any fragments and run-together sentences you revised are punctuated correctly.

For help with punctuation, see Chapters 43–47.

Mechanics

1. Read your revised paragraph for any errors in capitalization.
2. Be sure to check your capitalization in any fragments or run-together sentences you revised.

For help with capitalization, see Chapter 48.

Word Choice and Spelling

Word Choice

1. Find any words used incorrectly in your revised paragraph.
2. Correct any errors you find.

For help with confused words, see Chapter 54.

Spelling

1. Use spell-check and a dictionary to check your spelling.
2. Correct any misspelled words.

For help with spelling, see Chapter 55.

Now rewrite your paragraph again with your editing corrections.

PRACTICING COMPARISON AND CONTRAST

Reading Suggestions

In Chapter 25, you will find two essays that follow the guidelines you have studied in this chapter: "The Barrio" by Ernesto Galarza compares various features of American and Mexican cultures, and "A Fable for Tomorrow" by Rachel Carson discusses how we are slowly destroying our planet. You might want to read these selections before writing any more comparison/contrast papers. As you read, notice how the writers make their points through well-thought-out, detailed comparisons and contrasts.

Writing Workshop

Guidelines for Writing a Comparison/Contrast Paragraph

1. State the point you want to make with your comparison in your topic sentence.
2. Choose items to compare and contrast that will make your point most effectively.
3. Organize your paragraph either by topics or by points of comparison.

1. Explain the similarities and differences in these pictures. How can one place be so different and yet the same?

2. Discuss the similarities and differences between your high school life and your college life. Are your classes more difficult? Do you still hang out with your friends from high school? Are you treated differently by your parents, school officials, or old classmates? Have your expectations of yourself changed? Do you now have to juggle school and work?

3. You have been hired by your local newspaper to compare and contrast various aspects of daily life. For example, you might compare two musical groups, good drivers versus bad drivers, two malls, or two kinds of pets. Decide on the point you want to make before you begin writing.

4. Create your own comparison/contrast assignment (with the help of your instructor), and write a response to it.

Revising Workshop

Small Group Activity (5–10 minutes per writer)   Working in groups of three or four, each person should read his or her comparison/contrast to the other members of the group. Those listening should record their reactions on a copy of the Peer Evaluation Form in Appendix 2E. After your group goes through this process, give your evaluation forms to the appropriate writers so that each writer has two or three peer comment sheets for revising.

Paired Activity (5 minutes per writer)   Using the completed Peer Evaluation Forms, work in pairs to decide what you should revise in your paragraph. If time allows, rewrite some of your sentences, and have your partner check them.

Individual Activity   Rewrite your paper, using the revising feedback you received from other students.

Editing Workshop

Paired Activity (5–10 minutes per writer)   Swap papers with a classmate, and use the editing portion of your Peer Evaluation Form to identify as many grammar, punctuation, mechanics, and spelling errors as you can. If time allows, correct some of your errors, and have your partner check them. Record your grammar, punctuation, and mechanics errors in the Error Log (Appendix 6) and your spelling errors in the Spelling Log (Appendix 7).

Individual Activity   Rewrite your paper again using the editing feedback you received from other students.

Reflecting on Your Writing

When you have completed your own essay, answer these five questions:

1. What was most difficult about this assignment?
2. What was easiest?
3. What did you learn about comparison/contrast by completing this assignment?
4. What do you think are the strengths of your comparison/contrast paragraph? What are its weaknesses?
5. What did you learn from this assignment about your own writing process—about preparing to write, about writing the first draft, about revising, and about editing?

Chapter 11

Dividing and Classifying

Three things are necessary for becoming a good
writer: a good head, a thick skin, and a soft heart.

—Austin J. App

Dividing and classifying play important roles in our daily lives. Think of
how we all organize our environment:

Our coursework is separated into different binders and notebooks
The names in our address book are divided up alphabetically
Our shirts, socks, and sweaters all get their own bureau drawers
Our garden supplies and household tools have separate locations in
the garage

In fact, division and classification come so naturally to us that we sometimes
aren't even aware we are using them. Imagine going to a grocery store that
doesn't group its merchandise logically: Dairy products wouldn't be together; salad dressings might be randomly scattered throughout the store;
some breakfast foods could be in the deli section—and who knows where
the rest might be? The result would be total chaos, and finding what you
were looking for would be frustrating and time-consuming.

Dividing and classifying are actually mirror images of each other.
Dividing is sorting into smaller categories, and **classifying** is grouping into
larger categories. Division moves from one category to many, while classifying moves in the opposite direction, from many categories to one. For
example, the general category of food can be divided or sorted into soups,
salads, dairy products, beef, chicken, and so on. In like manner, soups, salads,
dairy products, beef, and chicken can be grouped into the single category of
food. To classify, you need to find the common trait that all the items share.

Here is a paragraph from *Entrepreneur* magazine that is based on division
and classification. Written by Debra Phillips, the essay, "Tween Beat," puts

the youngest consumers into three categories to discuss their buying power. Notice how division and classification work together in this paragraph.

> In his widely hailed research on child-age consumers, author and Texas A&M University marketing professor James McNeal points out that there's not one but three different children's markets. First and foremost, there's the market created by kids' direct spending. Second, there's the market stemming from kids' influence over their family's purchases. Finally, there's the market of the future —that is, courting kids to eventually become loyal adult consumers. With so much at stake, it's easy to see why so many eyes are on the tween-age kids of the baby boomers. They are the present; they are also the future.

Before continuing in this chapter, take a moment to write your own division/classification paragraph. Save your work because you will use it later in this chapter.

✎ WRITE YOUR OWN DIVISION/CLASSIFICATION

We all have lots of friends, and we naturally divide them into categories, whether we realize it or not. What categories do your friends fall into? Write a paragraph that introduces your categories and then explains why specific friends fit into each category.

HOW TO WRITE A DIVISION/CLASSIFICATION PARAGRAPH

To write a division/classification paragraph, keep in mind that the same items can be divided and classified many different ways. No two kitchens are exactly alike, and your friends probably don't organize their closets the same way you do. Methods of organizing schoolwork also vary from person to person. Similarly, in writing, you can divide and classify a topic differently, but following the guidelines listed here will help you create an effective division/classification paragraph.

1. ***Decide on your overall purpose for writing, and state it in your topic sentence.*** Dividing and classifying are not very interesting in themselves unless you are trying to make a point. In other words, division and classification should be the means of communicating a coherent message. This message is the heart of your topic sentence.

    In Debra Phillips's paragraph, for example, Phillips is using division and classification to show that the younger generation affects the economy more than most people realize. She does this by using James McNeal's division of child consumers into three categories—direct spending, influences on family buying, and future consumers.

2. ***Divide your topic into categories (division); explain each category with details and examples (classification).*** Since division and classification are so closely related, you will often use both of them in a single paragraph. In fact, each one actually helps explain the other. When you choose examples, remember that they must share a common trait. You should not, for instance, classify cars on the basis of safety features and use air bags, antilock brakes, and leather seats as your examples because leather seats have nothing to do with safety.

In her paragraph, Debra Phillips uses a combination of division and classification. She establishes three categories for her topic (division) and then explains how children fit into these categories (classification). All the examples share a common trait—they all refer to types of buying markets.

3. ***Organize your categories so that they help you communicate your message clearly.*** Being logical is really the only requirement for organizing a division/classification paragraph. You want to move smoothly from one category to another with transitions that help your readers understand your reasoning.

The paragraph on child consumers is organized according to the degree of influence children have on the buying market. Phillips's first category is a small market of children's direct purchases. This market is certainly not as large as the group of children who influence their parents' purchases. Finally, in the future, when these children are grown, they will have enormous buying power of their own. So Phillips's categories move from small to large and from present to future.

DISCOVERING HOW DIVISION AND CLASSIFICATION WORK

Two additional examples will help you understand more clearly the choices you have to make when you write division/classification paragraphs. The first, by Sarah Hodgson, divides dogs' personalities into five categories and explains each. As you read it, see if you can find all five categories.

Some people may think that only humans have a real personality. Anyone who has ever had a dog knows better. Dogs, like us, have their own personalities. Some are extremely funny. I call this rowdy bunch *The Comedians*. They can be frustrating as heck, constantly dancing on the edge of good behavior. But in your most serious or sad moments, they'll make you laugh.

Then we have *The Eager Beavers*, the dogs many of us dream of. They'll do anything that warrants approval. Sounds fantastic, but they'll be bad, too, if that gets attention, so even the Eager Beavers can find themselves on the "B" list if their owners aren't careful. There are also *The Sweet Peas* of the planet, quiet souls who prefer the sidelines over the spotlight. Taking the sweet thing a step too far are those dogs who are *Truly Timid*. Almost anything will freak them out. Poor creatures, they require a lot of understanding. And then there is *The Boss*. This fellow thinks a little too highly of himself. He needs lots of training to tame his egotism. Take a look at where your dog fits in, because like us, they all learn differently!

1. This paragraph doesn't simply classify the personalities of dogs for its own sake. It has a broader message. What is Hodgson's general purpose in this paragraph?

   _____

   _____

2. Does this paragraph use both division and classification?

   _____

   When does Hodgson move from one to many (division)? From many to one (classification)?

   Division: _____

   Classification: _____

3. Different methods of organization work well with different topics. How is this paragraph organized?

   _____

The next example divides and classifies the various abilities of the human brain. It is from an essay titled "Smart Genes?" by Michael Lemonick. What is the author's purpose in this paragraph?

   When everything is going right, these different systems work together seamlessly. If you're taking a bicycle ride, for example, the memory of how to operate the bike comes from one set of neurons [nerve cells]; the memory of how to get from here to the other side of town comes from another; the nervous feeling you have left over from taking a bad spill last time comes from still another. Yet you are never aware that your mental experience has been assembled, bit by bit, like some invisible edifice [structure] inside your brain.

1. What is Lemonick's general message in this paragraph?

    _____

2. When does this paragraph move from one to many (division)? From many to one (classification)?

    Division: _____

    Classification: _____

    _____

3. How does Lemonick organize his paragraph?

    _____

REVISING AND EDITING A STUDENT PARAGRAPH

Here is a division/classification paragraph written by LaKesha Montgomery. Her paragraph focuses on the different types of interior decorators she has come across in her experience. Can you figure out when she is using division and when she is using classification?

^{1}I learned that interior decorators really fall into three different categories. ^{2}I also found out that they work hard after decorating my new apartment. ^{3}First is an interior decorator who specializes in residences. ^{4}This person has to work closely with people and try to get into there lifestyles. ^{5}So that he or she can help the customer make decisions. ^{6}The next type of interior decorator sells estate furniture. ^{7}He or she works in an upscale store called a gallery. ^{8}His or her main responsibility is to acquire all kinds of merchandise from estate sales and than sell it to those people who our interested in these more valuable pieces. ^{9}I certainly wasn't in this category. ^{10}I don't even know how I learned about this type of interior decorator. ^{11}Some interior decorators specialize in office décor. ^{12}They enjoy working with exotic schemes. ^{13}And making peoples stark office space come alive.

This paragraph is LaKesha's first draft, which now needs to be revised and edited. First, apply the Revising Checklist on next page to the content of LaKesha's draft. When you are satisfied that her ideas are fully developed and well organized, use the Editing Checklist on page 165 to correct her grammar and mechanics errors. Answer the questions after each checklist. Then write your suggested changes directly on LaKesha's draft.

REVISING CHECKLIST ✔

TOPIC SENTENCE
- ✔ Does the topic sentence convey the paragraph's controlling idea?
- ✔ Does the topic sentence appear as the first or last sentence of the paragraph?

DEVELOPMENT
- ✔ Does the paragraph contain *specific* details that support the topic sentence?
- ✔ Does the paragraph include *enough* details to explain the topic sentence fully?

UNITY
- ✔ Do all the sentences in the paragraph support the topic sentence?

ORGANIZATION
- ✔ Is the paragraph organized logically?

COHERENCE
- ✔ Do the sentences move smoothly and logically from one to the next?

Topic Sentence

1. What general message is LaKesha trying to communicate in this paragraph?

_____

2. Put brackets around LaKesha's topic sentence. Does it capture her main point?

_____

3. Expand LaKesha's topic sentence.

_____

_____

Development

1. Do the details in the paragraph describe all three types of interior decorators?

_____

2. Where do you need more information?

_____

3. Add a closing sentence to LaKesha's paragraph.

_____

Unity

1. Read each of LaKesha's sentences with her topic sentence (revised, if necessary) in mind.
2. Cross out the two sentences that are not directly related to LaKesha's topic sentence.

Organization

1. Read LaKesha's paragraph again to see if all the sentences are arranged logically.
2. List the main categories LaKesha explains in this paragraph.

_____

_____

_____

3. Move the one category that seems to be out of order.
4. Identify LaKesha's method of organization:

_____

Coherence

For a list of transitions, see pages 46–47.

1. Circle three transitions, repetitions, synonyms, or pronouns LaKesha uses.

For a list of pronouns, see pages 364–365.

2. Explain how one of these makes LaKesha's paragraph easier to read.

_____

Now rewrite LaKesha's paragraph with your revisions.

EDITING CHECKLIST ✔

SENTENCES

✔ Does each sentence have a main subject and verb?

✔ Do all subjects and verbs agree?

✔ Do all pronouns agree with their nouns?

✔ Are modifiers as close as possible to the words they modify?

PUNCTUATION AND MECHANICS

✔ Are sentences punctuated correctly?

✔ Are words capitalized properly?

WORD CHOICE AND SPELLING

✔ Are words used correctly?

✔ Are words spelled correctly?

Sentences

Subjects and Verbs

1. Underline the subjects once and verbs twice in your revision of LaKesha's paragraph. Remember that sentences can have more than one subject-verb set.

2. Does each of the sentences have at least one subject and verb that can stand alone?

For help with subjects and verbs, see Chapter 30.

_____

3. Did you find and correct LaKesha's two fragments? If not, find and correct them now.

For help with fragments, see Chapter 31.

Subject-Verb Agreement

1. Read aloud the subjects and verbs you underlined in your revision of LaKesha's paragraph.

2. Correct any subjects and verbs that do not agree.

For help with subject-verb agreement, see Chapter 35.

Pronoun Agreement

1. Find any pronouns in your revision of LaKesha's paragraph that do not agree with their nouns.

2. Correct any pronouns that do not agree with their nouns.

For help with pronoun agreement, see Chapter 39.

Modifier Errors

For help with modifier errors, see Chapter 42.

1. Find any modifiers in your revision of LaKesha's paragraph that are not as close as possible to the words they modify.

2. Did you find and correct LaKesha's one modifier error? If not, find and correct it now.

Punctuation and Mechanics

Punctuation

For help with punctuation, see Chapters 43–47.

1. Read your revision of LaKesha's paragraph for any errors in punctuation.

2. Find the two fragments you revised, and make sure they are punctuated correctly.

3. Did you find and correct the apostrophe error in LaKesha's paragraph? If not, find and correct it now.

Mechanics

For help with capitalization, see Chapter 48.

1. Read your revision of LaKesha's paragraph for any errors in capitalization.

2. Be sure to check LaKesha's capitalization in the fragments you revised.

Word Choice and Spelling

Word Choice

For help with confused words, see Chapter 54.

1. Find any words used incorrectly in your revision of LaKesha's paragraph.

2. Did you find and correct her three confused words?

   If not, find and correct them now.

Spelling

For help with spelling, see Chapter 55.

1. Use spell-check and a dictionary to check the spelling in your revision of LaKesha's paragraph.

2. Correct any misspelled words.

Now rewrite LaKesha's paragraph again with your editing corrections.

REVISING AND EDITING YOUR OWN PARAGRAPH

Returning to the division/classification paragraph you wrote earlier in this chapter, revise and edit your own writing. The checklists will help you apply what you have learned to your own paragraph.

REVISING CHECKLIST ✓

TOPIC SENTENCE
- ☐ Does the topic sentence convey the paragraph's controlling idea?
- ☐ Does the topic sentence appear as the first or last sentence of the paragraph?

DEVELOPMENT
- ☐ Does the paragraph contain *specific* details that support the topic sentence?
- ☐ Does the paragraph include *enough* details to explain the topic sentence fully?

UNITY
- ☐ Do all the sentences in the paragraph support the topic sentence?

ORGANIZATION
- ☐ Is the paragraph organized logically?

COHERENCE
- ☐ Do the sentences move smoothly and logically from one to the next?

Topic Sentence

1. What is the main point or general message in your paragraph?

_____

2. Put brackets around your topic sentence. Does it capture your main point?

_____

3. How can you change it if necessary to introduce all the ideas in your paragraph?

_____

Development

1. Does your paragraph use both division and classification? Where does it divide? Where does it classify?

<table>
<tr><td align="center">Dividing</td><td align="center">Classifying</td></tr>
<tr><td>_____</td><td>_____</td></tr>
<tr><td>_____</td><td>_____</td></tr>
<tr><td>_____</td><td>_____</td></tr>
</table>

2. Add any categories or details that will make your paragraph clearer.

Unity

1. Read each of your sentences with your topic sentence in mind.
2. Drop or rewrite any sentences not directly related to your topic sentence.

Organization

1. Read your paragraph again to see if all the sentences are arranged logically.
2. List some of your examples in the order they appear. Then identify your method of organization.

<table>
<tr><td>_____</td><td>_____</td></tr>
<tr><td>_____</td><td>_____</td></tr>
<tr><td>_____</td><td>_____</td></tr>
<tr><td>_____</td><td>_____</td></tr>
</table>

Method of organization: _____

Coherence

For a list of transitions, see pages 46–47.

1. Circle three transitions, repetitions, synonyms, or pronouns you use.
2. Explain how one of these makes your paragraph easier to read.

For a list of pronouns, see pages 364–365.

Now rewrite your paragraph with your revisions.

EDITING CHECKLIST ✔

SENTENCES

☐ Does each sentence have a main subject and verb?

☐ Do all subjects and verbs agree?

☐ Do all pronouns agree with their nouns?

☐ Are modifiers as close as possible to the words they modify?

PUNCTUATION AND MECHANICS

☐ Are sentences punctuated correctly?

☐ Are words capitalized properly?

WORD CHOICE AND SPELLING

☐ Are words used correctly?

☐ Are words spelled correctly?

Sentences

Subjects and Verbs

1. Underline the subjects once and verbs twice in your revised paragraph. Remember that sentences can have more than one subject-verb set.

2. Does each of your sentences have at least one subject and verb that can stand alone?

For help with subjects and verbs, see Chapter 30.

3. Correct any fragments you have written.

4. Correct any run-together sentences you have written.

For help with fragments, see Chapter 31.

For help with run-togethers, see Chapter 32.

Subject-Verb Agreement

1. Read aloud the subjects and verbs you underlined in your revised paragraph.

2. Correct any subjects and verbs that do not agree.

For help with subject-verb agreement, see Chapter 35.

Pronoun Agreement

1. Find any pronouns in your revised paragraph that do not agree with their nouns.

2. Correct any pronouns that do not agree with their nouns.

For help with pronoun agreement, see Chapter 39.

Modifier Errors

For help with modifier errors, see Chapter 42.

1. Find any modifiers in your revised paragraph that are not as close as possible to the words they modify.
2. Rewrite sentences if necessary so that your modifiers are as close as possible to the words they modify.

Punctuation and Mechanics

Punctuation

For help with punctuation, see Chapters 43–47.

1. Read your revised paragraph for any errors in punctuation.
2. Make sure any fragments and run-together sentences you revised are punctuated correctly.

Mechanics

For help with capitalization, see Chapter 48.

1. Read your revised paragraph for any errors in capitalization.
2. Be sure to check your capitalization in any fragments or run-together sentences you revised.

Word Choice and Spelling

Word Choice

For help with confused words, see Chapter 54.

1. Find any words used incorrectly in your revised paragraph.
2. Correct any errors you find.

Spelling

For help with spelling, see Chapter 55.

1. Use spell-check and a dictionary to check your spelling.
2. Correct any misspelled words.

Now rewrite your paragraph again with your editing corrections.

PRACTICING DIVISION AND CLASSIFICATION

Reading Suggestions

In Chapter 26, you will find two essays that follow the guidelines you have studied in this chapter. "Rapport: How to Ignite It" by Camille Lavington divides and classifies personality types by communication styles, and "Categories of Time Use" by Edwin Bliss divides and classifies tasks to help people make better use of their time. You might want to read these selections before writing another division/classification paper. As you read, notice how the writers use these rhetorical modes to make their points.

Writing Workshop

> **Guidelines for Writing a Division/Classification Paragraph**
>
> 1. Decide on your overall purpose for writing, and state it in your topic sentence.
> 2. Divide your topic into categories (division); explain each category with details and examples (classification).
> 3. Organize your categories so that they help you communicate your message clearly.

1. Place yourself in this picture, and tell someone who isn't looking at the picture about the different types of products you see as you move through the outdoor market. In other words, use division and classification to describe the market.
2. Think of the many occasions in your life that require different types of clothes. For example, you would never wear to a funeral what you wear to the beach. Group the routine events in your life, and explain how various clothes in your wardrobe are appropriate for specific types of events.
3. Think of the various jobs you will be qualified for when you finish college. Classify these jobs into a few categories, and explain your interest in each category.
4. Create your own division/classification assignment (with the help of your instructor), and write a response to it.

Revising Workshop

Small Group Activity (5–10 minutes per writer)   Working in groups of three or four, each person should read his or her division/classification to the other members of the group. Those listening should record their reactions on a copy of the Peer Evaluation Form in Appendix 2F. After your group goes through this process, give your evaluation forms to the appropriate writers so that each writer has two or three peer comment sheets for revising.

Paired Activity (5 minutes per writer)   Using the completed Peer Evaluation Forms, work in pairs to decide what you should revise in your paragraphs. If time allows, rewrite some of your sentences, and have your partner check them.

Individual Activity   Rewrite your paper, using the revising feedback you received from other students.

Editing Workshop

Paired Activity (5–10 minutes per writer)   Swap papers with a classmate, and use the editing portion of your Peer Evaluation Forms to identify as many grammar, punctuation, mechanics, and spelling errors as you can. If time allows, correct some of your errors, and have your partner check them. Record your grammar, punctuation, and mechanics errors in the Error Log (Appendix 6) and your spelling errors in the Spelling Log (Appendix 7).

Individual Activity   Rewrite your paper again, using the editing feedback you received from other students.

Reflecting on Your Writing

When you have completed your own essay, answer these five questions:
1. What was most difficult about this assignment?
2. What was easiest?
3. What did you learn about division and classification by completing this assignment?
4. What do you think are the strengths of your division/classification paragraph? What are its weaknesses?
5. What did you learn from this assignment about your own writing process—about preparing to write, about writing the first draft, about revising, and about editing?

Defining

> Words are the tools with which we work. . . .
> Everything depends on our understanding of them.

— Felix Frankfurter

Part of our daily communication process is asking people for clarification and definitions.

"What do you mean by that?"

"Can you clarify 'unfair'?"

"Can you explain what you mean by 'hyper'?"

"Can someone tell me what HTML is?"

Definitions keep the world running efficiently. Whenever we communicate—in spoken or written form—we use words we all understand. If we did not work from a set of shared definitions, we would not be able to communicate at all. We use definitions to explain concrete things (crayfish, DVD, laser beam), to identify places and events (Grand Canyon, Empire State Building, Cinco de Mayo celebration), and to discuss complex ideas (democracy, ambition, happiness).

Definition is the process of explaining a word, an object, or an idea in such a way that the audience knows as precisely as possible what you mean. A good definition of a word, for example, focuses on the special qualities of the word that set it apart from similar words. In the following paragraph, Mary Pipher defines the concept of family. She uses humorous, realistic examples to explain the responsibilities and rewards of being part of a family. See if you can pick out the main points of her definition.

Families are the people for whom it matters if you have a cold, are feuding with your mate, or are training a new puppy. Family members use magnets to fasten the newspaper clippings about your bowling team on the refrigerator door. They save your drawings and homemade pottery. They like to hear stories about when you were young. They'll help you can tomatoes or change the oil in your car. They're the people who will come visit you in the hospital, will talk to you when you call with "a dark night of the soul," and will loan you money to pay the rent if you lose your job. Whether or not they are biologically related to each other, the people who do these things are family.

Before continuing in this chapter, take a moment to write a definition of your own. Save your work because you will use it later in this chapter.

WRITE YOUR OWN DEFINITION

Everyone has a personal definition of the word "student." What is your definition of this word? Explain it in a paragraph.

HOW TO WRITE A DEFINITION PARAGRAPH

Definitions vary in length from short summaries (such as dictionary entries) to longer, extended pieces (such as essays and whole books written on complex concepts like "courage"). In addition, definitions can be objective or factual (as in a textbook) or subjective (combined with personal opinion). Pipher's definition of "family" is very subjective. Whether short or long, objective or subjective, a good definition meets certain basic requirements. The following guidelines will help you write an effective definition paragraph.

1. *State your purpose in your topic sentence.* Sometimes a definition is used by itself (as in a classified ad for a job opening). More often, definitions are used in other types of writing, such as process analysis, comparison/contrast, and division/classification. In any case, the topic sentence in a definition paragraph should state your purpose as clearly as possible.

   In Mary Pipher's paragraph, Pipher lays out her purpose right away in her topic sentence: "Families are the people for whom it matters if you have a cold, are feuding with your mate, or are training a new puppy." She explains this definition in the rest of her paragraph.

2. *Decide how you want to define your term or idea.* Definitions are the building blocks of communication. Therefore, you want to be sure your audience understands how you're using certain words and key terms. Consider your audience, and define the term in a way that your readers

will understand. The three possibilities are by synonym, by category, or by negation.

By synonym: The simplest way to define a word or term is to provide a synonym or word that has a similar meaning. This synonym should be easier to understand than the word being defined. For example, "A *democracy* is a *free society.*"

By category: Defining by category is a two-step process. First, you put the word you are defining into a specific class or category: "A *democracy* is a form of government." Then you need to state how the word is different from other words in that category: "A *democracy* is a form of government based on individual freedom that is developed *by* the people and *for* the people."

By negation: When you define a word by negation, you say what the word is *not* before stating what it is. For example, "A *democracy* is not a socialist form of government. Rather it is based on freedom and independence."

In her paragraph, Pipher uses the second method to define her term. First, she puts the term *family* in the category of *people.* Then she explains how members of a family are different from other people. Your family cares "if you have a cold, are feuding with your mate, or are training a new puppy."

3. ***Use examples to expand on your definition.*** These examples should show your word in action. Concrete examples are an option for accomplishing this task.

In Pipher's paragraph, the author uses examples to expand on her definition of the word "family." Every example is concrete, appealing to one of the five senses, and action-oriented.

> Family members use magnets to fasten the newspaper clippings about your bowling team on the refrigerator door.
>
> They save your drawings and homemade pottery.
>
> They like to hear stories about when you were young.
>
> They'll help you can tomatoes or change the oil in your car.
>
> They're the people who will come visit you in the hospital, will talk to you when you call with "a dark night of the soul," and will loan you money to pay the rent if you lose your job.

By the end of the paragraph, you have a very clear sense of what "family" means to Mary Pipher.

4. ***Organize your examples to communicate your definition as clearly as possible.*** Your examples should progress in some logical order—from

most serious to least serious, from least important to most important, chronologically, or spatially. What's important is that they move in some recognizable way from one to the next.

In her paragraph, Pipher arranges her examples from least crucial (putting your bowling score on the refrigerator) to most crucial (loaning you money when you lose your job). Pipher's method of organization is subtle but important to the flow of the paragraph.

DISCOVERING HOW DEFINITION WORKS

Two more examples will help you understand more clearly how good definition paragraphs work. The first, by Nancy Mairs, defines what it is to be handicapped in society today. What is the main point of her definition?

> I am a cripple. I choose this word to name me. I choose from among several possibilities, the most common of which are "handicapped" and "disabled." I made the choice a number of years ago, without thinking, unaware of my motives for doing so. Even now, I'm not sure what those motives are, but I recognize that they are complex and not entirely flattering. People—crippled or not—wince at the word "cripple," as they do not at "handicapped" or "disabled." Perhaps I want them to wince. I want them to see me as a tough customer, one to whom the fates/gods/viruses have not been kind, but who can face the brutal truth of her existence squarely. As a cripple, I swagger.

1. What is this paragraph defining?

   _____

2. Does this author rely on a synonym, a category, or a negation to start off her paragraph? Explain your answer.

   _____

   _____

3. What examples does Mairs use to develop her definition? List some here.

   _____

   _____

4. How does Mairs organize her examples: from one extreme to another, chronologically, or spatially?

_____

_____

Explain your answer.

_____

_____

The next example defines the word "khaki." It is from an essay titled "Up Through the Ranks" by David Feld. What is Feld's approach to this definition?

> The word khaki is Urdu, a dialect of Hindustani spoken in Afghanistan. It means dust-colored. From dark tannish green to light taupe verging on cream, there is as much variance in khaki as there are shades of the earth. In fact, one of the trousers' great attractions is that they almost beg to be dirty. Virtually any type of dirt can be simply brushed off, but khakis, because of their colorations, often don't even look soiled, when, in fact, they are quite filthy.

1. What is this paragraph defining?

_____

2. Does this author rely on a synonym, a category, or a negation at the beginning of this paragraph? Explain your answer.

_____

_____

3. What examples does Feld use to develop his definition? List some here.

_____

_____

_____

4. How does Feld organize his examples: from one extreme to another, chronologically, or spatially?

_____

Explain your answer.

_____

_____

REVISING AND EDITING A STUDENT PARAGRAPH

Here is a definition paragraph written by Inez Morales. Her paragraph defines "success." After you read her definition, see if you can restate her definition in your own words.

[1]To me, success is having an education, a decent job, and a happy, healthy family. [2]In order to be successful in life people must first get a college degree. [3]This education will prepare them for whatever situation in life that may come up. [4]I believe that having professional jobs like doctors, lawyers, and teachers help show a level of success. [5]When people work in professional jobs, they has the ability to build bigger homes, and buy better cars. [6]They are able to travel to different parts of the world with their families. [7]Many of my friends whose parents have professional jobs don't enjoy traveling. [8]They also don't have large families. [9]The last element of success are having a happy and healthy family. [10]Without an education, people will not be qualified for well-paying jobs. [11]I believe this is the formula for making it if people have all three of these in their lives, then they have success.

This paragraph is Inez's first draft, which now needs to be revised and edited. First, apply the Revising Checklist below to the content of Inez's draft. When you are satisfied that her ideas are fully developed and well organized, use the Editing Checklist on pages 180–181 to correct her grammar and mechanics errors. Answer the questions after each checklist. Then write your suggested changes directly on Inez's draft.

REVISING CHECKLIST ✔

TOPIC SENTENCE
- ✔ Does the topic sentence convey the paragraph's controlling idea?
- ✔ Does the topic sentence appear as the first or last sentence of the paragraph?

DEVELOPMENT
- ✔ Does the paragraph contain *specific* details that support the topic sentence?
- ✔ Does the paragraph include *enough* details to explain the topic sentence fully?

UNITY
- ✔ Do all the sentences in the paragraph support the topic sentence?

ORGANIZATION
- ✔ Is the paragraph organized logically?

COHERENCE
- ✔ Do the sentences move smoothly and logically from one to the next?

Topic Sentence

1. What is Inez defining?

_____

2. Put brackets around Inez's topic sentence. Does it explain what she is defining?

_____

3. Make sure it introduces all the ideas in Inez's paragraph.

Development

1. Do the details in the paragraph define success?

_____

2. Does Inez rely on synonyms, categories, or negation to develop her definition?

_____

3. Where do you need more information?

_____

4. Add at least one other detail to Inez's paragraph.

Unity

1. Read each of Inez's sentences with her topic sentence (revised, if necessary) in mind.

2. Cross out the two sentences not directly related to Inez's topic sentence.

Organization

1. Read Inez's paragraph again to see if all the sentences are arranged logically.

2. List some of the examples in Inez's paragraph in the order they appear.

_____

_____

_____

_____

_____

_____

3. Move the one example that seems to be out of order.

4. Identify Inez's method of organization:

_____

Coherence

For a list of transitions, see pages 46–47.

1. Circle three transitions Inez uses.

2. Add another transition to Inez's paragraph.

Now rewrite Inez's paragraph with your revisions.

EDITING CHECKLIST ✔

SENTENCES

✔ Does each sentence have a main subject and verb?

✔ Do all subjects and verbs agree?

✔ Do all pronouns agree with their nouns?

✔ Are modifiers as close as possible to the words they modify?

> **PUNCTUATION AND MECHANICS**
> ✔ Are sentences punctuated correctly?
> ✔ Are words capitalized properly?
>
> **WORD CHOICE AND SPELLING**
> ✔ Are words used correctly?
> ✔ Are words spelled correctly?

Sentences

Subjects and Verbs

1. Underline the subjects once and verbs twice in your revision of Inez's paragraph. Remember that sentences can have more than one subject-verb set.

2. Does each of the sentences have at least one subject and verb that can stand alone?

For help with subjects and verbs, see Chapter 30.

3. Did you find and correct Inez's run-together sentence?
   If not, find and correct it now.

For help with run-togethers, see Chapter 32.

Subject-Verb Agreement

1. Read aloud the subjects and verbs you underlined in your revision of Inez's paragraph.

2. Did you find and correct the three subjects and verbs that don't agree?

   If not, find and correct them now.

For help with subject-verb agreement, see Chapter 35.

Pronoun Agreement

1. Find any pronouns in your revision of Inez's paragraph that do not agree with their nouns.

2. Correct any pronouns that do not agree with their nouns.

For help with pronoun agreement, see Chapter 39.

Modifier Errors

1. Find any modifiers in your revision of Inez's paragraph that are not as close as possible to the words they modify.

2. Rewrite sentences if necessary so that the modifiers are as close as possible to the words they modify.

For help with modifier errors, see Chapter 42.

Punctuation and Mechanics

Punctuation

For help with punctuation, see Chapters 43–47.

1. Read your revision of Inez's paragraph for any errors in punctuation.

2. Find the run-together sentence you revised, and make sure it is punctuated correctly.

3. Did you find and correct the two comma errors in Inez's paragraph? If not, find and correct them now.

Mechanics

For help with capitalization, see Chapter 48.

1. Read your revision of Inez's paragraph for any errors in capitalization.

2. Be sure to check Inez's capitalization in the run-together sentence you revised.

Word Choice and Spelling

Word Choice

For help with confused words, see Chapter 54.

1. Find any words used incorrectly in your revision of Inez's paragraph.

2. Correct any errors you find.

Spelling

For help with spelling, see Chapter 55.

1. Use spell-check and a dictionary to check the spelling in your revision of Inez's paragraph.

2. Correct any misspelled words.

Now rewrite Inez's paragraph again with your editing corrections.

REVISING AND EDITING YOUR OWN PARAGRAPH

Returning to the definition paragraph you wrote earlier in this chapter, revise and edit your own writing. The checklists will help you apply what you have learned to your own paragraph.

REVISING CHECKLIST ✔

TOPIC SENTENCE
- [ ] Does the topic sentence convey the paragraph's controlling idea?
- [ ] Does the topic sentence appear as the first or last sentence of the paragraph?

DEVELOPMENT

☐ Does the paragraph contain *specific* details that support the topic sentence?

☐ Does the paragraph include *enough* details to explain the topic sentence fully?

UNITY

☐ Do all the sentences in the paragraph support the topic sentence?

ORGANIZATION

☐ Is the paragraph organized logically?

COHERENCE

☐ Do the sentences move smoothly and logically from one to the next?

Topic Sentence

1. What are you defining?

_____

2. Put brackets around your topic sentence. Does it explain what you are defining?

_____

3. Make sure it introduces all the ideas in your paragraph.

Development

1. Do your details help you define your term or concept?

_____

2. Do you rely on synonyms, categories, or negation to develop your definition?

_____

3. Where do you need more information?

_____

_____

4. Add at least one other detail to your paragraph.

Unity

1. Read each of your sentences with your topic sentence in mind.
2. Drop or rewrite any sentences not directly related to your topic sentence.

Organization

1. Read your paragraph again to see if all the sentences are arranged logically.
2. What method of organization did you use?

_____

3. What word clues from your paragraph tell your readers how it is organized?

_____

Coherence

For a list of transitions, see pages 46–47.

1. Circle three transitions.
2. Add one transition to your paragraph, and explain how it makes your paragraph easier to read.

_____

_____

Now rewrite your paragraph with your revisions.

EDITING CHECKLIST ✔

SENTENCES

☐ Does each sentence have a main subject and verb?

☐ Do all subjects and verbs agree?

☐ Do all pronouns agree with their nouns?

☐ Are modifiers as close as possible to the words they modify?

PUNCTUATION AND MECHANICS

☐ Are sentences punctuated correctly?

☐ Are words capitalized properly?

> WORD CHOICE AND SPELLING
> ☐ Are words used correctly?
> ☐ Are words spelled correctly?

Sentences

Subjects and Verbs

1. Underline the subjects once and verbs twice in your revised paragraph. Remember that sentences can have more than one subject-verb set.

2. Does each of your sentences have at least one subject and verb that can stand alone?

For help with subjects and verbs, see Chapter 30.

_____

3. Correct any fragments you have written.

For help with fragments, see Chapter 31.

4. Correct any run-together sentences you have written.

For help with run-togethers, see Chapter 32.

Subject-Verb Agreement

1. Read aloud the subjects and verbs you underlined in your revised paragraph.

2. Correct any subjects and verbs that do not agree.

For help with subject-verb agreement, see Chapter 35.

Pronoun Agreement

1. Find any pronouns in your revised paragraph that do not agree with their nouns.

2. Correct any pronouns that do not agree with their nouns.

For help with pronoun agreement, see Chapter 39.

Modifier Errors

1. Find any modifiers in your revised paragraph that are not as close as possible to the words they modify.

2. Rewrite sentences if necessary so that your modifiers are as close as possible to the words they modify.

For help with modifier errors, see Chapter 42.

Punctuation and Mechanics

Punctuation

1. Read your revised paragraph for any errors in punctuation.

2. Make sure any fragments and run-together sentences you revised are punctuated correctly.

For help with punctuation, see Chapters 43–47.

Mechanics

For help with capitalization, see Chapter 48.

1. Read your revised paragraph for any errors in capitalization.
2. Be sure to check your capitalization in any fragments or run-together sentences you revised.

Word Choice and Spelling

Word Choice

For help with confused words, see Chapter 54.

1. Find any words used incorrectly in your revised paragraph.
2. Correct any errors you find.

Spelling

For help with spelling, see Chapter 55.

1. Use spell-check and a dictionary to check your spelling.
2. Correct any misspelled words.

Now rewrite your paragraph again with your editing corrections.

PRACTICING DEFINITION

Reading Suggestions

In Chapter 27, you will find two essays that follow the guidelines you have studied in this chapter: "Workers" by Richard Rodriguez uses definition to explain the complexities of hard labor. "What Is Poverty?" by Jo Goodwin Parker defines poverty in its most gruesome details. You might want to read these selections before writing another definition. As you read, notice how the writers make their points through well-chosen examples and details.

Writing Workshop

Guidelines for Writing a Definition Paragraph

1. State your purpose in your topic sentence.
2. Decide how you want to define your term or idea.
3. Use examples to expand on your definition.
4. Organize your examples to communicate your definition as clearly as possible.

1. Define "parenthood" from your point of view.
2. Define "relaxation" or "stress," depending on your mood today.
3. Define one of the following abstract terms: *knowledge, fear, love, inferiority, wonder, pride, self-control, discipline, anger, freedom, violence, assertiveness, fellowship, friendship, courtesy, kindness.*
4. Create your own definition assignment (with the help of your instructor), and write a response to it.

Revising Workshop

Small Group Activity (5–10 minutes per writer)   Working in groups of three or four, each person should read his or her definition to the other members of the group. Those listening should record their reactions on a copy of the Peer Evaluation Form in Appendix 2G. After your group goes through this process, give your evaluation forms to the appropriate writers so that each writer has two or three peer comment sheets for revising.

Paired Activity (5 minutes per writer)   Using the completed Peer Evaluation Forms, work in pairs to decide what you should revise in your paragraphs. If time allows, rewrite some of your sentences, and have your partner check them.

Individual Activity   Rewrite your paper using the revising feedback you received from other students.

Editing Workshop

Paired Activity (5–10 minutes per writer)   Swap papers with a classmate, and using the editing portion of your Peer Evaluation Forms, identify as many grammar, punctuation, mechanics, and spelling errors as you can. If time allows, correct some of your errors, and have your partner check them. Record your grammar, punctuation, and mechanics errors in the Error Log (Appendix 6) and your spelling errors in the Spelling Log (Appendix 7).

Individual Activity   Rewrite your paper again using the editing feedback you received from other students.

Reflecting on Your Writing

When you have completed your own essay, answer these five questions:

1. What was most difficult about this assignment?
2. What was easiest?
3. What did you learn about definition by completing this assignment?
4. What do you think are the strengths of your definition paragraph? What are its weaknesses?
5. What did you learn from this assignment about your own writing process—about preparing to write, about writing the first draft, about revising, and about editing?

ANALYZING CAUSES AND EFFECTS

How do I know what I think until I see what I say?

—E. M. FORSTER

We all analyze causes and effects without even realizing it. Consider the following thoughts that might have crossed your mind:

Why you find someone attractive

The reasons you thought a movie was good

The effects of cutting your English class

Your reaction to a political debate

The consequences of going out with your friends instead of studying for an exam

Wanting to know why something happens is a natural interest that surfaces early in life—"Why can't I play outside today?" Not only do we want to know *why*, but we also want to know *what* will happen as a result of our actions. In like manner, your college courses often want you to analyze causes and effects. For example, an essay exam in a psychology course might ask "Why are some people superstitious?" Or a history question might be "What were the positive effects of the Spanish-American War?"

When we work with **causes and effects,** we are searching for connections and reasons. To understand a **cause,** we look to the past for reasons why something is the way it is. To discover an **effect,** we look to the future to figure out what the possible results of a particular action might be. In other words, we break an action or situation into parts and look at how these different parts relate to each other so that we can better understand the world around us.

In a book titled *Immigrant Kids*, Russell Freedman analyzes why the children of immigrants reject their parents' language and customs. He then discusses the results of this rejection. Can you see the difference between the causes and effects in this paragraph?

> The children became Americanized much faster than their parents. Often this caused painful conflicts in immigrant families. A gap appeared between the children and their parents. The parents spoke English with heavy accents, if they spoke it at all. They clung to Old World customs and beliefs. The kids spoke English all day with their friends. They thought in American terms. More than anything else, they wanted to be accepted as equals in their adopted land. In their anxiety to become fully "American," some immigrant children rejected their Old World heritage and the traditional values of their parents. They felt embarrassed or even ashamed by their parents' immigrant ways.

Before continuing in this chapter, take a moment to analyze an event in your own life. Save your work because you will use it later in this chapter.

WRITE YOUR OWN CAUSE/EFFECT ANALYSIS

Why did you choose the college you are attending today? Explain in a paragraph the events that led up to your decision and the results you expect from attending this college.

HOW TO WRITE A CAUSE/EFFECT PARAGRAPH

Writing about causes and effects requires careful critical thinking. To do this well, you need to discover connections between two or more events or ideas and explain the connection. Although this is a complex form of writing, good cause/effect paragraphs follow a few simple guidelines.

1. *Write a topic sentence that makes a clear statement about what you are going to analyze.* This should always be the first step in a cause/effect essay. You need to decide what you are analyzing and whether you are going to focus on causes (activities leading up to the event), effects (the results of an event), or both. These decisions will give focus and coherence to the rest of your paragraph.

   In Russell Freedman's paragraph, Freedman writes a very clear topic sentence: "The children became Americanized much faster than their parents." His topic sentence suggests that he will be discussing both the causes and effects of this observation.

2. ***Choose facts and details to support your topic sentence.*** These facts and details are the causes and effects that fully explain your topic sentence. To generate this material, try to anticipate your readers' questions and then answer them in your paragraph.

   In Freedman's paragraph, the author cites two *results* of Americanization at the beginning of the paragraph:

   > often caused painful conflicts
   >
   > gaps appeared between children and parents

   Then he discusses seven *causes* of this situation—two from the parents' side of the conflict:

   > spoke English with heavy accents
   >
   > clung to Old World customs

   and five from the children's side:

   > spoke English all day long
   >
   > thought in American terms
   >
   > wanted to be accepted as equals
   >
   > rejected Old World customs
   >
   > were embarrassed by their parents' immigrant ways

3. ***Make sure you include the real causes and effects of your topic.*** Just as you wouldn't stop reading halfway through a good murder mystery, you shouldn't stop too early in your analysis of causes and effects. For example, a student might fail a biology exam because she was sick. However, if you dig a little deeper, you may find that she missed several lectures, didn't study very much, and is exhausted holding down two jobs. Similarly, failing the exam probably has many effects: She may quit one job, promise herself to attend class regularly, and study harder for the next test. In other words, the actual causes and effects may not be the most obvious ones. This digging for the basic causes and effects will help you avoid confusing causes and effects with coincidences.

   In the sample paragraph, Freedman keeps digging for the "real" reasons for the conflict and tension in immigrant families. He first lists ways children try to become more American and finally realizes that they are basically embarrassed by their heritage.

4. ***Organize your material so that it communicates your message as clearly as possible.*** You should present your details in a logical order— perhaps chronologically or from one extreme to another. Chronological order follows a time sequence; from one extreme to another could involve any two extremes.

Freedman organizes his paragraph from least serious to most serious according to the two different groups he is discussing. He first takes up the parents' point of view (from accent to customs) and then deals with the children's side (from their speaking English all day to their feelings of embarrassment and shame).

DISCOVERING HOW CAUSE AND EFFECT WORK

Two additional sample paragraphs will help you understand more clearly how good cause-and-effect reasoning works. The first, by Drew Appleby, examines the causes and effects of specific behaviors in the classroom. See if you can separate the causes from the effects in this paragraph.

Sometimes the behavior of students and that of faculty becomes circular, with each contributing to the undesirable response of the other. For example, students yawn, gaze around the room, and otherwise look bored. The instructor reads this behavior as students not caring and concludes, "If they're not interested, why should I try to be interesting? I'll just do it and get it over with." So, there's nothing but lecture, endless instructor talk, and more students get bored and yawn and gaze around.

1. What is Appleby analyzing in this paragraph?

   _____

2. Does Appleby's topic sentence capture this focus? Explain your answer.

   _____

   _____

3. What causes and effects does Appleby cite? How does each relate to the topic sentence?

   Causes   **Relation to Topic Sentence**

   _____   _____

   _____   _____

Effects

_____   _____

_____   _____

_____   _____

4. Do you feel that Appleby gets to the real source of student-faculty classroom behavior? Explain your answer.

_____

_____

5. How does Appleby organize the details in his paragraph: chronologically or one extreme to another?

_____

In this next example, Robert Hine writes about his life when surgery restored his eyesight after many years of blindness. In this paragraph, Hine discusses points of contact among humans. Does the author deal with both causes and effects in this paragraph?

> We assume that the face is the primary means of human contact. "Face-to-face" is a basic term in the language . . . . It refers to one-on-one relationships, fundamental in the building of strong traditional communities. What then for the blind? Because they do not see faces, are they excluded from community? Obviously not. The blind do not need to "face" one another (though they often do so, turning toward the voice as a gesture of respect or an effort to conform). Theirs is the special bonding based either on their own internal images from voices or on some spiritual sense. Though faces are newly precious to me, for myself or for my community, I realize that the blind have their own form of face-to-face relationships.

1. What is Hine analyzing in this paragraph?

_____

Does Hine's topic sentence capture this focus? Explain your answer.

_____

_____

2. What one cause and one effect does Hine cite? How does each relate to the topic sentence?

Cause	Relation to Topic Sentence

Effect	

3. Do you feel that Hine gets to the real causes and effects connected with face-to-face relationships among the blind? Explain your answer.

_____

_____

_____

4. How does Hine organize the details in his paragraph: chronologically or from one extreme to another?

_____

_____

REVISING AND EDITING A STUDENT PARAGRAPH

Here is a cause/effect paragraph written by a student named Matthew Machias. His paragraph analyzes the causes and effects of his experience with jury duty. Do you think Matthew gets to the real causes and effects of the jury's verdict in this paragraph?

[1]Serving on a jury and determining someone's future are the toughest tasks I've ever had to do. [2]We had finished listening to both sides present evidence, examine witnesses, and summarize their arguments. [3]We had looked at photographs of the terrible automobile accident, shots of the wreckage, close-ups of the defendant's best friend, and even photos of him being taken away. [4]We heard that Grant (the defendant) had been driving while intoxicated on Highway 281 at 2 a.m. after a party. [5]His blood alcohol level was .11. [6]Well over the legal limit. [7]Grant had been convicted of drunk driving on previous occasions during 1998–99. [8]Grant didn't know that his actions would lead to his best friend's death. [9]Grant had completed

a special program for drunk drivers in mid-May. [10]I've heard those programs don't work well. [11]I don't know why those programs keep running. [12]Grant was driving over 80 mph while drunk, even though his license had been suspended. [13]When Grant's friend got in the car with him that night, was Grant's friend partly to blame for his own death. [14]What a tough question this is? [15]Even though the twenty-two-year-old defendant looked like a nice person, he was guilty. [16]Grant and his friend knew what they were doing when he drove to the party that night. [17]He knew what he was doing when he took that first drink. [18]Grant's friend trusted him. [19]That was the last decision he was ever able to make. [20]After we filed back into the jury box. [21]The foreman read our verdict of second-degree murder. [22]I knew that the group's judgment was the right one, even though I still felt sorry for the defendant.

This paragraph is Matthew's first draft, which now needs to be revised and edited. First, apply the Revising Checklist below to the content of Matthew's draft. When you are satisfied that his ideas are fully developed and well organized, use the Editing Checklist on page 197 to correct his grammar and mechanics errors. Answer the questions after each checklist. Then write your suggested changes directly on Matthew's draft.

REVISING CHECKLIST ✔

TOPIC SENTENCE
- ✔ Does the topic sentence convey the paragraph's controlling idea?
- ✔ Does the topic sentence appear as the first or last sentence of the paragraph?

DEVELOPMENT
- ✔ Does the paragraph contain *specific* details that support the topic sentence?
- ✔ Does the paragraph include *enough* details to explain the topic sentence fully?

UNITY
- ✔ Do all the sentences in the paragraph support the topic sentence?

ORGANIZATION
- ✔ Is the paragraph organized logically?

COHERENCE
- ✔ Do the sentences move smoothly and logically from one to the next?

Topic Sentence

1. What is Matthew analyzing in his paragraph?

   _____

2. Put brackets around Matthew's topic sentence. Does it capture the paragraph's focus?

   _____

3. Make sure it introduces all the ideas in Matthew's paragraph.

Development

1. Do the details in the paragraph refer to specific causes and effects?

   _____

2. Where does Matthew deal with causes? Where does he deal with effects?

Causes	Effects
_____	_____
_____	_____
_____	_____
_____	_____
_____	_____

Unity

1. Read each of Matthew's sentences with his topic sentence (revised, if necessary) in mind.
2. Cross out the two sentences not directly related to Matthew's topic sentence.

Organization

1. Read Matthew's paragraph again to see if all the sentences are arranged logically.

2. Identify Matthew's method of organization.

_____

3. Move the one example that seems to be out of order.

Coherence

1. Circle three pronouns Matthew uses.

2. Change three references to Grant to pronouns.

For a list of pronouns, see pages 364–365.

Now rewrite Matthew's paragraph with your revisions.

EDITING CHECKLIST ✔

SENTENCES

✔ Does each sentence have a main subject and verb?

✔ Do all subjects and verbs agree?

✔ Do all pronouns agree with their nouns?

✔ Are modifiers as close as possible to the words they modify?

PUNCTUATION AND MECHANICS

✔ Are sentences punctuated correctly?

✔ Are words capitalized properly?

WORD CHOICE AND SPELLING

✔ Are words used correctly?

✔ Are words spelled correctly?

Sentences

Subject and Verbs

1. Underline the subjects once and verbs twice in your revision of Matthew's paragraph. Remember that sentences can have more than one subject-verb set.

For help with subjects and verbs, see Chapter 30.

2. Does each of the sentences have at least one subject and verb that can stand alone?

_____

For help with fragments, see Chapter 31.

3. Did you find and correct Matthew's two fragments? If not, find and correct them now.

Subject-Verb Agreement

For help with subject-verb agreement, see Chapter 35.

1. Read aloud the subjects and verbs you underlined in your revision of Matthew's paragraph.

2. Correct any subjects and verbs that do not agree.

Pronoun Agreement

For help with pronoun agreement, see Chapter 39.

1. Find any pronouns in your revision of Matthew's paragraph that do not agree with their nouns.

2. Did you find and correct the four pronoun agreement errors in Matthew's paragraph? If not, find and correct them now.

Modifier Errors

For help with modifier errors, see Chapter 42.

1. Find any modifiers in your revision of Matthew's paragraph that are not as close as possible to the words they modify.

2. Rewrite sentences if necessary so that the modifiers are as close as possible to the words they modify.

Punctuation and Mechanics

Punctuation

For help with punctuation, see Chapters 43–47.

1. Read your revision of Matthew's paragraph for any errors in punctuation.

2. Find the two fragments you revised, and make sure they are punctuated correctly.

3. Did you find and correct two errors in end punctuation in Matthew's paragraph?

If not, find and correct them now.

Mechanics

For help with capitalization, see Chapter 48.

1. Read your revision of Matthew's paragraph for any errors in capitalization.

2. Be sure to check Matthew's capitalization in the fragments you revised.

Word Choice and Spelling

Word Choice

1. Find any words used incorrectly in your revision of Matthew's paragraph.

2. Correct any errors you find.

For help with confused words, see Chapter 54.

Spelling

1. Use spell-check and a dictionary to check the spelling in your revision of Matthew' paragraph.

2. Correct any misspelled words.

For help with spelling, see Chapter 55.

Now rewrite Matthew's paragraph again with your editing corrections.

REVISING AND EDITING YOUR OWN PARAGRAPH

Returning to the cause/effect paragraph you wrote earlier in this chapter, revise and edit your own writing. The checklists will help you apply what you have learned to your own paragraph.

REVISING CHECKLIST ✔

TOPIC SENTENCE
- ☐ Does the topic sentence convey the paragraph's controlling idea?
- ☐ Does the topic sentence appear as the first or last sentence of the paragraph?

DEVELOPMENT
- ☐ Does the paragraph contain *specific* details that support the topic sentence?
- ☐ Does the paragraph include *enough* details to explain the topic sentence fully?

UNITY
- ☐ Do all the sentences in the paragraph support the topic sentence?

ORGANIZATION
- ☐ Is the paragraph organized logically?

COHERENCE
- ☐ Do the sentences move smoothly and logically from one to the next?

Topic Sentence

1. What are you analyzing in your paragraph?

   _____

2. Underline your topic sentence. Does it capture the focus of your paragraph?

   _____

3. Make sure it introduces all the ideas in your paragraph.

Development

1. Do the details in your paragraph refer to specific causes and effects?

   _____

2. Where do you deal with causes? Where do you deal with effects?

   Causes   **Effects**

   _____   _____

   _____   _____

   _____   _____

   _____   _____

   _____   _____

Unity

1. Read each of your sentences with your topic sentence in mind.
2. Drop or rewrite any sentences not directly related to your topic sentence.

Organization

1. Read your paragraph again to see if all the sentences are arranged logically.
2. What method of organization did you use for your paragraph?

   _____

3. What word clues from your paragraph tell your readers how it is organized?

_____

Coherence

1. Circle three pronouns you use.

2. Add at least one pronoun to your paragraph, and explain how it makes your paragraph easier to read.

For a list of pronouns, see pages 364–365.

_____

_____

Now rewrite your paragraph with your revisions.

EDITING CHECKLIST ✔

SENTENCES
☐ Does each sentence have a main subject and verb?

☐ Do all subjects and verbs agree?

☐ Do all pronouns agree with their nouns?

☐ Are modifiers as close as possible to the words they modify?

PUNCTUATION AND MECHANICS
☐ Are sentences punctuated correctly?

☐ Are words capitalized properly?

WORD CHOICE AND SPELLING
☐ Are words used correctly?

☐ Are words spelled correctly?

Sentences

Subject and Verbs

1. Underline the subjects once and verbs twice in your revised paragraph. Remember that sentences can have more than one subject-verb set.

For help with subjects and verbs, see Chapter 30.

2. Does each of your sentences have at least one subject and verb that can stand alone?

For help with fragments, see Chapter 31.

For help with run togethers, see Chapter 32.

3. Correct any fragments you have written.
4. Correct any run-together sentences you have written.

Subject-Verb Agreement

For help with subject-verb agreement, see Chapter 35.

1. Read aloud the subjects and verbs you underlined in your revised paragraph.
2. Correct any subjects and verbs that do not agree.

Pronoun Agreement

For help with pronoun agreement, see Chapter 39.

1. Find any pronouns in your revised paragraph that do not agree with their nouns.
2. Correct any pronouns that do not agree with their nouns.

Modifier Errors

For help with modifier errors, see Chapter 42.

1. Find any modifiers in your revised paragraph that are not as close as possible to the words they modify.
2. Rewrite sentences if necessary so that your modifiers are as close as possible to the words they modify.

Punctuation and Mechanics
Punctuation

For help with punctuation, see Chapters 43–47.

1. Read your revised paragraph for any errors in punctuation.
2. Make sure any fragments and run-together sentences you revised are punctuated correctly.

Mechanics

For help with capitalization, see Chapter 48.

1. Read your revised paragraph for any errors in capitalization.
2. Be sure to check your capitalization in any fragments and run-together sentences you revised.

Word Choice and Spelling
Word Choice

For help with confused words, see Chapter 54.

1. Find any words used incorrectly in your revised paragraph.
2. Correct any errors you find.

Spelling

1. Use spell-check and a dictionary to check your spelling.

2. Correct any misspelled words.

Now rewrite your paragraph again with your editing corrections.

For help with spelling, see Chapter 55.

PRACTICING CAUSE AND EFFECT

Reading Suggestions

In Chapter 28, you will find two essays that follow the guidelines you have studied in this chapter. In "Shedding the Weight of My Dad's Obsession," Linda Lee Andujar analyzes a lifelong problem with her father, and in "Life Sentences," Corky Clifton analyzes the role of writing in a prisoner's life. You might want to read these selections before writing another cause/effect paper. As you read, notice how the writers make their points through well-thought-out, detailed reasoning.

Writing Workshop

Guidelines for Writing a Cause/Effect Paragraph

1. Write a topic sentence that makes a clear statement about what you are going to analyze.

2. Choose facts and details to support your topic sentence.

3. Make sure you include the real causes and effects of your topic.

4. Organize your material so that it communicates your message as clearly as possible.

1. Write an explanation of how the area in the picture on the previous page became such a wasteland. Analyze what happened before this picture was taken. Why did it happen? Or focus on what might happen in this area in the future.

2. Write a paragraph about an important event that changed your attitude toward an authority figure in your life (a parent, a religious leader, a teacher, a club sponsor, a supervisor or boss). What brought about the change? What were the results of the change?

3. Choose a major problem you see in society today, and analyze its causes and effects. Can you propose a solution to this problem?

4. Create your own cause/effect assignment (with the help of your instructor), and write a response to it.

Revising Workshop

Small Group Activity (5–10 minutes per writer)   Working in groups of three or four, each person should read his or her cause/effect analysis to the other members of the group. Those listening should record their reactions on a copy of the Peer Evaluation Form in Appendix 2H. After your group goes through this process, give your evaluation forms to the appropriate writers so that each writer has two or three peer comment sheets for revising.

Paired Activity (5 minutes per writer)   Using the completed Peer Evaluation Forms, work in pairs to decide what you should revise in your paragraphs. If time allows, rewrite some of your sentences, and have your partner check them.

Individual Activity   Rewrite your paper using the revising feedback you received from other students.

Editing Workshop

Paired Activity (5–10 minutes per writer)   Swap papers with a classmate, and using the editing portion of your Peer Evaluation Forms, identify as many grammar, punctuation, mechanics, and spelling errors as you can. If time allows, correct some of your errors, and have your partner check them. Record your grammar, punctuation, and mechanics errors in the Error Log (Appendix 6) and your spelling errors in the Spelling Log (Appendix 7).

Individual Activity   Rewrite your paper again using the editing feedback you received from other students.

Reflecting on Your Writing

When you have completed your own essay, answer these five questions:

1. What was most difficult about this assignment?

2. What was easiest?

3. What did you learn about analyzing causes and effects by completing this assignment?

4. What do you think are the strengths of your cause/effect paragraph? What are its weaknesses?

5. What did you learn from this assignment about your own writing process—about preparing to write, about writing the first draft, about revising, and about editing?

14

ARGUING

Remember, no one is obligated to take your word for anything.

—M. L. STEIN

When was the last time you tried to talk someone into doing something? Was it when you wanted

your wife to go to a movie you were excited to see,

your parents to let you use the car,

your sister to lend you money,

a professor to give you a little more time to submit a paper, or

the garage mechanic to fix your car without charging you more than the car was worth?

So much of what we say or do is an attempt to convince someone to do something. If you dress up for a job interview, you are trying to persuade the employer that you should be hired. If you argue with a friend about gun control, you are trying to persuade your friend to agree with you. And think of all the television, magazine, and billboard ads that are trying to talk you into buying a certain product. Life is filled with opportunities to argue with others and persuade them of your point of view.

The purpose of **arguing** is to persuade your readers to take some action or to think or feel a certain way. So arguing and persuading work closely together. Because we live in a society that allows us to voice our opinions freely, learning how to express our thoughts in a polite and reasonable way is one goal we should all strive for. The ability to argue well is a powerful tool.

In the following paragraph, Jesse Jackson argues for the continuation of affirmative action. In it, he tries to help people see the value in such "creative justice." Does he persuade you?

If our goal is educational and economic equity and parity—and it is—then we need affirmative action to catch up. We are behind as a result of discrimination and denial of opportunity. There is one white attorney for every 680 whites, but only one black attorney for every 4,000 blacks; one white physician for every 659 whites, but only one black physician for every 5,000 blacks; and one white dentist for every 1,900 whites, but only one black dentist for every 8,400 blacks. Less than 1 percent of all engineers—or of all practicing chemists—is black. Cruel and uncompassionate injustice created gaps like these. We need creative justice and compassion to help us close them.

Before continuing in this chapter, take a moment to write your own argument paragraph. Save your work because you will use it later in this chapter.

✎ WRITE YOUR OWN ARGUMENT

Choose a controversial issue on your campus, and write a paragraph that presents your opinion about it. When writing your paragraph, be sure to back up your opinion with reasons.

HOW TO WRITE AN ARGUMENT PARAGRAPH

When you are writing an argument, you must present evidence that convinces your readers to agree with you on a particular topic. This isn't always as easy as it sounds. All too often your reader will have a different opinion. Your evidence, therefore, must be accurate and logical. In fact, evidence is the most important ingredient in an argument. Without supporting evidence, your paragraph will be nothing more than a statement of your opinion. Convincing evidence, however, helps your readers understand and perhaps agree with your views. The following guidelines will help you organize and develop a good argument/persuasion paragraph.

1. **State your opinion on the issue in the topic sentence.** This sentence should state your position on an issue that can be argued and does not have a clear answer. It sets up your point of view and prepares your readers for the evidence you plan to give them.

   Jesse Jackson starts his paragraph with a sentence that readers might dispute: "If our goal is educational and economic equity and parity—and it is—then we need affirmative action to catch up." Jackson's first sentence sets up the rest of his paragraph, in which he will have to present material that supports his position on this issue.

2. ***Find out as much as you can about your audience before you write.***
   Knowing your audience's background and feelings toward your topic
   will help you choose supporting details and examples. If you are trying
   to convince people in two different age groups not to smoke, you might
   tell teenagers that cigarettes make their breath rancid, their teeth
   yellow, and their clothes smell bad. On the other hand, you might persuade parents and other adults to stop smoking with some long-term
   statistics on lung and heart disease in smokers.

   In Jackson's paragraph, he addresses the public as "we" in his first
   sentence, including himself in his reference. He then proceeds to talk
   directly to his audience. He concludes with another reference to "we,"
   reminding his audience that his readers and he are facing this issue
   together. Jackson's knowledge of his audience will help him develop
   the rest of his paragraph, making effective choices as he writes.

3. ***Choose appropriate evidence that supports your topic sentence.***
   Evidence usually takes the form of (a) facts, (b) statistics, (c) statements
   from authorities, or (d) examples and personal stories. You can use one
   of these types of evidence or a combination of them in any argument
   paragraph. Opinions—your own or other people's—are not evidence.

   In Jackson's paragraph, the author cites five pieces of evidence that
   fall into two of these categories:

Evidence	Type
We are behind as a result of discrimination and denial of opportunity.	statement from authority
There is one white attorney for every 680 whites, but only one black attorney for every 4,000 blacks.	statistic
There is one white physician for every 659 whites, but only one black physician for every 5,000.	statistic
There is one white dentist for every 1,900 whites, but only one black dentist for every 8,400 blacks.	statistic
Less than 1 percent of all engineers—or of all practicing chemists—is black.	statistic

4. ***Organize your evidence so that it supports your argument as effectively as possible.*** The organization of your material in an argument
   paragraph depends to a great extent on the opinions of your readers.
   Your paragraph should be arranged from general to particular, from
   particular to general, or from one extreme to another. When you know
   that your readers already agree with you, you should arrange your

paragraph from a general statement to particular examples or from most to least important. This way, your audience will move through your argument with you from beginning to end, and you will be building on their loyalty and enthusiasm. When you are dealing with readers who probably disagree with you, you should work from details and examples to a single general statement or from least to most important. With this method of organization, you can lead your readers through your reasoning step by step as you use your examples to pull them into your way of thinking.

In his paragraph, Jackson starts with a general statement and then organizes his statistics from smallest (one white attorney for every 680 whites, but only one black attorney for every 4,000 blacks) to largest (less than 1 percent of all engineers—or of all practicing chemists—is black). He is trying to persuade his readers that they really can't ignore the fact that "discrimination and denial of opportunity" still exist in American society and furthermore that they should take action against such injustice.

DISCOVERING HOW ARGUMENT WORKS

Two additional sample paragraphs will help you understand more clearly how good arguments work. The first, by Marie Winn, argues that TV watching is an addiction. See if you can identify her evidence.

Not unlike drugs or alcohol, the television experience allows the participant to blot out the real world and enter into a pleasurable and passive mental state. The worries and anxieties of reality are as effectively deferred by becoming absorbed in a television program as by going on a "trip" induced by drugs or alcohol. And just as alcoholics are only vaguely aware of their addiction, feeling that they control their drinking more than they really do ("I can cut it out any time I want—I just like to have three or four drinks before dinner"), people similarly overestimate their control over television watching. Even as they put off other activities to spend hour after hour watching television, they feel they could easily resume living in a different, less passive style. But somehow or other, while the television set is present in their homes, the click doesn't sound. With television pleasures available, those other experiences seem less attractive, more difficult somehow.

1.   What is Winn's topic sentence?

_____

_____

Does it state her opinion about a certain issue?

_____

Is it debatable? (Does it have more than one side?)

_____

2. Whom do you think Winn is addressing in this paragraph? How did you come to this conclusion?

_____

3. What evidence does the author use to support her topic sentence? How would you classify her major pieces of evidence (facts, statistics, statements from authorities, or examples/personal stories)?

Evidence	Type
_____	_____
_____	_____
_____	_____
_____	_____
_____	_____

4. How does Winn organize her paragraph: general to particular, particular to general, or one extreme to another?

_____

_____

The next paragraph is a statement from a commission report on the quality of education in U.S. schools. Its information has often been used as evidence that we need to reform our educational system. What type of evidence does the report furnish? Do you find it convincing?

We must emphasize that the variety of student aspirations, abilities, and preparation requires that appropriate content be available to satisfy diverse needs. Attention must be directed to both the nature of the content available and to the needs of particular learners. The most gifted students, for example, may need a curriculum enriched and accelerated beyond even the needs of other students of high ability. Similarly, educationally disadvantaged students may require special curriculum materials, smaller classes, or individual tutoring to help them master the material presented. Nevertheless, there remains a common expectation: We must demand the best effort and performance from all students, whether they are gifted or less able, affluent or disadvantaged, whether destined for college, the farm, or industry.

1. What is the paragraph's topic sentence?

   _____

   _____

   _____

   Does it state the authors' opinion about a certain issue?

   _____

   Is it debatable? (Does it have more than one side?)

   _____

2. Whom do you think the authors are addressing in this paragraph? How did you come to this conclusion?

   _____

   _____

   _____

3. The authors offer three statements to support their topic sentence. What are these statements? How would you classify each statement (fact, statistic, statement from an authority, or example/personal story)?

Evidence	Type
_____	_____
_____	_____
_____	_____

4. How do the authors organize the evidence in this paragraph?

_____

_____

REVISING AND EDITING A STUDENT PARAGRAPH

Here is a paragraph written by Anthony Barone arguing against home schooling for children. Notice how this student writer organizes and presents his evidence on this subject.

> [1]Being educated at home is not in the best interest of children. [2]I do not think it should be allowed unless a child is sick or lives to far from school to go home every day. [3]Most parents say the world is too dangerous for their children who teach they're kids at home. [4]Parents also need to consider that children do not learn to work together by staying home, they need to be around other children to learn how to argue, how to solve problems, and how to develop a strong value system. [5]But if one child is unsafe. [6]All children are unsafe that I know. [7]The community should get together and make the area safe for these children. [8]Children can learn more then academic subjects in school they can also learn about life. [9]Parents should volunteer at there child's school. [10]And pass their knowledge on to other children too.

This paragraph is Anthony's first draft, which now needs to be revised and edited. First, apply the Revising Checklist below to the content of Anthony's draft. When you are satisfied that his ideas are fully developed and well organized, use the Editing Checklist on pages 214–215 to correct his grammar and mechanics errors. Answer the questions after each checklist. Then write your suggested changes directly on Anthony's draft.

REVISING CHECKLIST ✔

TOPIC SENTENCE
- ✔ Does the topic sentence convey the paragraph's controlling idea?
- ✔ Does the topic sentence appear as the first or last sentence of the paragraph?

DEVELOPMENT
✔ Does the paragraph contain *specific* details that support the topic sentence?
✔ Does the paragraph include *enough* details to explain the topic sentence fully?

UNITY
✔ Do all the sentences in the paragraph support the topic sentence?

ORGANIZATION
✔ Is the paragraph organized logically?

COHERENCE
✔ Do the sentences move smoothly and logically from one to the next?

Topic Sentence

1. What is the subject of Anthony's paragraph?

_____

2. What is his opinion on this subject?

_____

3. Put brackets around Anthony's topic sentence. Does it communicate the subject and his opinion on it?

_____

4. Make sure it introduces all the ideas in Anthony's paragraph.

Development

1. What types of support does Anthony supply for his topic sentence?

Evidence	Type
_____	_____
_____	_____
_____	_____

2. Where do you need more information?

_____

_____

Unity

1. Read each of Anthony's sentences with his topic sentence (revised, if necessary) in mind.

2. Drop or rewrite any of his sentences not directly related to his topic sentence.

Organization

1. Read Anthony's paragraph again to see if all sentences are arranged logically.

2. Identify Anthony's method of organization.

_____

3. Move the one example that seems to be out of order.

Coherence

For a list of transitions, see pages 46–47.

1. Circle three transitions, repetitions, synonyms, or pronouns Anthony uses.

For a list of pronouns, see pages 364–365.

2. Change at least one of these in Anthony's paragraph, and explain how your change makes the paragraph easier to read.

Now rewrite Anthony's paragraph with your revisions.

ⒺDITING CHECKLIST ✔

SENTENCES
- ✔ Does each sentence have a main subject and verb?
- ✔ Do all subjects and verbs agree?
- ✔ Do all pronouns agree with their nouns?
- ✔ Are modifiers as close as possible to the words they modify?

> **PUNCTUATION AND MECHANICS**
> ✔ Are sentences punctuated correctly?
> ✔ Are words capitalized properly?
>
> **WORD CHOICE AND SPELLING**
> ✔ Are words used correctly?
> ✔ Are words spelled correctly?

Sentences

Subjects and Verbs

1. Underline the subjects once and verbs twice in your revision of Anthony's paragraph. Remember that sentences can have more than one subject-verb set.

2. Does each of Anthony's sentences have at least one subject and verb that can stand alone?

For help with subjects and verbs, see Chapter 30.

3. Did you find and correct Anthony's two fragments? If not, find and correct them now.

For help with fragments, see Chapter 31.

4. Did you find and correct Anthony's two run-together sentences? If not, find and correct them now.

For help with run-togethers, see Chapter 31.

Subject-Verb Agreement

1. Read aloud the subjects and verbs you underlined in your revision of Anthony's paragraph.

2. Correct any subjects and verbs that do not agree.

For help with subject-verb agreement, see Chapter 35.

Pronoun Agreement

1. Find any pronouns in your revision of Anthony's paragraph that do not agree with their nouns.

2. Correct any pronouns that do not agree with their nouns.

For help with pronoun agreement, see Chapter 39.

Modifier Errors

1. Find any modifiers in your revision of Anthony's paragraph that are not as close as possible to the words they modify.

2. Did you find and correct Anthony's two modifier errors? If not, find and correct them now.

For help with modifier errors, see Chapter 42.

Punctuation and Mechanics

Punctuation

For help with punctuation, see Chapters 43–47.

1. Read your revision of Anthony's paragraph for any errors in punctuation.

2. Find the two run-together sentences and two fragments that you revised, and make sure they are punctuated correctly.

Mechanics

For help with capitalization, see Chapter 48.

1. Read your revision of Anthony's paragraph for any errors in capitalization.

2. Be sure to check Anthony's capitalization in the fragments and run-together sentences you revised.

Word Choice and Spelling

Word Choice

For help with confused words, see Chapter 54.

1. Find any words used incorrectly in your revision of Anthony's paragraph.

2. Did you find and correct the four words Anthony uses incorrectly? If not, find and correct them now.

Spelling

For help with spelling, see Chapter 55.

1. Use spell-check and a dictionary to check the spelling in your revision of Anthony's paragraph.

2. Correct any misspelled words.

Now rewrite Anthony's paragraph again with your editing corrections.

REVISING AND EDITING YOUR OWN PARAGRAPH

Returning to the argument paragraph you wrote earlier in this chapter, revise and edit your own writing. The checklists will help you apply what you have learned to your own paragraph.

REVISING CHECKLIST ✔

TOPIC SENTENCE
- ☐ Does the topic sentence convey the paragraph's controlling idea?
- ☐ Does the topic sentence appear as the first or last sentence of the paragraph?

DEVELOPMENT

☐ Does the paragraph contain *specific* details that support the topic sentence?

☐ Does the paragraph include *enough* details to explain the topic sentence fully?

UNITY

☐ Do all the sentences in the paragraph support the topic sentence?

ORGANIZATION

☐ Is the paragraph organized logically?

COHERENCE

☐ Do the sentences move smoothly and logically from one to the next?

Topic Sentence

1. What is the subject of your paragraph?

_____

2. What is your opinion on this subject?

_____

_____

3. Put brackets around your topic sentence. Does it communicate your subject and opinion?

_____

4. Make sure it introduces all the ideas in your paragraph.

Development

1. What type of support do you supply for your topic sentence?

Evidence	Type
_____	_____
_____	_____

_____   _____

_____   _____

_____   _____

2. Where do you think you need to give more information?

_____

_____

Unity

1. Read each of your sentences with your topic sentence in mind.
2. Drop or rewrite any sentences not directly related to your topic sentence.

Organization

1. Read your paragraph again to see if all the sentences are arranged logically.
2. How did you organize the evidence in your paragraph?

_____

3. What word clues from your paragraph tell your readers how it is organized?

_____

Coherence

For a list of transitions, see pages 46–47.

For a list of pronouns, see pages 364–365.

1. Circle three transitions, repetitions, synonyms, or pronouns you use.
2. Change at least one of these in your paragraph, and explain how your change makes your paragraph easier to read.

_____

_____

Now rewrite your paragraph with your revisions.

❸DITING CHECKLIST ✔

SENTENCES
☐ Does each sentence have a main subject and verb?

☐ Do all subjects and verbs agree?

☐ Do all pronouns agree with their nouns?

☐ Are modifiers as close as possible to the words they modify?

PUNCTUATION AND MECHANICS
☐ Are sentences punctuated correctly?

☐ Are words capitalized properly?

WORD CHOICE AND SPELLING
☐ Are words used correctly?

☐ Are words spelled correctly?

Sentences

Subjects and Verbs

1. Underline the subjects once and verbs twice in your revised paragraph. Remember that sentences can have more than one subject-verb set.

   For help with subjects and verbs, see Chapter 30.

2. Does each of your sentences have at least one subject and verb that can stand alone?

3. Correct any fragments you have written.

   For help with fragments, see Chapter 31.

4. Correct any run-together sentences you have written.

   For help with run-togethers, see Chapter 32.

Subject-Verb Agreement

1. Read aloud the subjects and verbs you underlined in your revised paragraph.

   For help with subject-verb agreement, see Chapter 35.

2. Correct any subjects and verbs that do not agree.

Pronoun Agreement

1. Find any pronouns in your revised paragraph that do not agree with their nouns.

   For help with pronoun agreement, see Chapter 39.

2. Correct any pronouns that do not agree with their nouns.

Modifier Errors

For help with modifier errors, see Chapter 42.

1. Find any modifiers in your revised paragraph that are not as close as possible to the words they modify.
2. Rewrite sentences if necessary so that your modifiers are as close as possible to the words they modify.

Punctuation and Mechanics

Puncutation

For help with punctuation, see Chapters 43–47.

1. Read your revised paragraph for any errors in punctuation.
2. Make sure any fragments and run-together sentences you revised are punctuated correctly.

Mechanics

For help with capitalization, see Chapter 48.

1. Read your revised paragraph for any errors in capitalization.
2. Be sure to check your capitalization in any fragments or run-together sentences you revised.

Word Choice and Spelling

Word Choice

For help with confused words, see Chapter 54.

1. Find any words used incorrectly in your revised paragraph.
2. Correct any errors you find.

Spelling

For help with spelling, see Chapter 55.

1. Use spell-check and a dictionary to check your spelling.
2. Correct any misspelled words.

Now rewrite your paragraph again with your editing corrections.

PRACTICING ARGUMENT

Reading Suggestions

In Chapter 29, you will find three essays that follow the guidelines you have studied in this chapter. The first is an essay by Dwight van Avery called "Why Study English?" which discusses the relationship between studying English and success in life. The other two essays are about hate crime laws: "Hate Crime Laws Are Necessary" and "Hate Crime Laws Are Unnecessary," both published in *Opposing Viewpoints*. You might want to read these selections before writing another argument paragraph. As you read, notice how the writers make their points through clear, well-chosen evidence.

Writing Workshop

Guidelines for Writing an Argument Paragraph

1. State your opinion on the issue in the topic sentence.
2. Find out as much as you can about your audience before you write.
3. Choose appropriate evidence that supports your topic sentence.
4. Organize your evidence so that it supports your argument as effectively as possible.

1. Explain how this ad is trying to persuade people to buy cigarettes. How does it appeal to its viewers? What line of reasoning does it follow? Write a paragraph about what the ad would say if it could talk directly to you.
2. We all have strong opinions on controversial issues. A newspaper or newscast might remind you of some of these subjects. Choose a current controversial issue, and, presenting your evidence in an essay, try to convince your classmates that your opinion is right.
3. Persuade the leader of an organization that your position on an important topic affecting the organization is the best choice. To find a topic, think of your own work experience, or talk to someone who has work experience. Organize your evidence as effectively as possible.
4. Create your own argument/persuasion assignment (with the help of your instructor), and write a response to it.

Revising Workshop

Small Group Activity (5–10 minutes per writer)   Working in groups of three or four, each person should read his or her argument to the other members of the group. Those listening should record their reactions on a copy of the Peer Evaluation Form in Appendix 2I. After your group goes through this process, give your evaluation forms to the appropriate writers so that each writer has two or three peer comment sheets for revising.

Paired Activity (5 minutes per writer)   Using the completed Peer Evaluation Forms, work in pairs to decide what you should revise in your paragraphs. If time allows, rewrite some of your sentences, and have your partner check them.

Individual Activity   Rewrite your paper using the revising feedback you received from other students.

Editing Workshop

Paired Activity (5–10 minutes per writer)   Swap papers with a classmate, and using the editing portion of your Peer Evaluation Forms, identify as many grammar, punctuation, mechanics, and spelling errors as you can. If time allows, correct some of your errors, and have your partner check them. Record your grammar, punctuation, and mechanics errors in the Error Log (Appendix 6) and your spelling errors in the Spelling Log (Appendix 7).

Individual Activity   Rewrite your paper again using the editing feedback you received from other students.

Reflecting on Your Writing

When you have completed your own essay, answer these five questions:
1. What was most difficult about this assignment?
2. What was easiest?
3. What did you learn about argument by completing this assignment?
4. What do you think are the strengths of your argument paragraph? What are its weaknesses?
5. What did you learn from this assignment about your own writing process—about preparing to write, about writing the first draft, about revising, and about editing?

ESSAYS: PARAGRAPHS IN CONTEXT

Everyone agrees that a writer's sense of purpose usefully directs choices about what to say and where and how to say it.

—C. H. KNOBLAUCH

Part III explains what an essay is. It tells you not only how to identify an essay but also how to write one—step by step. It provides both a professional model and a student model for you to work with. Then it helps you apply specific revising and editing guidelines to a student essay and to your own writing.

CHAPTER 15

RECOGNIZING AN ESSAY

In content, essays are "nonfiction." That is, they are about real-life subjects rather than made-up ones. Most essays focus on one specific subject, a single purpose, and a particular audience (for example, telling college students how to get a good job). For an essay to be successful, its method of development must suit its purpose and appeal to its target audience. A successful essay gets the reaction from the readers that its author hopes for, whether this response is to appreciate a special scene, identify with someone's grief, or leap to action on a controversial issue.

Although essays may differ a great deal in design, organization, and content, they share certain features that distinguish them from other types of writing. At the simplest level, the way an essay looks on the page tells its audience "Here's an essay!" First, an essay usually has a title that names its general subject. Longer, more complex essays may also have subtitles. When writers move from one topic to another, they start a new paragraph by indenting a few spaces. In addition, most essays contain a thesis statement (a controlling idea for the entire essay) in the introduction. Several body paragraphs explain and support that thesis, and a conclusion draws the essay to a close.

The following essay, by Scott Russell Sanders, is from a book titled *Hunting for Hope*.

FIDELITY

by Scott Russell Sanders

1   A cause needn't be grand, it needn't impress a crowd, to be worthy of our commitment. I knew a man, a lifelong Quaker, who visited prisoners in our county jail, week in and week out, for decades. He would write letters for them, carry messages for them, fetch them clothing or books. But mainly

he just offered himself, a very tall and spare and gentle man, with a full shock of white hair in his later years and a rumbling voice that never wasted a word. He didn't ask whether the prisoners were innocent or guilty of the charges that had landed them in jail. All that mattered was that they were in trouble. He didn't preach to them, didn't pick and choose between the likable and the nasty, didn't look for any return on his time. Nor did he call attention to his kindness; I had known him for several years before I found out about his visits to the jail. Why did he go spend time with outcasts, every week without fail, when he could have been golfing or shopping or watching TV? "I go," he told me once, "in case everyone else has given up on them. I never give up."

Never giving up is a trait we honor in athletes, in soldiers, in climbers   2
marooned by avalanches, in survivors of shipwreck, in patients recovering from severe injuries. If you struggle bravely against overwhelming odds, you're liable to wind up on the evening news. A fireman rescues three children from a burning house, then goes back inside a fourth time to rescue the dog. A childless washerwoman in the deep South, who never dreamed of going to college herself, lives modestly and saves her pennies and in old age donates everything she's saved, over a hundred thousand dollars, for university scholarships. A pilot flies his flimsy plane through a blizzard, searching for a pickup truck in which a woman is trapped; gliding and banking through a whirl of white, he catches signals from her cellular phone, ever so faint; the snow blinds him, the wind tosses him around, his fuel runs low, but he circles and circles, homing in on that faint signal; then just before dark he spies the truck, radios the position to a helicopter crew, and the woman is saved. What kept him searching? "I hadn't found her yet," he tells the camera. "I don't quit so long as I have gas."

Striking examples of perseverance catch our eye, and rightly so. But in   3
less flashy, less newsworthy forms, fidelity to a mission or a person or an occupation shows up in countless lives all around us, all the time. It shows up in parents who will not quit loving their son no matter how much trouble he causes, in parents who will not quit loving their daughter even after she dyes her hair purple and tattoos her belly and runs off with a rock band. It shows up in couples who choose to mend their marriages instead of filing for divorce. It shows up in farmers who stick to their land through droughts and hailstorms and floods. It shows up in community organizers who struggle year after year for justice, in advocates for the homeless and the elderly, in volunteers at the hospital or library or women's shelter or soup kitchen. It shows up in the unsung people everywhere who do their jobs well, not because a supervisor is watching or because they are paid gobs of money but because they know their work matters.

4   When Jesse was in sixth grade, early in the school year, his teacher was diagnosed as having breast cancer. She gathered the children and told them frankly about the disease, about the surgery and therapy she would be undergoing, and about her hopes for recovery. Jesse came home deeply impressed that she had trusted them with her news. Before going to the hospital, she laid out lesson plans for the teacher who would be replacing her. Although she could have stayed home for the rest of the year on medical leave while the substitute handled her class, as soon as she healed from the mastectomy, she began going in to school one afternoon a week, then two, then a full day, then two days and three, to read with the children and talk with them and see how they were getting on. When a parent worried aloud that she might be risking her health for the sake of the children, the teacher scoffed, "Oh, heavens no! They're my best medicine." Besides, these children would only be in sixth grade once, and she meant to help them all she could while she had the chance. The therapy must have worked, because seven years later she's going strong. When Ruth and I see her around town, she always asks about Jesse. Is he still so funny, so bright, so excited about learning? Yes he is, we tell her, and she beams.

5   I have a friend who builds houses Monday through Friday for people who can pay him and then builds other houses on Saturday, with Habitat for Humanity, for people who can't pay him. I have another friend who bought land that had been stripped of topsoil by bad farming, and who is slowly turning those battered acres into a wildlife sanctuary by halting erosion and spreading manure and planting trees. A neighbor of ours who comes from an immigrant family makes herself available night and day to international students and their families, unriddling for them the puzzles of living in this new place. Other neighbors coach soccer teams, visit the sick, give rides to the housebound, go door to door raising funds for charity, tutor dropouts, teach adults to read; and they do these things not just for a month or a season but for years.

6   There's a man in our town who has been fighting the U.S. Forest Service for two decades, trying to persuade them to quit clear-cutting, quit selling timber at a loss, quit breaking their own rules in the Hoosier National Forest. All the while, those who make money from tearing up the woods call for more cutting, more road-building, more board feet. This man makes no money from carrying on his crusade, but he makes plenty of enemies, many of whom own chain saws and guns. He won't back down, though, because he loves the forest and loves the creatures that depend on the forest. Hearing him talk, you realize that he sees himself as one of those creatures, like any warbler or fox.

I could multiply these examples a hundredfold without ever leaving my   7
county. Most likely you could do the same in yours. Any community worth
living in must have a web of people faithful to good work and to one
another, or that community would fall apart.

Before continuing, take a moment to record some of your own thoughts
and observations. Save your work because you will use it later in Part III.

✎ WRITE YOUR OWN ESSAY

Think of someone you admire. Why do you look up to this person?
What has he or she done that you admire? Write an essay explaining
your feelings, observations, and thoughts about this special person.

CHAPTER 16

How to Read an Essay

To learn how essays actually function, you should look at them from two different perspectives—from both reading and writing. In each case, you are studying an essay from a different angle so you can clearly understand how essays work. As you progress through these next two chapters, you will see that reading and writing are companion activities that help people create meaning. When you read an essay, you work with the writer to understand his or her message; in other words, you convert words and sentences into ideas and thoughts. When you write an essay, your job is to put your own thoughts into language that communicates your message to your reader(s). In either case, you are in a partnership with the text to create meaning from the words on the page.

Every time you read an essay in this book, you will also be preparing to write your own essay. For this reason, you should pay careful attention to both the content (subject matter) and the form (language, sentence structure, organization, and development of ideas) of each essay you read. In fact, the more aware you are of each author's techniques and strategies, the more rapidly your own writing process will mature and improve.

The questions after each essay in Part IV teach you a specific way of approaching your reading that can help you understand what you read and discover the relationship of the writer's ideas to one another and to your own thoughts. These questions can also help clarify for you the connection between the writer's topic, his or her means of expression, and your own composing process. In other words, the questions are designed to help you understand and generate ideas, discover various choices the writers make in composing their essays, and then realize the freedom you have to make related choices in your own writing. Such an approach to the process of reading takes some of the mystery out of reading and writing and makes them manageable tasks at which anyone can succeed.

A good way to approach your reading is to discover for yourself exactly how an essay works. You will then understand more clearly the choices you can make as a writer. To accomplish this goal, choose an essay from Part IV of this book, and answer the questions that follow. Once you grapple with these questions, you will learn for yourself the various features at work in a good essay and be able to apply this new knowledge to your own writing.

The essay of your choice: _____

Author: _____

Page: _____

Answer each question in as much detail as you can.

1. What is the subject of this essay?

   _____

   _____

2. What is its thesis statement?

   _____

   _____

3. Does the thesis state the author's position on the subject?

   _____

4. How does the writer capture the readers' attention in the introduction?

   _____

   Is this strategy effective for this subject? Why or why not?

   _____

5. How many body paragraphs does the author include in this essay?

   _____

   List the topic sentence of each body paragraph:

   _____

   _____

_____

_____

_____

_____

_____

_____

_____

_____

6. Does the author use enough specific details to communicate his or her message?

_____

7. Do the sentences in each paragraph support the topic sentence?

_____

8. Is the essay organized logically?

_____

_____

9. Do the sentences and paragraphs move smoothly and logically from one to the next?

_____

_____

10. What strategy does the author use to conclude the essay?

_____

_____

Is this strategy effective? Explain your answer.

_____

11. How does the title relate to the author's thesis statement?

    _____

    Is this an effective title? Explain your answer.

    _____

    _____

12. Did you find the essay interesting?

    _____

    _____

Practice 1   What type of reading (novels, magazine, short stories, essays, comic books, etc.) do you like most?

_____

Practice 2   What do you like most about reading?

_____

_____

Practice 3   What do you like least about reading?

_____

_____

Practice 4   What did you learn about reading in this chapter that can help you with your writing?

_____

_____

CHAPTER 17 · HOW TO WRITE AN ESSAY

As you learned in the previous chapter, writing is a companion activity to reading. In fact, you can learn a great deal about how to write by reading. When you read an essay, you can see how the writer thinks and puts words together to create meaning. Then, when you write, you are putting your own thoughts into words so that you can communicate a specific message to your reader(s). In both cases, you must work together with the words to create meaning.

Writing an essay is very similar to writing a paragraph, although we call some elements of an essay by different names than we use for similar elements in a paragraph. The following chart demonstrates the correspondences:

Paragraph	Essay
Topic sentence	Introduction with thesis statement
Examples, details, support	Body paragraphs
Concluding sentence	Concluding paragraph

Keeping these similarities in mind, you will learn in this chapter how to construct a good essay. Laying out some clear guidelines is the best place to start.

1. ***Choose a subject.*** You might be choosing a subject from infinite possibilities or selecting a topic from a set of writing assignments. Whatever the case, make sure you decide on a topic that you can handle comfortably within the length required. That means you might choose a subject, like pets, and then narrow the subject further to fulfill the assignment:

   General subject: pets

   More specific: dogs

   More specific: golden retrievers

   More specific: training your golden retriever

This limited subject would be perfect for a short essay.

In the essay in Chapter 15, Scott Sanders might have started with a general topic like "good deeds," limited it to the idea that good deeds don't have to be "grand," and finally settled on the message that a cause doesn't have to be "grand" to be worthwhile.

2. ***Write a thesis statement about your subject.*** Just as a topic sentence is the controlling idea of a paragraph, a thesis statement provides the controlling idea for an essay. It guides the writing of your entire essay. Like a high-powered telescope pointed at a distant star, your thesis statement focuses on a single aspect of your subject.

Your essay's thesis statement is also a contract between you and your readers. The thesis statement tells your readers what the main idea of your essay will be and what the body paragraphs will be about. If you don't deliver what your thesis statement promises, your readers will be confused and disappointed.

To write a thesis statement, begin by stating your position on your topic. This sentence moves you from the broad subject of your essay to your own perspective or feeling about the topic.

Topic:	Training your golden retriever
Thesis statement:	Training your golden retriever is important for your dog's safety and for your enjoyment of each other.

In this case, the writer states a position (training is important) and gives reasons for this position (safety and enjoyment).

When you feel you have a good working thesis statement, turn it into a question as an exercise to guide you through your draft. Then the rest of your essay should answer this question.

Thesis question:	In what ways is training your golden retriever important for your dog's safety and for your enjoyment of each other?

Usually, the thesis statement is the final sentence in the introduction. This placement gives the reader a road map for reading the rest of your essay.

Scott Sanders's controlling idea or thesis appears at the beginning of his first paragraph:

"A cause needn't be grand, it needn't impress a crowd, to be worthy of our commitment."

Sanders's body paragraphs after this statement explain this thesis. His entire essay is about the benefits of performing selfless acts and being true to a cause or mission to help others in some way.

3. **Construct an introduction that leads up to your thesis statement.**
   The introduction to an essay is your chance to make a great first
   impression. Just like a firm handshake and a warm smile in a job interview, an essay's introduction should capture your readers' interest, set
   the tone for your essay, and state your specific purpose. Introductions
   often take on a funnel shape: they typically begin with general information and then narrow the focus to your position on a particular issue.
   Regardless of your approach, your introduction should "hook" your
   readers by grabbing their attention.

   Some effective ways of catching your audience's attention and giving necessary background information are (1) to furnish a quotation;
   (2) to tell a story that relates to your topic; (3) to provide a revealing
   fact, statistic, or definition; (4) to offer an interesting comparison; or
   (5) to ask an intriguing question. Always make sure your introduction
   gives your readers all the information they need in order to follow your
   train of thought.

   Sanders's introduction is a single paragraph. It starts out with his
   thesis statement, which is followed by a story about a man who visited
   prisoners and did specific chores for them for several years. The paragraph ends with a question and answer. This introduction uses a brief
   story, a question, and a quotation to draw its readers into the essay.

4. **Develop as many supporting paragraphs or body paragraphs as necessary to explain your thesis statement.** Following the introductory
   paragraph, an essay includes several body paragraphs that support and
   explain the essay's thesis. Each body paragraph deals with a topic that
   is directly related to your thesis statement.

   At least one supporting paragraph should cover each topic in your
   essay. Supporting paragraphs, also called "body" paragraphs, usually
   include a topic sentence, which is a general statement about the paragraph's content, plus examples or details that support the topic sentence.
   See the chapters in Part II for methods of developing and organizing
   these paragraphs.

   Indenting and starting a new paragraph gives your readers important information. It tells them you are moving to a new idea that will
   be developed in its own paragraph.

   Sanders's essay contains five body paragraphs, each making a separate point that is directly related to the essay's thesis:

Paragraph	Point
2	We value never giving up.
3	"Fidelity" shows up in all kinds of people.

4   A teacher is diagnosed with breast cancer.

5   Neighbors help the needy.

6   People choose causes that they feel strongly about.

Like the foundation of a solid building, these paragraphs provide support for the position Sanders takes in his thesis statement. The stronger the supporting paragraphs are, the stronger the essay.

5. ***Write a concluding paragraph.*** The concluding paragraph is the final paragraph of an essay. In its most basic form, it should summarize the main points of your essay and remind readers of your thesis statement. It should also reflect the introduction.

The best conclusions expand on these basic requirements and conclude the essay with one of these creative strategies: They will (1) ask a question that provokes new ideas, (2) predict the future, (3) offer a solution to a problem, or (4) call the reader to action. Each of these options sends a specific message and creates a slightly different effect at the end of an essay. The most important responsibility of the last paragraph, however, is to bring the essay to a close.

Sanders's conclusion summarizes his main point—

"I could multiply these examples a hundredfold without ever leaving my county";

extends his observations to other areas—

"Most likely you could do the same in yours";

and ends by echoing his thesis and highlighting his main points—

"Any community worth living in must have a web of people faithful to good work and to one another, or that community would fall apart."

Overall, his conclusion summarizes and calls his readers to action.

6. ***Give your essay a catchy title.*** Now that you have written a draft, you should think of a title for your essay. Much like wearing your best clothes to a job interview, your title is what your reader sees first. Titles are phrases, usually no more than a few words, placed at the beginning of your essay that suggest or sum up the subject, purpose, or focus of your essay. The title chosen for this book, *Mosaics*, reflects a specific view of the writing process—a collection of brightly colored individual pieces that fit together to form a complete whole. Whereas this title vividly conveys the textbook's purpose, the title for this chapter is a more straightforward label: "How to Write an Essay." These are just two of many approaches to creating a title.

Besides forecasting an essay's purpose, a good title catches an audience's attention. For instance, Sanders's title, "Fidelity," gets his readers' attention because they are bound to be curious about this author's use of this single word. That's exactly what a title should do—make your readers want to read your essay.

7. ***Revise and edit your essay.*** Revising and editing an essay are very similar to revising and editing a paragraph. A few more simple guidelines are necessary, but the process is the same. You should first apply the revising guidelines to your writing until you are satisfied with the content. Then go through the editing guidelines one by one and correct any grammar and mechanics errors in your final draft.

Sanders probably went through similar revising and editing strategies several times before his essay was published. Most professional writers consider revising and editing essential parts of the entire writing process.

Practice 1 What type of writing (essays, short stories, poems, lists, memos, journals, letters, etc.) do you enjoy most?

_____

Practice 2 What do you like best about writing?

_____

_____

Practice 3 What do you like least about writing?

_____

_____

Practice 4 What did you learn about writing in this chapter that can help you with your reading?

_____

_____

DEVELOPMENT

- ✔ Do the body paragraphs adequately support the thesis statement?
- ✔ Does each body paragraph have a focused topic sentence?
- ✔ Does each body paragraph contain *specific* details that support the topic sentence?
- ✔ Does each body paragraph include *enough* details to explain the topic sentence fully?

UNITY

- ✔ Do the essay's topic sentences relate directly to the thesis statement?
- ✔ Do the details in each body paragraph support its topic sentence?

ORGANIZATION

- ✔ Is the essay organized logically?
- ✔ Is each body paragraph organized logically?

COHERENCE

- ✔ Are transitions used effectively so that paragraphs move smoothly and logically from one to the next?
- ✔ Do the sentences move smoothly and logically from one to the next?

Thesis Statement

1. What is Jolene's main idea in this essay?

   _____

2. Put brackets around the last sentence in Jolene's introduction. Does it introduce her main idea?

   _____

3. Rewrite Jolene's thesis statement if necessary so that it states her main point and introduces her topics.

   _____

   _____

Basic Elements

1. Give Jolene's essay an alternate title.

   _____

2. Rewrite Jolene's introduction so that it captures the readers' attention and builds up to the thesis statement at the end of the paragraph.

   _____

   _____

   _____

   _____

3. Does each of Jolene's body paragraphs deal with only one topic?

   _____

4. Rewrite Jolene's conclusion using at least one suggestion from Chapter 17, #5.

   _____

   _____

   _____

   _____

Development

1. Write out Jolene's thesis statement (revised, if necessary), and list her four topic sentences below it.

   Thesis statement: _____

   Topic 1: _____

   _____

   Topic 2: _____

   _____

Topic 3: _____

_____

Topic 4: _____

_____

2. Do Jolene's topics adequately support her thesis statement?

_____

3. Does each body paragraph have a focused topic sentence?

_____

4. Are Jolene's examples specific?

_____

Add another more specific detail to one of the examples in her essay.

5. Does she offer enough examples to make her point?

_____

Add at least one new example to strengthen Jolene's essay.

Unity

1. Read each of Jolene's topic sentences with her thesis statement (revised, if necessary) in mind. Do they go together?

_____

2. Revise them if necessary so they are directly related.
3. Read each of Jolene's sentences with its topic sentence in mind.
4. Drop or rewrite any sentences not directly related to their topic sentence.

Organization

1. Review your list of Jolene's topics in item 1 under "Development," and decide if her body paragraphs are organized logically.

2. What is her method of organization?

_____

3. Look closely at Jolene's body paragraphs to see if all her sentences are arranged logically within paragraphs.

4. Move any sentences that are out of order.

Coherence

For a list of transitions, see pages 46–47.

1. Circle five transitions Jolene uses.

2. Explain how two of these make Jolene's essay easier to read.

_____

_____

Now rewrite Jolene's essay with your revisions.

EDITING CHECKLIST ✔

SENTENCES

✔ Does each sentence have a main subject and verb?

✔ Do all subjects and verbs agree?

✔ Do all pronouns agree with their nouns?

✔ Are modifiers as close as possible to the words they modify?

PUNCTUATION AND MECHANICS

✔ Are sentences punctuated correctly?

✔ Are words capitalized properly?

WORD CHOICE AND SPELLING

✔ Are words used correctly?

✔ Are words spelled correctly?

Sentences

Subjects and Verbs

For help with subjects and verbs, see Chapter 30.

1. In paragraph 1 of your revision, underline Jolene's subjects once and verbs twice. Remember that sentences can have more than one subject-verb set.

2. Does each sentence have at least one subject and verb that can stand alone?

3. Correct any fragments you find.

For help with fragments, see Chapter 31.

4. Correct any run-together sentences you find.

For help with run-togethers, see Chapter 32.

Subject-Verb Agreement

1. Read aloud the subjects and verbs you underlined in Jolene's first paragraph.

For help with subject-verb agreement, see Chapter 35.

2. Correct any subjects and verbs that do not agree.

3. Now read aloud all the subjects and verbs in the rest of her revised paragraphs.

4. Correct any subjects and verbs that do not agree.

Pronoun Agreement

1. Find any pronouns in your revision of Jolene's essay that do not agree with their nouns.

For help with pronoun agreement, see Chapter 39.

2. Correct any pronouns that do not agree with their nouns.

Modifier Errors

1. Find any modifiers in your revision of Jolene's essay that are not as close as possible to the words they modify.

For help with modifier errors, see Chapter 42.

2. Rewrite sentences if necessary so that modifiers are as close as possible to the words they modify.

Punctuation and Mechanics

Punctuation

1. Read your revision of Jolene's essay for any errors in punctuation.

For help with punctuation, see Chapters 43–47.

2. Make sure any fragments and run-together sentences you revised are punctuated correctly.

Mechanics

1. Read your revision of Jolene's essay for any errors in capitalization.

For help with capitalization, see Chapter 48.

2. Be sure to check her capitalization in any fragments or run-together sentences you revised.

Word Choice and Spelling

Word Choice

For help with confused words, see Chapter 54.

1. Find any words used incorrectly in your revision of Jolene's essay.

2. Correct any errors you find.

Spelling

For help with spelling, see Chapter 55.

1. Use spell-check and a dictionary to check the spelling in your revision of Jolene's essay.

2. Correct any misspelled words.

Now rewrite Jolene's paragraph again with your editing corrections.

REVISING AND EDITING YOUR OWN ESSAY

Returning to the essay you wrote at the end of Chapter 15, revise and edit your own writing. The checklists here will help you apply what you have learned to your own writing.

REVISING CHECKLIST ✔

THESIS STATEMENT

☐ Does the thesis statement contain the essay's controlling idea and appear as the last sentence of the introduction?

BASIC ELEMENTS

☐ Does the title draw in the readers?

☐ Does the introduction capture the readers' attention and build up to the thesis statement effectively?

☐ Does each body paragraph deal with a single topic?

☐ Does the conclusion bring the essay to a close in an interesting way?

DEVELOPMENT

☐ Do the body paragraphs adequately support the thesis statement?

☐ Does each body paragraph have a focused topic sentence?

☐ Does each body paragraph contain *specific* details that support the topic sentence?

☐ Does each body paragraph include *enough* details to explain the topic sentence fully?

UNITY

☐ Do the essay's topic sentences relate directly to the thesis statement?

☐ Do the details in each body paragraph support its topic sentence?

ORGANIZATION

☐ Is the essay organized logically?

☐ Is each body paragraph organized logically?

COHERENCE

☐ Are transitions used effectively so that paragraphs move smoothly and logically from one to the next?

☐ Do the sentences move smoothly and logically from one to the next?

Thesis Statement

1. What is the main idea you are trying to convey in your essay?

   _____

2. Put brackets around the last sentence in your introduction. Does it convey your main idea?

   _____

3. Rewrite your thesis statement if necessary so that it states your main point and introduces your topics.

   _____

Basic Elements

1. Give your essay a title if it doesn't have one.

2. Does your introduction capture your readers' attention and build up to your thesis statement at the end of the paragraph?

   _____

3. Does each of your body paragraphs deal with only one topic?

   _____

4. Does your conclusion follow some of the suggestions offered in Part I?

   _____

Development

1. Write out your thesis statement (revised, if necessary) and your topic sentences.

   Thesis Statement: _____

   Topic Sentences: _____

   _____

   _____

   _____

2. Do your topics adequately support your thesis statement?

   _____

3. Does each body paragraph have a focused topic sentence?

   _____

4. Are your examples specific?

   _____

   Add another more specific detail to an example in your essay.

5. Do you give enough examples to make your point?

   _____

   Add at least one new example to your essay.

Unity

1. Read each of your topic sentences with your thesis statement in mind. Do they go together?
2. Revise them if necessary so that they are directly related.
3. Drop or rewrite any sentences in your body paragraphs not directly related to their topic sentence.

Organization

1. Read your essay again to see if all the paragraphs are arranged logically.
2. Review the list of your topics in item 1 under "Development." Then identify your method of organization.

   _____

3. Is the order you chose for your paragraphs the most effective approach to your topic?

   _____

4. Move any paragraphs that are out of order.
5. Look closely at your body paragraphs to see if all the sentences are arranged logically within paragraphs.
6. Move any sentences that are out of order.

Coherence

For a list of transitions, see pages 46–47.

1. Circle five transitions you use.
2. Explain how two of these make your essay easier to read.

   _____

   _____

Now rewrite your essay with your revisions.

EDITING CHECKLIST ✔

SENTENCES

☐ Does each sentence have a main subject and verb?
☐ Do all subjects and verbs agree?
☐ Do all pronouns agree with their nouns?
☐ Are modifiers as close as possible to the words they modify?

PUNCTUATION AND MECHANICS

☐ Are sentences punctuated correctly?
☐ Are words capitalized properly?

> WORD CHOICE AND SPELLING
> ☐ Are words used correctly?
> ☐ Are words spelled correctly?

Sentences

Subjects and Verbs

1. In a paragraph of your choice, underline the subjects once and verbs twice. Remember that sentences can have more than one subject-verb set.

2. Does each of your sentences have at least one subject and verb that can stand alone?

For help with subjects and verbs, see Chapter 30.

3. Correct any fragments you have written.
4. Correct any run-together sentences you have written.

For help with fragments, see Chapter 31.

For help with run-togethers, see Chapter 32.

Subject-Verb Agreement

1. Read aloud the subjects and verbs you underlined in the paragraph of your choice.
2. Correct any subjects and verbs that do not agree.
3. Now read aloud the subjects and verbs in the rest of your revised essay.
4. Correct any subjects and verbs that do not agree.

For help with subject-verb agreement, see Chapter 35.

Pronoun Agreement

1. Find any pronouns in your revised essay that do not agree with their nouns.
2. Correct any pronouns that do not agree with their nouns.

For help with pronoun agreement, see Chapter 39.

Modifier Errors

1. Find any modifiers in your revised essay that are not as close as possible to the words they modify.
2. Rewrite sentences if necessary so that your modifiers are as close as possible to the words they modify.

For help with modifier errors, see Chapter 42.

Punctuation and Mechanics

Punctuation

For help with punctuation, see Chapters 43–47.

1. Read your revised essay for any errors in punctuation.
2. Make sure any fragments and run-together sentences you revised are punctuated correctly.

Mechanics

For help with capitalization, see Chapter 48.

1. Read your revised essay for any errors in capitalization.
2. Be sure to check your capitalization in any fragments or run-together sentences you revised.

Word Choice and Spelling

Word Choice

For help with confused words, see Chapter 54.

1. Find any words used incorrectly in your revised essay.
2. Correct any errors you find.

Spelling

For help with spelling, see Chapter 55.

1. Use spell-check and a dictionary to check your spelling.
2. Correct any misspelled words.

Now rewrite your essay again with your editing corrections.

WRITING WORKSHOP

CHAPTER 20

Guidelines for Writing an Essay

1. Choose a subject.
2. Write a thesis statement about your subject.
3. Construct an introduction that leads up to your thesis statement.
4. Develop as many supporting paragraphs or body paragraphs as necessary to explain your thesis statement.
5. Write a concluding paragraph.
6. Give your essay a catchy title.
7. Revise and edit your essay.

1. Find someone who does community service or volunteer work as in the photo on the previous page. What type of service does this person do? Why is the person attracted to this type of work? Who does he or she help? What does this activity do for the community? What does it do for you?

2. You have been asked by the editor of your campus newspaper to relate your weirdest experience. Write an essay about this experience, including what you learned from it.

3. Analyze a relationship you have with another person by explaining its causes and effects.

4. Come up with your own essay assignment (with the help of your instructor), and write a response to it.

Revising Workshop

Small Group Activity (5–10 minutes per writer)   Working in groups of three or four, each person should read his or her essay to the other members of the group. Those listening should record their reactions on a copy of the Peer Evaluation Form in Appendix 3A. After your group goes through this process, give your evaluation forms to the appropriate writers so that each writer has two or three peer comment sheets for revising.

Paired Activity (5 minutes per writer)   Using the completed Peer Evaluation Forms, work in pairs to decide what you should revise in your essay. If time allows, rewrite some of your sentences, and have your partner look at them.

Individual Activity   Rewrite your paper, using the revising feedback you received from other students.

Editing Workshop

Paired Activity (5–10 minutes per writer)   Swap papers with a classmate, and use the editing portion of your Peer Evaluation Forms to identify as many grammar, punctuation, mechanics, and spelling errors as you can. If time allows, correct some of your errors, and have your partner look at them. Record your grammar, punctuation, and mechanics errors in the Error Log (Appendix 6) and your spelling errors in the Spelling Log (Appendix 7).

Individual Activity   Rewrite your paper again, using the editing feedback you received from other students.

Reflecting on Your Writing

When you have completed your own essay, answer these five questions:

1. What was most difficult about this assignment?
2. What was easiest?
3. What did you learn about writing essays by completing this assignment?
4. What do you think are the strengths of your essay? What are its weaknesses?
5. What did you learn from this assignment about your own writing process—about preparing to write, about writing the first draft, about revising, and about editing?

IV

FROM READING TO WRITING

There is no way to write unless you read and read a lot.

—WALTER J. ONG

Part IV is a collection of essays that demonstrate the rhetorical modes you are studying in this book. Each chapter focuses on a different rhetorical strategy and includes two essays that show the strategy at work with other strategies. After each essay are questions that check your understanding of the selection. By charting your correct and incorrect responses to these questions in Appendix 6, you will discover your general level of comprehension.

CHAPTER 21 DESCRIBING

In the following selections, the writers provide detailed and accurate descriptions that enable readers to see for themselves the actions and events the authors experienced. In the excerpt from *The Joy Luck Club* by Amy Tan, a young girl observes the sights, sounds, smells, textures, and tastes that she encounters when she arrives at her new home. The second selection, an essay called "Longing to Die of Old Age," by Alice Walker, considers the right of human beings to die a natural death.

Amy Tan
MAGPIES

Focusing Your Attention

1. Think of a place you are very familiar with: your room, your home, your school, your place of employment, a garden, a restaurant. Then make a list of the sights, sounds, textures, smells, and tastes that come into your mind as you think of that place.

2. In the excerpt you are about to read, a young girl recounts the many sights, sounds, smells, textures, and tastes that she encountered when she first arrived at her new home. Think of an occasion when you entered a place for the first time. What sights, sounds, textures, smells, and tastes made the strongest impressions on you?

Expanding Your Vocabulary

The following words are important to your understanding of this essay.

British Concession: areas that the Chinese allowed the British to occupy (paragraph 1)

concubines: women who were part of a man's household and were expected to fulfill his needs (paragraph 14)

mourning: representing grief over a person's death (paragraph 17)

I know from the beginning our new home would not be an ordinary 1
house. My mother had told me we would live in the household of Wu Tsing,
who was a very rich merchant. She said this man owned many carpet fac-
tories and lived in a mansion located in the British Concession of Tientsin,
the best section of the city where Chinese people could live. We lived not
too far from Paima Di, Racehorse Street, where only Westerners could live.
And we were also close to little shops that sold only one kind of thing: only
tea, or only fabric, or only soap.

The house, she said, was foreign-built; Wu Tsing liked foreign things 2
because foreigners had made him rich. And I concluded that was why my
mother had to wear foreign-style clothes, in the manner of newly rich
Chinese people who liked to display their wealth on the outside. And even
though I knew all this before I arrived, I was still amazed at what I saw.

The front of the house had a Chinese stone gate, rounded at the top, 3
with big black lacquer doors and a threshold you had to step over. Within
the gates I saw the courtyard, and I was surprised. There were no willows
or sweet-smelling cassia trees, no garden pavilions, no benches sitting by
a pond, no tubs of fish. Instead, there were long rows of bushes on both
sides of a wide brick walkway, and to each side of those bushes was a big
lawn area with fountains. And as we walked down the walkway and got
closer to the house, I saw this house had been built in the Western style. It
was three stories high, of mortar and stone, with long metal balconies on
each floor and chimneys at every corner.

When we arrived, a young servant woman ran out and greeted my 4
mother with cries of joy. She had a high scratchy voice: "Oh Taitai, you've
already arrived! How can this be?" This was Yan Chang, my mother's personal maid, and she knew how to fuss over my mother just the right
amount. She had called my mother Taitai, the simple honorable title of
Wife, as if my mother were the first wife, the only wife.

Yan Chang called loudly to other servants to take our luggage, called 5
another servant to bring tea and draw a hot bath. And then she hastily
explained that Second Wife had told everyone not to expect us for another
week at least. "What a shame! No one to greet you! Second Wife, the others, gone to Peking to visit her relatives. Your daughter, so pretty, your same
look. She's so shy, eh? First Wife, her daughters . . . gone on a pilgrimage to
another Buddhist temple. . . . Last week, a cousin's uncle, just a little crazy,
came to visit, turned out not to be a cousin, not an uncle, who knows who
he was. . . ."

As soon as we walked into that big house, I became lost with too many 6
things to see: a curved staircase that wound up and up, a ceiling with faces
in every corner, then hallways twisting and turning into one room then
another. To my right was a large room, larger than I had ever seen, and it

was filled with stiff teakwood furniture: sofas and tables and chairs. And at the other end of this long, long room, I could see doors leading into more rooms, more furniture, then more doors. To my left was a darker room, another sitting room, this one filled with foreign furniture: dark green leather sofas, paintings with hunting dogs, armchairs, and mahogany desks. And as I glanced in these rooms, I would see different people, and Yan Chang would explain: "This young lady, she is Second Wife's servant. That one, she is nobody, just the daughter of cook's helper. This man takes care of the garden."

7   And then we were walking up the staircase. We came to the top of the stairs, and I found myself in another large sitting room. We walked to the left, down a hall, past one room, and then stepped into another. "This is your mother's room," Yan Chang told me proudly. "This is where you will sleep."

8   And the first thing I saw, the only thing I could see at first, was a magnificent bed. It was heavy and light at the same time: soft rose silk and heavy, dark, shiny wood carved all around with dragons. Four posts held up a silk canopy, and at each post dangled large silk ties holding back curtains. The bed sat on four squat lion's paws, as if the weight of it had crushed the lion underneath. Yan Chang showed me how to use a small step stool to climb onto the bed. And when I tumbled onto the silk coverings, I laughed to discover a soft mattress that was ten times the thickness of my bed in Ningpo.

9   Sitting in this bed, I admired everything as if I were a princess. This room had a glass door that led to a balcony. In front of the window door was a round table of the same wood as the bed. It too sat on carved lion's legs and was surrounded by four chairs. A servant had already put tea and sweet cakes on the table and was now lighting the houlu, a small stove for burning coal.

10   It was not that my uncle's house in Ningpo had been poor. He was actually quite well-to-do. But this house in Tientsin was amazing. And I thought to myself, My uncle was wrong. There was no shame in my mother's marrying Wu Tsing.

11   While thinking this, I was startled by a sudden clang! clang! clang! followed by music. On the wall opposite the bed was a big wooden clock with a forest and bears carved into it. The door on the clock had burst open, and a tiny room full of people was coming out. There was a bearded man in a pointed cap seated at a table. He was bending his head over and over again to drink soup, but his beard would dip in the bowl first and stop him. A girl in a white scarf and blue dress was standing next to the table, and she was bending over and over again to give the man more of this soup. And next to the man and girl was another girl with a skirt and short jacket. She was swinging her arm back and forth, playing violin music. She

always played the same dark song. I can still hear it in my head after these many years—ni-ah! nah! nah! nah! nah-ni-nah!

This was a wonderful clock to see, but after I heard it that first hour, then 12 the next, and then always, this clock became an extravagant nuisance. I could not sleep for many nights. And later, I found I had an ability: To not listen to something meaningless calling to me.

I was so happy those first few nights, in this amusing house, sleeping in 13 the big soft bed with my mother. I would lie in this comfortable bed, think-ing about my uncle's house in Ningpo, realizing how unhappy I had been, feeling sorry for my little brother. But most of my thoughts flew to all the new things to see and do in this house.

I watched hot water pouring out of pipes not just in the kitchen but also 14 into washbasins and bathtubs on all three floors of the house. I saw cham-ber pots that flushed clean without servants having to empty them. I saw rooms as fancy as my mother's. Yan Chang explained which ones belonged to First Wife and the other concubines, who were called Second Wife and Third Wife. And some rooms belonged to no one. "They are for guests," said Yan Chang.

On the third floor were rooms for only the men servants, said Yan 15 Chang, and one of the rooms even had a door to a cabinet that was really a secret hiding place from sea pirates.

Thinking back, I find it hard to remember everything that was in that 16 house; too many good things all seem the same after a while. I tired of any-thing that was not a novelty. "Oh, this," I said when Yan Chang brought me the same sweet meats as the day before. "I've tasted this already."

My mother seemed to regain her pleasant nature. She put her old 17 clothes back on, long Chinese gowns and skirts now with white mourning bands sewn at the bottoms. During the day, she pointed to strange and funny things, naming them for me: bidet, Brownie camera, salad fork, nap-kin. In the evening, when there was nothing to do, we talked about the servants: who was clever, who was diligent, who was loyal. We gossiped as we cooked small eggs and sweet potatoes on top of the houlu just to enjoy their smell. And at night, my mother would again tell me stories as I lay in her arms falling asleep.

If I look upon my whole life, I cannot think of another time when I felt 18 more comfortable: when I had no worries, fears, or desires, when my life seemed as soft and lovely as lying inside a cocoon of rose silk.

Thinking Critically About Content

1. List two details from this essay for each of the five senses: seeing, hear-ing, touching, smelling, and tasting. How do these details *show* rather than tell the readers the narrator's impressions of her new house?

2. In one or more complete sentences, state the main character's point of view.

3. What does the narrator mean when she says, "If I look upon my whole life, I cannot think of another time when I felt more comfortable: when I had no worries, fears, or desires, when my life seemed as soft and lovely as lying inside a cocoon of rose silk" (paragraph 18)? Why do you think she is so comfortable in these surroundings?

Thinking Critically About Purpose and Audience

4. What dominant impression does the writer create in this description? How does this impression change throughout the essay?

5. Do you think readers who have never been to China can appreciate and enjoy this essay? Explain your answer.

6. What specific observations are most interesting to you? Why? In what ways do these observations help you imagine the entire scene?

Thinking Critically About Paragraphs

7. If a paragraph is unified, all of its sentences are related to one central idea. Based on this explanation, is paragraph 12 unified? Explain your answer.

8. Look closely at paragraph 17, and explain how it is organized. (Refer to pages 24–31 for information on organization.)

9. Choose one body paragraph, and decide if it has enough details. What is the most interesting detail in the paragraph?

10. Write a paragraph describing the inner feelings of the main character when she finally settles into her new home.

Alice Walker

LONGING TO DIE OF OLD AGE

Focusing Your Attention

1. Do you consider yourself healthy? What keeps you healthy? Do you care about your health?

2. Have you thought about how you might want to die? The essay you are about to read claims that we should all be able to die naturally of old age. Do you agree with this notion? How do you feel when disease gets in the way of this process?

Expanding Your Vocabulary

The following words are important to your understanding of this essay.

enslaved person: slave (paragraph 1)

longevity: long life (paragraph 1)

organic: natural (paragraph 3)

congested: crowded (paragraph 5)

collard greens: a leafy vegetable (paragraph 7)

indelible: permanent (paragraph 12)

self-induced: brought on by one's own actions (paragraph 13)

aberration: abnormality (paragraph 13)

Mrs. Mary Poole, my "4-greats" grandmother, lived the entire nineteenth century, from around 1800 to 1921, and enjoyed exceptional health. The key to good health, she taught (this woman who as an enslaved person was forced to carry two young children, on foot, from Virginia to Georgia), was never to cover up the pulse at the throat. But, with the benefit of hindsight, one must believe that for her, as for generations of people after her, in our small farming community, diet played as large a role in her longevity and her health as loose clothing and fresh air. 1

For what did the old ones eat? 2

Well, first of all, almost nothing that came from a store. As late as my own childhood, in the fifties, at Christmas we had only raisins and perhaps bananas, oranges, and a peppermint stick, broken into many pieces, a sliver for each child; and during the year, perhaps, a half-dozen apples, nuts, and a bunch of grapes. All extravagantly expensive and considered rare. You ate *all* of the apple, sometimes, even the seeds. Everyone had a vegetable garden; a garden as large as there was energy to work it. In these gardens people raised an abundance of food: corn, tomatoes, okra, peas and beans, squash, peppers, which they ate in summer and canned for winter. There was no chemical fertilizer. No one could have afforded it, had it existed, and there was no need for it. From the cows and pigs and goats, horses, mules, and fowl that people also raised, there was always ample organic manure. 3

Until I was grown, I never heard of anyone having cancer. 4

In fact, at first cancer seemed to be coming from far off. For a long time if the subject of cancer came up, you could be sure cancer itself wasn't coming any nearer than to some congested place in the North, then to Atlanta, seventy-odd miles away, then to Macon, forty miles away, then to Monticello, twenty miles away.... The first inhabitants of our community to 5 die of acknowledged cancer were almost celebrities, because of this "foreign" disease. But now, twenty-odd years later, cancer has ceased to be viewed as a visitor and is feared instead as a resident. Even the children die of cancer now, which, at least in the beginning, seemed a disease of the old.

6   Most of the people I knew as farmers left the farms (they did not own the land and were unable to make a living working for the white people who did) to rent small apartments in the towns and cities. They ceased to have gardens, and when they did manage to grow a few things they used fertilizer from boxes and bottles, sometimes in improbable colors and consistencies, which they rightly suspected, but had no choice but to use. Gone were their chickens, cows, and pigs. Gone their organic manure.

7   To their credit, they questioned all that happened to them. Why must we leave the land? Why must we live in boxes with hardly enough space to breathe? (Of course, indoor plumbing seduced many a one.) Why must we buy all our food from the store? Why is the price of food so high—and so tasteless? The collard greens bought in the supermarket, they said, "tasted like water."

8   The United States should have closed down and examined its every intention, institution, and law on the very first day a black woman observed that the collard greens tasted like water. Or when the first person of any color observed that store-bought tomatoes tasted more like unripened avocados than tomatoes.

9   The flavor of food is one of the clearest messages the Universe ever sends to human beings; and we have by now eaten poisoned warnings by the ton.

10   When I was a child growing up in middle Georgia in the forties and fifties, people still died of old age. Old age was actually a common cause of death. My parents inevitably visited dying persons over the long or short period of their decline; sometimes I went with them. Some years ago, as an adult, I accompanied my mother to visit a very old neighbor who was dying a few doors down the street, and though she was no longer living in the country, the country style lingered. People like my mother were visiting her constantly, bringing food, picking up and returning laundry, or simply stopping by to inquire how she was feeling and to chat. Her house, her linen, her skin all glowed with cleanliness. She lay propped against pillows so that by merely turning her head she could watch the postman approaching, friends and relatives arriving, and, most of all, the small children playing beside the street, often in her yard, the sound of their play a lively music.

11   Sitting in the dimly lit, spotless room, listening to the lengthy but warm-with-shared-memories silences between my mother and Mrs. Davis was extraordinarily pleasant. Her white hair gleamed against her kissable

black skin, and her bed was covered with one of the most intricately pat-
terned quilts I'd ever seen—a companion to the dozen or more she'd stored
in a closet, which, when I expressed interest, she invited me to see.

I thought her dying one of the most reassuring events I'd ever wit- 12
nessed. She was calm; she seemed ready; her affairs were in order. She
was respected and loved. In short, Mrs. Davis was having an excellent
death. A week later, when she had actually died, I felt this all the more
because she had left, in me, the indelible knowledge that such a death is
possible. And that cancer and nuclear annihilation are truly obscene alter-
natives. And surely, teaching this very vividly is one of the things an excellent death is supposed to do.

To die miserably of self-induced sickness is an aberration we take as 13
normal; but it is crucial that we remember and teach our children that
there are other ways.

For myself, for all of us, I want a death like Mrs. Davis's. One in which 14
we will ripen and ripen further, as richly as fruit, and then fall slowly into
the caring arms of our friends and other people we know. People who will
remember the good days and the bad, the names of lovers and grandchil-
dren, the time sorrow almost broke, the time loving friendship healed.

It must become a right of every person to die of old age. And if we 15
secure this right for ourselves, we can, coincidentally, assure it for the
planet. And that, as they say, will be excellence, which is, perhaps, only
another name for health.

Thinking Critically About Content

1. What did the narrator's great-great-great-great grandmother think
   the key to good health was?

2. Find at least one detail for each of the five senses. Does Walker
   draw on any one sense more than the others?

3. Why does Walker "want a death like Mrs. Davis's" (paragraph 14)?

Thinking Critically About Purpose and Audience

4. What dominant impression does Walker create in this essay?

5. Who do you think Walker's primary audience is?

6. Explain your understanding of this essay's title.

Thinking Critically About Paragraphs

7. What is the topic sentence of paragraph 12? Do all the sentences in
   that paragraph relate to its topic sentence? Explain your answer.

8. If a paragraph is coherent, it is considered logical and easy to read.
   Often, well-chosen transitions help a writer achieve coherence.

(Refer to pages 46–47 for a list of transitions.) Underline three transitions Walker uses in paragraph 10. How do these words help this paragraph read smoothly? Explain your answer.

9. How are the details organized in paragraph 5? (See Part I for more information on organization.)

10. Write a paragraph describing what you think the secret to longevity is.

Writing Topics: Describing

Before you begin to write, you might want to review the writing process in Part I.

1. In the first selection, Amy Tan draws on impressions from all the senses to show how her main character observes her new home. Think of a place that is very important to you, a place that is a part of your life now or that was a part of your life in the past. Write a description of that place, drawing on as many of the senses as possible—seeing, hearing, touching, smelling, and tasting—so that your reader can experience this place the way you did.

2. How healthy are you? Write a description of the foods that you eat and the exercise that you get in a normal week. In what ways are you taking good care of yourself so that you have a chance for a long, healthy life?

3. What do you think are the most important features of a good description? Why are they important? What effect do they have on you?

NARRATING

CHAPTER 22

In the following essays, the authors tell stories that are realistic and moving. In "Eleven," Sandra Cisneros recalls the humiliation she suffered in front of her classmates as a result of an insensitive teacher. In the second selection, "Choosing the Path with Honor," Michael Arredondo tells a moving story about his education.

Sandra Cisneros

ELEVEN

Focusing Your Attention

1. Can you recall a time when you felt embarrassed in front of your classmates? What details do you recall?

2. In the story you are about to read, "Eleven" refers to the age of the main character in the story. Try to remember what your life was like when you were eleven years old; you would have been in the fifth or sixth grade. Were you particularly sensitive about your looks? Did you worry about what your friends thought of you or whether or not you were popular? Have you become more or less self-conscious about these issues as you have gotten older?

Expanding Your Vocabulary

The following word is important to your understanding of this story.

rattling: moving around and making noise (paragraph 5)

What they don't understand about birthdays and what they never tell   1
you is that when you're eleven, you're also ten, and nine, and eight, and
seven, and six, and five, and four, and three, and two, and one. And when
you wake up on your eleventh birthday, you expect to feel eleven, but you

don't. You open your eyes and everything's just like yesterday, only it's today. And you don't feel eleven at all. You feel like you're still ten. And you are—underneath the year that makes you eleven.

2   Like some days you might say something stupid, and that's the part of you that's still ten. Or maybe some days you might need to sit on your mama's lap because you're scared, and that's the part of you that's five. And maybe one day when you're all grown up, maybe you will need to cry like if you're three, and that's okay. That's what I tell Mama when she's sad and needs to cry. Maybe she's feeling three.

3   Because the way you grow old is kind of like an onion or like the rings inside a tree trunk or like my little wooden dolls that fit one inside the other, each year inside the next one. That's how being eleven years old is.

4   You don't feel eleven. Not right away. It takes a few days, weeks even, sometimes even months before you say Eleven when they ask you. And you don't feel smart eleven, not until you're almost twelve. That's the way it is.

5   Only today I wish I didn't have only eleven years rattling inside me like pennies in a tin Band-Aid box. Today I wish I was one hundred and two instead of eleven because if I was one hundred and two I'd have known what to say when Mrs. Price put the red sweater on my desk. I would've known how to tell her it wasn't mine instead of just sitting there with that look on my face and nothing coming out of my mouth.

6   "Whose is this?" Mrs. Price says, and she holds the red sweater up in the air for all the class to see. "Whose? It's been sitting in the coatroom for a month."

7   "Not mine," says everybody. "Not me."

8   "It has to belong to somebody," Mrs. Price keeps saying, but nobody can remember. It's an ugly sweater with red plastic buttons and a collar and sleeves all stretched out like you could use it for a jump rope. It's maybe a thousand years old, and even if it belonged to me I wouldn't say so.

9   Maybe because I'm skinny, maybe because she doesn't like me, that stupid Sylvia Saldívar says, "I think it belongs to Rachel." An ugly sweater like that, all raggedy and old, but Mrs. Price believes her. Mrs. Price takes the sweater and puts it right on my desk, but when I open my mouth nothing comes out.

10   "That's not, I don't, you're not . . . Not mine," I finally say in a little voice that was maybe me when I was four.

11   "Of course it's yours," Mrs. Price says. "I remember you wearing it once." Because she's older and the teacher, she's right and I'm not.

12   Not mine, not mine, not mine, but Mrs. Price is already turning to page thirty-two, and math problem number four. I don't know why, but all of a sudden I'm feeling sick inside, like the part of me that's three wants to come

out of my eyes, only I squeeze them shut tight and bite down on my teeth real hard and try to remember today I am eleven, eleven. Mama is making a cake for me for tonight, and when Papa comes home everybody will sing Happy birthday, happy birthday to you.

But when the sick feeling goes away and I open my eyes, the red sweater's still sitting there like a big red mountain. I move the red sweater to the corner of my desk with my ruler. I move my pencil and books and eraser as far from it as possible. I even move my chair a little to the right. Not mine, not mine, not mine. 13

In my head I'm thinking how long till lunchtime, how long till I can take the red sweater and throw it over the schoolyard fence, or leave it hanging on a parking meter, or bunch it up into a little ball and toss it in the alley. Except when math period ends Mrs. Price says loud and in front of everybody, "Now, Rachel, that's enough," because she sees I've shoved the red sweater to the tippy-tip corner of my desk and it's hanging all over the edge like a waterfall, but I don't care. 14

"Rachel," Mrs. Price says. She says it like she's getting mad. "You put that sweater on right now and no more nonsense." 15

"But it's not—" 16

"Now!" Mrs. Price says. 17

This is when I wish I wasn't eleven, because all the years inside of me— ten, nine, eight, seven, six, five, four, three, two, and one—are pushing at the back of my eyes when I put one arm through one sleeve of the sweater that smells like cottage cheese, and then the other arm through the other and stand there with my arms apart like if the sweater hurts me and it does, all itchy and full of germs that aren't even mine. 18

That's when everything I've been holding in since this morning, since when Mrs. Price put the sweater on my desk, finally lets go, and all of a sudden I'm crying in front of everybody. I wish I was invisible but I'm not. I'm eleven and it's my birthday today and I'm crying like I'm three in front of everybody. I put my head down on the desk and bury my face in my stupid clown-sweater arms. My face all hot and spit coming out of my mouth because I can't stop the little animal noises from coming out of me, until there aren't any more tears left in my eyes, and it's just my body shaking like when you have the hiccups, and my whole head hurts like when you drink milk too fast. 19

But the worst part is right before the bell rings for lunch. That stupid Phyllis Lopez, who is even dumber than Sylvia Saldívar, says she remembers the red sweater is hers! I take it off right away and give it to her, only Mrs. Price pretends like everything's okay. 20

Today I'm eleven. There's a cake Mama's making for tonight, and when Papa comes home from work we'll eat it. There'll be candles and presents 21 and everybody will sing Happy birthday, happy birthday to you, Rachel, only it's too late.

22   I'm eleven today. I'm eleven, ten, nine, eight, seven, six, five, four, three, two, and one, but I wish I was one hundred and two. I wish I was anything but eleven, because I want today to be far away already, far away like a runaway balloon, like a tiny o in the sky, so tiny-tiny you have to close your eyes to see it.

Thinking Critically About Content

1. Why do you think Cisneros pays such close attention to Rachel's age and to the fact that it is her birthday?

2. What does Rachel mean when she says that although there will be a cake and candles and presents and singing that evening at her home, "it's too late" (paragraph 21)?

3. What details does Cisneros use to show that Rachel is far more sensitive and intelligent than her teacher, Mrs. Price, thinks she is?

Thinking Critically About Purpose and Audience

4. What do you think Cisneros's purpose is in this essay? Explain your answer.

5. What type of audience do you think would most understand and appreciate this recollection?

6. Does the writer succeed in making the audience feel the pain and hurt of an eleven-year-old? How does she accomplish this?

Thinking Critically About Paragraphs

7. In this story, Cisneros adopts the point of view of an eleven-year-old girl, using the language, thought processes, and behavior of a child that age. Paragraph 19 is an especially good example of the author's point of view in this essay. How would this paragraph be different if it were told by Rachel as an adult remembering the incident?

8. In this essay, Cisneros uses several comparisons called *similes*. A simile uses "like" or "as" in a comparison between two unlike items. These comparisons help us understand an item the author is trying to explain. Here are some examples:

    > Because the way you grow old is kind of like an onion or like the rings inside a tree trunk or like my little wooden dolls that fit one inside the other, each year inside the next one. That's how being eleven years old is. (paragraph 3)

    Find two more similes, and explain why they are effective.

9. Record three specific details from paragraph 9. What do they add to the paragraph?

10. Rachel feels terribly frustrated because her teacher simply does not understand the significance of making Rachel claim ownership for the ugly red sweater. Pretend you are Mrs. Price, and rewrite this event from her point of view, portraying her frustration over Rachel's behavior.

Michael Arredondo
CHOOSING THE PATH WITH HONOR

Focusing Your Attention

1. Have you ever had a goal that was very hard for you to reach? What was it?

2. This narrative is about a person who had a dream since he was six years old that he didn't know if he could achieve. Have you ever had a dream that seemed impossible? What have you done to keep that dream alive?

Expanding Your Vocabulary

The following words are important to your understanding of this essay.

ruptured: burst (paragraph 1)

fragmented: broken into pieces (paragraph 2)

deployed: sent off (paragraph 15)

fibrilators: medical tools that help control an abnormal heartbeat (paragraph 17)

ablation: process of melting away (paragraph 17)

empowering: enabling (paragraph 23)

predominantly: mainly (paragraph 27)

I get my Shawnee blood from my mother's side of the family. Her father   1
was Shawnee, and her mother was Turtle Mountain Chippewa. My father's family is from Mexico. My great, great grandfather, David Dushane, was chief of the Eastern Shawnee in the 1940s, who died in 1976 of a ruptured appendix. The Shawnee were involuntarily placed in Oklahoma. But of

course we were promised the land would always be ours and it would never be owned by whites.

2   As we all know, in 1907 Oklahoma, land of the Red people, home of the Red people, became the 46th state. The Shawnee were fragmented into three tribes, the Loyal, the Absentee, and the Eastern extreme.

3   We have about 1,000 tribal members, and if my math is correct there it's only two to three percent that are fluent in our language. There is no way to learn our language unless you go home. There is no other way to learn the language. You have to go home and attend language class on Wednesday nights. Being a student here at Cornell, it is just impossible for me to be in Oklahoma on Wednesday nights. I understand the elders reasoning for doing that. However, it is a difficult thing to accept.

4   The Shawnee never received a reservation. Instead, we received offers to buy tracts of land for individual ownership.

5   I have two older sisters, and my father took a look at the poverty, high unemployment, poor health, and the welfare system and said, "I cannot raise my family here. I need to go where I can do the best for them." So he moved us to Albuquerque, New Mexico. You know, they say if you don't like Mexicans and you don't like Indians, don't go to Albuquerue.

6   So we fit right in there, and that is where we grew up. My mom's parents were also there. My grandfather sat me down as he would from time to time and told me about all the bad things I would hear about being Native.

7   As my life unfolded, I saw that it was indeed true. I did hear those things. In paralleling Sitting Bull's words, in his time, he told me that I had been born into a white man's world and that I would be walking on a white man's road.

8   He said, "You should acquire the white man's medicine and his skills and his planning and you bring them back to us. We will be waiting for you."

9   I have been trying my whole life to get to college. It has been quite a long road. I learned about college while watching TV. I caught about the last five minutes of a TV program, and I went and found my mom after it was over, and I asked her what an Ivory Leaf school was.

10   She was chuckling for about as long as you are, and she told me that it was a school that you could go to if you had a lot of money. I asked her if we had enough.

11   She looked at me, and she said, "It might be a little while." So this college thing sounded pretty good, and if I was going to go, I was definitely going to go to the best, because that was what the TV program said.

12   So I went out, and I got all the jobs a little kid can get at that age. I raked leaves and picked up old cans and that sort of thing. They were all too

happy to pay me to do odd jobs to contribute to my Ivory Leaf school fund. After some time, I put all this money together and took it to my mom, and I asked her if I had enough yet to go to the best school.

She didn't bother to count it. She only looked at me, and she said, "You know, it might be a while." So this continued for some time, but I noticed that a very indirect and subtle message began to appear. Over time as I got older, it came to be a very direct message. I was told by various people in the school system that certain programs, institutions, and educational opportunities weren't for me. Weren't for Indians. Weren't for people of color. And that perhaps I should make other plans. 13

So I quit talking about it so much, and by the time I got to high school, I quit talking about it altogether. In four years of high school, I did not have one teacher, one administrator, one coach, one advisor, one counselor ask me if I wanted to go to college. Not one. 14

So after high school, I joined the U.S. Navy to get the G.I. bill so I could go to college, because I knew my parents couldn't help me. Shortly thereafter I was deployed to the Gulf War. Being medical personnel in the Gulf on the USS Iwo Jima put me in a pretty bad position. We had what was termed the worst accident in the history of the Gulf War. I had never seen and I hope I never see again bodies that were burned that bad, beyond recognition. Using their dental records to identify their remains, preparing them to be shipped back home, I could only stop and think, this is not what I had in mind. I just wanted to get money to go to school. 15

But you know what they say, join the service, see the world, get money for your education. When I got back from the Gulf, I applied and was accepted to the cardiovascular school of medicine in Bethesda, Maryland. To give you a very brief idea of what a cardiovascular technologist does, we function in place of a physician assistant to the cardiologist. We scrub in with the physician at the table in the OR. We are a cross between a physician's assistant and first assistant in the operating room. 16

Along with the doctor, we know all the procedures that clear out the blockages in the heart. We know how to program and implant internal fibrillators that will restore an abnormal heartbeat. We know how to map the electricity inside the heart, find the abnormal pathways and fry them out with radio frequency ablation to restore normal rhythms. 17

I really love what I do, what I have been doing for ten years already. When I got out of the Navy five years ago, I was 26. I had to stop and think, do I still want to be assisting physicians in ten years? In ten years, I could be a physician. 18

So I had three goals ahead of me. I needed to get out of debt. I am a skydiver. I have been skydiving for six years now, and I stopped counting 19 jumps at 200, which is a whole other story. But I had to master a significant amount of debt. I needed to get in school, because as we all know, being outside of the school system and getting to the point where you are sitting down in the classroom and taking classes can be quite a hurdle.

20   I also wanted to find a way to finance my education and cost of living. I looked around for about six months. I found a job in Seattle, and I move up there. In a year I pounded down about 17 grand worth of debt, and I got into school.

21   I reduced my hours to part-time at work, which in my field is about 30 hours a week. And while taking chemistry, calculus, physics, organic chemistry, biology and all those sorts of classes, I found that it was becoming just too much, the stress of my work and my classes.

22   So I wrote a letter to the richest man in the world, explaining my plight to accomplish my third goal. The richest man in the world wrote me back and said, I understand your situation. I understand what you have been up against. I understand that not very many people have given you a chance. I'll take a chance on you.

23   It's really been quite a thing to think that somebody that I don't even know has decided to back me like that. For every semester that I successfully complete, along my pathway, I get funding from the Bill and Linda Gates Foundation, and it covers my tuition, my books and my fees, cost of living, groceries and electricity bill, food plan. It's really quite a deal. It is one of the most empowering things that has ever happened to me.

24   So, this last spring, a letter came in the mail from an Ivory Leaf school.

25   I opened that letter up, and it told me that the dream that I had inside for 25 years, the dream of a six year old child, had finally come true.

26   This past summer, I sold most of what I owned and loaded the rest in a U-Haul and took six days to drive out here to Cornell, to finish my pre-med requirements. I am here at Cornell.

27   The Native students here, we face our own issues. We wonder if we got accepted for our blood. I've talked with other Native people, not here at Cornell, that feel perhaps we have sold out, come to a predominantly white institution, that what we need is to attend our own schools and tribal colleges.

28   When you look at all the physicians in the United States, divide them up by race, and point to all of them that are Indian, it's one tenth of one one-hundredth. When you look at all of the applicants in the Cornell pre-med pool every year, out of everybody that applies to medical school from Cornell University every year, on the average 81 percent get in. Those are huge numbers when you compare that to other institutions.

I came here to increase my chances, to take the road that gives me the best chance to accomplish my dream. Unfortunately the reality is that if I blow my grades, I blow my ride. It's that simple. 29

I imagine with my heritage I could just as well work for indigenous people from Mexico. But I wasn't nurtured that way. I know that in the end, when I stand before the Creator and look him in the eye, I know that I have chosen the more narrow, more difficult path, but one with great honor. 30

That will be my message to those that are yet to come, not to be self-serving. To pick that most difficult path, to come back and serve your own, to be proud of who you are, be proud of being Indian and where you come from. To be humble before the creator, to listen to the children, for they will be sitting where you sit and I will sit. They'll be the only ones. 31

Thinking Critically About Content

1. What race is the author? When do we learn this fact?

2. What is the author's dream for his future?

3. According to Arredondo, what was "one of the most empowering things that has ever happened to me" (paragraph 23)?

Thinking Critically About Purpose and Audience

4. Explain your understanding of this essay's title.

5. Who do you think Arredondo's primary audience is?

6. Arredondo uses a very informal tone in this essay, which makes the readers feel he is actually talking to us. Do you feel this is an effective way to get his message across? Explain your answer.

Thinking Critically About Paragraphs

7. Find four details in Arredondo's essay that help us understand the difficult time the author had getting to college.

8. How does Arredondo organize his details in paragraph 22? Is this an effective order for this paragraph?

9. Why does Arredondo focus on children in his final paragraph? Is this an effective ending to his essay?

10. Write a paragraph describing what you think Arredondo's mother was thinking the first time he asked her about college.

Writing Topics: Narrating

Before you begin to write, you might want to review the writing process in Part I.

1. If being 11, according to Cisneros, is also being 10, 9, 8, 7, 6, and so on, what is being 20? 30? Choose an age above 11, and write a narrative to explain it to other students in your class.

2. How clear are your goals? Arredondo set his career objectives at six years old and then worked 25 years just to get into pre-med school. What are your main goals in life? How do you plan to reach them? Explain your goals for the future.

3. What do you think are the most important features of a good story? Why are they important? What effect do they have on you?

ILLUSTRATING

The two essays in this chapter show how authors use examples in essays. The first essay, "Homeless Woman Living in a Car," written by someone who adopts the name Diane because she doesn't want to be identified, uses examples to catalog the horrors of her lifestyle. In the second essay, "Walk On By," Brent Staples uses some examples from his own experience to send a warning to kids in gangs.

"Diane"
HOMELESS WOMAN LIVING IN A CAR

Focusing Your Attention

1. Can you think of a time when you reached "rock bottom" in your life? How did you feel? What caused you to fall so low? How did you handle the situation?

2. The essay you are about to read is written by a woman from Orange County in California who is currently homeless. She has a job, but it doesn't pay enough to cover a place to live. What do you think it feels like to be homeless?

Expanding Your Vocabulary

The following words are important to your understanding of this essay.

anonymity: the state of being unknown or unidentified (paragraph 1)

prosperous: wealthy (paragraph 2)

abyss: bottomless pit (paragraph 3)

mourn: feel sorrow over a death or a serious loss (paragraph 6)

prospects: chances, possibilities, expectations (paragraph 6)

dementia: madness, loss of mental functioning (paragraph 7)

Alzheimer's: disease affecting the central nervous system (paragraph 7)

annuity: sum of money payable annually or at regular intervals (paragraph 8)

irony: unexpected twist (paragraph 13)

array: display (paragraph 24)

amenities: pleasant features (paragraph 24)

warily: watchfully, suspiciously (paragraph 25)

tenancy: residence (paragraph 25)

shroud: cover (paragraph 25)

adrenaline: natural stimulant produced by the body (paragraph 26)

precariously: dangerously (paragraph 37)

excruciating: extremely painful (paragraph 41)

1   I need anonymity, so call me Diane.

2   I try not to be seen as I watch you prosperous-looking people walking from your cars to your offices. If you saw me, your faces would mirror your suspicion and disapproval.

3   Yet I was one of you. And at least some of you are dancing on the same tightrope over the same abyss into which I have fallen.

4   None of you know I am here in the car just a few feet away from you—or what it is like once you get here. I can tell you, courtesy of a typewriter for which no one would pay me five desperately needed dollars.

5   Last night my money added up to $38.67, so I found a cheaper motel. But tonight I will start sleeping in my car. I must eat on $6.23 for the next 10 days. Then there will be a paycheck—enough to keep me in a motel again for about a week. After that, it will be back to the car until the next payday.

6   Yes, I work for a living, but this job may end soon. And since the pay isn't enough for a deposit on an apartment or even a room, it would be hard to mourn its loss. Except that I have no money, no home, no evident prospects.

7   My downward spiral from a middle-class Orange County lifestyle began a few years ago. I was divorced and in my 50s, earning $40,000 a year as an editor, when my mother died of cancer. As the only child, I was left to care for an aged father advancing steadily into the dementia of Alzheimer's.

8   I quit my job, moved to his apartment in Florida and cared for him for two years. We survived on my savings and his annuity. And in 1989 he

died, leaving me broke and drained of self-confidence and the ability to concentrate.

News reports told of high unemployment among "older workers," 9 meaning anyone over 40. I was 57. Where did I fit in?

I didn't. 10

Now I drive through the streets of Newport Beach looking for a place to 11 spend the night.

There seems something wrong with each street-side parking space. 12 Here is a house whose windows look directly into my car. Here a space is too near an intersection with heavy traffic. To remain anywhere, I must remain invisible. Yet the one quiet area is also isolated. There is danger in isolation.

Finally, I drive slowly past the Sheraton hotel, with its many parked cars 13 and empty parking spaces. It seems so civilized. I used to come here for business lunches when I worked across the street. Aware of the irony, I check into a space facing the street.

The back seat of my 5-year-old Oldsmobile is too short for sleeping, but 14 the front seats recline. My legs dangle toward the brake and accelerator, yet it seems comfortable enough to think of getting some sleep.

I drop my seat back, but tense whenever footsteps approach. I dread 15 waking to find someone staring at me, so a large, black, cotton knit jacket I place over my head makes me feel nicely invisible. If I were dressed entirely in black, I'd be even less visible. From now on, I shall prepare for the night like a cat burglar.

I sleep soundly for two hours, then fitfully for the next hour and a half. To 16 avoid discovery, I must leave before daylight.

This is the first night of what will become four months of living out of my 17 car—long hours of solitude, physical discomfort, boredom, and sometimes hunger.

But it will teach me much about myself—and that line beyond which 18 lies permanent hopelessness.

When I awaken, the night sky is beginning to pale. I drive toward 19 McDonald's and sit impatiently in a parking lot for its 6 o'clock opening. I can wait for coffee, but I need the restroom. I take my dish-washing detergent along and manage a passable sponge bath.

After one of the most boring days and nights of my life, I wake up the 20 next morning and drive to Ralph's and spend 69 cents of my remaining $2.56 for a can of tuna. Carrying my tuna back to the car, I find a wallet full of cash and credit cards in the parking lot. I take it to the market manager. As I walk back to my car, I wonder: How hungry or desperate would I have to be to have kept that wallet? I don't know, but I'm not there now, and I'm thankful.

21   I awaken the next morning at 4:30 after sleeping almost five hours.

22   This is a go-to-work day for me. I work a 40-hour week in four days. But while most people yearn for quitting time, I now look forward to the hours in the office, that place of blissful luxury.

23   It has hot water, coffee, tea, drinking water, a newspaper, a restroom, my own chair, and a place to leave the car. I hope I will be alert enough to do a good day's work.

24   I manage to perform well. Only in the warm, airless afternoon do I suddenly drop off over my papers and yank instantly awake. I pull through the fog, pour more coffee, and focus on my work. The irony is I work for a firm that publishes books advertising apartment rentals and their vast array of comforts and amenities.

25   Back in my car, one night late, I awaken abruptly. I hear the sound of a key being slowly worked into my door lock and turned, just inches from my ear. My scalp tingles. The key does not work and is slowly withdrawn. I listen warily. I can lunge for the horn if need be. That could bring someone out of the hotel—and probably end my tenancy at the Sheraton. I wait, unmoving and unseeing under my nighttime shroud.

26   In a few minutes, I hear a key working the lock of a nearby car door or trunk. It opens and soon closes softly. Then it is quiet. I lie awake, adrenaline rushing, and finally sleep fitfully. This is a cold wash of reality: I am no more immune from danger than anyone else.

27   This payday has loomed larger in my mind with each passing day. I feel increasing urgency to buy some fresh food, to have a bed to sleep in for a few nights, to soak in a tub. Such expectation allowed me very little sleep last night.

28   But the paychecks from out of state are delayed; they won't be here until tomorrow.

29   Tonight I eat my last saved slice of bread and margarine. And, with a wary eye on the gas tank, which reads empty, I drive to the Sheraton yet again.

30   The paychecks arrive. I check into a motel and almost instantly fall asleep, unable to enjoy the luxury of tub and television until tomorrow.

31   I wish I had discovered earlier how much money can be saved by sleeping in the car. It's the only way I know now to save enough to rent a room near my office. Allowing for a night at a motel once a week to catch up on sleep, for laundry, and for general self-repair, it will probably take two months or so to save up.

32   But will I be able to keep up the rent?

When I returned to California from Florida, I finally landed a low- 33
paying but full-time job and was promised rapid advancement. Now I find
that the promises are not going to be kept by the corporation that bought
this company.

I decide to take a stand: Live up to the promises the company made me, 34
or I quit. They praise me but won't budge. I quit, and they look surprised. It
was hardly noble or heroic. When you are already living out of your car, it
is easier to give up a job. If you have a home, you can imagine losing it.

The downward spiral continues in earnest. The auto life had a rhythm 35
based on paydays. But now there are no more paychecks to come.

My son, who lives in Tennessee, is suspicious. He's been aware that I'm 36
having money problems, but my lack of a permanent phone number and
address prompts him to ask me outright if I'm sleeping in my car. I've tried
carefully to keep this from him. I don't want to burden him and his family
with my financial problems. So when he asks, I laugh it off.

The gas tank is precariously low. I start walking almost everywhere.   37

It's harder to look for a new job. Without motel room telephones and the 38
workplace, there is no way to leave call-back numbers when responding to
ads. I can walk major distances, but it means arriving hot, sweaty, and too
tired to impress anybody.

I walk as much as 25 miles a day. Now, after seven days of exceptional 39
walking, my left knee is stunningly painful, and the right knee echoes the
pain. There are other unfamiliar pains running down the front of my legs.
But if I don't start walking, I won't get a gallon of gas into the car, and I won't
get any food.

So I grit my teeth and walk, overriding the pain with necessity. For the 40
next three days, I continue to walk many miles. The pain fills every part of
my brain.

Now I am hobbling, so crippled that I can hardly get in and out of the 41
car. One day of rest makes no improvement, nor do two, nor three.
Movement is excruciating.

I have come to a critical time. My days have become a self-defeating 42
spiral of nonaccomplishment. Everything I do now is devoted to simple
survival. If I don't do something to halt it, I could be on my way into a
rougher homelessness. But what can I do?

Thinking Critically About Content

1. The anonymous author "Diane" used to be an active member of
   middle-class America. What caused Diane's downfall?

2. What examples from this essay illustrate most clearly what characterizes Diane's life as a "homeless woman living in a car"?

3. Does this essay change your thinking about homelessness? In what ways?

Thinking Critically About Purpose and Audience

4. Why do you think the author wrote this article? Why do you think she wanted to stay anonymous?

5. What type of audience do you think would most understand and appreciate this essay?

6. Are you one of the people who, according to Diane, is "dancing on the same tightrope over the same abyss into which I have fallen" (paragraph 3)?

Thinking Critically About Paragraphs

7. In this essay, the author writes in the present tense as if she is currently going through these experiences. Yet in paragraph 17, the author says, "This is the first night of what will become four months of living out of my car." What is her perspective on her homelessness?

8. Look closely at paragraph 31. Is it unified? Do the examples the author uses in this paragraph support its topic sentence? Explain your answer.

9. How does the writer organize her details in paragraph 7? Is this an effective order?

10. Write a paragraph that answers Diane's question, "But what can I do?" (paragraph 42).

Brent Staples

WALK ON BY

Focusing Your Attention

1. Do you intimidate people with any of your behavior? Are you intimidated by anyone in particular?

2. The essay you are about to read discusses the image of African American males as criminals or suspects. It is written by someone who doesn't deserve this reputation. Have you ever been blamed for something you didn't do? What were you blamed for? Why were you blamed?

Expanding Your Vocabulary

The following words are important to your understanding of this essay.

affluent: wealthy (paragraph 1)

impoverished: poor (paragraph 1)

uninflammatory: giving no cause for concern (paragraph 1)

billowing: waving (paragraph 1)

menacingly: dangerously (paragraph 1)

unwieldy: large, unmanageable (paragraph 2)

insomnia: sleeplessness (paragraph 2)

wayfarers: wanderers, travelers (paragraph 2)

dismayed: horrified (paragraph 2)

accomplice: associate, helper (paragraph 2)

tyranny: cruelty (paragraph 2)

errant: out of place (paragraph 2)

crowd cover: presence of large numbers of people (paragraph 4)

SoHo: a neighborhood of Manhattan, south of Houston Street (paragraph 4)

taut: strained, intense (paragraph 4)

ruthless: cruel (paragraph 5)

extols: praises (paragraph 5)

panhandlers: beggars (paragraph 5)

warrenlike: crowded (paragraph 6)

bandolier style: over one shoulder (paragraph 6)

lethality: deadliness (paragraph 7)

flailings: flinging one's arms in the air (paragraph 8)

mark: victim (paragraph 8)

cowered: cringed (paragraph 8)

valiant: brave, courageous (paragraph 8)

bravado: false bravery (paragraph 9)

perilous: dangerous (paragraph 10)

proprietor: owner (paragraph 11)

Doberman pinscher: a large breed of dog (paragraph 11)

skittish: easily frightened (paragraph 13)

congenial: friendly (paragraph 13)
constitutionals: walks (paragraph 14)
Beethoven: 1770–1827, a German composer (paragraph 14)
Vivaldi: 1678–1741, an Italian composer (paragraph 14)

1   My first victim was a woman—white, well dressed, probably in her early twenties. I came upon her late one evening on a deserted street in Hyde Park, a relatively affluent neighborhood in an otherwise mean, impoverished section of Chicago. As I swung onto the avenue behind her, there seemed to be a discreet, uninflammatory distance between us. Not so. She cast back a worried glance. To her, the youngish black man—a broad six feet two inches with a beard and billowing hair, both hands shoved into the pockets of a bulky military jacket—seemed menacingly close. After a few more quick glimpses, she picked up her pace and was soon running in earnest. Within seconds she disappeared into a cross street.

2   That was more than a decade ago. I was 22 years old, a graduate student newly arrived at the University of Chicago. It was in the echo of that terrified woman's footfalls that I first began to know the unwieldy inheritance I'd come into—the ability to alter public space in ugly ways. It was clear that she thought herself the quarry of a mugger, a rapist, or worse. Suffering a bout of insomnia, however, I was stalking sleep, not defenseless wayfarers. As a softy who is scarcely able to take a knife to a raw chicken—let alone hold it to a person's throat—I was surprised, embarrassed, and dismayed all at once. Her flight made me feel like an accomplice in tyranny. It also made it clear that I was indistinguishable from the muggers who occasionally seeped into the area from the surrounding ghetto. That first encounter, and those that followed, signified that a vast, unnerving gulf lay between nighttime pedestrians—particularly women—and me. And I soon gathered that being perceived as dangerous is a hazard in itself. I only needed to turn a corner into a dicey situation, or crowd some frightened, armed person in a foyer somewhere, or make an errant move after being pulled over by a policeman. Where fear and weapons meet—and they often do in urban America—there is always the possibility of death.

3   In the first year, my first away from my hometown, I was to become thoroughly familiar with the language of fear. At dark, shadowy intersections in Chicago, I could cross in front of a car stopped at a traffic light and elicit the *thunk, thunk, thunk, thunk* of the driver—black, white, male, or

female—hammering down the door locks. On less traveled streets after dark, I grew accustomed to but never comfortable with people who crossed to the other side of the street rather than pass me. Then there were the standard unpleasantries with police, doormen, bouncers, cab drivers, and others whose business it is to screen out troublesome individuals *before* there is any nastiness.

I moved to New York nearly two years ago, and I have remained an 4
avid night walker. In central Manhattan, the near-constant crowd cover minimized tense one-on-one street encounters. Elsewhere—visiting friends in SoHo, where sidewalks are narrow and tightly spaced, buildings shut out the sky—things can get very taut indeed.

Black men have a firm place in New York mugging literature. Norman 5
Podhoretz in his famed (or infamous) 1963 essay, "My Negro Problem—and Ours," recalls growing up in terror of black males; they "were tougher than we were, more ruthless," he writes—and as an adult on the Upper West Side of Manhattan, he continues, he cannot constrain his nervousness when he meets black men on certain streets. Similarly, a decade later, the essayist and novelist Edward Hoagland extols a New York where once "Negro bitterness bore down mainly on other Negroes." Where some see mere panhandlers, Hoagland sees "a mugger who is clearly screwing up his nerve to do more than just *ask* for money." But Hoagland has "the New Yorker's quick-hunch posture for broken-field maneuvering," and the bad guy swerves away.

I often witness that "hunch posture" from women after dark on the war- 6
renlike streets of Brooklyn where I live. They seem to set their faces on neutral and, with their purse straps strung across their chests bandolier style, they forge ahead as though bracing themselves against being tackled. I understand, of course, that the danger they perceive is not a hallucination. Women are particularly vulnerable to street violence, and young black males are drastically overrepresented among the perpetrators of that violence. Yet these truths are no solace against the kind of alienation that comes of being ever the suspect, against being set apart, a fearsome entity with whom pedestrians avoid making eye contact.

It is not altogether clear to me how I reached the ripe old age of 22 with- 7
out being conscious of the lethality nighttime pedestrians attributed to me. Perhaps it was because in Chester, Pennsylvania, the small, angry industrial town where I came of age in the 1960s, I was scarcely noticeable against a backdrop of gang warfare, street knifings, and murders. I grew up one of the good boys, had perhaps a half-dozen fist fights. In retrospect, my shyness of combat has clear sources.

8   Many things go into the making of a young thug. One of those things is the consummation of the male romance with the power to intimidate. An infant discovers that random flailings send the baby bottle flying out of the crib and crashing to the floor. Delighted, the joyful babe repeats those motions again and again, seeking to duplicate the feat. Just so, I recall the points at which some of my boyhood friends were finally seduced by the perception of themselves as tough guys. When a mark cowered and surrendered his money without resistance, myth and reality merged—and paid off. It is, after all, only manly to embrace the power to frighten and intimidate. We, as men, are not supposed to give an inch of our lane on the highway; we are to seize the fighter's edge in work and in play and even in love; we are to be valiant in the face of hostile forces.

9   Unfortunately, poor and powerless young men seem to take all this nonsense literally. As a boy, I saw countless tough guys locked away; I have since buried several. They were babies, really—a teenage cousin, a brother of 22, a childhood friend in his mid-twenties—all gone down in episodes of bravado played out in the streets. I came to doubt the virtues of intimidation early on. I chose, perhaps even unconsciously, to remain a shadow—timid, but a survivor.

10   The fearsomeness mistakenly attributed to me in public places often has a perilous flavor. The most frightening of these confusions occurred in the late 1970s and early 1980s when I worked as a journalist in Chicago. One day, rushing into the office of a magazine I was writing for with a deadline story in hand, I was mistaken for a burglar. The office manager called security and, with an ad hoc posse, pursued me through the labyrinthine halls, nearly to my editor's door. I had no way of proving who I was. I could only move briskly toward the company of someone who knew me.

11   Another time I was on assignment for a local paper and killing time before an interview. I entered a jewelry store on the city's affluent Near North Side. The proprietor excused herself and returned with an enormous red Doberman pinscher straining at the end of a leash. She stood, the dog extended toward me, silent to my questions, her eyes bulging nearly out of her head. I took a cursory look around, nodded, and bade her good night. Relatively speaking, however, I never fared as badly as another black male journalist. He went to nearby Waukegan, Illinois, a couple of summers ago to work on a story about a murderer who was born there. Mistaking the reporter for the killer, police hauled him from his car at gunpoint and but for his press credentials would probably have tried to book him. Such episodes are not uncommon. Black men trade tales like this all the time.

In "My Negro Problem—and Ours," Podhoretz writes that the hatred he   12
feels for blacks makes itself known to him through a variety of avenues—
one being his discomfort with that "special brand of paranoid touchiness"
to which he says blacks are prone. No doubt he is speaking here of black
men. In time, I learned to smother the rage I felt at so often being taken for
a criminal. Not to do so would surely have led to madness—via that special
"paranoid touchiness" that so annoyed Podhoretz at the time he wrote the
essay.

I began to take precautions to make myself less threatening. I move   13
about with care, particularly late in the evening. I give a wide berth to nervous people on subway platforms during the wee hours, particularly when
I have exchanged business clothes for jeans. If I happen to be entering a
building behind some people who appear skittish, I may walk by, letting
them clear the lobby before I return, so as not to seem to be following them.
I have been calm and extremely congenial on those rare occasions when
I've been pulled over by the police.

And on late-evening constitutionals along streets less traveled by, I   14
employ what has proved to be an excellent tension-reducing measure: I
whistle melodies from Beethoven and Vivaldi and the more popular classical composers. Even steely New Yorkers hunching toward nighttime desti-
nations seem to relax, and occasionally they even join in the tune. Virtually
everybody seems to sense that a mugger wouldn't be warbling bright,
sunny selections from Vivaldi's *Four Seasons*. It is my equivalent of the
cowbell that hikers wear when they know they are in bear country.

Thinking Critically About Content

1. According to Staples, what reputation do African American men have?

2. When did the author become aware of this reputation?

3. What is Staples's opinion of "young thugs" (paragraph 8)? How did you come to this conclusion?

Thinking Critically About Purpose and Audience

4. What do you think Staples's purpose is in this essay?

5. Who do you think Staples's primary audience is?

6. Which of Staples's examples convince you that people are some-times intimidated by African American men?

Thinking Critically About Paragraphs

7. What is the topic sentence of paragraph 3? Do all the sentences in that paragraph support that topic sentence? Explain your answer.

8. Staples begins his essay with the words "My first victim." What is he implying by these words? Is this an effective beginning? Explain your answer.

9. What is the organization of paragraph 9? Is this an effective order for these details? Explain your answer.

10. Write a paragraph using examples to explain one of your opinions about society today.

Writing Topics: Illustrating

Before you begin to write, you might want to review the writing process in Part I.

1. Contemporary American society rewards compulsive, fast-moving people. But some people just can't keep up for any number of reasons. Have you ever felt the way Diane says she feels in her essay? Was your reason for not keeping up as legitimate as Diane's? Discuss any similarities you see between yourself and Diane.

2. What are some of the main dangers on the streets in your hometown? What characterizes these dangers? How do you deal with them?

3. What do you think writers should consider first when choosing examples to support a topic sentence? Why are these criteria most important when working with examples?

ANALYZING A PROCESS

The following essays explain different events or processes; in other words, they tell you how to do something or how something happened the way it did. The first, "Getting Out of Debt (and Staying Out)" by Julia Bourland, offers practical suggestions for getting and staying out of debt. It demonstrates how to do something. "Coming Over," by Russell Freedman, explains what people had to go through at Ellis Island to immigrate to the United States around the turn of the twentieth century. It demonstrates the how-something-happened process analysis.

Julia Bourland
GETTING OUT OF DEBT (AND STAYING OUT)

Focusing Your Attention

1. Think of a time when you had to explain to someone how to do something. Was it an easy or difficult task? Did the person understand you? Was the person able to follow your directions?

2. In the process analysis essay you are about to read, the writer tells us how to manage money and control debt. Do you manage your money efficiently? Have you ever been in debt? Do you know how to avoid debt?

Expanding Your Vocabulary

The following words are important to your understanding of this essay.

assumption: a claim (paragraph 1)
incurred: gained (paragraph 1)
deferring: putting off (paragraph 2)
vulnerable: capable of being hurt (paragraph 5)

meager: small (paragraph 8)

insatiable: unsatisfied (paragraph 8)

conscientious: careful (paragraph 8)

inundated: swamped (paragraph 8)

gingerly: with caution (paragraph 8)

diligent: hardworking (paragraph 9)

accrue: gain (paragraph 10)

amassed: gathered (paragraph 10)

uber-exorbitant: very extreme (paragraph 15)

1   I'm going to make the bold assumption that you have incurred a little debt during your great entrance into adulthood, from either student loans, devilish credit cards, or that car loan you recently signed with its 36 easy installment payments. If you haven't tasted debt, you are abnormally perfect and unAmerican and can just skip on down to the next section on retirement planning and chill out until the rest of us catch up with you.

2   Some debt, such as student loans, is money well borrowed and an investment in your future. Because of their relatively low interest rates, manageable (though seemingly eternal) repayment plans, and reasonable deferment options, student loans should not be the source of midnight panic attacks during your second semester of senior year, even if you've incurred thousands and thousands of dollars to fund your education and still don't have a job that suggests that all the debt was worth it. If you haven't graduated yet, toward the end of your final semester, your college student loan officer will give you all the dirty details of your repayment schedule (hopefully armed with ample tissue for the tears that are certain to flood your contacts), as well as tell you how to defer paying back your loans if you aren't employed by the time your repayment grace period is up, as was my case. The cheery thing I discovered about deferring repayment is that the groovy government actually paid the interest I owed during my six-month deferment. That's not the case with all student loans, but you'll find that out when you start reading the fine print.

3   If you're like me, you may have several loans to repay. Again, you probably got (or will get) the skinny from your financial aid administrator at college, but in case he or she is on drugs, I'll summarize. There are a few consolidation plans that can make the whole process of paying back your loans less horrifying. Consolidating means that you will be able to merge all of your loans into one giant superloan that offers a low interest rate, as well as various options for shortening or lengthening your repayment

schedule (which will increase or decrease the amount you owe each month, thereby increasing or decreasing the amount of interest you ultimately end up paying). But the best reason to consolidate your loans is that you will receive only one bill every month, which means you have to think and stress about all the student loan money you owe only once every 30 days! I highly recommend consolidation, if only for that.

If you have several loans from one financial institution, contact   4
your lender directly about its consolidation options, or try these two programs: Federal Direct Consolidation Loan Program (800–557–7392; www.ed.gov/directloan) and Student Loan Marketing Association (a.k.a. Sallie Mae) Smart Loan Account (800–524–9100; www.salliemae.com).

Student loans are much less threatening and guilt-provoking than   5
credit card debt, to which we 20-somethings are painfully vulnerable. There are so many things we want and need. Credit card companies seize upon our vulnerability, especially during college, sending us application after application with such enticing incentives as a *free water bottle, a two-pound bag of M&Ms, a 10% discount* on first purchases, *free checks* to spend anywhere we please, our very own *head shot* on the card, a 4.9% *introductory interest rate,* and *bonus airline miles.* My first advice on the whole matter of credit card debt is to avoid it like the devil! I know many honest, smart girls who've become submerged in debt through the seductive power of plastic.

Our society once thrived without credit, so it *is* possible to stay out of   6
debt as we begin our adult lives. But since you will probably experiment with credit despite the danger, memorize these eight guidelines compliments of those who've battled the plastic demons:

1. No Department Store Credit Cards

In-store credit usually carries a much higher interest rate than credit   7
cards issued by banks. If you don't pay your debt back right away, what you buy is going to cost you much more than you bargained for. The only exception is if you have money to pay off your debt as soon as the bill arrives, and signing up for a card gives you a substantial discount on your first purchase. In these cases, get the card (and discount), pay your bill in full, and immediately cancel the card and shred it into a million pieces, lest you be tempted to use it again without the discount and money to pay for it. Note: If the discount isn't more than $10 or 20, don't even bother, because when you sign on, you'll probably get put on some annoying direct-mail list that will be sold to a bunch of trashy companies who will send you junk mail every single day.

2. One Card Only

8   The fewer little plastic rectangles you have, the less you'll be tempted to live beyond your meager means (and the fewer hysteria-provoking bills you'll receive). Ideally, you should use your card only for items that you know you can pay off with your next paycheck or for unavoidable emergencies, like getting new brakes for your clunker or fillings for your insatiable sweet tooth. The ideal cards have fixed annual percentage rates ranging from 9 to 12 percent, or less if you can find them, no annual fee, and a grace period that doesn't start charging interest on what you buy until the bill's due date. If you are a conscientious customer, you will be inundated with appealing offers for new cards boasting Platinum status and $25,000 credit lines. When you receive these, gingerly toss them into the recycling bin. Opening them will only lead you into trouble. There is one exception to this rule, but I'll get to that when we talk about transferring balances. First, a few more basic tips.

3. Use Your ATM Credit/Debit Card Instead

9   If you're diligent about balancing your checkbook, there's no reason to fear the credit card capabilities of your ATM card, which most banks are offering these days. Keep the receipt for whatever you purchase with your card as you would had you withdrawn money from the bank, and record the amount in your checkbook ledger as you would a check. Your debit card is just as convenient as a credit card, but your purchase won't accrue interest, which will save you money. Definitely use your debit card instead of a real credit card when grocery shopping or buying little things at the pharmacy, unless you like the idea of paying 18 percent interest on cereal and tampons. Trust your elders: the interest on all the little things makes them as costly as a raging girl's night out.

4. Pay Back as Much as You Can, as Soon as You Can

10   If we take the *minimum* payment request on our monthly statements to heart, we may not pay off our account in full until we qualify for social security. That's because interest continues to accrue on our balance each month. If we don't pay off everything we owe, the remainder plus the interest we've amassed will be charged interest the following month, and the month after that, which means our balance continues to grow at the speed of our card's annual percentage rate (APR) despite the fact that we pay our minimum due every month and have hidden our credit card in the closet under five shoe boxes. That's how credit card companies make so much

money and why we should avoid getting into debt in every humanly possible (but legal) way.

If you have debt from several sources, pay back whatever has higher 11 interest rates first—usually your credit cards—then tackle the typically lower-rated student loan and car loan debts. If your credit card debt is spiraling out of control, you could refinance your student or car loans so that you will owe less on them each month, using the extra money to pay off your credit cards. Then, when your costlier debts have been paid off (and cards dumped in the nearest incinerator), you can designate all your funds to paying back your temporarily neglected student and car loans as quickly as you can.

5. Trash Those Credit Card Checks That Come with Your Statement, and Shun Cash Advances from the ATM

Both checks and cash advances will cost you dearly, since many card 12 companies tack on an additional finance charge to your bill when you use them, plus impose an interest rate for the amount you borrow that's much higher than the rate you have for normal purchases. That means that if you withdraw $100 from your card at a bank or ATM or use one of those checks for your rent, you'll be paying back your credit card company a lot more than the amount you borrowed.

6. Switch to a Card with a Lower Interest Rate

I said earlier that you should throw away offers for additional credit 13 cards, and that is a good rule unless you are carrying a balance on a card (or cards) with an outrageous interest rate, say more than 12 percent. In that case, it's a good financial move to transfer your balance(s) to one card with the lowest rate you can find. Some offer temporary introductory interest rates as low as 2.9 percent on all transferred balances; when you apply, make sure you note the expiration date for those low rates on your calendar, and have another card offer lined up and ready to take on the load when the time comes. I know this sounds tedious, but careful organization and diligence will save you money as you attempt to pay the whole balance off.

If you play credit card musical chairs, keep three things in mind. First, 14 some balance transfer offers have associated fees or finance charges that aren't exactly highlighted in their promotions. Always inquire about transfer fees, and try to talk them out of it; many issuers are willing to waive the fees upon request. Second, even after you transfer your balance in full, the account remains open. To close it, you must officially cancel. The issuing bank won't automatically cancel a zero-balance account, so if you don't, your access to that credit line will remain on your credit report. That could be problematic later on when you're applying for a mortgage and have thousands of dollars worth of potential debt in your financial profile— something that makes lenders skittish. The other reason to cancel is to avoid the temptation to start using that clean slate of credit that your old card suddenly presents. And the third caveat: When you transfer your balance, do not use this new card to purchase new things. Declare it a debt repayment card only, and stick that shiny piece of plastic in the file where you keep your monthly statements. Here's why:

15   When you charge new items on a card that has adopted old debt, many card issuers apply a different (and uber-exorbitant) interest rate to those new purchases. The higher interest rate will remain on the amount of your new purchases until your entire debt has been repaid. Therefore, when you are trying to pay off a large debt, you should try to have two credit cards—one with a very low balance-transfer interest rate for your main debt and another with a reasonable interest rate on new purchases that you will use for emergencies only, since you are, after all, trying to get out of the hole, not rack up new debt. A good resource for finding low-rate, no-fee cards is a company called CardWeb.com, Inc., which publishes a newsletter called CardTrak that lists these desirable cards. You can access the newsletter and other credit card consumer information on its website (www.cardweb.com) or by calling (800) 344–7714.

7. Apply for a Secured Credit Card If Your Credit Is Screwed

16   If you have damaged your credit rating by defaulting on a loan or debt, your main priority (besides coming up with a repayment plan that suits all your creditors) is to rebuild your credit. Secured credit cards can help. You give the issuer a certain sum of money up front, which is kept in an account for you as a security deposit. Depending on the terms of your agreement, you can then charge a specified amount on that card. Once you've proved that you can repay your debts in this secured way, you may be offered a new card with real credit that doesn't require you to put up money ahead of time. CardWeb.com, Inc. (cited in the previous entry) can provide a list of secured credit cards as well as low-rate, no-fee cards.

17   If you are in a bad situation and creditors are calling you about monster debt that you can't currently pay off, don't pack up and move to North Dakota, thinking creditors won't be able to find you—they will. A couple of nonprofit credit counseling organizations can help with debt-repayment planning

assistance: Consumer Credit Counseling Services, associated with the National Foundation for Consumer Credit (800–388–2227; www.nfcc.org), and Debt Counselors of America (800–698–5182; www.dca.org).

8. Check Your Credit Report

I've already expounded on why a clean credit report is so important, so 18 I won't beat that dead horse, but I will add that it's wise to check up on your report every now and then to make sure there are no surprises (or mistakes) that need mending. There are three agencies that compile credit reports, and they all get their information separately, so what one company says is part of your credit history may differ from what another company includes. You can get copies of your credit report from each company for $8 or less, depending on your state of residence. If you have had bad credit in the past but believe you've been exonerated (usually after seven years), you should make sure all three companies are showing you in the proper light.

The three agencies keeping tabs are Experian (formerly TRW) (888–397– 19 3742; www.experian.com/ecommerce/consumercredit.html); Equifax (800–685–1111; www.econsumer.equifax.com); and Trans Union (800–888–4213; www.transunion.com/CreditReport/).

Thinking Critically About Content

1. According to Bourland, what types of debt are worthwhile?

2. What are Bourland's eight guidelines for avoiding credit card debt? Summarize each guideline.

3. How can you check your credit rating?

Thinking Critically About Purpose and Audience

4. What do you think Bourland's purpose is in writing this essay?

5. Who do you think Bourland's primary audience is? Does debt play any part in their lives?

6. Which of Bourland's guidelines are most likely to help you now and in the future? Explain your answer.

Thinking Critically About Paragraphs

7. Summarize Bourland's essay. Make sure you cover all her main points.

8. Choose a paragraph from this essay, and explain why it is well developed.

9. How is the information in paragraph 3 organized? Why is this an effective order for this topic?

10. Write a paragraph trying to convince a bill collector that you will pay a specific overdue bill next month.

Russell Freedman

COMING OVER

Focusing Your Attention

1. If you could immigrate to another country, which one would you go to and why?

2. The following essay chronicles the experiences of Europeans trying to immigrate into the United States around 1900. Do you know any recent immigrants to the United States? What did they do to get into the United States? Was it a traumatic experience for them?

Expanding Your Vocabulary

The following words are important to your understanding of this essay.

impoverished: poor (paragraph 1)

fervent: intense (paragraph 1)

narrows: a strait connecting two bodies of water (paragraph 6)

jabbered conversation: rapid talk that can't be understood (paragraph 6)

din: continuous noise (paragraph 6)

flustered: confused (paragraph 6)

indomitable: unable to be conquered (paragraph 15)

1   In the years around the turn of the [twentieth] century, immigration to America reached an all-time high. Between 1880 and 1920, 23 million immigrants arrived in the United States. They came mainly from countries of Europe, especially from impoverished towns and villages in southern and eastern Europe. The one thing they had in common was a fervent belief that in America life would be better.

2   Most of these immigrants were poor. Somehow they managed to scrape together enough money to pay for their passage to America. Many

immigrant families arrived penniless. Others had to make the journey in stages. Often the father came first, found work, and sent for his family later. Immigrants usually crossed the Atlantic as steerage passengers. Reached by steep, slippery stairways, the steerage lay deep down in the hold of the ship. It was occupied by passengers paying the lowest fare.

Men, women, and children were packed into dark, foul-smelling com-   3
partments. They slept in narrow bunks stacked three high. They had no showers, no lounges, and no dining rooms. Food served from huge kettles was dished into dinner pails provided by the steamship company. Because steerage conditions were crowded and uncomfortable, passengers spent as much time as possible up on deck.

The voyage was an ordeal, but it was worth it. They were on their way   4
to America.

The great majority of immigrants landed in New York City at America's   5
busiest port. They never forgot their first glimpse of the Statue of Liberty.

Edward Corsi, who later became United States Commissioner of   6
Immigration, was a 10-year-old Italian immigrant when he sailed into New York harbor in 1907:

> My first impression of the New World will always remain etched in my memory, particularly that hazy October morning when I first saw Ellis Island. The steamer *Florida*, fourteen days out of Naples, filled to capacity with 1600 natives of Italy, had weathered one of the worst storms in our captain's memory; and glad we were, both children and grown-ups, to leave the open sea and come at last through the Narrows into the Bay.
>
> My mother, my stepfather, my brother, Giuseppe, and my two sisters, Liberta and Helvetia, all of us together, happy that we had come through the storm safely, clustered on the foredeck for fear of separation and looked with wonder on this miraculous land of our dreams.
>
> Giuseppe and I held tightly to Stepfather's hands, while Liberta and Helvetia clung to Mother. Passengers all about us were crowding against the rail. Jabbered conversation, sharp cries, laughs and cheers—a steadily rising din filled the air. Mothers and fathers lifted up babies so that they too could see, off to the loft, the Statue of Liberty. . . .
>
> Finally the *Florida* veered to the left, turning northward into the Hudson River, and now the incredible buildings of lower Manhattan came very close to us.
>
> The officers of the ship . . . went sliding up and down the decks shouting orders and directions and driving the immigrants before them. Scowling and gesturing, they pushed and pulled the passengers, herding us into separate groups as though we were animals. A few moments later we came to our dock, and the long journey was over.

7   But the journey was not yet over. Before they could be admitted to the United States, immigrants had to pass through Ellis Island, which became the nation's chief immigrant processing center in 1892. There they would be questioned and examined. Those who could not pass all the exams would be detained; some would be sent back to Europe. And so their arrival in America was filled with great anxiety. Among the immigrants, Ellis Island was known as "Heartbreak Island."

8   When their ship docked at a Hudson River pier, the immigrants had numbered identity tags pinned to their clothing. Then they were herded onto special ferryboats that carried them to Ellis Island. Officials hurried them along, shouting "Quick! Run! Hurry!" in half a dozen languages.

9   Filing into an enormous inspection hall, the immigrants formed long lines separated by iron railings that made the hall look like a great maze.

10   Now the examinations began. First, the immigrants were examined by two doctors of the United States Health Service. One doctor looked for physical and mental abnormalities. When a case aroused suspicion, the immigrant received a chalk mark on the right shoulder for further inspection: L for lameness, H for heart, X for mental defects, and so on.

11   The second doctor watched for contagious and infectious diseases. He looked especially for infections of the scalp and at the eyelids for symptoms of trachoma, a blinding disease. Since trachoma caused more than half of all medical detentions, this doctor was greatly feared. He stood directly in the immigrant's path. With a swift movement, he would grab the immigrant's eyelid, pull it up, and peer beneath it. If all was well, the immigrant was passed on.

12   Those who failed to get past both doctors had to undergo a more thorough medical exam. The others moved on to the registration clerk, who questioned them with the aid of an interpreter: What is your name? Your nationality? Your occupation? Can you read and write? Have you ever been in prison? How much money do you have with you? Where are you going?

13   Some immigrants were so flustered that they could not answer. They were allowed to sit and rest and try again.

14   About one immigrant out of every five or six was detained for additional examinations or questioning.

15   The writer Angelo Pellegrini has recalled his own family's detention at Ellis Island:

> We lived there for three days—Mother and we five children, the youngest of whom was three years old. Because of the rigorous physical examination that we had to submit to, particularly of the eyes, there was this

terrible anxiety that one of us might be rejected. And if one of us was, what would the rest of the family do? My sister was indeed momentarily rejected; she had been so ill and had cried so much that her eyes were absolutely bloodshot, and Mother was told, "Well, we can't let her in." But fortunately, Mother was an indomitable spirit and finally made them understand that if her child had a few hours' rest and a little bite to eat, she would be all right. In the end we did get through.

Most immigrants passed through Ellis Island in about one day. Carrying   16
all their worldly possessions, they left the examination hall and waited on the dock for the ferry that would take them to Manhattan, a mile away. Some of them still faced journeys overland before they reached their final destination. Others would head directly for the teeming immigrant neighborhoods of New York City.

Thinking Critically About Content

1. What common belief did the American immigrants share?
2. Make a chart of the stages of the immigration process in 1900, starting with receiving identity tags.
3. Why were families who wanted to move to the United States so anxious when they reached Ellis Island?

Thinking Critically About Purpose and Audience

4. What do you think the purpose of this essay is?
5. Who would be most interested in this essay?
6. Does the excerpt by Edward Corsi (paragraph 6) capture the excitement the new immigrants probably felt when they saw Ellis Island for the first time?

Thinking Critically About Paragraphs

7. Why do you think Freedman includes the paragraph written by Angelo Pellegrini (paragraph 15)? Do the details in this paragraph support its topic sentence? Explain your answer.
8. This essay has a number of well-chosen transitions in every paragraph to help move the readers through the author's ideas. Look closely at paragraph 10, and underline three transition words or phrases. (Refer to pages 16–17 for information on transitions.)
9. What is the topic sentence of paragraph 7? Do all the sentences in that paragraph support this topic sentence? Explain your answer.

10. Pretend (if necessary) you and your family came to the United States from another country. Write a paragraph explaining the process you went through to get admitted to the country. If any members of your family actually went through the immigration process to be into the United States, you might want to talk to them before you write.

Writing Topics: Analyzing a Process

Before you begin to write, you might want to review the writing process in Part I.

1. In the first essay, Julia Bourland discusses debt as a normal part of life. Have you ever thought of debt in this way? Explain a process from your experience that is another normal part of life.

2. Think of something in life that you want as much as the Europeans described in Freedman's essay wanted to come to the United States. Then explain your plan for achieving this goal or accomplishing this mission you have set for yourself.

3. Which type of process analysis do you find more interesting—how-to essays or background explanations? Explain your answer.

COMPARING AND CONTRASTING

The following essays show how comparison and contrast work in a complete essay. The first, "The Barrio" by Ernesto Galarza, is from his book *Barrio Boy*, which traces Galarza's move from Tepic, Mexico, to California. The second essay, "A Fable for Tomorrow" by Rachel Carson, compares and contrasts our past environment with the future through an imaginary town.

Ernesto Galarza
THE BARRIO

Focusing Your Attention

1. Have you ever watched someone merge two cultures or tried to blend two cultures yourself? What are the advantages of merging cultures? What are the disadvantages?

2. In the essay you are about to read, the writer compares and contrasts various characteristics of American and Latin American life from the perspective of someone who has come to America for the first time. What do you think are some of the differences between these two cultures? Some of the similarities?

Expanding Your Vocabulary

The following words are important to your understanding of this essay.

barrio: Spanish-speaking neighborhood (title)

mercados: marketplaces (paragraph 1)

chiquihuite: basket (paragraph 1)

pilón: sugar candy (paragraph 1)

Mazatlán: a city in Mexico (paragraph 1)

Judases: images of the disciple who betrayed Jesus (paragraph 2)

Holy Week: the week leading up to Easter (paragraph 2)

promenades: parades (paragraph 2)

plaza: public square (paragraph 2)

cathedral: large church (paragraph 2)

Palacio de Gobierno: town hall (paragraph 2)

vecindades: close-knit neighborhoods (paragraph 3)

mirth: fun, laughter (paragraph 4)

boisterous: noisy (paragraph 4)

compadre: godfather (paragraph 5)

comadre: godmother (paragraph 5)

cherubs: angels depicted as babies with wings (paragraph 5)

mica: a mineral (paragraph 5)

atole: a drink (paragraph 5)

corridos: songs (paragraph 5)

paddy wagon: police van (paragraph 6)

IOUs: debts (paragraph 8)

pochos: Mexicans living in the United States who grew up in the United States (paragraph 9)

chicanos: Mexicans living in the United States who grew up in Mexico (paragraph 9)

1   We found the Americans as strange in their customs as they probably found us. Immediately we discovered that there were no *mercados* and that when shopping you did not put the groceries in a *chiquihuite*. Instead, everything was in cans or in cardboard boxes, or each item was put in a brown paper bag. There were neighborhood grocery stores at the corners and some big ones uptown, but no *mercado*. The grocers did not give children a *pilón*, they did not stand at the door and coax you to come in and buy, as they did in Mazatlán. The fruits and vegetables were displayed on counters instead of being piled up on the floor. The stores smelled of fly spray and oiled floors, not of fresh pineapple and limes.

2   Neither was there a plaza, only parks which had no bandstands, no concerts every Thursday, no Judases exploding on Holy Week, and no promenades of boys going one way and girls the other. There were no parks in the *barrio*, and the ones uptown were cold and rainy in winter,

and in summer there was no place to sit except on the grass. When there were celebrations, nobody set off rockets in the parks, much less on the street in front of your house to announce to the neighborhood that a wedding or a baptism was taking place. Sacramento did not have a *mercado* and a plaza with the cathedral to one side and the Palacio de Gobierno on another to make it obvious that there and nowhere else was the center of the town.

It was just as puzzling that the Americans did not live in *vecindades*, like our block on Leandro Valle. Even in the alleys, where people knew one another better, the houses were fenced apart, without central courts to wash clothes, talk, and play with the other children. Like the city, the Sacramento *barrio* did not have a place which was the middle of things for everyone.

In more personal ways, we had to get used to the Americans. They did not listen if you did not speak loudly, as they always did. In the Mexican style, people would know that you were enjoying their jokes tremendously if you merely smiled and shook a little, as if you were trying to swallow your mirth. In the American style, there was little difference between a laugh and a roar, and until you got used to them you could hardly tell whether the boisterous Americans were roaring mad or roaring happy.

The older people of the *barrio*, except in those things which they had to do like the Americans because they had no choice, remained Mexican. Their language at home was Spanish. They were continuously taking up collections to pay somebody's funeral expenses or to help someone who had had a serious accident. Cards were sent to you to attend a burial where you would throw a handful of dirt on top of the coffin and listen to tearful speeches at the graveside. At every baptism, a new *compadre* and a new *comadre* joined the family circle. New Year greeting cards were exchanged, showing angels and cherubs in bright colors sprinkled with grains of mica so that they glistened like gold dust. At the family parties the huge pot of steaming tamales was still the center of attention, the *atole* served on the side with chunks of brown sugar for sucking and crunching. If the party lasted long enough, someone produced a guitar; the men took over and the singing of *corridos* began.

In the *barrio* there were no individuals who had official titles or who were otherwise recognized by everybody as important people. The reason must have been that there was no place in the public business of the city of Sacramento for the Mexican immigrants. We only rented a corner of the city and as long as we paid the rent on time everything else was decided at City Hall or the County Court House, where Mexicans went only when they were in trouble. Nobody from the *barrio* ever ran for mayor or city council-man. For us, the most important public officials were the policemen who walked their beats, stopped fights, and hauled drunks to jail in a paddy wagon we called *La Julia*.

7   The one institution we had that gave the *colonia* some kind of image was the *Comisión Honorífica*, a committee picked by the Mexican Consul in San Francisco to organize the celebration of the *Cinco de Mayo* and the Sixteenth of September, the anniversaries of the battle of Puebla and the beginning of our War of Independence. These were the two events which stirred everyone in the *barrio*, for what we were celebrating was not only the heroes of Mexico but also the feeling that we were still Mexicans our-selves. On these occasions, there was a dance preceded by speeches and a concert. For both the *cinco* and the sixteenth, queens were elected to preside over the ceremonies.

8   Between celebrations, neither the politicians uptown nor the *Comisión Honorífica* attended to the daily needs of the *barrio*. This was done by volunteers—the ones who knew enough English to interpret in court, on a visit to the doctor, a call at the county hospital, and who could help make out a postal money order. By the time I had finished the third grade at the Lincoln School, I was one of these volunteers. My services were not profes-sional, but they were free, except for the IOU's I accumulated from families who always thanked me with "God will pay you for it."

9   My clients were not *pochos*, Mexicans who had grown up in California, probably had even been born in the United States. They had learned to speak English of sorts and could still speak Spanish, also of sorts. They knew much more about the Americans than we did, and much less about us. The *chicanos* and the *pochos* had certain feelings about one another. Concerning the *pochos*, the *chicanos* suspected that they considered them-selves too good for the *barrio* but were not, for some reason, good enough for the Americans. Toward the *chicanos*, the *pochos* acted superior, amused at our confusions but not especially interested in explaining them to us. In our family, when I forgot my manners, my mother would ask me if I was turning *pochito*.

10   Turning *pocho* was a half-step toward turning American. And America was all around us, in and out of the *barrio*. Abruptly we had to forget the ways of shopping in a *mercado* and learn those of shopping in a corner grocery or in a department store. The Americans paid no attention to the Sixteenth of September, but they made a great commotion about the Fourth of July. In Mazatlán, Don Salvador had told us, saluting and march-ing as he talked to our class, that the *Cinco de Mayo* was the most glorious date in human history. The Americans had not even heard about it.

Thinking Critically About Content

1. Explain three differences between American and Latin American customs.

2. What difference between these customs is most interesting to you? Why?

3. What does Galarza mean when he says, "Turning *pocho* was a half-step toward turning American" (paragraph 10)?

Thinking Critically About Purpose and Audience

4. What is Galarza's purpose in writing this essay?

5. Who do you think is his primary audience?

6. Why does Galarza call his essay "The Barrio"? What is his point of view toward the barrio?

Thinking Critically About Paragraphs

7. Explain how the topic sentence works in paragraph 4. Does it supply the controlling idea for the entire paragraph?

8. Choose a paragraph from this essay, and underline all of its transitional words and phrases. Do these transitions help move the reader through the paragraph? Explain your answer. (Refer to pages 46–47 for information on transitions.)

9. Galarza sprinkles Spanish words throughout his essay. What effect does the addition of Spanish words have on the essay?

10. Write a paragraph responding to some of Galarza's observations. What are some of his confusions?

Rachel Carson

A FABLE FOR TOMORROW

Focusing Your Attention

1. What do you find most appealing about your immediate environment outside? Are any of these natural elements in danger from pollution or general misuse?

2. In the essay you are about to read, the author warns us through a fable that we are destroying our environment day by day. What activities do you see in your area that are destructive to the planet? What activities do you see that are constructive?

Expanding Your Vocabulary

The following words are important to your understanding of this essay.

prosperous: wealthy (paragraph 1)

migrants: birds flying between their summer and winter nesting places (paragraph 2)

blight: disease (paragraph 3)

maladies: illnesses (paragraph 3)

moribund: approaching death (paragraph 4)

droned: buzzed (paragraph 5)

anglers: fishermen (paragraph 6)

granular: grainy (paragraph 7)

specter: ghost (paragraph 9)

stark: bleak, grim (paragraph 9)

1   There was once a town in the heart of America where all life seemed to live in harmony with its surroundings. The town lay in the midst of a checkerboard of prosperous farms, with fields of grain and hillsides of orchards where, in spring, white clouds of bloom drifted above the green fields. In autumn, oak and maple and birch set up a blaze of color that flamed and flickered across a backdrop of pines. Then foxes barked in the hills and deer silently crossed the fields, half hidden in the mists of the fall mornings.

2   Along the roads, laurel, viburnum and alder, great ferns and wildflowers delighted the traveler's eye through much of the year. Even in winter the roadsides were places of beauty, where countless birds came to feed on the berries and on the seed heads of the dried weeds rising above the snow. The countryside was, in fact, famous for the abundance and variety of its bird life, and when the flood of migrants was pouring through in spring and fall, people traveled from great distances to observe them. Others came to fish the streams, which flowed clear and cold out of the hills and contained shady pools where trout lay. So it had been from the days many years ago when the first settlers raised their houses, sank their wells, and built their barns.

3   Then a strange blight crept over the area and everything began to change. Some evil spell had settled on the community; mysterious maladies swept the flocks of chickens; the cattle and sheep sickened and died. Everywhere was a shadow of death. The farmers spoke of much illness among their families. In the town, the doctors had become more and more

puzzled by new kinds of sickness appearing among their patients. There had been several sudden and unexplained deaths not only among adults but even among children, who would be stricken suddenly while at play and die within a few hours.

There was a strange stillness. The birds, for example—where had they 4 gone? Many people spoke of them, puzzled and disturbed. The feeding stations in the backyards were deserted. The few birds seen anywhere were moribund; they trembled violently and could not fly. It was a spring without voices. On the mornings that had once throbbed with the dawn chorus of robins, catbirds, doves, jays, wrens, and scores of other bird voices, there was now no sound; only silence lay over the fields and woods and marsh.

On the farms the hens brooded, but no chicks hatched. The farmers 5 complained that they were unable to raise any pigs—the litters were small, and the young survived only a few days. The apple trees were coming into bloom but no bees droned among the blossoms, so there was no pollination and there would be no fruit.

The roadsides, once so attractive, were now lined with browned and 6 withered vegetation as though swept by fire. These, too, were silent, deserted by all living things. Even the streams were now lifeless. Anglers no longer visited them, for all the fish had died.

In the gutters under the eaves and between the shingles of the roofs, a 7 white granular powder still showed a few patches; some weeks before it had fallen like snow upon the roofs and the lawns, the fields and streams.

No witchcraft, no enemy action had silenced the rebirth of new life in 8 this stricken world. The people had done it themselves.

This town does not actually exist, but it might easily have a thousand 9 counterparts in America or elsewhere in the world. I know of no community that has experienced all the misfortunes I describe. Yet every one of these disasters has actually happened somewhere, and many real communities have already suffered a substantial number of them. A grim specter has crept upon us almost unnoticed, and this imagined tragedy may easily become a stark reality we all shall know.

Thinking Critically About Content

1. What do you think Carson means by the reference to all life living "in harmony with its surroundings" (paragraph 1)?

2. What is the "grim specter" that has "crept upon us almost unnoticed" (paragraph 9)? Why is the author so concerned about this specter?

3. Do you see any evidence of Carson's concerns in your immediate environment? Explain your answer.

Thinking Critically About Purpose and Audience

4. Why do you think Carson wrote this essay?

5. Who would be most interested in this essay?

6. How does this essay make you feel about the environment in the United States?

Thinking Critically About Paragraphs

7. What examples does Carson use in paragraph 4 to explain her topic sentence? Do these examples get her point across in this paragraph?

8. If a paragraph is unified, all of its sentences refer to the idea expressed in the topic sentence. In paragraph 2, four sentences follow the topic sentence. How do these four sentences relate to the paragraph's topic sentence?

9. Carson begins her essay like a fable and keeps that stance through the entire essay. Is the fable a good format for her message? Explain your answer.

10. Write a short fable about an environmental issue. It can be either a positive or a negative story.

Writing Topics: Comparing and Contrasting

Before you begin to write, you might want to review the writing process in Part I.

1. In the first essay, Ernesto Galarza talks about the differences he sees on a daily basis between two cultures. Compare and contrast your family's rituals and practices with those of another family.

2. Expand the fable you wrote in response to question 10 after Rachel Carson's essay by adding more characters and more examples.

3. What process do you have to go through to come up with an interesting comparison or contrast? How is it different from the process you go through for other rhetorical modes?

DIVIDING AND CLASSIFYING

CHAPTER 26

The essays that follow show both division and classification at work. The first, "Rapport: How to Ignite It" by Camille Lavington, divides and classifies types of people. In the second, "Categories of Time Use," Edwin Bliss breaks common tasks into five categories.

Camille Lavington
RAPPORT: HOW TO IGNITE IT

Focusing Your Attention

1. Do you get along easily with others? Do you like different types of people?

2. The essay you are about to read classifies the different personality traits in people. What are your dominant personality traits? What impression do you usually make on people? How do you know you make this particular impression?

Expanding Your Vocabulary

The following words are important to your understanding of this essay.

rapport: chemistry between people (title)

reticent: reserved, shy (paragraph 2)

Henry Kissinger: U.S. secretary of state during the Nixon administration (paragraph 2)

out of sync: out of step, out of alignment (paragraph 2)

persona: image, public identity (paragraph 2)

affinity: liking, attraction (paragraph 4)

endowed: gifted (paragraph 4)

remedied: fixed, corrected (paragraph 6)

hyperactive: energetic (paragraph 9)

intrusive: pushy (paragraph 9)

paradoxically: surprisingly, contrary to what was expected (paragraph 9)

reservoir: supply (paragraph 9)

eliciting: bringing forth, drawing out (paragraph 13)

vogue: trend, fad, style (paragraph 13)

osmosis: effortless learning, absorption (paragraph 17)

ESP: intuition, insight (paragraph 17)

cosmic: coming from the universe (paragraph 17)

charismatic: charming (paragraph 17)

nonconformity: difference from the norm (paragraph 17)

prudent: cautious (paragraph 21)

affluent: wealthy (paragraph 22)

monster: huge (paragraph 23)

superiority complex: the feeling that one is more important than other people (paragraph 23)

frivolities: matters of little importance (paragraph 23)

cerebral: intellectual (paragraph 24)

stick-in-the-mud: an old-fashioned or unprogressive person (paragraph 24)

from the heart: based on emotion (paragraph 25)

from the gut: based on intuition or insight rather than reason (paragraph 25)

empathetic: kindly, sensitive to the feelings of others (paragraph 25)

modified: adapted, changed (paragraph 25)

got strokes: was praised or rewarded (paragraph 25)

spontaneous: impulsive (paragraph 26)

all is not hearts and flowers: the situation is not entirely positive (paragraph 26)

psychoanalyze: try to explain the thoughts and emotions of others (paragraph 26)

benchmarks: criteria, milestones, points of reference (paragraph 29)

It happens in a flash, based entirely on surface cues, but people use   1
first impressions to make sometimes irreversible judgments.

So don't be reticent about the talent you've been given. It's your obliga-   2
tion to share it with the world, and your personality is the driving force
behind your talent. As Henry Kissinger once said, history is fueled not by
impersonal forces, but by personalities. If yours is out of sync, it may need
some work. That doesn't mean adopting a phony persona; it simply means
adjusting your communicating style in order to relate better to others.

Understanding your own personality makes it easier to spot someone   3
with whom you'd like to connect. There are simple signs that signal personality types, and you can recognize them—even in strangers.

We are all a combination of many personality traits, but most people   4
have a stronger affinity for one. Or you may be one of those rarely gifted
individuals who are *evenly* endowed in *every* style.

Introverts are deep thinkers who prefer time alone to read, or stare at   5
their computer screens, or gaze into outer space. They strive for, and
appreciate, excellence. Ironically, introverts often have meaningful friendships. These are their positive qualities. But, as with all personality types,
there are negative aspects: Introverts have a tendency to be suspicious
and worried. Introverts can also be intellectual snobs who are unaccepting
of others and perfectionists to a fault. They may be self-centered and have
friends who are jealous of them.

Much of introversion is caused by shyness and lack of experience. Of all   6
the personality traits, I think that introversion is the one characteristic that
most needs to be remedied. Why? Introversion borders on selfishness. By
hanging back during interactions with others, introverts are protecting
themselves. A conversation is like a canoe that requires the exertion of both
participants to keep moving forward; an introvert isn't engaging his pad-
dle. It's everyone's job to contribute to relationships and to make others
comfortable.

Extroverts aren't perfect, but society tends to reward their behavior.   7
They have many good qualities, including their friendliness and magnet-
ism. Energetic and sparkling, they inspire others. They like people, variety,
and action. Extroverts like to chat a lot. They get their energy from other
people.

You won't see an extrovert going to the movies alone, eating dinner   8
alone, taking a vacation alone. Extroverts are born leaders. It should come
as no surprise that most CEOs and politicians are extroverts.

Still, extroverts can be hyperactive and intrusive. They need to be the   9
center of attention at all times, and have a habit of boasting. They're looking
for a vote of confidence from the outside, even if they have to solicit it.

Paradoxically, this is sometimes because they don't tap into their own reservoir of strength and thus haven't learned their own value.

10   The easiest way to achieve rapport with others is to remember that time together is either a learning or an entertaining experience. With this attitude, you'll always be eager to draw people into any dialogue by inviting them to add a comment or an opinion—rather than draining other people's energy by dominating or shortchanging the conversation.

11   Lock two extroverts in a room, and each will complain that the other is a poor conversationalist. (An extrovert thinks a good conversationalist is someone who is interested in what *he* has to say.)

12   **Sensers** are just-the-facts people, and they get that way by using their objective senses, rather than their intuition, to gather information. A senser relies on his eyes and ears for clues. Practical and bottom-line oriented, sensers are doers who want action and want it now. They are competitive and highly organized, and they set high standards for themselves.

13   Sensers are master manipulators who have a talent for eliciting the response they want from people; many actors, comedians, and salespeople are sensers for just that reason. Sensers prefer to wear comfortable clothing, but peer pressure means so much to them that they will give in to the current vogue and wear what people they admire are wearing.

14   On the negative side, sensers can be self-involved, arrogant, and status-seeking. They tend to act first and think later. Also, they can be domineering and lacking in trust.

15   Sometimes you will be thrown off by a senser's easygoing manner because of his sense of humor, but don't waste his time. Get to the point quickly; remember that he's action-oriented and looking for short-term personal gain. If you have no previous knowledge about his temperament, take a look around for clues. A senser decorates his walls and bookshelves with personal trophies and memorabilia that remind him of his conquests.

16   You will lose points if you ever try to upstage a senser. This type, of all of the others, wants to be the center of interest, as indicated by all of the personal trophies on his walls.

17   **Intuitors** make up a scant 10% of the population. So you're dealing with a rare bird. Albert Einstein is the classic intuitor—a genius who didn't speak until he was six years old. Intuitors gather information through a sort of osmosis, absorbing ESP signals and cosmic energy. Creative, imaginative, and original, they are driven by inspiration and a powerful intellect. Intuitors see the big picture in spite of a tenuous grasp of the details. Intuitors can be quite charismatic, although they tend to be unaware of their effect on people. They are also magnets to each other—finding their

counterparts in the arts, sciences, wherever. Their nonconformity makes them dress in unusual combinations. In fact, they'll wear anything.

On the other hand, intuitors can drive others to madness. At times 18 they're unrealistic and impractical. They're allergic to focusing on details. Fantasy-bound, they can be long on vision and short on action.

To approach an intuitor, spark her curiosity. When picking the brain of 19 an intuitor, ask her to problem-solve without following any rules. You want to hear her unedited ideas.

If you're trying to impress an intuitor, don't waste time. You'll lose her 20 attention if you give her a lot of background. Instead, respect her right-brain ability to jump to the heart of the matter in a flash.

Thinkers are the mainstay of society. They make life better because of 21 their strong work ethic and high standards. Deliberate, prudent, and objective thinkers dwell in the world of rationality and analysis. Thinkers like to sleep on it. Many are effective communicators, possibly because they consider carefully before they speak. They make good jurors, who wait until closing arguments are concluded before weighing the evidence carefully. Their checkbooks are balanced.

Thinkers tend to like tailored, conservative clothing. If they're affluent, 22 they have a tie that shows they met the rigid qualifications for entry to a top-ranked school. Teaching is a profession often favored by thinkers.

Thinkers can get trapped in their love of analysis, becoming overcau- 23 tious and indecisive. They can be frustrating in a relationship by being too rigid, impersonal, and unemotional. Some of them walk around with monster superiority complexes, trying at every turn to prove they're smarter than others. Some don't care how they look, because they're trying to send a message: *I have too big a brain to concern myself with frivolities like appearance.* But they're not out to hurt anyone; they forget their own feelings as well as the feelings of others. Thinkers often forget to stop and smell the roses.

These cerebral types can sound like sticks-in-the-mud, but don't take 24 them lightly. Some of the finest minds in the world fall into this category. Put this trait together with extroversion and you've got one remarkable leader.

Feelers operate from the heart and the gut. They're warm and always 25 observing interactions among people and interpreting them: *Why didn't she invite me to that meeting? Was that look he gave me a sign of disapproval?* Feelers read between the lines. They are nurturing and empathetic. Their need for an emotional response can have an odd side effect: Whatever childhood behavior got attention from their parents is the one they'll pursue in a modified form as adults—so a feeler child who got strokes for bringing home straight A's will turn into a feeler adult who works overtime at the office.

26   Feelers are not trendsetters; they are more comfortable in the mainstream, following traditional values. They like colorful clothes that reflect their emotions. They are loyal, spontaneous, and persuasive. But all is not hearts and flowers. Feelers overreact and get defensive if things don't go their way. Their need to psychoanalyze everyone gets them into trouble as they over-personalize every interaction, stirring up conflict. Some are guilt-ridden, ruled by thoughts of what they've done wrong.

27   **Judges** aren't any more judgmental than the rest of us. Any personality type can be judgmental.

28   If you are a judge, you like to think you have some control over life. Judges are structured and organized; they want to finish things and move along. They set standards for themselves and for others and follow them. Judges are surprised every time someone fails to live up to his or her agreement, as if that were unusual. Judges set goals and meet them—thriving on the resulting sense of closure.

29   Dealing with a judge is simple: Make a commitment, and live up to it. Set goals, and use benchmarks to measure your performance by objective standards. Fail to meet a judge's expectations of you, and you'll travel a rocky road.

30   **Perceivers** are always receptive to more information or stimulation before acting. They take each day as it comes and don't kick themselves for letting chores slide into tomorrow. Perceivers generally grew up in either an unstructured environment or a very structured one against which they rebel as adults. These people can be very kind to others because they're kind to themselves. They don't become angry because you're late or take offense if you ask them a personal question. They see life as a process. A lot of artistic people fall into this category.

31   Pressure tactics just don't work with perceivers, but perceivers are so easy to be around that they are certainly worth rewarding with a little patience.

32   Once you've discovered what makes the other person tick—which traits are getting in the way of good communication between the two of you—then you have to decide what to do with that information.

Thinking Critically About Content

1. What are the eight different personality types that Lavington outlines in her essay?

2. Are these personality traits evenly distributed in you, or is one dominant? Explain your answer.

3. Do you agree with Lavington when she says, "Don't be reticent about the talent you've been given. It's your obligation to share it with the world" (paragraph 2)?

Thinking Critically About Purpose and Audience

4. What do you think Lavington's purpose is in this essay?

5. Who do you think is her primary audience?

6. When did you last make an important judgment based on a first impression of someone? Was your impression fairly accurate?

Thinking Critically About Paragraphs

7. Explain how the topic sentence works in paragraph 7. Does it supply the controlling idea for the entire paragraph? Are the other sentences in this paragraph related to the topic sentence?

8. Why do you think Lavington discusses these personality types in this particular order? What is her rationale for moving from one type to the next?

9. How does Lavington start her essay? Is it effective?

10. Write an alternative conclusion to Lavington's essay.

Edwin Bliss

CATEGORIES OF TIME USE

Focusing Your Attention

1. Do you use your time wisely? Where could you improve your time management skills?

2. In the essay you are about to read, the author lays out five categories of tasks for organizing our daily lives. These categories will help you realize that each chore and activity in your life has a different status. Do you find that you get to all the tasks that you need to complete in a particular day? Or do you procrastinate beyond your deadlines? Explain your answer.

Expanding Your Vocabulary

The following words are important to your understanding of this essay.

escalated: increased rapidly (footnote to paragraph 2)

simultaneously: at the same time (paragraph 3)

precedence: priority (paragraph 3)
preliminary: initial, beginning (paragraph 6)
clamor: shout (paragraph 8)
marginally: only slightly (paragraph 10)
diversionary: distracting (paragraph 10)
subjective: differing from person to person (paragraph 13)
Ernest Hemingway: 1899–1961, an American writer (paragraph 14)
theological: related to religion (paragraph 14)
scrutiny: inspection, examination (paragraph 14)
in vain: without success (paragraph 15)
allocating: assigning (paragraph 15)

1   *Tasks* can be broken down into five categories:

1. Important and Urgent
2. Important but Not Urgent
3. Urgent but Not Important
4. Busy Work
5. Wasted Time

1. Important and Urgent

2   These are the tasks that *must* be done immediately or in the near future. Examples: Your boss demands a certain report by 10 A.M. tomorrow. Or your engine blows a gasket. Or the labor pains are three minutes apart. Or it's April 15, and you haven't finished your income tax form.*

3   Now, unless these situations all develop simultaneously (God forbid!), you can cope with them. Because of their urgency and their importance, they take precedence over everything else, and procrastination is out of the question. It is not here that we find our time management problems.

2. Important but Not Urgent

4   Attention to this category is what divides effective individuals from ineffective ones.

---

*This is an example of a task that began in Category 2 and escalated to Category 1 now that you have reached the deadline.

Most of the really important things in our lives are not urgent. They can   5
be done now or later. In many cases they can be postponed forever, and in
too many cases they are. These are the things we "never get around to."

Examples: that special course you want to take to upgrade your profes-   6
sional skills; that new project you would like to suggest to your boss after
you find time to do the preliminary fact-finding; that article you've been
meaning to write; that diet you've intended to begin; that annual medical
checkup you've planned to get for the past three years; that visit to a
lawyer to have your will drawn; that retirement program you've been
planning to establish.

All of these tasks have one thing in common: Despite their importance,   7
affecting as they do your health, your wealth, and your family's welfare,
they will be postponed indefinitely unless you yourself initiate action. If
your activities are keyed to other people's priorities or to system-imposed
deadlines that make things "urgent," you will never get around to your
own priorities.

3. Urgent but Not Important

In this category are those things that clamor for immediate action but   8
that we would assign a low priority if we examined them objectively.

For example, someone asks you to chair a fund drive or to give a   9
speech or to attend a meeting. You might consider each of these low priority, but someone is standing in front of you waiting for an answer and you
accept because you cannot think of a graceful way to decline. Then,
because these tasks have built-in time limits, they get done, while
Category 2 items get moved to the back burner.

4. Busy Work

There are many tasks that are marginally worth doing but are neither   10
urgent nor important. We often do them ahead of more important things
because they are *diversionary*—they provide a feeling of activity and
accomplishment while giving us an excuse to put off tackling those
Category 2 tasks that have a far greater benefit.

One aerospace executive, for example, told me of going to his office   11
the previous Saturday morning to do some work he had been postponing.
He decided first to organize the materials on his desk. Having done so, he
decided that while he was at it he might as well straighten up the desk
drawers. He spent the rest of the morning reorganizing drawers and files.

"I left the office feeling vaguely disappointed that I hadn't accomplished   12
what I went in for," he said, "but I consoled myself with the thought that I

had been very busy doing some worthwhile things. I realize now that I was playing games with myself—working on low-priority tasks to give myself an excuse for further delay on the far more essential task I originally had assigned myself."

5. Wasted Time

13   The definition of wasted time is subjective, of course.

14   Ernest Hemingway is quoted as having defined "immoral" as "anything you feel bad after." I don't know whether that definition will stand up to theological scrutiny, but I do think it can be applied to wasted time. Television viewing, for example, can be time well spent if we come away feeling that we have been enlightened or entertained. But if afterward we feel that the time would have been better spent mowing the lawn or playing tennis or reading a good book, then we can chalk up that time as wasted.*

15   People who scramble madly to get control of their time often look in vain for things in this category upon which to blame their inefficiency. I am convinced, however, that with most people this is not where the problem lies. It lies rather with allocating too much time to things in Categories 3 and 4 rather than to those in Category 2.

*By any sane person's standards, about 95 percent of all television viewing must be put in this category, which is something to think about the next time you reach for that remote control.

Thinking Critically About Content

1. Explain Bliss's five categories of time use.

2. Based on Bliss's explanation, do you complete Category 2 tasks in a timely manner? Explain your answer.

3. List the tasks you perform in a typical day, and classify each in terms of Bliss's categories. Do his categories cover all of your tasks? Would you add any other categories to his essay? Explain your answer.

Thinking Critically About Purpose and Audience

4. Why do you think Bliss wrote this essay?

5. Who would be most interested in this essay?

6. Does this essay make you feel more or less stressed than you already do about time management? Explain your answer.

Thinking Critically About Paragraphs

7. What examples does Bliss use to explain Category 5? Add two more examples to this list.

8. Underline five transitions in the final three paragraphs. Then explain how they make the discussion of Category 5 smooth and coherent. (Refer to pages 46–47 for more information on transitions.)

9. Choose one paragraph, and decide whether or not it has enough details. Explain your answer.

10. Write an alternate introduction to Bliss's essay.

Writing Topics: Dividing and Classifying

Before you begin to write, you might want to review the writing process in Part I.

1. In the first essay, Camille Lavington divides and classifies the personality types she sees in the human race. Using her essay as a reference, explain what category you fit into and why you fit there.

2. Using Edwin Bliss's categories, divide a typical week of your homework into categories. Then explain each category.

3. How do division and classification work together? Refer to one of the reading assignments in Chapter 26 to respond to this question.

DEFINING

Here are two essays that show how definition works in the context of a full essay. "Workers" by Richard Rodriguez provides a clear definition of who workers are and what real work is. The second essay, "What Is Poverty?" by Jo Goodwin Parker, defines poverty from the author's personal experience.

Richard Rodriguez

WORKERS

Focusing Your Attention

1. Do you think different types of people are attracted to different types of jobs? What kind of job are you attracted to?

2. The essay you are about to read discusses laborers. Have you ever done hard labor? Did you work with other people? What kind of work did you do? How did you fit in?

Expanding Your Vocabulary

The following words are important to your understanding of this essay.

Stanford: a prestigious university near Palo Alto, California (paragraph 1)

uncoiled: unwound (paragraph 1)

menial: low, uninteresting, and undignified (paragraph 1)

Princeton: a prestigious university in New Jersey (paragraph 4)

skepticism: doubt, suspicion (paragraph 4)

bracero: contracted seasonal Mexican farm laborer brought into the United States (paragraph 4)

tedious: tiresome, boring (paragraph 5)

ember: hot piece of ash or coal (paragraph 5)

luxuriating in: enjoying (paragraph 5)

exotics: foreigners (paragraph 9)

subdued: hesitant, lacking intensity (paragraph 9)

Mark Rothko: 1923–1970, contemporary artist (paragraph 9)

oppressed: exploited, forced to suffer (paragraph 9)

los pobres: poor people (paragraph 9)

aliens: noncitizens (paragraph 10)

debris: rubbish (paragraph 10)

fatalistic: accepting, unresisting (paragraph 10)

patrón: boss (paragraph 12)

gringo: white man (paragraph 16)

ludicrous: laughable, foolish (paragraph 16)

torso: upper body (paragraph 17)

parody: caricature, similar but amusing image (paragraph 17)

dandy: a man who pays excessive attention to his appearance (paragraph 18)

taunts: criticisms, insults (paragraph 18)

gaudy: flashy (paragraph 18)

nouveau riche: newly rich people often lacking in social refinement (paragraph 18)

masque: costume party (paragraph 19)

unionize: organize into a labor union (paragraph 21)

uncanny: eerie, mysterious (paragraph 23)

pathos: pity (paragraph 23)

It was at Stanford, one day near the end of my senior year, that a friend 1
told me about a summer construction job he knew was available. I was
quickly alert. Desire uncoiled within me. My friend said that he knew I had
been looking for summer employment. He knew I needed some money.
Almost apologetically he explained: It was something I probably wouldn't
be interested in, but a friend of his, a contractor, needed someone for the
summer to do menial jobs. There would be lots of shoveling and raking
and sweeping. Nothing too hard. But nothing more interesting either. Still,
the pay would be good. Did I want it? Or did I know someone who did?

2   I did. Yes, I said, surprised to hear myself say it.

3   In the weeks following, friends cautioned that I had no idea how hard physical labor really is. ("You only *think* you know what it is like to shovel for eight hours straight.") Their objections seemed to me challenges. They resolved the issue. I became happy with my plan. I decided, however, not to tell my parents. I wouldn't tell my mother because I could guess her worried reaction. I would tell my father only after the summer was over, when I could announce that, after all, I did know what "real work" is like.

4   The day I met the contractor (a Princeton graduate, it turned out), he asked me whether I had done any physical labor before. "In high school, during the summer," I lied. And although he seemed to regard me with skepticism, he decided to give me a try. Several days later, expectant, I arrived at my first construction site. I would take off my shirt to the sun. And at last grasp desired sensation. No longer afraid. At last become like a *bracero*. "We need those tree stumps out of here by tomorrow," the contractor said. I started to work.

5   I labored with excitement that first morning—and all the days after. The work was harder than I could have expected. But it was never as tedious as my friends had warned me it would be. There was too much physical pleasure in the labor. Especially early in the day, I would be most alert to the sensations of movement and straining. Beginning around seven each morning (when the air was still damp but the scent of weeds and dry earth anticipated the heat of the sun), I would feel my body resist the first thrusts of the shovel. My arms, tightened by sleep, would gradually loosen; after only several minutes, sweat would gather in beads on my forehead and then—a short while later—I would feel my chest silky with sweat in the breeze. I would return to my work. A nervous spark of pain would fly up my arm and settle to burn like an ember in the thick of my shoulder. An hour, two passed. Three. My whole body would assume regular movements; my shoveling would be described by identical, even movements. Even later in the day, my enthusiasm for primitive sensation would survive the heat and the dust and the insects pricking my back. I would strain wildly for sensation as the day came to a close. At three-thirty, quitting time, I would stand upright and slowly let my head fall back, luxuriating in the feeling of tightness relieved.

6   Some of the men working nearby would watch me and laugh. Two or three of the older men took the trouble to teach me the right way to use a pick, the correct way to shovel. "You're doing it wrong, too . . . hard," one man scolded. Then proceeded to show me—what persons who work with their bodies all their lives quickly learn—the most economical way to use one's body in labor.

"Don't make your back do so much work," he instructed. I stood impa-   7
tiently listening, half listening, vaguely watching, then noticed his work-
thickened fingers clutching the shovel. I was annoyed. I wanted to tell him
that I enjoyed shoveling the wrong way. And I didn't want to learn the right
way. I wasn't afraid of back pain. I liked the way my body felt sore at the
end of the day.

I was about to, but, as it turned out, I didn't say a thing. Rather it was at   8
that moment I realized that I was fooling myself if I expected a few weeks of
labor to gain me admission to the world of the laborer. I would not learn in
three months what my father had meant by "real work." I was not bound to
this job; I could imagine its rapid conclusion. For me, the sensations were to
be feared. Fatigue took a different toll on their bodies—and minds.

It was, I know, a simple insight. But it was with this realization that I took   9
my first step that summer toward realizing something even more important
about the "worker." In the company of carpenters, electricians, plumbers,
and painters at lunch, I would often sit quietly, observant. I was not shy in
such company. I felt easy, pleased by the knowledge that I was casually
accepted, my presence taken for granted by men (exotics) who worked
with their hands. Some days the younger men would talk and talk about
sex, and they would howl at women who drove by in cars. Other days the
talk at lunchtime was subdued; men gathered in separate groups. It
depended on who was around. There were rough, good-natured workers.
Others were quiet. The more I remember that summer, the more I realize
that there was no single *type* of worker. I am embarrassed to say I had not
expected such diversity. I certainly had not expected to meet, for example,
a plumber who was an abstract painter in his off hours and admired the
work of Mark Rothko. Nor did I expect to meet so many workers with college
diplomas. (They were the ones who were not surprised that I intended to
enter graduate school in the fall.) I suppose what I really want to say here
is painfully obvious, but I must say it nevertheless: The men of that summer
were middle-class Americans. They certainly didn't constitute an
oppressed society. Carefully completing their work sheets, talking about
the fortunes of local football teams, planning Las Vegas vacations, comparing the gas mileage of various makes of campers—they were not *los
pobres* my mother had spoken about.

On two occasions, the contractor hired a group of Mexican aliens. They   10
were employed to cut down some trees and haul off debris. In all, there
were six men of varying age. The youngest in his late twenties; the oldest
(his father?) perhaps sixty years old. They came and they left in a single old
truck. Anonymous men. They were never introduced to the other men at
the site. Immediately upon their arrival, they would follow the contractor's

directions, start working—rarely resting—seemingly driven by a fatalistic sense that work which had to be done was best done as quickly as possible.

11   I watched them sometimes. Perhaps they watched me. The only time I saw them pay me much notice was one day at lunchtime when I was laughing with the other men. The Mexicans sat apart when they ate, just as they worked by themselves. Quiet. I rarely heard them say much to each other. All I could hear were their voices calling out sharply to one another, giving directions. Otherwise, when they stood briefly resting, they talked among themselves in voices too hard to overhear.

12   The contractor knew enough Spanish, and the Mexicans—or at least the oldest of them, their spokesman—seemed to know enough English to communicate. But because I was around, the contractor decided one day to make me his translator. (He assumed I could speak Spanish.) I did what I was told. Shyly I went over to tell the Mexicans that the *patrón* wanted them to do something else before they left for the day. As I started to speak, I was afraid with my old fear that I would be unable to pronounce the Spanish words. But it was a simple instruction I had to convey. I could say it in phrases.

13   The dark sweating faces turned toward me as I spoke. They stopped their work to hear me. Each nodded in response. I stood there. I wanted to say something more. But what could I say in Spanish, even if I could have pronounced the words right? Perhaps I just wanted to engage them in small talk, to be assured of their confidence, our familiarity. I thought for a moment to ask them where in Mexico they were from. Something like that. And maybe I wanted to tell them (a lie, if need be) that my parents were from the same part of Mexico.

14   I stood there.

15   Their faces watched me. The eyes of the man directly in front of me moved slowly over my shoulder, and I turned to follow his glance toward *el patrón* some distance away. For a moment I felt swept up by that glance into the Mexicans' company. But then I heard one of them returning to work. And then the others went back to work. I left them without saying anything more.

16   When they had finished, the contractor went over to pay them in cash. (He later told me that he paid them collectively—"for the job," though he wouldn't tell me their wages. He said something quickly about the good rate of exchange "in their own country.") I can still hear the loudly confident voice he used with the Mexicans. It was the sound of the *gringo* I had heard as a very young boy. And I can still hear the quiet, indistinct sounds of the Mexican, the oldest, who replied. At hearing that voice, I was sad for

the Mexicans. Depressed by their vulnerability. Angry at myself. The adventure of the summer seemed suddenly ludicrous. I would not shorten the distance I felt from *los pobres* with a few weeks of physical labor. I would not become like them. They were different from me.

After that summer, a great deal—and not very much really—changed 17 in my life. The curse of physical shame was broken by the sun; I was no longer ashamed of my body. No longer would I deny myself the pleasing sensations of my maleness. During those years when middle-class black Americans began to assert with pride "Black is beautiful," I was able to regard my complexion without shame. I am today darker than I ever was as a boy. I have taken up the middle-class sport of long-distance running. Nearly every day now I run 10 or 15 miles, barely clothed, my skin exposed to the California winter rain and wind or the summer sun of late afternoon. The torso, the soccer player's calves and thighs, the arms of the twenty-year-old I never was, I possess now in my thirties. I study the youthful parody shape in the mirror: the stomach lipped tight by muscle; the shoulders rounded by chin-ups; the arms veined strong. This man. A man. I meet him. He laughs to see me, what I have become.

The dandy. I wear double-breasted Italian suits and custom-made 18 English shoes. I resemble no one so much as my father—the man pictured in those honeymoon photos. At that point in life when he abandoned the dandy's posture, I assume it. At the point when my parents would not consider going on vacation, I register at the Hotel Carlyle in New York and the Plaza Athénée in Paris. I am as taken by the symbols of leisure and wealth as they were. For my parents, however, those symbols became taunts, reminders of all they could not achieve in one lifetime. For me, those same symbols are reassuring reminders of public success. I tempt vulgarity to be reassured. I am filled with the gaudy delight, the monstrous grace of the nouveau riche.

In recent years, I have had occasion to lecture in ghetto high schools. 19 There I see students of remarkable style and physical grace. (One can see more dandies in such schools than one ever will find in middle-class high schools.) There is not the look of casual assurance I saw students at Stanford display. Ghetto girls mimic high-fashion models. Their dresses are of bold, forceful color; their figures elegant, long; the stance theatrical. Boys wear shirts that grip at their overdeveloped muscular bodies. (Against a powerless future, they engage images of strength.) Bad nutrition does not yet tell. Great disappointment, fatal to youth, awaits them still. For the moment, movements in school hallways are dancelike, a procession of postures in a sexual masque. Watching them, I feel a kind of envy. I wonder how different my adolescence would have been had I been free. . . . But no, it is my parents I see—their optimism during those years when they were entertained by Italian grand opera.

20   The registration clerk in London wonders if I have just been to Switzerland. And the man who carries my luggage in New York guesses the Caribbean. My complexion becomes a mark of my leisure. Yet no one would regard my complexion the same way if I entered such hotels through the service entrance. That is only to say that my complexion assumes its significance from the context of my life. My skin, in itself, means nothing. I stress the point because I know there are people who would label me "disadvantaged" because of my color. They make the same mistake I made as a boy, when I thought a disadvantaged life was circumscribed by particular occupations. That summer I worked in the sun may have made me physically indistinguishable from the Mexicans working nearby. (My skin was actually darker because, unlike them, I worked without wearing a shirt. By late August my hands were probably as tough as theirs.) But I was not one of *los pobres*. What made me different from them was an attitude of *mind*, my imagination of myself.

21   I do not blame my mother for warning me away from the sun when I was young. In a world where her brother had become an old man in his twenties because he was dark, my complexion was something to worry about. "Don't run in the sun," she warns me today. I run. In the end, my father was right—though perhaps he did not know how right or why—to say that I would never know what real work is. I will never know what he felt at his last factory job. If tomorrow I worked at some kind of factory, it would go differently for me. My long education would favor me. I could act as a public person—able to defend my interests, to unionize, to petition, to speak up—to challenge and demand. (I will never know what real work is.) I will never know what the Mexicans knew, gathering their shovels and ladders and saws.

22   Their silence stays with me now. The wages those Mexicans received for their labor were only a measure of their disadvantaged condition. Their silence is more telling. They lack a public identity. They remain profoundly alien. Persons apart. People lacking a union obviously, people without grounds. They depend upon the relative good will or fairness of their employers each day. For such people, lacking a better alternative, it is not such an unreasonable risk.

23   Their silence stays with me. I have taken these many words to describe its impact. Only: the quiet. Something uncanny about it. Its compliance. Vulnerability. Pathos. As I heard their truck rumbling away, I shuddered, my face mirrored with sweat. I had finally come face to face with *los pobres*.

Thinking Critically About Content

1. How does Rodriguez define *real work?* What does he mean when he says, "I would never know what real work is" (paragraph 21)?

2. What did Rodriguez learn about the other workers at the construction site? What did he learn about himself from this experience?

3. What does Rodriguez mean when he says, "my complexion assumes its significance from the context of my life" (paragraph 20)?

Thinking Critically About Purpose and Audience

4. Why do you think Rodriguez wrote this essay?

5. Who do you think is his primary audience?

6. Have you ever learned an important lesson from a summer job? What was the job? What did you learn? Explain your answer.

Thinking Critically About Paragraphs

7. Paragraph 16 ends rather than begins with its controlling idea. Explain how Rodriguez develops this particular paragraph.

8. How is paragraph 4 organized? Why do you think Rodriguez puts these details in this particular order?

9. Choose one paragraph, and explain its tone or mood.

10. Write a summary of this essay for your English class.

Jo Goodwin Parker

WHAT IS POVERTY?

Focusing Your Attention

1. How do you generally feel about people who are less fortunate than you? Why do you feel this way?

2. In the essay you are about to read, the author defines poverty from her own experience. How would you define poverty? On what do you base your definition?

Expanding Your Vocabulary

The following words are important to your understanding of this essay.

> **stench:** stink, foul odor (paragraph 1)
>
> **privy:** toilet (paragraph 2)

grits: cornmeal mush (paragraph 4)

oleo: margarine (paragraph 4)

devour: eat (paragraph 5)

antihistamines: medications for colds and allergies (paragraph 5)

repossessed: taken away for failing to make installment payments (paragraph 8)

surplus commodities program: a government-run program that provides poor families with certain basic products free of charge (paragraph 11)

1   You ask me what is poverty? Listen to me. Here I am, dirty, smelly, and with no "proper" underwear on and with the stench of my rotting teeth near you. I will tell you. Listen to me. Listen without pity. I cannot use your pity. Listen with understanding. Put yourself in my dirty, worn out, ill-fitting shoes, and hear me.

2   Poverty is getting up every morning from a dirt-and-illness-stained mattress. The sheets have long since been used for diapers. Poverty is living in a smell that never leaves. This is a smell of urine, sour milk, and spoiling food sometimes joined with the strong smell of long-cooked onions. Onions are cheap. If you have smelled this smell, you did not know how it came. It is the smell of the outdoor privy. It is the smell of young children who cannot walk the long dark way in the night. It is the smell of the milk which has gone sour because the refrigerator long has not worked, and it costs money to get it fixed. It is the smell of rotting garbage. I could bury it, but where is the shovel? Shovels cost money.

3   Poverty is being tired. I have always been tired. They told me at the hospital when the last baby came that I had chronic anemia caused from poor diet, a bad case of worms, and that I needed a corrective operation. I listened politely—the poor are always polite. The poor always listen. They don't say that there is no money for iron pills or better food or worm medicine. The idea of an operation is frightening and costs so much that, if I had dared, I would have laughed. Who takes care of my children? Recovery from an operation takes a long time. I have three children. When I left them with "Granny" the last time I had a job, I came home to find the baby covered with fly specks and a diaper that had not been changed since I left. When the dried diaper came off, bits of my baby's flesh came with it. My other child was playing with a sharp bit of broken glass, and my oldest was playing alone at the edge of a lake. I made twenty-two dollars a week, and a good nursery school costs twenty dollars a week for three children. I quit my job.

4   Poverty is dirt. You can say in your clean clothes coming from your clean house, "Anybody can be clean." Let me explain about housekeeping

with no money. For breakfast I give my children grits with no oleo or corn-bread without eggs and oleo. This does not use up many dishes. What dishes there are, I wash in cold water and with no soap. Even the cheapest soap has to be saved for the baby's diapers. Look at my hands, so cracked and red. Once I saved for months to buy a jar of Vaseline for my hands and the baby's diaper rash. When I had saved enough, I went to buy it and the price had gone up two cents. The baby and I suffered on. I have to decide every day if I can bear to put my cracked sore hands into the cold water and strong soap. But you ask, why not hot water? Fuel costs money. If you have a wood fire it costs money. If you burn electricity, it costs money. Hot water is a luxury. I do not have luxuries. I know you will be surprised when I tell you how young I am. I look so much older. My back has been bent over the wash tubs every day for so long I cannot remember when I ever did anything else. Every night I wash every stitch my school age child has on and just hope her clothes will be dry by morning.

Poverty is staying up all night on cold nights to watch the fire, knowing   5
one spark on the newspaper covering the walls means your sleeping child dies in flames. In summer, poverty is watching gnats and flies devour your baby's tears when he cries. The screens are torn, and you pay so little rent you know they will never be fixed. Poverty means insects in your food, in your nose, in your eyes, and crawling over you when you sleep. Poverty is hoping it never rains because diapers won't dry when it rains and soon you are using newspapers. Poverty is seeing your children forever with runny noses. Paper handkerchiefs cost money, and all your rags you need for other things. Even more costly are antihistamines. Poverty is cooking without food and cleaning without soap.

Poverty is asking for help. Have you ever had to ask for help, knowing   6
your children will suffer unless you get it? Think about asking for a loan from a relative, if this is the only way you can imagine asking for help. I will tell you how it feels. You find out where the office is that you are supposed to visit. You circle that block four or five times. Thinking of your children, you go in. Everyone is busy. Finally, someone comes out, and you tell her that you need help. That never is the person you need to see. You go see another person, and after spilling the whole shame of your poverty all over the desk between you, you find that this isn't the right office after all—you must repeat the whole process, and it never is any easier at the next place.

You have asked for help, and after all it has a cost. You are again told to   7
wait. You are told why, but you don't really hear because of the red cloud of shame and the rising cloud of despair.

Poverty is remembering. It is remembering quitting school in junior   8
high because "nice" children had been so cruel about my clothes and my smell. The attendance officer came. My mother told him I was pregnant. I

wasn't, but she thought I could get a job and help out. I had jobs off and on, but never long enough to learn anything. Mostly, I remember being married. I was so young then. I am still young. For a time, we had all the things you have. There was a little house in another town, hot water and everything. Then my husband lost his job. There was unemployment insurance for a while, and what few jobs I could get. Soon, all our nice things were repossessed and we moved back here. I was pregnant then. This house didn't look so bad when we first moved in. Every week it gets worse. Nothing is ever fixed. We now had no money. There were a few odd jobs for my husband, but everything went for food then, as it does now. I don't know how we lived through three years and three babies, but we did. I'll tell you something, after the last baby died, I destroyed my marriage. It had been a good one, but could you keep on bringing children in this dirt? Did you ever think how much it costs for any kind of birth control? I knew my husband was leaving the day he left, but there were no goodbyes between us. I hope he has been able to climb out of this mess somewhere. He never could hope with us to drag him down.

9   That's when I asked for help. When I got it, you know how much it was? It was, and is, seventy-eight dollars a month for the four of us; that is all I ever can get. Now you know why there is no soap, no needles and thread, no hot water, no aspirin, no worm medicine, no hand cream, no shampoo. None of these things forever and ever and ever. So that you can see clearly, I pay twenty dollars a month rent, and most of the rest goes for food. For grits and cornmeal, and rice and milk and beans. I try my best to use only the minimum electricity. If I use more, there is that much less for food.

10   Poverty is looking into a black future. Your children won't play with my boys. They will turn to other boys who steal to get what they want. I can already see them behind the bars of their prison instead of behind the bars of my poverty. Or will they turn to the freedom of alcohol or drugs and find themselves enslaved. And my daughter? At best, there is for her a life like mine.

11   But you say to me, there are schools. Yes, there are schools. My children have no extra books, no magazines, no extra pencils, or crayons, or paper and most important of all, they do not have health. They have worms, they have infections, they have pink-eye all summer. They do not sleep well on the floor or with me in my one bed. They do not suffer from hunger, my seventy-eight dollars keeps us alive, but they do suffer from malnutrition. Oh yes, I do remember what I was taught about health in school. It doesn't do much good. In some places there is a surplus commodities program. Not here. The county said it cost too much. There is a school lunch program. But I have two children who will already be damaged by the time they get to school.

But, you say to me, there are health clinics. Yes, there are health clinics, 12
and they are in the town. I live out here eight miles from town. I can walk
that far (even if it is sixteen miles both ways), but can my little children? My
neighbor will take me when he goes; but he expects to get paid, one way or
another. . . . I bet you know my neighbor. He is that large man who spends
his time at the gas station, the barbershop, and the corner store complain-
ing about the government spending money on the immoral mothers of ille-
gitimate children.

Poverty is an acid that drips on pride until all pride is worn away. 13
Poverty is a chisel that chips on honor until honor is worn away. Some of
you say that you would do something in my situation, and maybe you
would, for the first week or the first month, but for year after year after year?

Even the poor can dream. A dream of a time when there is money. 14
Money for the right kinds of foods, for worm medicine, for iron pills, for
toothbrushes, for hand cream, for hammer and nails and a bit of screening,
for a shovel, for a bit of paint, for some sheeting, for needles and thread.
Money to pay in money for a trip to town. And, oh, money for hot water and
money for soap. A dream of when asking for help does not eat away the
last bit of pride. When the office you visit is as nice as the offices of other
governmental agencies, when there are enough workers to help you
quickly, when workers do not quit in defeat and despair. When you have to
tell your story to only one person and that person can send you for other
help and you don't have to prove your poverty over and over again.

I have come out of my despair to tell you this. Remember I did not come 15
from another place or another time. Others like me are all around you.
Look at us with an angry heart; anger will help you help me. Anger that
will let you tell of me. The poor are always silent. Can you be silent too?

Thinking Critically About Content

1. Parker develops her definition of poverty with a series of examples
   from her own life. Which of these examples communicates most
   clearly to you what poverty is? Explain your answer.

2. Explain the meaning of Parker's final paragraph. What is the main
   message of this paragraph?

3. Do you think the level of poverty that Parker describes is still a
   major part of our society? Give evidence for your answer.

Thinking Critically About Purpose and Audience

4. Why do you think Parker wrote this essay?

5. Who do you think is Parker's audience in this essay? Explain your
   answer.

6. Does this essay make you feel more or less pity for those who live below the poverty line? Explain your answer.

Thinking Critically About Paragraphs

7. What do you think Parker is saying in her first paragraph? Why do you think she starts her essay this way?

8. Parker's style is very curt and to the point in this essay. Instead of transitions, she uses parallel lists and pronouns to give her paragraphs coherence. Look specifically at paragraph 11. Underline the words and phrases that are in list form. (Refer to pages 608–613 for information on parallel structure.) Then explain the feeling these lists create in the paragraph.

9. Many of Parker's paragraphs start with a definition of poverty, "Poverty is . . ." What effect does this repetition have on the essay as a whole?

10. Paragraph 13 is a collection of metaphors that explain poverty. Metaphors are comparisons expressed without using "like" or "as" with words that cannot be taken literally. Make sure you understand the two metaphors Parker uses in the first two sentences. Then rewrite this paragraph in your own words.

Writing Topics: Defining

Before you begin to write, you might want to review the writing process in Part I.

1. In the first essay, Richard Rodriguez defines *work*. Write your own definition of *work* or of another aspect of life, such as *pleasure, recreation,* or *sport*.

2. Using Jo Goodwin Parker's method of development through examples, define *wealth*.

3. Now that you have studied different approaches to the process of definition, what makes a definition effective or useful for you? Apply what you have studied about definition to your answer.

ANALYZING CAUSES AND EFFECTS

28

The two essays in this chapter show cause and effect at work. The first essay, "Shedding the Weight of My Dad's Obsession," deals with the lifelong burden of an insensitive father. In the second essay, "Life Sentences," Corky Clifton explains why he made a desperate attempt to escape from prison when he was an inmate in the Louisiana State Penitentiary.

Linda Lee Andujar

SHEDDING THE WEIGHT OF MY DAD'S OBSESSION

Focusing Your Attention

1. Do you have a personal problem that plagues you consistently? What is this problem?

2. The essay you are about to read explains how the author finally shed an emotional burden she carried since her childhood. How do you deal with emotional problems? Where did you learn your "survival skills"? What do you do to find security and safety when you are upset about something?

Expanding Your Vocabulary

The following words are important to your understanding of this essay.

Bluebird: entry-level organization for future Girl Scouts (paragraph 1)

clambered: climbed awkwardly (paragraph 4)

timber: quality of life (paragraph 5)

authoritarian regimens: strict regulations (paragraph 5)

incarceration: imprisonment (paragraph 7)

skirmish: battle (paragraph 8)

amphetamines: stimulants that lessen appetite (paragraph 9)

diuretics: drugs that increase the production of urine (paragraph 9)

metabolism: bodily process that changes food into energy (paragraph 11)

1   Instead of selling the Camp Fire candy, I ate it. Eight boxes of it. Each Bluebird in our fourth-grade troop was assigned 12 boxes of chocolate candy to sell for a dollar a box. I sold four boxes to my family and then ran out of ideas for selling the rest.

2   As the days passed and the stack of candy remained in a corner of my room, the temptation to eat it overwhelmed my conscience. Two months after we'd been given the goodies, the troop leader announced that the drive was over and we were to bring in our sales money, along with any unsold candy, to the next Tuesday meeting. I rushed home in a panic and counted $4 in my sales money envelope and 12 boxes of candy gone.

3   I thought of the piggy bank filled with silver dollars that my father kept on a shelf in his closet. It was a collection that he added to but never spent. I tried to push this financial resource out of my mind, but Tuesday was approaching, and I still had no money.

4   By Monday afternoon I had no choice. I tiptoed into my parents' bedroom, pulled the vanity chair from Mother's dressing table, and carried it to the walk-in closet. There was the piggy bank smiling down at me from the high shelf. After stacking boxes on the chair, I reached up and laid hands on the bank. When I had counted out eight silver dollars, I returned the pig to its place and clambered down. For days I felt bad about my theft, but what I felt even guiltier about was eating all those treats.

5   Throughout my childhood, my parents weighed me every day, and Daddy posted the numbers on my bedroom door. He never called me fat, but I came to learn every synonym. He discussed every health aspect of obesity endlessly. The daily tone and timber of our household was affected by Dad's increasingly authoritarian regimens.

6   I remember one Friday night, months after the candy caper. I heard the garage door rumble shut, and I knew that Daddy was home. He came in the back door, kissed Mother, and asked what my weight was for the day. Mother admitted that I was still a pound over the goal he had set. "Get a pillow and a book, Linda," he said.

7   He firmly ushered me to the bathroom, then shut and locked the door behind me. As the door was closing, I caught a glimpse of Mother and my sister looking on as though they were witnessing an execution. For the next two days, the only time I was allowed out was for meals. It was late Sunday

evening when I was finally released from my cell, supposedly taught a lesson by my incarceration.

The bathroom episode was one skirmish in a long war that had begun 8 when, unlike my older sister, I failed to shed the "baby fat" many children are born with. Although I was cheerful, affectionate, and good-natured, none of these qualities interested my father. He had one slender child—he meant to have two. It was simply a matter of my self-discipline.

My slightly chubby figure had become a target for my physician 9 father's frustration as he struggled to establish his medical practice. Dad told me constantly that if I was a pound overweight, I would be teased at school and nobody would like me. I stayed away from the other kids, fearing harsh words that never came. When I was 16, Daddy came up with the ultimate punishment: any day that I weighed more than 118 pounds (the weight my father had deemed ideal for my 5-foot, 4-inch frame) I'd have to pay him. In an attempt to shield me from this latest tactic, my exhausted, loving mother secretly took me to an internist friend of the family who prescribed what he described as "diet pills"—amphetamines and diuretics. Although the pills caused unpleasant side effects like lightheadedness, taking them landed me a slim figure and, two years later, an engineer husband.

I quit the hated amphetamines at 27 and accepted my divorce as a 10 result of my weight gain. I became a single, working mother devoted to raising my son and daughter. Over time, I realized that people liked my smile and my laugh and, contrary to my father's predictions, didn't shun me because of my size.

Many years ago, at my annual physical, I mentioned to my doctor that I 11 couldn't eat the same quantity of food that normal people eat without getting bigger. He kindly reassured me that people do indeed have different metabolisms, some more efficient than others. This discussion ultimately helped me to accept my size and shed the emotional burden carried over from my childhood.

My sister and her husband have a daughter who was pudgy as a child. 12 They asked me what they should do about her weight "problem." My reply, "Don't make it an issue. Let her find her own weight level." To their great credit, they did.

Thinking Critically About Content

1. What is Andujar analyzing in this essay?
2. The author is very honest and open about the causes and effects of her weight problem. What is the most fundamental cause and the ultimate effect?

3. What does Andujar seem upset about when she says, "Although I was cheerful, affectionate, and good-natured, none of these qualities interested my father" (paragraph 8).

Thinking Critically About Purpose and Audience

4. What do you think Andujar's purpose is in this essay?

5. Who do you think is her primary audience?

6. Explain the essay's title.

Thinking Critically About Paragraphs

7. Andujar opens her essay with the story about the Camp Fire candy. Do you think this is an effective beginning? Explain your answer.

8. Paragraph 5 gives us a hint of what the real problem is in Andujar's life. How does the writer organize her details in that paragraph?

9. What is the topic sentence of paragraph 9? Do all the sentences in that paragraph support this topic sentence? Explain your answer.

10. Write a paragraph about the role of a particular relative in your life. Are you very emotionally attached to this person? How did you become so close?

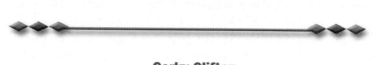

Corky Clifton

LIFE SENTENCES

Focusing Your Attention

1. Think of a time when you acted or did something without carefully analyzing the situation. What were the results?

2. In the essay you are about to read, the writer analyzes his reasons for risking his life to escape from prison. Think of the most difficult decision you have ever had to make. In what way did you analyze the situation and circumstances before you made the decision? Did you think about it for a long time? Discuss it with others? Write about it?

Expanding Your Vocabulary

The following words are important to your understanding of this essay.

disciplinary reports: reports of misconduct (paragraph 4)

D.A.: district attorney, prosecutor for the government (paragraph 4)

inflict: commit (paragraph 5)

Why did I escape? I suppose it was for the same reason that men have   1
fought wars and died for throughout history. I wanted to be free.

For 27 years, I have submitted to discipline, the rules, the harsh condi-   2
tions, the torment of my children growing from babies into men—without
ever seeing them. I've never had a visit from any of my family during these
27 years because, being from Ohio, no one could afford the trip here to
Louisiana.

I once thought, as most people do, that all you had to do in order to get   3
out of prison was just be good and they'll let you out someday. One does
not have to be in the prison system very long to learn what a joke that is.

If Jesus Christ himself was in here with a life sentence, he couldn't get   4
out unless he had money to put in the right places. I've always been a
pretty stubborn person, so even though I was told how the political and
Pardon Board system works, I freely submitted to all the prison rules and
discipline. After 12 years with a perfect record—no disciplinary reports—I
applied to the Pardon Board and was denied any consideration for relief.
So I waited 10 more years and applied again, still with an excellent prison
record. This time they wouldn't even hear my case. In 1983, I applied to the
board for the third time and the Pardon Board cut my time to 50 years.
However, the judge and D.A., retired, simply called the governor's legal
staff and told them they don't want me to be free—so, end of case. When I
applied for my pardon in 1983, the D.A. published an article in the newspaper saying I was a very dangerous man that would kill anyone who got
into my way. He said a lot of things which were all designed to turn public
opinion against me and justify his reason for protesting my release.

In spite of having to endure the torment of prison life all these years   5
without hope, I was still determined to better myself, no longer with any
hope that a nice record would get me my freedom but because the years of
discipline and hardships had molded my personality to the extent that I no
longer desired to do anything criminal. I could not even inflict revenge on
my enemies within prison.

I taught myself how to repair watches, and for more than 20 years I   6
repaired watches for other prisoners as well as guards. I also taught myself
how to paint pictures. At the 1988 Angola Arts & Crafts Festival, I won a
second place for one of my watercolors. Aside from all my other accom-
plishments within prison, I have only two disciplinary reports in 27 years. I
proved my honesty and sincerity many times over. Every time I made a
friend through correspondence, one of the first things they wanted to know
is how come I'm still in prison. I'm always tempted to use up several legal
pads trying to explain about the corrupt legal and political system here in
Louisiana. But who's gonna believe a man can be kept in here all his life
just because some big shot out there doesn't want him out? Well, I am one

example of it, and there are hundreds more lifers in here, many of them I know personally, who are in here for no other reason than because some big shot out there doesn't want them to go free. The only way you can get around that is *money*—in the right places.

7   Since the sheriff, the D.A., and/or the judge can dictate who can get out and who can't, then what's the purpose of a pardon board? Why the waste of taxpayers' money? I spent many years in here struggling for freedom. There are many people here in prison, as well as outside, who believe I should be free, but the judge and D.A. say they intend to see that I never go free, as long as I live. How am I supposed to handle that?

8   I'm not Charles Manson or some other mass murderer. I didn't torture or mutilate some child. When I was 23 years old, I killed a man in a robbery. That's bad enough. But the point is, hundreds of prisoners in here for the same and even worse crimes have been pardoned throughout all the years I've been here. The majority of them served only half or less time than I have.

9   Of course, it's no mystery to me why I'm still in prison. The judge and D.A. are keeping me here. But I say that's unfair—should, in fact, be illegal. They prosecuted and sentenced me 27 years ago, and that should be the end of their involvement in my case. They justify keeping me in here by claiming I am still the same dangerous man I was 27 years ago. If this were true, then I would like for someone to explain why, when I escaped a few weeks ago, I did not steal a car, knock someone in the head, or break into one of the many houses I passed.

10   On the night of April 15, when I finally made up my mind to escape, I knew the odds were against me. I was fifty-two years old and had already suffered two heart attacks. In those final few days before April 15, I fought many emotional battles with myself. I had a lot to lose, and I'd be letting down a lot of good people who'd put their trust in me. But desperation is pretty hard to win a rational argument with. My time was running out. Had run out, really, because I was certainly in no condition to run through that jungle in the Tunica Hills. But even against all odds, I went for it anyway.

11   I struggled through those hills, mountains really, for five days and six nights, sleeping on the ground, with no food and very little water. I ended up in Mississippi. I saw a lot of people, and I even talked to a few.

12   After a couple days I knew it would be impossible for me to get away unless I stole a car or knocked someone in the head. Not far from Woodville, Mississippi, I came across a house trailer. I sat in the bushes watching the trailer from about 50 yards away. I watched a woman drive up and unlock the door and go in alone. A few minutes later, she came out and washed

her car. I could have knocked her in the head, or even killed her, took her car, and been long gone. But I couldn't bring myself to do that.

I discovered that in reality I could no longer commit the crimes that I 13 once did. So here I stood in those bushes, watching that house trailer, that car, and that lady—my ticket to freedom—and discover I can't pay the price. I can't think of any words that could truly describe the dejection and hopelessness I felt at that moment. There was no way I could continue on as I had those five days past. There was just no strength left in my legs to go on. Resigned to my fate, I walked several hundred yards to the highway and gave myself up.

So now I am left with only two ways left to escape my torment. Just sit 14 here for God knows how many more years and wait on a natural death. Or I can avoid all those senseless years of misery and take my own life now.

Having to sit in this cell now for several weeks with nothing—even 15 being denied my cigarettes—I have thought a lot about suicide, and it seems to be the most humane way out of a prison I no longer care to struggle in. Suicide or endless torment. Which would you choose?

Thinking Critically About Content

1. What is Clifton analyzing in this essay? How does his title help focus his analysis?

2. Explain two causes and two effects of Clifton's escape from prison.

3. Why do you think Clifton ends this essay with a question? Is this an effective conclusion?

Thinking Critically About Purpose and Audience

4. Why do you think Clifton wrote this essay?

5. Who do you think Clifton's audience is in this essay? Explain your answer.

6. Did the fact that this excerpt was written by a convicted criminal have any effect on you? Explain your answer.

Thinking Critically About Paragraphs

7. In paragraph 2 of his essay, the author mentions the "torment" of not being able to see his children growing up, yet he doesn't mention the crime he committed until paragraph 8. Why do you think he presents his material in this order?

8. Which of Clifton's paragraphs deal with the causes of his escape? Which deal with the effects? Do you think this is a good balance for Clifton's purpose? Explain your answer.

9. How does Clifton organize the details in paragraph 12? Why do you think he chose this method of organization?

10. If you were the district attorney who prosecuted Corky Clifton, how would you respond to Clifton's analysis? Write your response to him in the form of a letter.

Writing Topics: Analyzing Causes and Effects

Before you begin to write, you might want to review the writing process in Part I.

1. Linda Andujar's father felt that her weight problem was simply a matter of self-discipline. What role does self-discipline play in most of our daily lives? Explain your answer.

2. In "Life Sentences," Corky Clifton explains that he is desperate to escape from prison. He can no longer stand "the torment." Have you ever wanted to escape from certain people or a specific situation in your life? How do you escape when you want to?

3. How would looking closely at causes and effects help you live a better life? How would the process of discovering causes and effects help you think through your decisions and problems more logically? Explain your answer.

ARGUING

The three essays in this chapter let you see argument at work in a full essay. The first essay, "Why Study English?" was written by Dwight Van Avery. In it, the author draws clear relationships between writing well and succeeding in life.

The next two essays present two positions on hate crime legislation. The first essay, written by Tamara Roleff, claims that hate crime laws are necessary for the preservation of a civilized society. The second essay, written by Brenda Stalcup, Tamara Roleff, and Mary Williams, argues that hate crime laws are not a deterrent to criminals, but a basic change in people's attitudes is necessary for hate crime to stop.

Dwight Van Avery

WHY STUDY ENGLISH?

Focusing Your Attention

1. Think of all the ways you use reading, writing, and speaking in a typical day. What percent of your day involves the use of words?

2. Van Avery says, "Every day in your future you will be called upon to speak and write, and when you open your mouth, or write a letter or report, you will be advertising your progress and your potential worth" (paragraph 17). Based on this statement, what is your "potential worth"?

Expanding Your Vocabulary

The following words are important to your understanding of this essay.

   emphatic: bold; said with force (paragraph 11)

   mimeographed: copied by using an inked stencil (paragraph 13)

   verbatim: word for word (paragraph 17)

dense: thick (paragraph 17)

authoritative: official (paragraph 19)

phenomena: occurrences (paragraph 19)

habituated: learned; familiarized (paragraph 37)

inadequacies: defects (paragraph 40)

accumulate: collect (paragraph 41)

unceasing: never-ending (paragraph 42)

1   If what Peter Drucker says is true, and we believe it is, you had better do something about your English.

2   Mr. Drucker wrote an article for the May 1952 *Fortune* called "How to Be an Employee." He said that the ability to express ideas in writing and in speaking heads the list of requirements for success.

3   "As soon as you move one step up from the bottom, your effectiveness depends on your ability to reach others through the spoken or written word. And the further away your job is from manual work, the larger the organization of which you are an employee, the more important it will be that you know how to convey your thoughts in writing or speaking. In the very large organizations, whether it is the government, the large business corporation, or the Army, this ability to express oneself is perhaps the most important of all the skills a man can possess."

4   It pleases us at General Electric to go on record as supporters of Mr. Drucker's statement. We know, of course, that there are many skills and personal qualifications leading to success. There is no doubt in our minds, for example, that you should have a genuine desire to exchange your best efforts in your employer's behalf for the chance to tackle increasingly more important, more challenging, and more rewarding assignments. We think that you should be able to look a fellow employee, including your boss, in the eye; that you should be reasonably neat and clean. But right now we have much to say about English.

5   The top engineer upstairs is on the telephone. He says to us, "Right before my eyes is a brief report made out by one of our young engineers. I have to guess what the fellow is driving at. I'm no English shark, but I find myself getting a little angry when I see four sentences tied together into one with commas. He has *principle* for *principal*, and he has also misspelled *accommodate* and *Cincinnati*. What if some of this fellow's bad sentences get into the hands of our customers?"

6   We sympathize, and we say somewhat lamely that it's up to him to suggest that the fellow hire a tutor.

The top engineer is wound up. "At the last meeting of our Association, 7 representatives of all the major companies complained about the way their younger men were putting down their words—and futures—on paper. Can't someone tell us what to do?"

We reach for an answer. "When boys and girls began avoiding mathe- 8 matics like the plague," we remind him, "we began printing facts. It is now our duty and privilege to beat the drums for English! Our motives are partly selfish, because we want American business to succeed even more than it has in the past. But our motive is more than self-interest. We know because we rub shoulders with people, at work and in the community, that a solid background in English is prerequisite to happiness and well-being. Without a reasonably good command of English—as a means of communication— and without knowledge of what the best minds of all time have put into print, we are not educated for personal happiness, apart from the job, or for personal success in the exciting business of making a living."

"But I thought all boys and girls took English in high school and college?" 9

"Yes, they put in their time. Their teachers have spread the feast, but 10 some of them haven't been very hungry. Perhaps they will listen to us. Their teachers can tell them a thousand times that English is important, but they will say, 'Teacher means well, but she's trying to sell us on the importance of her subject.' Perhaps when a manufacturer of turbines, gen- erators, jet engines, lamps, room air coolers, toasters, refrigerators, and 200,000 other electrical products says English is of tremendous importance, they will listen. After all, English is almost as important as math in our busi- ness, isn't it?"

The engineer's answer is deliberately emphatic: "Change the word 11 *almost* to *just*, and, brother, you've said a mouthful! Tell them that English is important to them—and to us—because very soon their ability to read and to know and to remember what they have read, and to speak and to write well, will make all the difference, whether they and we or some other com- pany of their career choice will succeed together."

At one time or another, all of us try our hand at writing. 12

A group of engineers applies the new principle to the development of a 13 revolutionary type of gadget. The results of this effort are summed up in a typewritten report to the head of their department. The report is then mimeographed for the benefit of others in the organization.

The company prepares to put the new product on the market. Writers 14 prepare literature describing its virtues or explaining how to use it and keep it in working order.

This is indeed useful writing. No piece of company business can begin, 15 progress, and achieve its purpose without the use of words. Writing, together with reading, is as much an integral part of the electrical manufacturing business (or any business) as your bones are part of your body.

16   Every day in your future you will be called upon to speak and write, and when you open your mouth, or write a letter or report, you will be advertising your progress and your potential worth.

17   Here is a verbatim extract from a laboratory notebook:

> "Curt flew into the cloud, and I started the dispenser in operation. I dropped about three pounds (of dry ice) and then swung around and headed south.
>
> "About this time I looked toward the rear and was thrilled to see long streamers of snow falling from the base of the cloud through which we had just passed. I shouted to Curt to swing around, and as we did so we passed through a mass of glistening snow crystals! We made another run through a dense portion of the unseeded cloud, during which time I dispensed about three more pounds of crushed dry ice. . . . This was done by opening the window and letting the suction of the passing air remove it. We then swung west of the cloud and observed draperies of snow which seemed to hang for 2–3000 feet below us and noted the cloud drying up rapidly, very similar to what we observe in the cold box in the laboratory. . . . While still in the clouds as we saw the glinting crystals all over, I turned to Curt, and we shook hands as I said, 'We *did* it!' Needless to say, we were quite excited."

18   This extract is from the laboratory notebook of Vincent J. Schaefer. It is of historical significance because it describes the first artificial snow making outside the General Electric Research Laboratory. Without such a record, other men could not have understood the purpose, procedure, and effect; would not have had a starting point from which to take off on their own investigations.

19   Since its beginning in 1900, the Research Laboratory has published nearly 2000 papers in technical journals, and these have recorded new facts, new basic discoveries, and new theories. Many are recognized the world over as classics and are cited as authoritative references in their fields. Some opened up wholly new fields for exploration. Others cast new light on known phenomena. Some disclosed new tools for research.

20   But the recording of ideas and facts is not confined only to the engineering and scientific laboratories. Each year, thousands of General Electric mechanics, stenographers, accountants, and others write down their suggestions for improving company products and procedures. To each whose suggestion is adopted is given a certain amount of money, but we suspect that the real gain—for company and employee—is the focusing of attention

upon those persons who can think of a better way and who can tell about it with words on paper.

We thought little of it at the time, but one night several of us were visiting 21 over the back fence, and a college boy, home for the summer, joined us. He told us how he was enjoying his summer job as helper on a General Electric truck. We asked him who his boss was and how he liked him. He gave us the name and said, simply, "I like him very much. He is a well-spoken man." We think that you, too, if you will stop to think, prefer well-spoken men and women.

You will probably grant that General Electric knows a thing or two 22 about its various specialties, but you may question whether our expertness extends to the English part of the education field. Let's get off the hook directly: your English teacher has probably forgotten more about the teaching of English than we will ever know. As a matter of fact, if someday your employer finds you wobbly in English, he will be critical of you, not some long-suffering teacher or parent.

One of our business colleagues, who would hate us if we gave away his 23 name, has an interesting background. Early in his growing-up years, he dropped schooling so he could earn enough money to buy a Stutz roadster. Eight years later, after working in a shoe factory, another powerful desire took possession of him. He wanted a Harvard degree. For one year he studied all the specified high school subjects; he read everything he could lay his hands on. Then he took all the required high school examinations and passed them with an average of 95 percent. At Harvard, he kept on reading everything he could squeeze into four years' time. To make a long story short, he's now doing better than all right.

Attitude makes all the difference! 24

If you are one of those "dese" and "dose" guys, and if it "don't make no 25 sense" to you that your school and your employer "wants" you to become a literate person, all the teaching skill and the modern facilities can't win you over.

Did you ever hear of a mental block? It's a massive barrier in your mind, 26 but like the Maginot Line, it can be penetrated.

That block may be mathematics or history or spelling or perhaps a feel- 27 ing that no one likes you or something else. Do you remember how you learned to swim? You had flailed the water and sunk like a stone. But then a fortunate stroke propelled you forward, and now it doesn't occur to you when you dive off the board that you may not be able to swim to shore.

Too, your mind may be blocked because you imagine all well-read, 28 literate persons are precious, prissy characters who go around spouting Shakespeare. There may be a few of those people, but that is not

Shakespeare's fault. We are just realistic enough to believe that some of the master poet's gracious writing style will rub off on you. We know that in a sense we become a part of what we read and that what we call writing style is born from our unconscious attempt to imitate what we like.

29   We hope it has occurred to you that English extends beyond a single classroom; that your success or failure in your other classrooms is largely due to your ability to read, to understand, to speak, and to write. English is just as all-embracing in a business organization. Whether we are at drafting board, desk, machine, or calling on customers, we are involved more or less in communication.

30   We say that English—especially to American boys and girls—is an easy language to learn. Making English behave may be a little troublesome. You can play safe by writing dull little sentences, and they, of course, are less frustrating to the reader than involved wrong sentences. But since the sentence you write or speak is what the reader or listener uses as a criterion in judging you, it is good sense to learn how to become its master.

31   We know from our experience at General Electric that too many of our younger employees say to themselves before spreading their wings for a flight with words, "But if I write that report the way I *feel* it should be written, my boss will think that I am a child." If an engineer, for example, is testing an insulating material and it chars and smells like burned string beans, we can think of no reason why he should not say so.

32   Our business world needs young people whose minds are packed with facts, but with the boldness of imagination to release them in a form that is easy and pleasant to take.

33   We have on our desk copies of the *General Electric Review* and the *Scientific American*—both written for thousands of top-flight engineers and scientists. The editors of both magazines know that factual reporting is necessary so that their readers, who are so brilliantly expert in many fields, will have confidence in the authority of their articles. But they know, too, that men and women, whatever their job or profession, are willing to begin and stay with an article only if it is well-written. Only you can guess how many books and articles you have thrown aside after tasting the first few paragraphs. Everyone who reads and listens is so very human.

34   Without interested readers, whether the magazine is *Scholastic* or *Scientific American*, its survival depends upon the skill and labor-of-love that editors and authors lavish upon it. Your survival, too, as the adult you are aiming to be, depends upon your ability, desire, and courage to put your best foot forward in a world that will judge you by your words as well as your actions.

Who is the next most important man or woman in your life? We aren't 35
thinking of the next prom date, but an understanding person who is sitting
at a desk studying a filled-in application blank. Whether he's a college
admissions or an employment officer, he hopes he is so right before saying
yes or *no.*

Can you live up to your expressed desires? Will you fit in? Have you 36
enough preparation, enough intellectual background? Can your brain
direct your hands in performing skills? Can you stand the pace of competition? Can you accept responsibility? Will you worry a workaday problem,
like a dog with a bone, till you have conquered it—and then brace yourself
for a tougher assignment?

If what you have said on the application blank shows a glimmer of hope, 37
you are brought in for a personal interview. This can be rough going if you
haven't habituated yourself to accurate and well-organized expression.

The interviewer across the desk from you has been charged by his 38
college or company to weigh your worth; he has accepted the responsibility of determining the future of the organization he represents—any good
organization is but the lengthened shadow of qualified people.

Your job interests. Your participation in school activities. Your subject 39
preferences. Your hobbies. Your ambitions. These and many other topics
are brought forward for you to discuss.

The minutes speed by. You summon up the skills of presentation you 40
have practiced in English and other classes. It strikes you, as you talk, that
in neither writing nor speaking can you conceal your inadequacies.

As you move up the success ladder, what you write and what you say 41
will determine in part your rate of climb. It is neither too early nor too late to
become practiced in the art of communication; certainly not too late to
accumulate background through reading experiences. . . .

We pause and listen to the unceasing whine of a motor across the yard. 42
In the distance, three green-gray columns of smoke are rushing upward
from three yellow-brick chimneys. We see them as symbols of mechanical
might controlled by the will, the wit, and the intelligence of earnest men.
And these men, adventurers and pioneers of industry, can move ahead
with their plans, because their own thought processes have been built
upon such logical disciplines as history and math—and English.

Thinking Critically About Content

1. What is Van Avery's main point about studying English?
2. Van Avery claims we are judged by words and by actions everywhere we go. Have you found this to be true? Explain your answer.

3. According to Van Avery, in what way is "a solid background in English . . . prerequisite to happiness and well-being" (paragraph 8)?

Thinking Critically About Purpose and Audience

4. What do you think Van Avery's purpose is in writing this essay?

5. Why do you think Van Avery introduces his role in General Electric?

6. An essential ingredient in writing an effective argument is to pull the readers into the situation. Does Van Avery accomplish this? Explain your answer.

Thinking Critically About Paragraphs

7. Van Avery starts his essay with a conversation about writing on the job. Is the printing of the actual dialogue at the beginning of this essay effective? Why or why not?

8. Van Avery often uses comparisons, called analogies, to make his point. Explain the comparison of reading and writing in business to bones in the human body (paragraph 15).

9. Why does Van Avery include an excerpt from Vincent J. Schaefer's laboratory notebook? Does this excerpt help the author make his point? In what ways?

10. Imagine that you are an employee at General Electric. Write a paragraph responding to Van Avery.

ARGUING A POSITION

Focusing Your Attention

1. If you were asked to take a strong position on a topic of great importance to you and society, what are some of the topics you would consider?

2. In the two essays that you will be reading, one writer tries to persuade the readers that hate crime laws are necessary to deter the perpetrators of these crimes, while the other essay tells the readers that hate crime laws are not the answer to America's discrimination problems. Although you have not yet read the essays, which one do you think you will agree with?

Tamara Roleff

HATE CRIME LAWS ARE NECESSARY

Expanding Your Vocabulary

The following words are important to your understanding of this essay.

assailants: attackers (paragraph 2)

perpetrators: persons guilty of a crime (paragraph 2)

genocide: mass murder of a race, people, or minority group (paragraph 4)

supremacist: a group that believes they are of the highest authority (paragraph 9)

jurisdiction: the right or power to control the law (paragraph 9)

forensic: used in courts of law or debate (paragraph 9)

Each year has its notorious hate crime incidents. June 1998 saw the   1
dragging death of James Byrd Jr., a black man from Jasper, Texas, by
white racists. Not long after, in October 1998, Matthew Shepard, a gay college student, was robbed, beaten into a coma, tied to a fence, and left to die
near Laramie, Wyoming. In July 1999, Benjamin Smith went on a racially
motivated shooting spree, killing a black former basketball coach and a
Korean college student and wounding nine other minorities in Indiana and
Illinois. A month later in Los Angeles, white supremacist Buford Furrow
shot and injured five people—including three children—at a Jewish community center and then killed a Filipino mail carrier, Joseph Lleto. In March
2000, Ronald Taylor, who is black, shot and killed three white men and
wounded two others in Wilkinsburg, Pennsylvania. Eight weeks later,
Richard Bauhammers, who is white, killed five minorities and wounded a
sixth near Pittsburgh, Pennsylvania.

These horrifying murders and assaults are fundamentally different   2
from other violent crimes. They are hate crimes: The victims were chosen
only because they were black, white, Asian, Jewish, or gay. Hate crimes
are particularly devastating because they are intended to terrorize as well
as physically harm the individual. Hate crimes make the victim feel isolated and unprotected; studies have shown that hate crimes have a greater
and longer-lasting psychological impact than other crimes. Research also
has found that the assailants in hate crimes are more violent and inflict
more serious injuries on their victims than the perpetrators of ordinary
assaults do.

The Damaging Effects of Hate Crimes

3   Hate crimes have a damaging effect on society as well. Senator Edward Kennedy of Massachusetts describes hate crimes as "modern day lynchings"[1] because their purpose is to threaten and terrorize not only the individual but the victim's entire minority group. Thus, a seemingly isolated act of violence can devastate a community and, in the most notorious cases, the entire nation. If society does not step in to reassure the targeted group that such acts will not be tolerated, relations between the victim group and the rest of society may deteriorate irreparably. Kennedy and Arlen Specter, the Republican senator from Pennsylvania who cosponsored federal hate crimes legislation with Kennedy in 1997, explain why hate crimes are so much more serious than other types of crime: "Random street crimes don't provoke riots; hate crimes can and sometimes do."[2]

4   History shows that, if the attacking group believes their actions are supported by the community at large, the results can be disastrous. The Holocaust against the Jews during World War II and the genocide of the ethnic Albanians in Kosovo and Muslims in Bosnia are proof that hate, left unchecked, can escalate into widespread violence and terror.

5   Messages of hate and intimidation also wreak havoc on the community because hate crimes endanger the principles the United States was founded on. As the editors of the *Los Angeles Times* write, hate crimes are "blows against the ideals of equality that this nation should hold most sacred."[3] When someone is beaten or killed because of his or her race, religion, or sexual orientation, it demonstrates the poor state of civil rights in America. A hate crimes law would ensure that people are not victimized simply because of how they look, what religion they practice, or who they love.

A Necessary Law

6   Hate crime laws define which groups have historically suffered victimization and discrimination and set guidelines to severely punish criminals who specifically target these groups. Because of the devastating effect of hate crimes on both the victims and society, those who commit hate crimes should receive stiffer sentences than other criminals. Penalty enhancement laws, which increase the severity of the sentence given to someone convicted of a hate crime, send a message to racists and bigots that society will not tolerate crimes that are committed because of the victim's race, religion, gender, or sexual orientation.

7   Penalty enhancement in sentencing is not unusual. Society has long considered a criminal's motive and intent in the sentencing process. For

example, motive and intent are important when deciding whether to charge a defendant with assault or aggravated assault or when deciding whether a homicide is a case of self-defense, manslaughter, second-degree murder, or first-degree murder. Penalty enhancement laws would allow society to express its outrage over hate crimes.

A federal hate crimes law is needed to expand the definition of what groups should be protected from hate crimes. A law passed during the civil rights era made it illegal to "injure, oppress, threaten, or intimidate"[4] a person because of the victim's race, color, religion, or national origin. This law needs to be expanded to include crimes that are committed on the basis of gender, sexual orientation, and disability. Many of the most vicious hate crimes committed in recent years have been committed against homosexuals or those whom the attackers believed to be homosexual. The federal hate crimes law should be expanded to include these groups because, as Kennedy argues, "The federal government . . . has a role in preventing violence against other disadvantaged groups who have historically been subject to abuse."[5] Former president Bill Clinton, who had pushed Congress to expand the federal hate crimes law since 1997, agrees, adding, "All Americans deserve protection from hate."[6]

The Federal Government Can Help

As hate groups exploit the Internet to spread their influence and message across state lines, more and more hate crimes are being committed by individuals who have ties to white supremacist organizations such as Aryan Nations, World Church of the Creator, Christian Identity, and others. The federal government can investigate and prosecute hate crimes committed by hate groups and their members more effectively than individual states can, yet the federal government lacks legal jurisdiction. Eric Holder Jr., the deputy attorney general for the United States, testified before Congress on why he believes a federal hate crimes law is necessary. According to Holder, a federal hate crimes law would

> authorize the federal government to share its law enforcement resources, forensic expertise, and civil rights experience with state and local officials. And in rare circumstances where state or local officials are unable or unwilling to bring appropriate criminal charges in state court or where federal law or procedure is significantly better suited to the vindication of the federal interest—the United States must be able to bring federal civil rights charges. In these special cases, the public is served when, after consultation with state and local authorities, prosecutors have a federal alternative as an option.[7]

10   A federal hate crimes law would give the government the ability and authority to protect Americans from hate crimes. Federal law prohibits the government's participation in prosecuting hate crimes unless the victim was engaged in one of six federally protected activities: voting, enrolling in or attending public school, serving on a jury, applying for employment or working, traveling or engaging in interstate commerce, or participating in a program, facility, or activity provided by any state or local government. For example, the government was able to provide resources for the prosecution of a hate crime murder that was committed on a public street in Lubbock, Texas, in 1994 because the government provided the funds to build the street. However, if the skinhead perpetrators had murdered their victim inside a house, the federal government would have been unable to help. Having to make such a distinction on where the crime takes place before the federal government can help just "doesn't make sense," Clinton argued. "It shouldn't matter where the murder was committed. It was still a hate crime. And the resources of the federal government were needed."[8]

Hate Will Not Be Tolerated

11   A hate crimes law is necessary for several reasons. It will ensure that all Americans, whatever their race, religion, gender, sexual orientation, or disability, are protected from hate crimes. It will allow the federal government to assist state governments with hate crime investigations and prosecutions. And perhaps most important, it will let bigots and racists know that hate is not acceptable. In a meeting with law enforcement officials, [former] Attorney General Janet Reno emphasized why hate crime laws are so important. Hate crime laws "let us continue to speak against haters and hatred," she explained. "Haters are cowards and when confronted they so often back down. When we are silent, they are emboldened."[9] Hate crime laws are a means of speaking out and letting haters know that hate will not be tolerated.

Notes

1. Edward Kennedy, "Statement of Senator Edward M. Kennedy: Hate Crimes Prevention Act Amendment," 16 June 2000, www.senate.gov/~kennedy/statements/00/06/2000620E04.html.

2. Edward M. Kennedy and Arlen Specter, "When Combating Hate Should Be a Federal Fight," *Washington Post*, 1 December 1997, A25.

3. *Los Angeles Times*, "Tackling the Haters," 21 July 1999, B6.

4. Quoted in Wyn Craig Wade, *The Fiery Cross: The Ku Klux Klan in America* (New York: Oxford University Press), 1987, 444.

5. Edward Kennedy, "Bill Summary of the Hate Crimes Prevention Act Amendment," 19 June 2000, www.senate.gov/~kennedy/statements/00/06/2000620E14.html.

6. Bill Clinton, remarks by the President at the White House Conference on Hate Crimes, Washington, D.C., 10 November 1997, www.whitehouse.gov/uri-res/l2R?urn:pdi://oma.eop.gov.us/1997/11/12/1.text.1.

7. Eric H. Holder Jr., testimony before the Committee on the Judiciary, U.S. House of Representatives, Concerning Hate Crimes, 4 August 1999, www.usdoj.gov/dag/testimony/dagjudic080499.htm.

8. Bill Clinton, remarks by the President on Hate Crimes, 25 April 2000, www.pub.whitehouse.gov/uri-res/l2R?urn:pdi://oma.eop.gov.us/2000/4/26/8.text.1.

9. Janet Reno, "Attorney General Reno Delivers Statement on Hate Crimes," 25 April 2000, wwws.elibrary.com.

Brenda Stalcup, Tamara Roleff, and Mary Williams

HATE CRIME LAWS ARE UNNECESSARY

Expanding Your Vocabulary

The following words are important to your understanding of this essay.

ethnicity: belonging to a group of people, sharing beliefs and customs (paragraph 1)

advocates: supporters (paragraph 1)

supremacist: a group that believes they are of the highest authority (paragraph 2)

discrimination: separation because of race or religion (paragraph 3)

diligently: carefully (paragraph 4)

retribution: punishment for evil or wrong-doing (paragraph 5)

interrogation: questioning (paragraph 6)

prosecutions: formal charges in court (paragraph 6)

embezzler: someone who steals from another something that is entrusted to him or her (paragraph 8)

bigot: person who is attached to his or her own beliefs or prejudices and who dislikes those who disagree (paragraph 9)

Whenever a hate crime makes the national news, such as the murders   1
of James Byrd Jr. in Jasper, Texas, and Matthew Shepard in Laramie,

Wyoming, the knee-jerk reaction of civil rights activists, the media, and liberal politicians is always the same: Pass a federal hate crimes law. A hate crimes law will prevent hate crimes, they claim. Hate crime laws are of two types. One defines which groups will receive "special" protection so that any crime committed against them can be labeled a "hate crime." The other is a penalty enhancement law, which requires that a defendant receive a stiffer sentence if it can be proved that the victim was chosen due to prejudice against his or her race, religion, national origin, and sometimes gender, disability, or sexual orientation. Congress passed a federal sentencing enhancement act in 1994 that increased the penalty for a federal crime by an average of one-third if the crime was motivated by hatred of a victim's race, color, religion, national origin, or ethnicity. Since then, Congress has been trying to expand the definition of a hate crime to include victims who are selected due to their gender, sexual orientation, or disability. If these traits are included in the federal hate crimes law or if states pass such a law, then more people will be protected from hate crimes, civil rights advocates claim. But hate crime laws, whether at the state or federal level, are not necessary.

Two Notorious Examples

2   Supporters of hate crime laws condemned the lack of such laws in Texas and Wyoming when Byrd and Shepard were murdered. Byrd, a black man, was tied by his ankles to a pickup truck and dragged to his death in June 1998 by three white men who had ties to white supremacist groups. A few months later, gay rights advocates demanded the passage of a hate crimes law in Wyoming after Shepard, a gay college student, was robbed, beaten, tied to a fence, and left to die in October 1998. Hate crimes law supporters imply that Byrd and Shepard would still be alive if Texas and Wyoming had had hate crime laws. Evidently the editors of the *New York Times* believe a hate crimes law would have made a difference in Shepard's life:

> He died in a coma yesterday, in a state without a hate crimes law. Its legislature had rejected the latest attempt to pass one in February [1998]. . . . His death makes clear the need for hate crime laws to protect those who survive and punish those who attack others.[1]

Not a Deterrent

3   Unfortunately, such reasoning is faulty. James Byrd's and Matthew Shepard's murders, as heinous as they were, would not have been prevented if their states had had a hate crimes law on the books. For example, Indiana and Illinois both have hate crime laws, but that didn't stop

Benjamin Smith, a white supremacist, from killing two minorities and wounding nine more in a hate-filled shooting spree in July 1999 in Bloomington and Skokie. California has a hate crimes law, and yet Buford Furrow, another white supremacist, shot children in a Jewish community center and killed a Filipino mail carrier in Los Angeles in August 1999. Hate crime laws cannot protect from harm those who are the subject of discrimination, no matter what the editors of the *New York Times* believe.

The violent acts that are included in hate crime statutes are crimes that   4
are already prosecuted under state criminal codes. Murder is murder. Designating Byrd's or Shepard's murder as a hate crime rather than an "ordinary" crime does not change the fact that both men are still dead. Nor does it mean that law enforcement and the judiciary will prosecute their cases any more diligently.

Crime and Punishment

The second claim in the *New York Times* editorial—that hate crime laws   5
are necessary to ensure that those who commit hate crimes are properly punished—isn't a valid argument either. In Texas, a state known to aggressively carry out the death penalty, two of Byrd's killers were sentenced to death, the third to life in prison. Nor would a hate crimes law have made a difference for Shepard's killers in Wyoming, both of whom were sentenced to life in prison. These murderers all received the harshest penalty available under the law. But evidently being sentenced to the chair or life in prison isn't enough for the *New York Times*. Richard Dooling, a lawyer and author, explains what must be on some people's minds when they argue for hate crime laws:

> Texas's death penalty apparently isn't harsh enough for this kind of crime; we need a federal hate-crimes bill to send a message. Now white supremacists will know they can't get off so easy. They will receive enhanced penalties under federal law, even if retribution must be administered in the afterlife.[2]

Since we all know you can't kill someone twice or punish him after his death, hate crime laws are therefore redundant and unnecessary.

Thought Control

If hate crime legislation becomes the law of the land, then every trial   6
could potentially become an examination of the defendant's thoughts and beliefs. For example, during a trial in Ohio, the prosecutor attempted to prove a campground dispute was the result of racial animosity by

maintaining that because the defendant wasn't a close friend of his black neighbor, he was prejudiced against blacks. Despite testifying that he did have black friends, the accused was confronted with such questions as: "And you lived next door [to her] for nine years and you don't even know her first name? Never had dinner with her? Never gone out and had a beer with her? You don't associate with her, do you? All these black people that you have described that are your friends, I want you to give me one person, just one who was really a good friend of yours."[3] Under hate crime laws, the limits of relevant evidence would be expanded to include what books the accused read, the organizations he or she belonged to, and whether the defendant had a diverse range of friends. Every action and inaction would become suspect, and interrogations and prosecutions could become routine if the nation adopts hate crime laws.

7   But perhaps most importantly, how can anyone *know* what someone else was thinking during the commission of a crime and then be able to *prove* it? And even if you could prove that hate was the motivation for a crime, it is unconstitutional to punish a person for it. Sentencing a criminal with extra punishment for his beliefs while punishing him for his actions violates the First Amendment's guarantee of free speech. Thus, hate crime laws are a form of thought control. Hateful thought will have become a criminal activity, which is the first step toward a totalitarian government.

8   No other crime merits an enhanced sentence based on the criminal's thoughts. Frank Morriss, a contributing editor for the weekly Catholic newspaper the *Wanderer*, notes that sentences are not enhanced if an embezzler hates his employer, or if a bank robber hates bankers. There is only one judge of a person's thoughts, he maintains: "God has the right to judge on the basis of our motives; it is an invasion of our personal freedom of will for government to do so."[4] Giving the government such power over our thoughts and ideas threatens our rights to live and think as we please.

What Is Needed

9   Hate crime laws are unnecessary, ineffective, and dangerous. When bigots act on their hate and prejudice, then their crimes should be vilified and punished as the law requires. But law enforcement and judicial officials must continue to diligently prosecute *all* crimes, whether or not they are based on hate. And instead of passing new hate crime laws, Americans need to loudly and forcefully condemn such despicable acts of violence. Only when attitudes have changed toward minorities, homosexuals, women, and others who are the subject of discrimination will behavior finally start to change. A hate crimes law won't do it.

Notes

1. *New York Times*, "Murdered for Who He Was," 13 October 1998, A22.

2. Richard Dooling, "Punish Crime, Not Hate," *Wall Street Journal*, 20 July 1998, A18.

3. Quoted in George Will, "Hate Crimes: An Extension of Identity Politics," *Conservative Chronicle*, 21 October 1998, 27.

4. Frank Morriss, "Senate Vote on Hate Crimes Sweeps Aside Serious Considerations," *Wanderer*, 5 August 1999, 4.

Thinking Critically About Content

1. What purpose do the references to specific crimes serve in each essay? How do they further each argument?

2. What is the main argument of each essay?

3. Why do you think each author quotes authorities and cites historical examples? Explain your reasoning.

Thinking Critically About Purpose and Audience

4. What type of audience do you think would be most interested in the topic of these two essays? Explain your answer.

5. What tone do the authors use in these essays?

6. Which essay do you agree with more? Did you agree with that position before you read the essay? If you changed your mind as a result of reading one of these essays, which part of the essay made you change your mind? Explain your answer.

Thinking Critically About Paragraphs

7. Discuss the authors' methods of organizing their ideas in paragraph 3 of the first essay compared to paragraph 3 of the second essay. How are their methods of organization different in these paragraphs? How are they the same?

8. Compare the conclusions in these two essays. Do these conclusions each reflect the main points of their essays?

9. Which paragraph is most convincing to you in each essay? What makes each one so convincing?

10. Write a paragraph explaining one of the ideas or facts that both essays agree on.

Writing Topics: Arguing and Persuading

Before you begin to write, you might want to review the writing process in Part I.

1. "Why Study English?" suggests that learning how to speak, write, and read well is perhaps the best formula for success in life. Choose another subject and explain the degree to which competence in that discipline will most likely affect someone's life.

2. The two essays on hate crimes are both concerned with controlling and reducing this type of crime. Think of another strategy for fighting hate crimes, and attempt to convince a group of your peers to try your solution to the problem. Gather as much evidence as you can before you begin to write.

3. How can being able to develop good arguments and persuade people of your point of view help you in real life? How might this ability give you the edge over other people in the job market?

THE HANDBOOK

This part of *Mosaics* provides you with a complete handbook for editing your writing. You can use it as a reference tool as you write or as a source of instruction and practice in areas where you need work.

This handbook consists of an introduction and eight units:

The chapters in each unit start with a self-test to help you identify your strengths and weaknesses in that area. Then the chapters teach specific sentence skills and provide exercises so you can practice what you have learned. Each chapter also asks you to write your own sentences and then work with another student to edit each other's writing. At the end of each unit, two review tests are provided that ask you to apply to sentences and paragraphs all that you have practiced in the unit.

The Editing Symbols on the inside back cover will give you marks for highlighting errors in your papers. In addition, the Error Log (Appendix 6) and Spelling Log (Appendix 7) will help you tailor the instruction to your own needs and keep track of your progress.

Introduction: Parts of Speech, Phrases, and Clauses

This handbook uses very little terminology. But sometimes talking about the language and the way it works is difficult without a shared understanding of certain basic grammar terms. For that reason, your instructor may ask you to study parts of this introduction to review basic grammar—parts of speech, phrases, and clauses. You might also use this introduction for reference.

This section has three parts:

Parts of Speech
Phrases
Clauses

PARTS OF SPEECH

Test Yourself

In the following paragraph, label the parts of speech listed here:

2 verbs (v)	2 adverbs (adv)
2 nouns (n)	2 prepositions (prep)
2 pronouns (pro)	2 conjunctions (conj)
2 adjectives (adj)	2 interjections (int)

The personality trait that I like best about myself is my healthy sense of humor. No matter how bad a situation is, I can usually find something funny to say to cheer everyone up. When Toby's ancient car was stolen, I told him it was a piece of junk anyway, and I felt sorry for the foolish person who stole it. Man, we laughed so hard, imagining the car thief broken down on the side of the road somewhere in town. Oh, there are some things that I don't even try to joke about, like death and diseases. A person would have to be extremely insensitive to joke about those situations.

(Answers are in Appendix 4.)

Every sentence is made up of a variety of words that play different roles. Each word, like each part of a coordinated outfit, serves a distinct function. These functions fall into eight categories:

1. Verbs
2. Nouns
3. Pronouns
4. Adjectives
5. Adverbs
6. Prepositions
7. Conjunctions
8. Interjections

Some words, such as *is*, can function in only one way—in this case, as a verb. Other words, however, can serve as different parts of speech depending on how they are used in a sentence. For example, look at the different ways the word *burn* can be used:

Verb: The farmers **burn** the fields after every harvest.
(*Burn* is a verb here, telling what the farmers do.)

Noun: Yolanda's **burn** healed well.
(*Burn* functions as a noun here, telling what healed.)

Adjective: My mom found two **burn** marks on the sofa.
(*Burn* is an adjective here, modifying the noun *marks*.)

Verbs

The **verb** is the most important word in a sentence because every other word depends on it in some way. Verbs tell what's going on in the sentence.

There are three types of verbs: action, linking, and helping. An **action verb** tells what someone or something is doing. A **linking verb** tells what someone or something is, feels, or looks like. Sometimes an action or linking verb has **helping verbs**—words that add information, such as when an action is taking place. A **complete verb** consists of an action or linking verb and all the helping verbs.

Action:	We **started** the fire too close to the tent.
Action:	Mark **voted** in the election.
Linking:	We **felt** really smart.
Linking:	It **was** the most embarrassing moment in my life.
Helping:	She **will be** arriving tomorrow.
Helping:	I **have** been so tired lately.
Complete Verb:	She **will be arriving** tomorrow.
Complete Verb:	I **have been** so tired lately.

REVIEWING VERBS

Define each of the following types of verbs, and give an example of each.

Action: _____

_____

Linking: _____

_____

Helping: _____

_____

What is a complete verb? Give an example with your definition.

_____

_____

P r a c t i c e 1 Identifying In each of the following sentences, under-line the complete verbs. Some sentences have more than one verb.

1. We left on our fishing expedition when we got off work.
2. My brother has felt guilty since he took my money.
3. People sometimes think more than they act.
4. The first sign of trouble came almost immediately.
5. Next weekend we will be going Christmas shopping at the mall.

P r a c t i c e   2   **Completing** Fill in each blank in the following paragraph with a verb.

Last weekend we (1) ___wanted___ to go shopping at a nearby outlet mall. Before we got out of the city limits, Maryl (2) _____ that she was really thirsty and Kurt (3) _____ hungry. So we stopped at the first convenience store we saw. While Kurt and Maryl were inside the store, I (4) _____ steam coming from under the hood of my car. After checking it out, I (5) _____ water leaking from the radiator, so we canceled the trip and went home.

P r a c t i c e   3   **Writing Your Own** Write a sentence of your own for each of the following verbs.

1. had been going _____

2. chuckled _____

3. appeared _____

4. did become _____

5. whispers _____

Nouns

People often think of **nouns** as "naming words" because they identify—or name—people (*friend, Brian, dad, officer*), places (*town, lake, Greenville*), or things (*tree, boat, table, belt*). Nouns also name ideas (*freedom, democracy*), qualities (*honesty, courage*), emotions (*fear, anxiety*), and actions (*competition, negotiations*). A **common noun** names something general (*actor, mountain, soda, restaurant*). A **proper noun** names something specific (*Julia Roberts, Mt. McKinley, Pepsi, Burger King*).

Hint: To test whether a word is a noun, try putting *a, an,* or *the* in front of it:

Nouns: a friend, an apple, the love
NOT Nouns: a silly, an around, the sing

This test does not work with proper nouns:

NOT   a Ken, the Seattle

REVIEWING NOUNS

What is a noun?

_____

_____

What is the difference between a common noun and a proper noun? Give an example of each.

Common noun: _____

_____

Proper noun: _____

_____

P r a c t i c e 4 Identifying Underline all the nouns in the following sentences.

1. Students in college have many responsibilities.
2. Before my friend ran in the marathon, she trained for months.
3. Last fall, my husband and I bought our first house.
4. David nodded his head while I presented my ideas.
5. Minnesota is known for its many lakes and excellent universities.

P r a c t i c e 5 Completing Fill in each blank in the following paragraph with a noun that will make each sentence complete.

My best (1) _friend_ is my brother Ben. He is 18, about six feet tall with curly brown hair. He is really a neat (2) _brother_. I have to say that he is unusual and does his own thing. For example, he likes to wear (3) _shorts_ during the wintertime. When he goes out, people usually point and stare. Ben just shakes his (4) _head_ and keeps on walking. But Ben's best qualities are his (5) _traits_ and his _determination_ to help people.

Practice 6 Writing Your Own Write a sentence of your own for each of the following nouns.

1. jury _The jury made its dicision_

2. point _The point of the paper was very colerent_

3. lateness _My lateness for class is getting worse_

4. determination _My detesmination for class is not very strong_

5. Michael Jordan _M. J. is an incredible basketball player_

Pronouns

Pronouns can do anything nouns can do. In fact, **pronouns** can take the place of nouns. Without pronouns, you would find yourself repeating nouns and producing boring sentences. Compare the following sentences, for example:

Maxine picked up **Maxine's** cell phone and called **Maxine's** friend Sam to say **Maxine** was on **Maxine's** way.

Maxine picked up **her** cell phone and called **her** friend Sam to say **she** was on **her** way.

There are many different types of pronouns, but you only need to focus on the following four types for now.

Most Common Pronouns

Personal (refer to people or things)

Singular:	*First Person:*	I, me, my, mine
	Second Person:	you, your, yours
	Third Person:	he, she, it, him, her, hers, his, its

Plural:	First Person:	we, us, our, ours
	Second Person:	you, your, yours
	Third Person:	they, them, their, theirs

Demonstrative (point out someone or something)

Singular:　this, that

Plural:　these, those

Relative (introduce a dependent clause)

who, whom, whose, which, that

Indefinite (refer to someone or something general, not specific)

Singular:　another, anybody, anyone, anything, each, either, everybody, everyone, everything, little, much, neither, nobody, none, no one, nothing, one, other, somebody, someone, something

Plural:　both, few, many, others, several

Either Singular or Plural:　all, any, more, most, some

Hint: When any of these words are used with nouns, they are pronouns used as adjectives.

Adjective:　She can have **some cookies.**
Pronoun:　She can have **some.**

Adjective:　I want **that car.**
Pronoun:　I want **that.**

Reviewing Pronouns

What is a pronoun?

Define the four most common types of pronouns, and give two examples of each.

Personal: _____

Demonstrative: _____

Relative: _____

Indefinite: _____

◆ **P r a c t i c e   7   Identifying** Underline all the pronouns in the following sentences. Don't underline pronouns that are really adjectives.

1. Some of the fruit was shipped from Florida.
2. I don't believe he could have committed such crimes.
3. Whoever took the last piece of pie should confess!
4. If we help each other, we can finish by Sunday.
5. This is the last time I spend any of my money calling a psychic hotline.

◆ **P r a c t i c e   8   Completing** In the following paragraph, replace the nouns in parentheses with pronouns.

Have you ever received an anonymous card or letter? I did. In fact, I received several cards. To this day I still don't know who sent (1) _____ (the cards). I remember when I got the first card. (2) _____ (The card) was written in a scratchy handwriting and signed "Your Secret Admirer." Of course, I asked my friends Amy and Beth whether (3) _____ (Amy and Beth) knew who had sent it. Though (4) _____ (Amy and Beth) denied it, I think Amy was more involved than (5) _____ (Amy) admits.

◆ **P r a c t i c e   9   Writing Your Own** Write a sentence of your own for each of the following pronouns.

1. they _____

2. anybody _____

3. those _____

4. who _____

5. few _____

Adjectives

Adjectives modify—or describe—nouns or pronouns. Adjectives generally make sentences clear and vivid.

Without Adjectives:	We had our rods, a cooler, and some sandwiches for the trip.
With Adjectives:	We had our **trusty fly** rods, a **white plastic** cooler, and **several tuna** sandwiches for the trip.

REVIEWING ADJECTIVES

What is an adjective?

_____

Give three examples of adjectives.

_____ _____ _____

◆ *P r a c t i c e 1 0* **Identifying** Underline all the adjectives in the following sentences.

1. Her long red hair bounced as she walked down the sunlit street.
2. Carl's successful career results from his hard work and pure determination.
3. Ali's poor old car needs two new tires and a complete under-the-hood check.
4. If you want to go on the camping trip, turn in the registration slip.
5. My little brother lost the remote control for our big-screen TV.

◆ *P r a c t i c e 1 1* **Completing** Fill in each blank in the following paragraph with an adjective.

We went to a (1) _____ play at the Little Theater on campus. It was a (2) _____ comedy written by a (3) _____ student at our school. The lead actor was a (4) _____ guy who kept everyone laughing with his (5) _____ faces and clever lines.

Practice 12   **Writing Your Own** Write a sentence of your own for each of the following adjectives.

1. sparkling _____

2. tasty _____

3. upset _____

4. fourth _____

5. thrilling _____

Adverbs

Adverbs modify—or describe—adjectives, verbs, and other adverbs. They do *not* modify nouns. Adverbs also answer the following questions:

How?	carefully, fast, quickly, slowly
When?	yesterday, lately, early, now
Where?	outside, here, there, deeply
How often?	usually, seldom, regularly, promptly
To what extent?	very, almost, too, hardly

Hint: Notice that adverbs often end in *-ly*. That might help you recognize them.

REVIEWING ADVERBS

What is an adverb?

_____

What are the five questions that adverbs answer?

_____ _____ _____ _____ _____

Give one example of an adverb that answers each question.

_____ _____ _____ _____ _____

P r a c t i c e 1 3   **Identifying** Underline all the adverbs in the following sentences.

1. My curious cat sat very quietly for a few seconds before she quickly pounced on the fly.
2. Steve was quite upset after badly missing the shot.
3. We will never do business with the Simpsons again.
4. Often Mr. Ringold asks, "Are you working hard or hardly working?"
5. I don't necessarily think we need to go there tomorrow.

P r a c t i c e 1 4   **Completing** Fill in each blank in the following paragraph with an adverb.

(1) _____ I decided to find a new job, a (2) _____ easy task, or so I thought. I began by (3) _____ going through the phone book and listing each business that I thought would be hiring (4) _____. After calling ten businesses that said they weren't hiring, I (5) _____ realized this job hunt would be more difficult than I first thought.

P r a c t i c e 1 5   **Writing Your Own** Write a sentence of your own for each of the following adverbs.

1. quickly _____

2. fast _____

3. sometimes _____

4. down _____

5. always _____

Prepositions

Prepositions indicate relationships among the ideas in a sentence. Something is *up, down, next to, behind, around, near,* or *under* something else. A preposition is always followed by a noun or a pronoun called the **object of the preposition.** Together, they form a **prepositional phrase.**

Preposition	+	Object	=	Prepositional Phrase
of	+	the supplies	=	of the supplies
for	+	the lake	=	for the lake

Here is a list of some common prepositions.

Common Prepositions

about	beside	into	since
above	between	like	through
across	beyond	near	throughout
after	by	next to	to
against	despite	of	toward
among	down	off	under
around	during	on	until
as	except	on top of	up
at	for	out	upon
before	from	out of	up to
behind	in	outside	with
below	in front of	over	within
beneath	inside	past	without

Hint: *To* + a verb (as in *to go, to come, to feel*) is not a prepositional phrase. It is a verb phrase, which we will deal with later in this unit.

REVIEWING PREPOSITIONS

What is a preposition?

_____

Give two examples of prepositions:

_____   _____

What is a prepositional phrase?

_____

_____

Give two examples of prepositional phrases:

_____   _____

Practice 16 **Identifying** Underline all the prepositions in the following sentences.

1. James said the concert <u>by</u> the college jazz band would take place during the last week of May.
2. Carlos was <u>with</u> us when we talked <u>after</u> the party.
3. <u>Before</u> the movie, we talked <u>among</u> ourselves <u>in</u> a downtown park.
4. Sharon was lying <u>on</u> the couch watching *Jeopardy* on TV when I walked <u>into</u> the room.
5. Colin looked <u>under</u> his bed and <u>inside</u> his closet, but he never found his math book.

Practice 17 **Completing** Fill in each blank in the following paragraph with a preposition.

One day as I waited (1) _____ the bus, a tall man sat down (2) _____ me on the bench and began talking (3) _____ the weather. I agreed that it certainly had been hot (4) _____ the city. As we were talking, a police officer came around the corner and began walking (5) _____ the sidewalk toward us. For some strange reason, the man quickly stood up and walked away.

Practice 18 **Writing Your Own** Write a sentence of your own for each of the following prepositions.

1. of _____

2. without _____

3. along _____

4. like _____

5. despite _____

Conjunctions

Conjunctions connect groups of words. Without conjunctions, most of our writing would be choppy and boring. The two types of conjunctions are easy to remember because their names state their purpose: *Coordinating conjunctions* link equal ideas, and *subordinating conjunctions* make one idea subordinate to—or dependent on—another.

Coordinating conjunctions connect parts of a sentence that are of equal importance or weight. These parts can be **independent clauses,** a group of words with a subject and verb that can stand alone as a sentence (see page 378). There are only seven coordinating conjunctions:

Coordinating Conjunctions

and, but, or, nor, for, so, yet

Coordinating*:*   I wanted to explore the caves, **and** Greg wanted to go up in a hot air balloon.

Coordinating: Our adventure turned into a nightmare, **but** we learned an important lesson.

Subordinating conjunctions join two ideas by making one dependent on the other. The idea introduced by the subordinating conjunction becomes a **dependent clause,** a group of words with a subject and a verb that cannot stand alone as a sentence (see page 378). The other part of the sentence is an independent clause.

Dependent Clause

Subordinating: I don't know <u>when I will return</u>.

Dependent Clause

Subordinating: <u>If we save enough money</u>, we can go to Disneyland.

Here are some common subordinating conjunctions.

Common Subordinating Conjunctions

after	because	since	until
although	before	so	when
as	even if	so that	whenever
as if	even though	than	where
as long as	how	that	wherever
as soon as	if	though	whether
as though	in order that	unless	while

REVIEWING CONJUNCTIONS

What is a coordinating conjunction?

_____

_____

Name the seven coordinating conjunctions.

_____   _____   _____   _____   _____   _____   _____

What is a subordinating conjunction?

_____

_____

Write a sentence using a subordinating conjunction.

_____

◆ Practice 19   Identifying Underline all the conjunctions in the following sentences.

1. I hate going grocery shopping, though I love to cook.
2. Whether or not you're ready for it, becoming a parent will change your life.
3. You can't rent a car unless you have a credit card.
4. Pedro would make a great attorney, and he would get paid to argue.
5. I thought this class was easy until we took the midterm.

◆ *P r a c t i c e 2 0* **Completing** Fill in each blank in the following paragraph with a conjunction.

(1) _____ I work two jobs and go to school, I have little spare time. Whenever possible, I try very hard to find time for myself. (2) _____ I have so many things to do, I sit down and write out everything in the order it has to be done. I try to make a schedule, (3) _____ I have a tendency to get side-tracked. For example, (4) _____ I have homework, it has to be my first priority. But (5) _____ work and school are finished, I make sure I save time for my friends.

◆ *P r a c t i c e 2 1* **Writing Your Own** Write a sentence of your own for each of the following conjunctions.

1. after _____

2. because _____

3. but _____

4. so _____

5. although _____

Interjections

Interjections are words that express strong emotion, surprise, or disappointment. An interjection is usually followed by an exclamation point or a comma.

Interjection: **Help!** The boat is drifting away.
Interjection: **Wow,** what an unbelievable game!

Other common interjections include *aha, awesome, great, hallelujah, neat, oh, oops, ouch, well, whoa, yeah,* and *yippee.*

REVIEWING INTERJECTIONS

What is an interjection?

_____

_____

Write a sentence using an interjection.

_____

Practice 22 Identifying Underline all the interjections in the following sentences.

1. Yeah! We got the best seats in the house!
2. Man, my legs are tired after running ten miles.
3. Oh, I almost forgot that I have a dentist appointment.
4. That was the best grade I've ever received in math. Hallelujah!
5. Ouch! I stubbed my toe.

Practice 23 Completing Fill in each blank in the following paragraph with an interjection.

(1) _____, was I tired last night! I woke up yesterday morning at the crack of dawn, climbed into the shower, and slipped on the bar of soap before I could even get my eyes completely open. (2) _____! Then I got into my car and, (3) _____, it wouldn't start. After calling a friend to give me a ride to work, I got to my desk to find an emergency project that needed to be completed before the end of my shift. (4) _____, I worked on it all day, though I had to stay late to finish it. (5) _____! I am so glad that day is over!

◆ *P r a c t i c e 2 4*   **Writing Your Own** Write a sentence of your own for each of the following interjections.

1. cool _____

2. help _____

3. good gracious _____

4. oh _____

5. oops _____

PHRASES

Test Yourself

Underline the phrases in the following sentences.

- After the concert, we decided to get some food.
- To get a good grade on the test, I know I have to study harder.
- Benito lives in the brick house at the end of the block behind the park.
- I am going to get a job this year.
- Do you want to see a movie with us?

(Answers are in Appendix 4.)

A **phrase** is a group of words that function together as a unit. Phrases cannot stand alone, however, because they are missing a subject, a verb, or both.

Phrases:	the black mountain bike, a happy person
Phrases:	turned up the music, cruised the mall, opened my present
Phrases:	after school, in the back room, by myself, on the green grass
Phrases:	telling us the answer, to be fooled

Notice that all these groups of words are missing a subject, a verb, or both.

REVIEWING PHRASES

What is a phrase?

_____

_____

Give two examples of phrases.

_____   _____

Practice 25 **Identifying** Underline 8 phrases in the following sentences.

1. Looking out the window, I watched the countryside from the train.
2. I like to do adventurous things like skydiving and rock climbing.
3. My favorite vacation was our trip to the Bahamas three years ago.
4. Customers should have completed their deposit slips.
5. Save energy by turning off the lights after everyone has left the room.

Practice 26 **Completing** Fill in each blank in the following paragraph with a phrase.

Sang went (1) _____ early because he had worked overtime yesterday afternoon. But since his roommate was cleaning the apartment, (2) _____, and (3) _____, Sang knew he would not be able to sleep. Tony, Sang's roommate, wanted everything clean because his parents (4) _____. His last chore was to get a can of air freshener (5) _____ and spray it around the apartment.

Practice 27 **Writing Your Own** Write a sentence of your own for each of the following phrases.

1. the timid first-grader _____

2. is sending out invitations _____

3. in the river _____

4. to attend college _____

5. energized by food and sleep _____

CLAUSES

Test Yourself

Underline the clauses in the following sentences.

- Mallory will get what she wants out of life because she is assertive.
- Since you don't have time to go to dinner, I'll bring you some food.
- If Rachel is going to leave first, she needs a map.
- We finished painting, and then we celebrated.
- I enjoyed the book the most when Harry Potter got the sorcerer's stone.

(Answers are in Appendix 4.)

Like phrases, **clauses** are groups of words. But unlike phrases, a clause always contains a subject and a verb. There are two types of clauses: *independent* and *dependent*.

An **independent clause** contains a subject and a verb and can stand alone and make sense by itself. Every complete sentence must have at least one independent clause.

Independent Clause: We planned our vacation very carefully.

Now look at the following group of words. It is a clause because it contains a subject and a verb. But it is a **dependent clause** because it is introduced by a word that makes it dependent, *since*.

Dependent Clause: **Since** we planned our vacation very carefully.

This clause cannot stand alone. It must be connected to an independent clause to make sense. Here is one way to complete the dependent clause and form a complete sentence.

        Dependent   Independent

Since we planned our vacation very carefully, we had a great time.

Hint: Subordinating conjunctions (such as *since, although, because, while*) and relative pronouns (*who, whom, whose, which, that*) make clauses dependent. (For more information on subordinating conjunctions, see page 373, and on relative pronouns, see page 365.)

REVIEWING CLAUSES

For a group of words to be a clause, it must have a _____

and a _____ .

What is an independent clause?

_____

_____

What is a dependent clause?

_____

_____

Name the two kinds of words that can begin a dependent clause.

_____ _____

Name five subordinating conjunctions.

_____ _____ _____ _____ _____

Name the five relative pronouns.

_____ _____ _____ _____ _____

Practice 28 **Identifying** Each of the following sentences is made up of two clauses. Circle the coordinating or subordinating conjunctions and relative pronouns. Then label each clause either independent (Ind) or dependent (Dep).

1. When Veronica got up, she made her bed and brushed her teeth.

2. The truck swerved toward his car, and Jason veered to the side of the road.

3. Unless you are planning to major in science, you don't need to take chemistry.

4. I am familiar with the person who won the contest.

5. Until he makes the team, Chan will continue to practice his swing.

◆ *Practice 29* **Completing** Add an independent or dependent clause that will complete each sentence and make sense.

Matt is an artist (1) who _____. (2) He _____. He buys supplies with half of his earnings, (3) and _____. His most recent drawing won a prize, (4) which _____. He says he will never sell it (5) because _____.

◆ *Practice 30* **Writing Your Own** Write five independent clauses. Then add at least one dependent clause to each independent clause.

_____

_____

_____

_____

_____

REVIEW

You might want to reread your answers to the questions in all the review boxes before you do the following exercises.

◆ *Review **P r a c t i c e** 1* **Identifying** Use the following abbreviations to label the underlined words in these sentences.

v	Verb	adv	Adverb
n	Noun	prep	Preposition
pro	Pronoun	conj	Conjunction
adj	Adjective	int	Interjection
ph	Phrase	cl	Clause

1. <u>Hey</u>, remember to meet with <u>your</u> <u>counselor</u> <u>before</u> choosing your <u>classes</u>.

2. Stacy <u>works</u> as a <u>telephone</u> salesperson and <u>has</u> to meet a <u>daily</u> quota.

3. An <u>education</u> enables people to obtain knowledge, <u>confidence</u>, <u>and</u> marketable skills.

4. <u>While</u> we <u>were eating</u> dinner at <u>Jake's Tex Mex</u>, my parents and <u>I</u> were discussing my <u>college</u> bills.

5. The <u>best</u> movie made <u>in 2002</u> was *Chicago*.

6. Men <u>who hunt wild game</u> are not <u>necessarily</u> <u>trying to destroy nature</u>.

7. My brother <u>lives</u> <u>in</u> Virginia because <u>he</u> is <u>in the Navy</u>.

8. There is <u>nothing</u> better than a <u>warm</u> fire on a <u>cold</u> day.

9. Tom <u>wanted</u> to date <u>Susan</u>, but <u>she</u> <u>is</u> dating Damian.

10. If you <u>maintain</u> a B+ average, you will <u>likely</u> qualify <u>for</u> grants <u>or</u> scholarships.

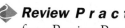 **Review P r a c t i c e 2 Completing** Fill in each blank in the following paragraph with an appropriate word, phrase, or clause, as indicated.

I saved money for six months to buy a new (1) _____ (noun) for my (2) _____ (adjective) car. I found a store where I could (3) _____ (verb) this product, (4) _____ (conjunction) I waited an extra week for it to go on sale. The store was located (5) _____ (preposition) town, but it was worth the drive. (6) _____ (interjection)! I had wanted this thing for a long time! On my next day off work, I (7) _____ (adverb) drove to the store and made the purchase. I talked to the salesperson for about an hour, and (8) _____ (pronoun) assured me I was making a wise purchase. But when (9) _____ (clause), the item I had saved so long for did not work properly, and I completely lost my temper. I picked the thing up and angrily threw it (10) _____ (phrase).

Review P r a c t i c e 3 Writing Your Own Write your own paragraph about your favorite pet. What did you name it? What kind of animal was it?

Review P r a c t i c e 4 Editing Your Writing Exchange paragraphs from Review Practice 3 with a classmate, and do the following:

1. Circle any words that are used incorrectly.
2. Underline any phrases that do not read smoothly.
3. Put an X in the margin where you find a dependent clause that is not connected to an independent clause.

Then return the paragraph to its writer, and use the information in the Introduction to edit your own paragraph. Record your errors on the Error Log in Appendix 6.

SUBJECTS AND VERBS

CHAPTER 30

✔ CHECKLIST for Identifying Subjects and Verbs

> ✔ Does each of your sentences contain a subject?
> ✔ Does each of your sentences contain a verb?

Test Yourself

Circle the subjects and underline the verbs in each sentence.

- We really liked the movie.
- Melissa and Giselle left early.
- She is in class.
- Clean your room.
- The Masons have never remodeled their kitchen.
- She checked the oil and put air in the tires.

(Answers are in Appendix 4.)

A sentence has a message to communicate, but for communication to take place, it must have a subject and a verb. The subject is the topic of the sentence or what the sentence is about. The verb is the sentence's motor. It moves the message forward to its destination. Without these two parts, the sentence is not complete.

SUBJECTS

To be complete, every sentence must have a subject. The **subject** tells who or what the sentence is about.

Subject
↓
She   never liked movies at all.

Mystery **novels**   appeal to everyone.

Compound Subjects

When two or more separate words tell what the sentence is about, the sentence has a **compound subject.**

Compound Subject: **Hamburgers** and **hotdogs** are my favorite foods.

Compound Subject: **Margaret** and **I** watch movies every night.

Hint: Note that *and* is not part of the compound subject.

Unstated Subjects

Sometimes a subject does not actually appear in a sentence but is understood. This occurs in commands and requests. The understood subject is always *you*, meaning either someone specific or anyone in general.

Command: Call your boss in the morning.

                        s

Unstated Subject: **(You)** call your boss in the morning.

Request: Pass me the salt, please.

                        s

Unstated Subject: **(You)** pass me the salt, please.

Subjects and Prepositional Phrases

The subject of a sentence cannot be part of a prepositional phrase. A **prepositional phrase** is a group of words that begins with a **preposition,** a word like *in, on, under, after,* or *from.* Here are some examples of prepositional phrases:

in the hall	**next to** me	**on** the stairs	**before** dinner
under your pillow	**with** Brad	**behind** the car	**instead of** you

after lunch   into the cave   around the block   across the street

from the mayor's   during the day   for the child   at home
office

(See page 370 for a more complete list of prepositions.)

If you are looking for the subject of a sentence, first cross out all the prepositional phrases. Then figure out what the sentence is about.

<del>After dinner</del>, my friend and I went home.

The classified ads <del>in the local newspaper</del> were misleading.

One <del>of our cows</del> got <del>into a neighboring pasture</del> last night.

REVIEWING SUBJECTS

What is a subject?

_____

What is a compound subject?

_____

_____

What is an unstated subject?

_____

How can you find the subject of a sentence?

_____

_____

◆ *P r a c t i c e 1* **Identifying** Cross out the prepositional phrases in each of the following sentences, and then underline the subjects.

1. The boxers stood in their corners.
2. One of the artists is showing his paintings at a gallery in New York City.
3. Manuel and Jack are both good guitar players.
4. After the first of the year, I will begin preparing my taxes.
5. Start working on your term paper immediately.

◈ *P r a c t i c e   2* **Completing** Fill in each blank in the following sentences with a subject without using a person's name.

1. _____ slept fitfully last night.

2. _____ strutted across the stage to a cheering crowd.

3. Sitting high above the pool, _____ thought about life.

4. Sometimes _____ comes out all wrong.

5. _____ are always backing out at the last moment.

◈ *P r a c t i c e   3* **Writing Your Own** Write five sentences of your own, and circle the subjects.

_____

_____

_____

_____

_____

VERBS

To be complete, a sentence must have a verb as well as a subject. A **verb** tells what the subject is doing or what is happening.

Verb
↓

She   never **liked** movies at all.
Mystery novels   **appeal** to everyone.

Action Verbs

An **action verb** tells what a subject is doing. Some examples of action verbs are *run, skate, discuss, hurt, allow, forget, pretend, hope, laugh, increase, listen,* and *hurry.*

Action Verb: The players **raced** down the court.

Action Verb: The bus **stopped** at the bus stop.

Linking Verbs

A **linking verb** connects the subject to other words in the sentence that say something about it. Linking verbs are also called **state-of-being verbs** because they do not show action. Rather, they say that something "is" a particular way. The most common linking verb is *be* (*am, are, is, was, were*).

Linking Verb: The cats **are** in the other room.

Linking Verb: He **was** very happy to see her.

Other common linking verbs are *become, feel, look, appear,* and *seem.*

Linking: She **became** a lawyer.

Linking: Mom **feels** sick.

Linking: His beard **looks** rough and scratchy.

Linking: Ashley and Jack **appear** very worried.

Linking: My brother **seems** happy with his choice of career.

Some words, like *smell* and *taste,* can be either action verbs or linking verbs.

Action: I **smell** a skunk.

Linking: This rose **smells** so fragrant.

Action: I **tasted** the stew.

Linking: It **tasted** very good.

Compound Verbs

Just as a verb can have more than one subject, some subjects can have more than one verb. These are called **compound verbs.**

Compound Verb: She **watches** and **feeds** his dog on the weekends.

Compound Verb: I **visit** my grandparents and **play** cards with them.

Hint: A sentence can have both a compound subject and a compound verb.

s   s   v   v

Gus and Burt ran from the car and dove into the water.

Helping Verbs

Often the **main verb** (the action verb or linking verb) in a sentence needs help to convey its meaning. **Helping verbs** add information, such as when an action took place. The **complete verb** consists of a main verb and all its helping verbs.

Complete Verb:	The horses <u>are galloping</u> to the finish line.
Complete Verb:	Angelica <u>**did** feel</u> angry.
Complete Verb:	They <u>**might** come</u> with us.
Complete Verb:	Maybe we <u>**should have** gone</u> to the library.
Complete Verb:	My favorite teacher <u>**used to** give</u> a quiz every week.
Complete Verb:	Duane <u>**will**</u> not <u>**be** graduating</u> this year.

Hint: Note that *not* isn't part of the helping verb. Similarly, *never, always, only, just,* and *still* are never part of the verb.

Complete Verb:	I <u>**have**</u> never <u>**been**</u> so insulted in my life.

The most common helping verbs are

be, am, is, are, was, were
have, has, had
do, did

Other common helping verbs are

may, might
can, could
will, would
should, used to, ought to

REVIEWING VERBS

What is a verb?

_____

What is the difference between action and linking verbs?

_____

_____

Give an example of a compound verb. _____

Give an example of a helping verb. _____

What is the difference between a subject and a verb?

_____

_____

P r a c t i c e 4 **Identifying** Underline the complete verbs in each of the following sentences.

1. The workers became tired early.
2. O, *The Oprah Magazine* has been recognized as a very popular magazine.
3. One young woman with too many problems left school early.
4. If she succeeds, she feels happy and fulfilled.
5. Don't encourage her.

P r a c t i c e 5 **Completing** Fill in each blank in the following sentences with a verb. Avoid using *is*, *are*, *was*, and *were* except as helping verbs.

1. Orlando _____ extremely lucky.
2. The field workers _____ tired.
3. My manager _____ crossword puzzles every day.

4. Both the instructors and the deans _____ patiently for the meeting to begin.

5. Computers _____ our daily lives.

◆ **P r a c t i c e   6   Writing Your Own** Write five sentences of your own, and underline all the verbs in each.

_____

_____

_____

_____

_____

CHAPTER REVIEW

You might want to reread your answers to the questions in all the review boxes before you do the following exercises.

◆ **Review P r a c t i c e   1   Identifying** Underline the subjects once and the verbs twice in each of the following sentences. Cross out the prepositional phrases first.

1. The competitors eyed one another warily and looked ready for the game.
2. Sculptors work from a variety of raw material.
3. David was quite a good piano player.
4. After April 15th, she will begin my campaign for office.
5. Every year, her parents put money into her college fund.
6. The first three scenes in the horror film were frightening.
7. The earth and the buildings shook and cracked.
8. The singer couldn't remember the right words to the song.
9. Professional athletes and movie stars have the highest paying jobs in America.
10. My brother doesn't like his current job.

◆ *Review* **P r a c t i c e** *2* **Completing** Fill in the missing subjects or verbs in each of the following sentences.

1. _____ got the best seats in the house.

2. Usually _____ just waited and hoped for someone else to volunteer.

3. Mark and Mabel _____ to stay at the fancy hotel.

4. Every day _____ leaves the house to go to work in the grocery store.

5. Carrying the grand piano _____ a difficult task.

6. Certainly, _____ returned a little later and _____ a midnight movie.

7. In the spring, we usually _____ our house really well and _____ a huge garage sale.

8. Most of the time, my uncle _____ does the cooking, and my aunt _____ takes care of the lawn.

9. I _____ not _____ to scream.

10. _____ often is caught reading newspapers and magazines.

◆ *Review* **P r a c t i c e** *3* **Writing Your Own** Write a paragraph explaining what you would do if you won the lottery.

◆ *Review* **P r a c t i c e** *4* **Editing Through Collaboration** Exchange paragraphs from Review Practice 3 with another student, and do the following:

1. Circle the subjects.

2. Underline the verbs.

Then return the paragraph to its writer, and edit any sentences in your own paragraph that do not have both a subject and a verb. Record your errors on the Error Log in Appendix 6.

CHAPTER 31

FRAGMENTS

✔ CHECKLIST for Identifying and Correcting Fragments

> ✔ Does each sentence have a subject?
> ✔ Does each sentence have a verb?

Test Yourself

Put an X by the sentences that are fragments.

- _____ We were hoping that the test would be easy.
- _____ Which he did not see at first.
- _____ She wanted to become a musician.
- _____ Running to catch the plane, with her suitcase flying.
- _____ Since the newspaper had reported it.

(Answers are in Appendix 4.)

One of the most common errors in college writing is the fragment. A fragment is a piece of a sentence that is punctuated as a complete sentence. But it does not express a complete thought. Once you learn how to identify fragments, you can avoid them in your writing.

ABOUT FRAGMENTS

A complete sentence must have both a subject and a verb. If one or both are missing or if the subject and verb are introduced by a dependent word, you have only part of a sentence, a **fragment.** Even if it begins with a capital letter and ends with a period, it cannot stand alone and must be corrected in your writing. The five most common types of fragments are explained in this chapter.

Type 1: Afterthought Fragments

He works out at the gym. **And runs several miles a week.**

Type 2: *-ing* Fragments

Finding no food in the refrigerator. LaKesha went to the store.

Type 3: *to* Fragments

The company sponsored a national training program. **To increase its sales by 20 percent.**

Type 4: Dependent-Clause Fragments

Since he bought a Chevy Blazer. His insurance has gone up.

Type 5: Relative-Clause Fragments

I climbed Mt. Everest. **Which is the tallest mountain in the world.**

Once you have identified a fragment, you have two options for correcting it. You can connect the fragment to the sentence before or after it, or make the fragment into an independent clause.

Ways to Correct Fragments

Correction 1:   *Connect the fragment to the sentence before or after it.*

Correction 2:   *Make the fragment into an independent clause:*

  (a) add the missing subject and/or verb, or

  (b) drop the subordinating word before the fragment.

We will discuss these corrections for each type of fragment.

REVIEWING FRAGMENTS

What is a sentence fragment?

_____

_____

What are the five types of fragments?

_____   _____

_____   _____

_____

What are the two ways to correct a fragment?

1. _____

2. _____

IDENTIFYING AND CORRECTING FRAGMENTS

The rest of this chapter discusses the five types of fragments and the corrections for each type.

Type 1: Afterthought Fragments

Afterthought fragments occur when you add an idea to a sentence but don't punctuate it correctly.

Fragment: He works out at the gym. **And runs several miles a week.**

The phrase *And runs several miles a week* is punctuated and capitalized as a complete sentence. Because this group of words lacks a subject, however, it is a fragment.

Correction 1:   *Connect the fragment to the sentence before or after it.*

Example: He works out at the gym **and** runs several miles a week.

Correction 2:   *Make the fragment into an independent clause.*

Example: He works out at the gym. **He** runs several miles a week.

The first correction connects the fragment to the sentence before it or after it. The second correction makes the fragment an independent clause with its own subject and verb.

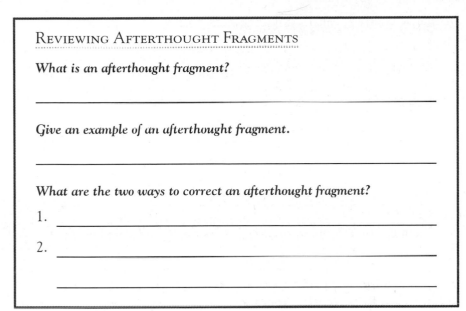

REVIEWING AFTERTHOUGHT FRAGMENTS

What is an afterthought fragment?

_____

Give an example of an afterthought fragment.

_____

What are the two ways to correct an afterthought fragment?

1. _____

2. _____

_____

P r a c t i c e   1 A **Identifying** Underline the afterthought fragments in each of the following sentences.

1. The competition was tough. We were all afraid to play them. Including me.

2. With his face against the window. He could see his keys lying on the end table.

3. She stayed up late last night. Now she's sleeping. In class.

4. Spring is my favorite time of year. With all the flowers in bloom. And lovers holding hands.

5. Aikio was very nervous. Before her job interview. I hope she calms down.

P r a c t i c e   1 B **Correcting** Correct the fragments in Practice 1A by rewriting each sentence.

P r a c t i c e   2 **Completing** Correct the following afterthought fragments using both correction 1 and correction 2. Rewrite any corrected sentences that you think could be smoother.

1. She found a beautiful vase at the yard sale. Also some antique chairs.

_____

2. Benny studied really hard. Lisa, too.

    _____

3. My mom makes the best brownies. Sometimes with walnuts and frosting.

    _____

4. They married December 6. In Las Vegas.

    _____

5. The mysterious woman stood in the doorway. And stared at him.

    _____

♦ *P r a c t i c e 3* **Writing Your Own** Write five afterthought fragments of your own, and correct them.

    _____

    _____

    _____

    _____

    _____

Type 2: *-ing* Fragments

Words that end in *-ing* are forms of verbs but cannot be the main verbs in their sentences. For an *-ing* word to function as a verb, it must have a helping verb with it (see page 388).

Fragment: **Finding no food in the refrigerator.** LaKesha went to the store.

Finding is not a verb in this sentence because it has no helping verb. Also, this group of words is a fragment because it has no subject.

Correction 1:   *Connect the fragment to the sentence before or after it.*

Example: **Finding no food in the refrigerator,** LaKesha went to the store.

Correction 2:   *Make the fragment into an independent clause.*

Example: **She found no food in the refrigerator.** LaKesha went to the store.

Hint: When you connect an *-ing* fragment to a sentence, insert a comma between the two sentence parts. You should insert the comma whether the *-ing* part comes at the beginning or the end of the sentence.

LaKesha went to the store, **finding no food in the refrigerator.**
Finding no food in the refrigerator, LaKesha went to the store.

REVIEWING *-ing* FRAGMENTS

How can you tell if an -ing word is part of a fragment or is a main verb?

_____

_____

Give an example of an -ing fragment.

_____

What are the two ways to correct an -ing fragment?

1. _____

2. _____

_____

What kind of punctuation should you use when you join an -ing fragment to another sentence?

_____

◆ *P r a c t i c e   **4 A**   **Identifying** Underline the *-ing* fragments in each of the following sentences.

1. Driving like a maniac. She made the trip in ten hours.
2. Yvonne joined a health club. Thinking that would motivate her to exercise.
3. Threatening the Florida coast. The hurricane grew in force.
4. Drew cleaned his house thoroughly. Vacuuming, dusting, and washing windows.
5. He's at the student union. Hanging out.

◆ *P r a c t i c e   **4 B**   **Correcting** Correct the fragments in Practice 4A by rewriting each sentence.

◆ *P r a c t i c e   **5**   **Completing** Correct each of the following *-ing* fragments using both methods. Remember to insert a comma when using correction 1.

1. We'll either walk or drive. Depending on the weather.

   _____

2. You can find him at home every night. Playing his electric guitar.

   _____

3. The car lurched and stopped suddenly. Spilling the soda on the seat.

   _____

4. Loving every minute on stage. She is a talented performer.

   _____

5. Mrs. Weeks volunteers at the hospital. Delivering flowers and cards to patients.

   _____

◆ *P r a c t i c e   **6**   **Writing Your Own** Write five *-ing* fragments of your own, and correct them.

_____

_____

_____

_____

_____

Type 3: *to* Fragments

When *to* is added to a verb (*to see, to hop, to skip, to jump*), the combination cannot be a main verb in its sentence. As a result, this group of words is often involved in a fragment.

Fragment: The company sponsored a national training program. **To increase its sales by 20 percent.**

Since *to* + a verb cannot function as the main verb of its sentence, *to increase its sales by 20 percent* is a fragment as it is punctuated here.

Correction 1:   *Connect the fragment to the sentence before or after it.*

Example: The company sponsored a national training program **to increase its sales by 20 percent.**

Correction 2:   *Make the fragment into an independent clause.*

Example: The company sponsored a national training program. **They decided to increase its sales by 20 percent.**

Hint: A *to* fragment can also occur at the beginning of a sentence. In this case, insert a comma between the two sentence parts when correcting the fragment.

To increase its sales by 20 percent, the company sponsored a national training program.

REVIEWING *to* FRAGMENTS

What does a to fragment consist of?

_____

Give an example of a to fragment.

_____

What are the two ways to correct a to fragment?

1. _____

2. _____

_____

Practice 7A   Identifying Underline the *to* fragments in each of the following sentences.

1. We want to stay home tonight. To see the MTV awards.
2. To get an A in English. That's Shonda's goal.
3. Would you please call Jerry? To remind him to bring his cooler.
4. The environmental group Greenpeace will be there. To protest whaling.
5. I have only one New Year's resolution. To stop smoking.

Practice 7B   Correcting Correct the fragments in Practice 7A by rewriting each sentence.

Practice 8   Completing Correct the following *to* fragments using both correction 1 and correction 2. Try putting the fragment at the beginning of the sentence instead of always at the end. Remember to insert a comma when you add the *to* fragment to the beginning of a sentence.

1. To improve her strength and flexibility. She has started a new exercise program.

_____

2. He works full time and takes classes at night. To get his degree in accounting.

   _____

3. Megan and Bethany are saving their money. To go to Florida for spring vacation.

   _____

4. To warn approaching ships. The captain sounded the foghorn.

   _____

5. He bought two pounds of coffee. To be sure he didn't run out.

   _____

P r a c t i c e   9 **Writing Your Own** Write five *to* fragments of your own, and correct them.

_____

_____

_____

_____

_____

Type 4: Dependent-Clause Fragments

A group of words that begins with a **subordinating conjunction** (see the following list) is called a **dependent clause** and cannot stand alone. Even though it has a subject and a verb, it is a fragment because it depends on an independent clause to complete its meaning. An **independent clause** is a group of words with a subject and a verb that can stand alone. (See page 378 for help with clauses.)

Here is a list of some commonly used subordinating conjunctions that create dependent clauses.

Subordinating Conjunctions

after	*because*	*since*	*until*
although	*before*	*so*	*when*
as	*even if*	*so that*	*whenever*
as if	*even though*	*than*	*where*
as long as	*how*	*that*	*wherever*
as soon as	*if*	*though*	*whether*
as though	*in order that*	*unless*	*while*

Fragment: <u>Since</u> he bought a Chevy Blazer. His insurance has gone up.

This sentence has a subject and a verb, but it is introduced by a subordinating conjunction, *since*. As a result, this sentence is a dependent clause and cannot stand alone.

Correction 1:   *Connect the fragment to the sentence before or after it.*

Example: **Since he bought a Chevy Blazer,** his insurance has gone up.

Correction 2:   *Make the fragment into an independent clause.*

Example: ~~Since~~ **He** bought a Chevy Blazer. His insurance has gone up.

Hint: If the dependent clause comes first, put a comma between the two parts of the sentence. If the dependent clause comes second, the comma is not necessary.

Since he bought a Chevy Blazer, his insurance has gone up.
His insurance has gone up **since he bought a Chevy Blazer.**

REVIEWING DEPENDENT-CLAUSE FRAGMENTS

What is a dependent-clause fragment?

_____

What types of words make a clause dependent?

_____   _____

What is an independent clause?

_____

Give an example of a dependent-clause fragment.

_____

What are the two ways to correct a dependent-clause fragment?

1. _____

2. _____

_____

◆ **P r a c t i c e   1 0 A   Identifying** Underline the dependent-clause fragments in each of the following sentences.

1. Let's wait under this awning. Until it stops raining.
2. We rented the apartment on Lee Street. So that I can walk to campus.
3. Ana took two aspirin. Because she has a headache.
4. If you are interested. I can show you how to install the new software.
5. Wait one minute, please. While I get my coat.

◆ **P r a c t i c e   1 0 B   Correcting** Correct the fragments in Practice 10A by rewriting each sentence.

◆ **P r a c t i c e   1 1   Completing** Correct the following dependent-clause fragments using both correction 1 and correction 2. When you use correction 1, remember to add a comma if the dependent clause comes first.

1. Although Jeff doesn't have any money. He manages to go to every Lakers game.

_____

2. As long as you're up. Would you please get me a Coke?

   _____

3. I don't watch much TV. Unless Oprah is on.

   _____

4. You can save a lot of money. If you clip coupons.

   _____

5. The checkbook is on the kitchen counter. Where I left it.

   _____

◆ *P r a c t i c e   1 2* **Writing Your Own** Write five dependent-clause fragments of your own, and correct them.

   _____

   _____

   _____

   _____

   _____

Type 5: Relative-Clause Fragments

   A **relative clause** is a dependent clause that begins with a relative pronoun: *who, whom, whose, which,* or *that.* When a relative clause is punctuated as a sentence, the result is a fragment.

   Fragment: I climbed Mt. Everest. **Which is the tallest mountain in the world.**

Which is the tallest mountain in the world is a clause fragment that begins with the relative pronoun *which.* This word automatically makes the words that follow it a dependent clause, so they cannot stand alone as a sentence.

Correction 1:   *Connect the fragment to the sentence before or after it.*

Example: I climbed Mt. Everest, **which** is the tallest mountain in the world.

Correction 2:   *Make the fragment into an independent clause.*

Example: I climbed Mt. Everest. **It** is the tallest mountain in the world.

REVIEWING RELATIVE-CLAUSE FRAGMENTS

How is a relative-clause fragment different from a dependent-clause fragment?

_____

_____

Give an example of a relative-clause fragment.

_____

What are the two ways to correct a relative-clause fragment?

1. _____

2. _____

◆ P r a c t i c e   1 3 A   Identifying Underline the relative-clause fragments in the following sentences.

1. For psychology, I have Professor Shannon. Whose wife also teaches psychology.
2. She takes courses online. Which allows her to also work full time.
3. Ronya is going to stay with her sister. Who lives in Brooklyn.
4. He's thinking of getting a laptop computer. That he can take on trips.
5. Traffic was bumper to bumper. Which always makes me impatient.

◀ *Practice 13B* **Correcting** Correct the fragments in Practice 13A by rewriting each sentence.

◀ *Practice 14* **Completing** Correct the following relative-clause fragments using both correction 1 and correction 2.

1. The shark circled the boat. Which made me very nervous.

   _____

2. She's dating Kevin. Whom I dated last year.

   _____

3. The movie stars Tom Hanks. Who has already won two Oscars.

   _____

4. He read every short story. That was published in 2004.

   _____

5. She watched the professor. Whose glasses kept slipping down his nose.

   _____

◀ *Practice 15* **Writing Your Own** Write five relative-clause fragments of your own, and correct them.

   _____

   _____

   _____

   _____

   _____

CHAPTER REVIEW

You might want to reread your answers to the questions in all the review boxes before you do the following exercises.

◆ *Review P r a c t i c e   1* **Identifying** Underline the fragments in the following paragraph.

The worst day of my life was last week. My sister promised to help me move into my new apartment. And didn't show up. Which I couldn't believe at first. When I called her to make arrangements, I should have known I was in trouble. Because she didn't sound like she was listening to me on the phone. This was my first clue. Anyway, I was counting on her. A big mistake. I kept expecting her to arrive all night. But she never came. I found out afterwards. That she forgot. This was what it was like growing up with her too. She remembered what she wanted to remember. And not any more. Which got her this far in life. But how much more can her family and friends forgive and forget?

◆ *Review P r a c t i c e   2* **Correcting** Correct all the fragments you underlined in Review Practice 1 by rewriting the paragraph.

◆ *Review P r a c t i c e   3* **Writing Your Own** Write a paragraph about your favorite restaurant. Where is this restaurant? What does it specialize in? Why do you like it? What is your favorite meal?

◆ *Review P r a c t i c e   4* **Editing Through Collaboration** Exchange paragraphs from Review Practice 3 with another student, and do the following:

1. Put brackets around any fragments that you find.
2. Identify the types of fragments that you find.

Then return the paper to its writer, and use the information in this chapter to correct any fragments in your own paragraph. Record your errors on the Error Log in Appendix 6.

CHAPTER 32

FUSED SENTENCES AND COMMA SPLICES

✔ CHECKLIST for Identifying and Correcting Fused Sentences and Comma Splices

> ✔ Are any sentences run together without punctuation?
> ✔ Are any sentences incorrectly joined with only a comma?

Test Yourself

Mark any incorrect sentences here with a slash between the independent clauses that are not joined properly.

- Jennifer was elected Academic President, I voted for her.
- The beach is a great getaway we're fortunate it's only 45 minutes away.
- He wanted to participate, but he wasn't sure of the rules.
- Casey is hard to get to know she hides her thoughts and feelings well.
- I hope I get into Dr. Jones's class, I hear he's the best teacher to get.

(Answers are in Appendix 4.)

When we cram two separate statements into a single sentence without correct punctuation, we create what are called a *fused sentences* and *comma splices*. These run-together sentences generally distort our message and cause problems for our readers. In this chapter, you will learn how to identify and avoid these errors in your writing.

IDENTIFYING FUSED SENTENCES AND COMMA SPLICES

Whereas a fragment is a piece of a sentence, **fused sentences** and **comma splices** are made up of two sentences written as one. In both cases, the first sentence runs into the next without the proper punctuation between the two.

Fused Sentence: The car slowly rolled to a stop we hopped out.

Comma Splice: The car slowly rolled to a stop, we hopped out.

Both of these sentences incorrectly join two independent clauses. The difference between them is one comma.

A **fused sentence** is two sentences "fused" or jammed together without any punctuation. Look at these examples:

Fused Sentence: Kinya's favorite event is the pole vault he always scores very high in it.

This example consists of two independent clauses with no punctuation between them:

1. Kinya's favorite event is the pole vault.
2. He always scores very high in it.

Fused Sentence: My brother loves to cook he doesn't like others to cook for him.

This example also consists of two independent clauses with no punctuation between them:

1. My brother loves to cook.
2. He doesn't like others to cook for him.

Like a fused sentence, a **comma splice** incorrectly joins two independent clauses. However, a comma splice puts a comma between the two independent clauses. The only difference between a fused sentence and a comma splice is the comma. Look at the following examples:

Comma Splice: Kinya's favorite event is the pole vault, he always scores very high in it.

Comma Splice: My brother loves to cook, he doesn't like others to cook for him.

Both of these sentences consist of two independent clauses. But a comma is not the proper punctuation to separate these two clauses.

REVIEWING FUSED SENTENCES AND COMMA SPLICES

What are the two types of run-together sentences?

_____   _____

What is the difference between them?

_____

_____

P r a c t i c e 1 Identifying Put a slash between the independent clauses that are not joined correctly.

1. Cedric goes out on a date every Saturday night he usually spends less than $20.
2. Toni Morrison wrote the novels *Beloved* and *The Bluest Eye* she won a Nobel Prize for literature.
3. The party begins at six, but the food isn't served until seven, there's a choice between chicken and beef.
4. The carnation is my favorite flower, but I still like the rose it is also beautiful.
5. Peanut butter and chocolate is my favorite ice cream flavor, but macadamia nuts in vanilla ice cream is a close second, the peanut butter makes my taste buds tingle.

P r a c t i c e 2 Identifying For each incorrect sentence in the following paragraph, put a slash between the independent clauses that are not joined properly.

The day I started my first job was the most frustrating day of my life. I arrived at the restaurant early no one showed me which door to enter so I stood outside banging on the wrong door for several minutes. One of the cooks heard me, he laughed and told the other employees. This embarrassed me from the start. I didn't know that my white shirt was wrong either, it had two pockets instead of one. Sherri, my manager, pointed this out. She said the personnel director should have told me about the dress code I said he had told me nothing but wear a white shirt. Anyway, the most frustrating part of the day was watching videos about setting a table, serving, and performing other duties. It was boring I had worked two years at the country club and knew what to do. I wanted to get out on the floor. The day was too long, I knew things had to get better!

◆ *P r a c t i c e 3* **Writing Your Own** Write five fused sentences. Then write the same sentences as comma splices.

_____

_____

_____

_____

_____

CORRECTING FUSED SENTENCES AND COMMA SPLICES

You have four different options for correcting your run-together sentences.

1. Separate the two sentences with a period, and capitalize the next word.

2. Separate the two sentences with a comma, and add a coordinating conjunction (*and, but, for, nor, or, so,* or *yet*).

3. Change one of the sentences into a dependent clause with a subordinating conjunction (such as *if, because, since, after,* or *when*) or a relative pronoun (*who, whom, whose, which,* or *that*).

4. Separate the two sentences with a semicolon.

Correction 1: Use a Period

Separate the two sentences with a period, and capitalize the next word.

Kinya's favorite event is the pole vault. **He** always scores very high in it.

My brother loves to cook. **He** doesn't like others to cook for him.

◆ *P r a c t i c e   4*   **Correcting** Correct all the sentences in Practice 1 using correction 1.

◆ *P r a c t i c e   5*   **Correcting** Correct the paragraph in Practice 2 using correction 1.

◆ *P r a c t i c e   6*   **Writing Your Own** Correct the sentences you wrote in Practice 3 using correction 1.

_____

_____

_____

_____

_____

Correction 2: Use a Coordinating Conjunction

Separate the two sentences with a comma, and add a coordinating conjunction (*and, but, for, nor, or, so,* or *yet*).

Kinya's favorite event is the pole vault, **so** he always scores very high in it.

My brother loves to cook, **but** he doesn't like others to cook for him.

◆ *P r a c t i c e   7*   **Correcting** Correct all the sentences in Practice 1 using correction 2.

◆ *P r a c t i c e   8*   **Correcting** Correct the paragraph in Practice 2 using correction 2.

◆ *P r a c t i c e* **9** **Writing Your Own** Correct the sentences you wrote in Practice 3 using correction 2.

_____

_____

_____

_____

Correction 3: Create a Dependent Clause

Change one of the sentences into a dependent clause with a subordinating conjunction (such as *if, because, since, after,* or *when*) or a relative pronoun (*who, whom, whose, which,* or *that*).

Kinya's favorite event is the pole vault **because** he always scores very high in it.

Even though my brother loves to cook, he doesn't like others to cook for him.

For a list of subordinating conjunctions, see page 373.

Hint: If you put the dependent clause at the beginning of the sentence, add a comma between the two sentence parts.

Because he always scores very high in it, Kinya's favorite event is the pole vault.

◆ *P r a c t i c e* **10** **Correcting** Correct all the sentences in Practice 1 using correction 3.

◆ *P r a c t i c e* **11** **Correcting** Correct the paragraph in Practice 2 using correction 3.

◆ *P r a c t i c e* **12** **Writing Your Own** Correct the sentences you wrote in Practice 3 using correction 3.

_____

_____

_____

_____

_____

Correction 4: Use a Semicolon

Separate the two sentences with a semicolon.

> Kinya's favorite event is the pole vault; he always scores very high in it.
>
> My brother loves to cook; he doesn't like others to cook for him.

You can also use a **transition,** a word or an expression that indicates how the two parts of the sentence are related, with a semicolon. A transition often makes the sentence smoother. It is preceded by a semicolon and followed by a comma.

> Kinya's favorite event is the pole vault; **as a result,** he always scores very high in it.
>
> My brother loves to cook; **however,** he doesn't like others to cook for him.

Here are some transitions commonly used with semicolons.

Transitions Used with a Semicolon Before and a Comma After

also	however	furthermore	instead
meanwhile	consequently	for example	similarly
in contrast	therefore	for instance	otherwise
of course	finally	in fact	nevertheless

◆ **P r a c t i c e   1 3   Correcting** Correct all the sentences in Practice 1 using correction 4.

◆ **P r a c t i c e   1 4   Correcting** Correct the paragraph in Practice 2 using correction 4.

◆ **P r a c t i c e   1 5   Writing Your Own** Correct the sentences you wrote in Practice 3 using correction 4.

REVIEWING METHODS OF CORRECTING FUSED SENTENCES
AND COMMA SPLICES

What are the four ways to correct a fused sentence or comma splice?

1. _____

2. _____

3. _____

4. _____

Why is correcting fused sentences and comma splices important?

_____

CHAPTER REVIEW

You might want to reread your answers to the questions in all the review boxes before you do the following exercises.

◆ *Review P r a c t i c e 1* **Identifying** Label each of the following sentences as fused (F), comma splice (CS), or correct (C).

1. _____ The small girls fidgeted in their colorful outfits they waited for their cue to go on stage.

2. _____ A hubcap came off the car as the car continued down the street.

3. _____ Alanna grabbed for the pen that worked she didn't want to forget his phone number.

4. _____ Stanley waited, but Tia never showed up, her car must have gotten stuck.

5. _____ Now that winter is approaching, the ski slopes will get very crowded.

6. _____ Both women would graduate at the end of the fall quarter, it was three weeks away.

7. _____ Sitting on top of flagpoles was an activity in the 1920s it was a great pastime.

8. _____ The library has over 1,000 journals, they can be found online.

9. _____ Some people get nervous when they meet movie stars, they're no different than regular people.

10. _____ Larissa is graduating with a degree in geology this year she's throwing a big party to celebrate.

◆ *Review P r a c t i c e* **2** **Completing** Correct the fused sentences and comma splices in Review Practice 1.

◆ *Review P r a c t i c e* **3** **Writing Your Own** Write a paragraph about a first in your life (for example, your first date, your first pizza, your first job).

◆ *Review P r a c t i c e* **4** **Editing Through Collaboration** Exchange paragraphs from Review Practice 3 with another student, and do the following:

1. Put brackets around any sentences that have more than one independent clause.

2. Circle the words that connect these clauses.

Then return the paper to its writer, and use the information in this chapter to correct any run-together sentences in your own paragraph. Record your errors on the Error Log in Appendix 6.

UNIT TESTS

Here are some exercises that test your understanding of all the material in this unit: Subjects and Verbs, Fragments, and Fused Sentences and Comma Splices.

Unit Test I

A. Underline the subjects once and the verbs twice in the following sentences. Cross out the prepositional phrases first. Then put the fragments in brackets ([ ]), and put a slash (/) between the run-together sentences.

1. She has transferred to Iowa State. After she went to our local community college.

2. I called the business office and inquired about my account balance the credit clerk told me that the company owed me money.

3. She bought a used Toyota. That she can drive between home and school.

4. Musicians and entertainers make great money after their "big break."

5. Before you make your plane reservations. Check the Internet prices.

6. Yesterday Val won the art contest at the mall it was judged by three professionals.

7. Mom planted a little garden this year. Some lettuce, spinach, and tomatoes.

8. Bowing and smiling. The actors appeared for yet another curtain call.

9. The school board conducted a poll 23 percent of the students like PE, but 37 percent dislike PE and the rest have no opinion.

10. Both of the children are in daycare.

11. All the kids love Mr. Kaufmann. Whose gingerbread cookies are a hit.

12. Agriculture is a very risky occupation. Since it depends on the weather.

13. Every year, her parents put money into her college fund.

14. To change your telephone message. Press SET and speak clearly.

15. If you're going to the store, we need cat food and paper towels. And something for dinner tonight.

16. You have all the ingredients here. To make a nutritious smoothie.

17. The twelve beautiful, mint green roses that I got during my wedding brunch were lovely, they lasted for two weeks after the event.

18. The first three scenes in the horror film were frightening.

19. Though Samuel signed up early, he still didn't get into summer school so many people applied.

20. On their vacation, Brent and Miranda felt and acted like royalty.

B. Correct the fragments and run-together sentences in Part A by rewriting each incorrect sentence.

Unit Test II

A. Underline the subjects once and the verbs twice in the following paragraph. Cross out the prepositional phrases first. Then put the fragments in brackets ([ ]), and put a slash (/) between the run-together sentences.

I went to the beach. During my summer vacation. My friends Christine and Jennifer went with me, we had such a great time. We spent one week at a hotel. Which was right on the beach. We had saved our money all spring. To be able to afford such a nice hotel room. Since we were so close. We spent nearly every moment at the beach. Christine would not play volleyball with us, she said that she was not good enough. Realizing we were just playing for fun. She soon joined our game. When our week was over. We were not ready to go home. I cannot wait for another vacation with Christine and Jennifer they are the best!

B. Correct the fragments and run-together sentences in Part A by rewriting the paragraph.

REGULAR AND
IRREGULAR VERBS

33

☑ CHECKLIST for Using Regular and Irregular Verbs

> ✔ Are regular verbs in their correct forms?
> ✔ Are irregular verbs in their correct forms?

Test Yourself

Underline the complete verb in each of the following sentences. Then mark an X if the form of the verb is incorrect.

- _____ We brang our new neighbor a pizza for dinner.
- _____ My brother married on February 14—Valentine's Day.
- _____ He drug the heavy suitcase down the street.
- _____ This CD costed $15.
- _____ My roommate's water bed has sprang a leak.

(Answers are in Appendix 4.)

All verbs are either regular or irregular. *Regular verbs* form the past tense and past participle by adding *-d* or *-ed* to the present tense. If a verb does not form its past tense and past participle this way, it is called an *irregular verb*.

REGULAR VERBS

Here are the principal parts (present, past, and past participle forms) of some regular verbs. They are **regular verbs** because their past tense and past participle end in *-d* or *-ed*. The past participle is the verb form often used with helping verbs like *have, has,* or *had*.

Some Regular Verbs

PRESENT TENSE	PAST TENSE	PAST PARTICIPLE (USED WITH HELPING WORDS LIKE *HAVE, HAS, HAD*)
talk	*talked*	*talked*
sigh	*sighed*	*sighed*
drag	*dragged*	*dragged*
enter	*entered*	*entered*
consider	*considered*	*considered*

The different forms of a verb tell when something happened—in the *present* (I *walk*) or in the *past* (I *walked*, I *have walked*, I *had walked*).

REVIEWING REGULAR VERBS

What is a regular verb?

_____

_____

Identify three forms of a regular verb.

_____   _____   _____

◆ **P r a c t i c e   1   Identifying** Put an X to the left of the incorrect verb forms in the following chart.

Present Tense	**Past Tense**	**Past Participle**
1. _____ skip	_____ skipt	_____ skipped
2. _____ paint	_____ painted	_____ painted
3. _____ danced	_____ dance	_____ danced

4. _____ play   _____ played   _____ playen

5. _____ cook   _____ cooked   _____ cooken

♦ *P r a c t i c e   2*   **Completing** Write the correct forms of the following regular verbs.

	Present Tense	Past Tense	Past Participle
1. act	_____	_____	_____
2. invent	_____	_____	_____
3. follow	_____	_____	_____
4. drag	_____	_____	_____
5. create	_____	_____	_____

♦ *P r a c t i c e   3*   **Writing Your Own** Write five sentences using at least five of the verb forms from Practice 2.

_____

_____

_____

_____

_____

IRREGULAR VERBS

Irregular verbs do not form their past tense and past participle with *-d* or *-ed*. That is why they are irregular. Some follow certain patterns (*sing, sang, sung; ring, rang, rung; drink, drank, drunk; shrink, shrank, shrunk*). But the only sure way to know the forms of an irregular verb is to spend time learning them. As you write, you can check a dictionary or the following list.

Irregular Verbs

PRESENT	PAST	PAST PARTICIPLE (USED WITH HELPING WORDS LIKE *HAVE, HAS, HAD*)
am	*was*	*been*
are	*were*	*been*
be	*was*	*been*
bear	*bore*	*borne, born*
beat	*beat*	*beaten*
begin	*began*	*begun*
bend	*bent*	*bent*
bid	*bid*	*bid*
bind	*bound*	*bound*
bite	*bit*	*bitten*
blow	*blew*	*blown*
break	*broke*	*broken*
bring	*brought* (not *brang*)	*brought* (not *brung*)
build	*built*	*built*
burst	*burst* (not *bursted*)	*burst*
buy	*bought*	*bought*
choose	*chose*	*chosen*
come	*came*	*come*
cost	*cost* (not *costed*)	*cost*
cut	*cut*	*cut*
deal	*dealt*	*dealt*
do	*did* (not *done*)	*done*
draw	*drew*	*drawn*
drink	*drank*	*drunk*
drive	*drove*	*driven*
eat	*ate*	*eaten*
fall	*fell*	*fallen*
feed	*fed*	*fed*
feel	*felt*	*felt*

fight	*fought*	*fought*
find	*found*	*found*
flee	*fled*	*fled*
fly	*flew*	*flown*
forget	*forgot*	*forgotten*
forgive	*forgave*	*forgiven*
freeze	*froze*	*frozen*
get	*got*	*got, gotten*
go	*went*	*gone*
grow	*grew*	*grown*
hang[1] (a picture)	*hung*	*hung*
has	*had*	*had*
have	*had*	*had*
hide	*hid*	*hidden*
hear	*heard*	*heard*
hurt	*hurt* (not *hurted*)	*hurt*
is	*was*	*been*
know	*knew*	*known*
lay	*laid*	*laid*
lead	*led*	*led*
leave	*left*	*left*
lend	*lent*	*lent*
lie[2]	*lay*	*lain*
lose	*lost*	*lost*
meet	*met*	*met*
pay	*paid*	*paid*
prove	*proved*	*proved, proven*
put	*put*	*put*
read [rēēd]	*read* [rĕd]	*read* [rĕd]
ride	*rode*	*ridden*
ring	*rang*	*rung*
rise	*rose*	*risen*
run	*ran*	*run*

say	*said*	*said*
see	*saw* (not *seen*)	*seen*
set	*set*	*set*
shake	*shook*	*shaken*
shine[3] (a light)	*shone*	*shone*
shrink	*shrank*	*shrunk*
sing	*sang*	*sung*
sink	*sank*	*sunk*
sit	*sat*	*sat*
sleep	*slept*	*slept*
speak	*spoke*	*spoken*
spend	*spent*	*spent*
spread	*spread*	*spread*
spring	*sprang* (not *sprung*)	*sprung*
stand	*stood*	*stood*
steal	*stole*	*stolen*
stick	*stuck*	*stuck*
stink	*stank* (not *stunk*)	*stunk*
strike	*struck*	*struck, stricken*
strive	*strove*	*striven*
swear	*swore*	*sworn*
sweep	*swept*	*swept*
swell	*swelled*	*swelled, swollen*
swim	*swam*	*swum*
swing	*swung*	*swung*
take	*took*	*taken*
teach	*taught*	*taught*
tear	*tore*	*torn*
tell	*told*	*told*
think	*thought*	*thought*
throw	*threw*	*thrown*
understand	*understood*	*understood*
wake	*woke*	*woken*

E DITING CHECKLIST ✔

SENTENCES

✔ Does each sentence have a main subject and verb?
✔ Do all subjects and verbs agree?
✔ Do all pronouns agree with their nouns?
✔ Are modifiers as close as possible to the words they modify?

PUNCTUATION AND MECHANICS

✔ Are sentences punctuated correctly?
✔ Are words capitalized properly?

WORD CHOICE AND SPELLING

✔ Are words used correctly?
✔ Are words spelled correctly?

FOLD HERE

FOLD HERE

REVISING CHECKLIST ✔

TOPIC SENTENCE
✔ Does the topic sentence convey the paragraph's controlling idea?
✔ Does the topic sentence appear as the first or last sentence of the paragraph?

DEVELOPMENT
✔ Does the paragraph contain *specific* details that support the topic sentence?
✔ Does the paragraph include *enough* details to explain the topic sentence fully?

UNITY
✔ Do all the sentences in the paragraph support the topic sentence?

ORGANIZATION
✔ Is the paragraph organized logically?

COHERENCE
✔ Do the sentences move smoothly and logically from one to the next?

wear	wore	worn
weave	wove	woven
win	won	won
wring	wrung	wrung
write	wrote	written

1. *Hang* meaning "execute by hanging" is regular: *hang, hanged, hanged.*
2. *Lie* meaning "tell a lie" is regular: *lie, lied, lied.*
3. *Shine* meaning "brighten by polishing" is regular: *shine, shined, shined.*

REVIEWING IRREGULAR VERBS

What is the difference between regular and irregular verbs?

_____

_____

What is the best way to learn how irregular verbs form their past tense and past participle?

_____

◆ **P r a c t i c e 4 Identifying** Put an X to the left of the incorrect verb forms in the following chart.

Present Tense	Past Tense	Past Participle
1. _____ bust	_____ bursted	_____ burst
2. _____ ring	_____ rung	_____ rung
3. _____ took	_____ taken	_____ taken
4. _____ sleep	_____ slept	_____ slepted
5. _____ drink	_____ drank	_____ drunk

◆ *P r a c t i c e* **5** **Completing** Write the correct forms of the following irregular verbs.

	Present Tense	Past Tense	Past Participle
1. hide	_____	_____	_____
2. sing	_____	_____	_____
3. bring	_____	_____	_____
4. write	_____	_____	_____
5. cost	_____	_____	_____

◆ *P r a c t i c e* **6** **Writing Your Own** Write five sentences using at least five of the verb forms from the chart in Practice 5.

_____

_____

_____

_____

_____

USING *LIE/LAY* AND *SIT/SET* CORRECTLY

Two pairs of verbs are often used incorrectly—*lie/lay* and *sit/set*.

Lie/Lay

	Present Tense	Past Tense	Past Participle
lie (recline or lie down)	lie	lay	(have, has, had) lain
lay (put or place down)	lay	laid	(have, has, had) laid

The verb *lay* always takes an object. You must lay something down:

Lay down *what?*
Lay down *your books.*

Sit/Set

	Present Tense	Past Tense	Past Participle
sit (get into a seated position)	sit	sat	(have, has, had) sat
set (put or place down)	set	set	(have, has, had) set

Like the verb *lay,* the verb *set* must always have an object. You must set something down:

> Set *what?*

> Set *the presents* over here.

REVIEWING *Lie/Lay* AND *Sit/Set*

What do lie and lay mean?

_____

What are the principal parts of lie and lay?

_____

What do sit and set mean?

_____

What are the principal parts of sit and set?

_____

Which of these verbs always take an object?

_____

◆ **Practice 7 Identifying** Choose the correct verb in the following sentences.

1. She has always (set, sat) in the front row.
2. Please (set, sit) the box of tissues on the nightstand.

3. You have (laid, lain) on the couch all morning.

4. At the concert, we (set, sat) with Howie and Carol.

5. The installers are coming to (lay, lie) the new carpeting.

◆ *P r a c t i c e* **8** **Completing** Fill in each blank in the following sentences with the correct form of *lie/lay* or *sit/set.*

1. I like to _____ next to the window on an airplane.

2. She has _____ out the clothes she will take on her trip.

3. _____ the box on the table.

4. I'm exhausted. I have to _____ down.

5. _____ the tray over here.

◆ *P r a c t i c e* **9** **Writing Your Own** Write five sentences using variations of *lie/lay* or *sit/set.*

_____

_____

_____

_____

_____

CHAPTER REVIEW

You might want to reread your answers to the questions in all the review boxes before you do the following exercises.

◆ *Review P r a c t i c e* **1** **Identifying** Write out the past tense and past participle of each verb listed here, and then identify the verb as either regular or irregular.

Present Tense	Past Tense	Past Participle	Type of Verb
1. react	_____	_____	_____
2. hesitate	_____	_____	_____

3. sing   _____   _____   _____

4. treat   _____   _____   _____

5. bring   _____   _____   _____

6. suffer   _____   _____   _____

7. read   _____   _____   _____

8. stink   _____   _____   _____

9. take   _____   _____   _____

10. speak   _____   _____   _____

◆ *Review P r a c t i c e 2* **Completing** Fill in each blank in the following sentences with a regular or irregular verb that makes sense.

1. No one believed that he had _____ the lottery.

2. I was so tired, I _____ home.

3. We _____ to the music until after midnight.

4. Because I have a cold, I have _____ in bed all day.

5. In the sixties, he _____ a beard and an outrageous afro.

6. Brian has always _____ a wonderful father to his daughter.

7. Every time the choir performs, my grandfather _____ to the concert.

8. Please _____ the groceries on the kitchen table.

9. She has _____ to the store to buy cheesecake.

10. At the football game, we _____ in the stands closest to the 50-yard line.

◆ *Review P r a c t i c e 3* **Writing Your Own** Write a paragraph explaining how active or inactive you are in life. What are the reasons for the choices you have made regarding your level of daily activity?

◆ ***Review Practice 4*** **Editing Through Collaboration** Exchange paragraphs from Review Practice 3 with another student, and do the following:

1. Circle any verb forms that are not correct.
2. Suggest a correction for these incorrect forms.

Then return the paper to its writer, and use the information in this chapter to correct the verb forms in your own paragraph. Record your errors on the Error Log in Appendix 6.

VERB TENSE

✔ CHECKLIST for Correcting Tense Problems

> ✔ Are present-tense verbs in the correct form?
> ✔ Are past-tense verbs in the correct form?
> ✔ Are *-ing* verbs used with the correct helping verbs?
> ✔ Are the forms of *be, do,* and *have* used correctly?

Test Yourself

Underline the complete verb in each sentence. Then mark an X if the form of the verb is incorrect.

- _____ We be planning on leaving in the morning.
- _____ The team chose an alligator as its mascot.
- _____ My sister practice the flute every day.
- _____ He don't look old enough to drive.
- _____ Over 1,000 students apply to my college this year.

(Answers are in Appendix 4.)

When we hear the word "verb," we often think of action. We also know that action occurs in time. We are naturally interested in whether something happened today or yesterday or if it will happen at some time in the future. The time of an action is indicated by the **tense** of a verb, specifically in the ending of a verb or in a helping word. This chapter discusses the most common errors in using verb tense.

PRESENT TENSE

One of the most common errors in college writing is reversing the present-tense endings—adding an *-s* where none is needed and omitting the *-s* where it is required. This error causes problems in subject-verb agreement. Make sure you understand this mistake, and then proofread carefully to avoid it in your writing.

Present Tense

Singular		Plural	
INCORRECT	CORRECT	INCORRECT	CORRECT
NOT *I talks*	*I talk*	**NOT** *we talks*	*we talk*
NOT *you talks*	*you talk*	**NOT** *you talks*	*you talk*
NOT *he, she, it talk*	*he, she, it talks*	**NOT** *they talks*	*they talk*

You also need to be able to spot these same errors in sentences.

Incorrect	Correct
Brad run to the store.	**Brad runs** to the store.
She like my tie.	**She likes** my tie.
You goes next.	**You go** next.
They plants a garden every year.	**They plant** a garden every year.

REVIEWING PRESENT-TENSE ERRORS

What is the most common error in using the present tense?

_____

_____

How can you prevent this error?

_____

◈ **P r a c t i c e   1 A   Identifying** Underline the present-tense errors in each of the following sentences.

1. Larry and Sara <u>wants</u> to join our study group. *WANT*
2. Rhoda <u>make</u> herself breakfast every morning. *Made*
3. At night, we <u>hears</u> coyotes and owls. *hear*
4. That jacket <u>look</u> good on you. *looks*
5. Our mail always <u>come</u> by noon. *come*

◈ **P r a c t i c e   1 B   Correcting** Correct the present-tense errors in Practice 1A by rewriting each sentence.

◈ **P r a c t i c e   2   Completing** Fill in each blank in the following paragraph with the correct present-tense verbs.

My mom always (1) __*wants*__ me to watch my little sister every time she goes out. Whether she goes to the store or on an errand, she always (2) __*nags*__ me in charge. I don't really mind, except sometimes my sister (3) __*gets*__ me into trouble because she doesn't like to listen to me. But I tend to let her do whatever she (4) __*pleases*__. This is probably why she doesn't listen to me all the time. We do have a lot of fun together, so in the end, I guess I (5) __*enjoy*__ the time we have together.

◈ **P r a c t i c e   3   Writing Your Own** Write a sentence of your own for each of the following present-tense verbs.

1. runs ~~I had~~ th My brother fun to stay in shape
2. feel Sunny days always make me feel good
3. bring I have to bring the groceries in.
4. believes RYAN believes he is the man.
5. wants My mom wants me not to go out on my 21st birthday.

PAST TENSE

Just as we know that a verb is in the present tense by its ending, we can tell that a verb is in the past tense by its ending. Regular verbs form the past tense by adding *-d* or *-ed*. But some writers forget the ending when they are writing the past tense. Understanding this problem and then proofreading carefully will help you catch this error.

Past Tense

Singular		Plural	
INCORRECT	CORRECT	INCORRECT	CORRECT
NOT *I talk*	*I talked*	**NOT** *we talk*	*we talked*
NOT *you talk*	*you talked*	**NOT** *you talk*	*you talked*
NOT *he, she, it talk*	*he, she, it talked*	**NOT** *they talk*	*they talked*

You also need to be able to spot these same errors in sentences.

Incorrect	Correct
He love the game.	**He loved** the game.
She try not to laugh.	**She tried** not to laugh.
The kids watch old movies for hours.	**The kids watched** old movies for hours.
Yes, **we study** for the test.	Yes, **we studied** for the test.

REVIEWING PAST-TENSE ERRORS

What is the most common sentence error made with the past tense?

_____

How can you prevent this error?

_____

Practice 4A **Identifying** Underline the past-tense errors in the following sentences.

1. We share a hot dog and a Coke at the game.
2. When she left, she lock the door.
3. He ignore the stop sign and almost kill himself.
4. Tina wrap the gift herself.
5. Anya and Sandra watch the little sailboat get smaller and smaller.

Practice 4B **Correcting** Correct the past-tense errors in Practice 4A by rewriting each sentence.

Practice 5 **Completing** Fill in each blank in the following paragraph with the correct past-tense verb.

Last year, our club held a fund-raiser to raise money for a local boys' club. We (1) _____ more than $5,000 by selling chocolate in tin tubs. We had all different kinds of chocolate, but the kind that (2) _____ the most was the chocolate turtles, which (3) _____ chocolate, caramel, and pecans. I actually (4) _____ five of these tins for my mom. We (5) _____ quite a lot of money for the boys' club. We are ready to beat last year's record this year.

Practice 6 **Writing Your Own** Write a sentence of your own for each of the following past-tense verbs.

1. ran _____

2. was _____

3. brought _____

4. thought _____

5. saw _____

USING HELPING WORDS WITH PAST PARTICIPLES

Helping words are used only with the past participle form, *not* with the past-tense form. It is therefore incorrect to use a helping verb (such as *is, was, were, have, has,* or *had*) with the past tense. Make sure you understand how to use helping words with past participles, and then proofread your written work to avoid making these errors.

Incorrect	Correct
He **has went.**	He **has gone.**
She **has chose** to stay home.	She **has chosen** to stay home.
I **have ate** at Jimmy's restaurant.	I **have eaten** at Jimmy's restaurant.
We **had flew** into Memphis.	We **had flown** into Memphis.

REVIEWING ERRORS WITH HELPING WORDS
AND PAST PARTICIPLES

What is the most common sentence error made with past participles?

_____

How can you prevent this error?

_____

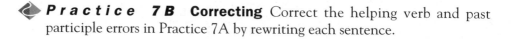 **Practice 7A Identifying** Underline the incorrect helping words and past participles in each of the following sentences.

1. Dawn had forgot that she promised to go with me.
2. The Wildcats have beat the Spartans every year since 2000.
3. He has broke the world record!
4. The lawyer has went to court.
5. You have drank all the orange juice.

Practice 7B Correcting Correct the helping verb and past participle errors in Practice 7A by rewriting each sentence.

◈ *P r a c t i c e* **8** **Completing** Fill in each blank in the following paragraph with helping verbs and past participles that make sense.

I thought you (1) _____ the money we talked about for spring break. But I guess you (2) _____ your mind. The last time we (3) _____ I thought our trip (4) _____. But I am glad to see it is on again. This time I (5) _____ to enjoy myself—whatever adjustments I have to make.

◈ *P r a c t i c e* **9** **Writing Your Own** Write a sentence of your own for each of the following helping words and past participles.

1. has run _____

2. have gone _____

3. had brought _____

4. is broken _____

5. have written _____

USING *-ing* VERBS CORRECTLY

Verbs ending in *-ing* describe action that is going on or that was going on for a while. To be a complete verb, an *-ing* verb is always used with a helping verb. Two common errors occur with *-ing* verbs:

1. Using *be* or *been* instead of the correct helping verb
2. Using no helping verb at all

Learn the correct forms, and proofread carefully to catch these errors.

Incorrect	Correct
The dog **be chasing** the cat.	The dog **is chasing** the cat.
	The dog **was chasing** the cat.
The dog **been chasing** the cat.	The dog **has been chasing** the cat.
	The dog **had been chasing** the cat.

We **drinking** Dr. Pepper.   We **are drinking** Dr. Pepper.

We **have been drinking** Dr. Pepper.

We **were drinking** Dr. Pepper.

We **had been drinking** Dr. Pepper.

REVIEWING *-ing* VERB ERRORS

What two kinds of errors occur with -ing verbs?

_____

_____

How can you prevent these errors?

_____

◆ **P r a c t i c e 1 0 A**   **Identifying** Underline the incorrect helping verbs and *-ing* forms in each of the following sentences.

1. Mrs. Trent been collecting teapots her whole life.
2. The ambulance be taking the victim to the hospital.
3. I been thinking that I should invite his family to dinner.
4. If you be following your dreams, you will be happy.
5. Stan's not here; he renewing his driver's license downtown.

◆ **P r a c t i c e 1 0 B**   **Correcting** Correct the verb form errors in Practice 10A by rewriting each sentence.

◆ **P r a c t i c e 1 1**   **Completing** Fill in each blank in the following paragraph with the correct helping verb and *-ing* form.

Today I can already tell I (1) _____ one of those days you wish you could start over. It began while I (2) _____ through my alarm. I then had only ten minutes to get to school before a test. All through the test, I felt like I (3) _____ to catch my breath because I still felt rushed. After I finished, I went to my car and actually found that a police officer (4) _____ me a ticket for parking illegally. I tried to persuade her to look the other way, but she wouldn't. At 10:45 in the morning, I (5) _____ to just lock myself in my house until tomorrow.

P r a c t i c e   1 2   Writing Your Own Write a sentence of your own for each of the following verbs.

1. is thinking _____

2. has been feeling _____

3. were going _____

4. was reading _____

5. had been jogging _____

PROBLEMS WITH *be*

The verb *be* can cause problems in both the present tense and the past tense. The following chart demonstrates these problems. Learn how to use these forms correctly, and then always proofread your written work carefully to avoid these errors.

The Verb *be*

Present Tense

Singular		Plural	
INCORRECT	CORRECT	INCORRECT	CORRECT
NOT *I be/ain't*	*I **am/am not***	**NOT** *we be/ain't*	*we **are/are not***
NOT *you be/ain't*	*you **are/are not***	**NOT** *you be/ain't*	*you **are/are not***
NOT *he, she, it be/ain't*	*he, she, it **is/is not***	**NOT** *they be/ain't*	*they **are/are not***

Past Tense

Singular		Plural	
INCORRECT	CORRECT	INCORRECT	CORRECT
NOT *I were*	*I* **was**	**NOT** *we was*	*we* **were**
NOT *you was*	*you* **were**	**NOT** *you was*	*you* **were**
NOT *he, she, it were*	*he, she, it* **was**	**NOT** *they was*	*they* **were**

REVIEWING PROBLEMS WITH *be*

What are two common errors made with be?

_____

_____

How can you prevent these errors?

_____

◆ **Practice 13A** **Identifying** Underline the incorrect forms of *be* in each of the following sentences.

1. She be in my dormitory, but we ain't friends.
2. We was hungry and freezing cold.
3. It ain't too late to change your mind.
4. You wasn't supposed to know about the party.
5. All in all, they was a good-natured group.

◆ **Practice 13B** **Correcting** Correct the incorrect forms of *be* in Practice 13A by rewriting each sentence.

◆ **Practice 14** **Completing** Fill in each blank in the following paragraph with the correct form of *be*.

Fishing (1) _____ the center of my dad's universe. He (2) _____ a good fisherman from the time he was a young boy. Fishing (3) _____ a sport that has been in my dad's family for years—his dad taught him, his dad's dad taught his dad, and so on. My dad taught me to fish when I (4) _____ three years old. We love to go out on long weekends. It is really more about being together than anything else. My dad (5) _____ always happiest when we are together on a fishing trip.

*P r a c t i c e   **15** **Writing Your Own** Write a sentence of your own for each of the following verbs.

1. was _____

2. is _____

3. am _____

4. were _____

5. are _____

PROBLEMS WITH *do*

Another verb that causes sentence problems in the present and past tenses is *do*. The following chart shows these problems. Learn the correct forms, and proofread to avoid errors.

The Verb *do*

Present Tense

Singular		Plural	
INCORRECT	CORRECT	INCORRECT	CORRECT
NOT I does	I **do**	**NOT** we does	we **do**
NOT you does	you **do**	**NOT** you does	you **do**
NOT he, she, it do	he, she, it **does**	**NOT** they does	they **do**

Past Tense

	Singular			Plural	
	INCORRECT	CORRECT		INCORRECT	CORRECT
NOT	*I done*	*I **did***	**NOT**	*we done*	*we **did***
NOT	*you done*	*you **did***	**NOT**	*you done*	*you **did***
NOT	*he, she, it done*	*he, she, it **did***	**NOT**	*they done*	*they **did***

REVIEWING PROBLEMS WITH *do*

What are two common errors made with do?

_____

_____

How can you prevent these errors?

_____

P r a c t i c e   1 6 A   **Identifying** Underline the incorrect forms of *do* in each of the following sentences.

1. She done the dishes today and yesterday.
2. She thinks she knows me, but she don't.
3. I done most of my research on the Internet.
4. Don't worry; it don't matter if you're late.
5. If he don't have the remote control, and you don't have it, where is it?

P r a c t i c e   1 6 B   **Correcting** Correct the incorrect forms of *do* in Practice 16A by rewriting each sentence.

P r a c t i c e   1 7   **Completing** Fill in each blank in the following paragraph with the correct form of *do*.

I (1) _____ my final presentation for sociology in less than five minutes. My teacher told us we could (2) _____ the reports in 10 to 15 minutes, but I talked so fast that I (3) _____ mine in only half the time. I always (4) _____ this to myself. I talk so fast that I speed up my oral reports. Usually the teachers are nice about my fast-talking performances and tell me I (5) _____ a good job.

◆ *P r a c t i c e   1 8*   **Writing Your Own** Write a sentence of your own for each of the following verbs.

1. do _____

2. did _____

3. does _____

4. did _____

5. do _____

PROBLEMS WITH *have*

Along with *be* and *do*, the verb *have* causes sentence problems in the present and past tenses. The following chart demonstrates these problems. Learn the correct forms, and proofread to avoid errors with *have*.

The Verb *have*

Present Tense

Singular		Plural	
INCORRECT	CORRECT	INCORRECT	CORRECT
NOT *I has*	*I* **have**	**NOT** *we has*	*we* **have**
NOT *you has*	*you* **have**	**NOT** *you has*	*you* **have**
NOT *he, she, it have*	*he, she, it* **has**	**NOT** *they has*	*they* **have**

Past Tense

Singular		Plural	
INCORRECT	CORRECT	INCORRECT	CORRECT
NOT *I has*	*I **had***	**NOT** *we has*	*we **had***
NOT *you have*	*you **had***	**NOT** *you has*	*you **had***
NOT *he, she, it have*	*he, she, it **had***	**NOT** *they has*	*they **had***

REVIEWING PROBLEMS WITH *have*

What are two common errors made with have?

_____

_____

How can you prevent these errors?

_____

◆ *P r a c t i c e* **1 9 A**   **Identifying** Underline the incorrect forms of *have* in each of the following sentences.

1. She have a wonderful sense of humor.
2. They has a great time at the movies.
3. You has some mail on the kitchen counter.
4. Lisa and Kayla has adopted a kitten from the shelter.
5. She have come to class late for a week.

◆ *P r a c t i c e* **1 9 B**   **Correcting** Correct the incorrect forms of *have* in Practice 19A by rewriting each sentence.

◆ *P r a c t i c e* **2 0**   **Completing** Fill in each blank in the following paragraph with the correct form of *have*.

I (1) _____ a fabulous spring break! My friends and I went to Padre Island and (2) _____ the best times of our

lives. Since we got home, we (3) _____ not stopped talking about all the people we met and parties we (4) _____.
We know for sure we are going back next year! Now all we (5) _____ to do is start saving our money for next year.

◆ *Practice* **21** **Writing Your Own** Write a sentence of your own for each of the following verbs.

1. has _____

2. have _____

3. had _____

4. have _____

5. had _____

CHAPTER REVIEW

You might want to reread your answers to the questions in all the review boxes before you do the following exercises.

◆ *Review Practice* **1** **Identifying** Underline the incorrect verb forms in the following sentences. Check problem areas carefully: Is an *-s* needed, or is there an unnecessary *-s* ending? Do all past-tense regular verbs end in *-d* or *-ed*? Is the past participle used with helping words? Is the correct helping verb used with *-ing* verbs? Are the forms of *be*, *do*, and *have* correct?

1. She be training for a new job at the bank.
2. Harper study very hard for the final exam.
3. She walk along the beach and pick up seashells.
4. We has a family reunion every Memorial Day.
5. That little frog been jumping from lily pad to lily pad all afternoon.
6. This is the second time she be reading that book.
7. My dog, Otto, goes everywhere I does.
8. He be bicycling to work every day.
9. We been standing at the bus stop when the storm struck.
10. She always have a backup file when she be working on the computer.

◆ ***Review P r a c t i c e   2* Writing Your Own** Write a paragraph describing your best friend. Be careful to use all verbs in the correct tense. Check in particular for errors with *be, do,* and *have.*

◆ ***Review P r a c t i c e   3* Editing Through Collaboration** Exchange paragraphs from Review Practice 3 with another student, and do the following:

1. Underline any incorrect tenses.
2. Circle any incorrect verb forms.

Then return the paper to its writer, and use the information in this chapter to correct any verb errors in your own paragraph. Record your errors on the Error Log in Appendix 6.

SUBJECT-VERB AGREEMENT

✅ CHECKLIST for Correcting Subject-Verb Agreement Problems

> ✔ Do all subjects agree with their verbs?

Test Yourself

Underline the subjects once and the complete verbs twice in the following sentences. Put an X by the sentence if its subject and verb do not agree.

- _____ Ben and Tess has become great friends.
- _____ Each of the nurses are with a patient.
- _____ Macaroni and cheese are my favorite food.
- _____ There are two trains to Baltimore in the morning.
- _____ Everyone are ready to leave.

(Answers are in Appendix 4.)

Almost every day, we come across situations that require us to reach an agreement with someone. For example, you and a friend might have to agree on which movie to see, or you and your manager might have to agree on how many hours you'll work in the coming week. Whatever the issue, agreement is essential in most aspects of life—including writing. In this chapter, you will learn how to resolve conflicts in your sentences by making sure your subjects and verbs agree.

SUBJECT-VERB AGREEMENT

Subject-verb agreement simply means that singular subjects must be paired with singular verbs and plural subjects with plural verbs. Look at this example:

Singular: **He lives** in Cleveland.

The subject *he* is singular because it refers to only one person. The verb *lives* is singular and matches the singular subject. Here is the same sentence in plural form:

Plural: **They live** in Cleveland.

The subject *they* is plural, more than one person, and the verb *live* is also plural.

REVIEWING SUBJECT-VERB AGREEMENT

What is the difference between singular and plural?

_____

What kind of verb goes with a singular subject?

_____

What kind of verb goes with a plural subject?

_____

◆ *P r a c t i c e 1* **Identifying** Underline the verb that agrees with its subject in each of the following sentences.

1. On her vacations, Sylvia (enjoys, enjoy) reading romance novels.
2. Jerry (has, have) a large coin collection.
3. During the day, the farm hands (works, work) in the fields.
4. Unfortunately, the paychecks (was, were) lost in the mail.
5. The twins (does, do) not look alike.

◆ *P r a c t i c e* **2** **Completing** Fill in each blank in the following sentences with a present-tense verb that agrees with its subject.

1. The new clothing styles _____ bad on me.

2. Bob _____ his mom to visit.

3. Every night the news _____ the latest disasters.

4. During the evening, Jake _____ for many hours.

5. The football team usually _____ its games.

◆ *P r a c t i c e* **3** **Writing Your Own** Write five sentences of your own, and underline the subjects and verbs. Make sure that your subjects and verbs agree.

_____

_____

_____

_____

_____

WORDS SEPARATING SUBJECTS AND VERBS

With sentences that are as simple and direct as *He lives in Cleveland*, checking that the subject and verb agree is easy. But problems can arise when words come between the subject and the verb. Often the words between the subject and verb are prepositional phrases. If you follow the advice given in Chapter 30, you will be able to find the subject and verb: *Cross out all the prepositional phrases in a sentence. The subject and verb will be among the words that are left.* Here are some examples:

$$\overset{s}{} \qquad \overset{v}{}$$

Prepositional Phrases: The **map** ~~of the Ozarks~~ **is** ~~in a small suitcase~~.

When you cross out the prepositional phrases, you can tell that the singular subject, *map*, and the singular verb, *is*, agree.

$$\overset{s}{}\qquad\qquad\overset{v}{}$$

Prepositional Phrases: Classes ~~at my college~~ **begin** ~~in August~~.

When you cross out the prepositional phrases, you can tell that the plural subject, *classes*, and the plural verb, *begin*, agree.

REVIEWING WORDS SEPARATING SUBJECTS AND VERBS

What words often come between subjects and verbs?

_____

What is an easy way to identify the subject and verb in a sentence?

_____

◆ *P r a c t i c e   4* **Identifying** Underline the subject once and the verb twice in each of the following sentences. Cross out the prepositional phrases first. Put an X to the left of any sentence in which the subject and verb do not agree.

1. _____ Her behavior in front of adults make us all sick.

2. _____ The blooming trees in the orchard are making me sneeze.

3. _____ Unlike John, Katie gives to the poor.

4. _____ The house in the mountains were for sale for one year.

5. _____ Oscar, along with his two sisters, are studying law.

◆ *P r a c t i c e   5* **Completing** Fill in each blank in the following sentences with a present-tense verb that agrees with its subject.

1. Many students at my college _____ business administration.

2. Angie, along with the entire math class, _____ the day could start over.

3. The police, despite many obstacles, _____ many criminals every day.

4. Most teachers at all grade levels _____ the work they do.

5. The buses in town _____ many students to school.

◆ *P r a c t i c e   6*   **Writing Your Own** Write five sentences of your own with at least one prepositional phrase in each, and underline the subjects and verbs. Make sure that your subjects and verbs agree.

_____

_____

_____

_____

_____

MORE THAN ONE SUBJECT

Sometimes a subject consists of more than one person, place, thing, or idea. These subjects are called **compound** (as discussed in Chapter 30). Follow these three rules when matching a verb to a compound subject:

1. When compound subjects are joined by *and*, use a plural verb.

   Plural: The **heat** and **humidity were** hard on Simone.

   The singular words *heat* and *humidity* together make a plural subject. Therefore, the plural verb *were* is needed.

2. When the subject appears to have more than one part but the parts refer to a single unit, use a singular verb.

   Singular: **Peanut butter and jelly is** Mindy's favorite sandwich.

   Peanut butter is one item and *jelly* is one item, but Mindy does not eat one without the other, so they form a single unit. Because they are a single unit, they require a singular verb—*is*.

3. When compound subjects are joined by *or* or *nor*, make the verb agree with the subject closest to it.

   Singular: Neither **leeches** nor miserable **weather was** enough to
              keep her from her goal.

   The part of the compound subject closest to the verb is *weather*, which is singular. Therefore, the verb must be singular—*was*.

   Plural: Neither miserable **weather** nor **leeches were** enough to
              keep her from her goal.

This time, the part of the compound subject closest to the verb is *leeches*, which is plural. Therefore, the verb must be plural—*were*.

REVIEWING SUBJECT-VERB AGREEMENT WITH MORE THAN ONE SUBJECT

Do you use a singular or plural verb with compound subjects joined by and*?*

_____

Why should you use a singular verb with a subject like macaroni and cheese*?*

_____

If one part of a compound subject joined by or *or* nor *is singular and the other is plural, how do you decide whether to use a singular or plural verb?*

_____

◆ *P r a c t i c e* **7 Identifying** Underline the verb that agrees with its subject in each of the following sentences. Cross out the prepositional phrases first.

1. The golfers and their caddies (looks, look) ready to play.
2. Ham and cheese (are, is) my favorite kind of sandwich.
3. Either the professor or his teaching assistants (grades, grade) exams.
4. The White Sox and the Cubs (is, are) both Chicago teams.
5. Checkers and chess (take, takes) a lot of concentration.

◆ *P r a c t i c e* **8 Completing** Fill in each blank in the following sentences with a present-tense verb that agrees with its subject. Avoid *is* and *are*. Cross out the prepositional phrases first.

1. Music and film _____ the senses with pleasure.
2. Either Omaha or Milwaukee _____ our choice for a weekend trip.

3. Ice cream and cake _____ me happy after a stressful day.

4. Neither my checkbook nor my credit cards _____ me out of debt when I have no money.

5. Teachers and counselors _____ the influence they have over their students.

◆ *P r a c t i c e   9*   **Writing Your Own**   Write a sentence of your own for each of the following compound subjects. Make sure that your subjects and verbs agree.

1. either the memo or the reports

   _____

2. jeans and coats

   _____

3. neither Jim nor Belinda

   _____

4. the mother and her baby girl

   _____

5. mashed potatoes and gravy

   _____

VERBS BEFORE SUBJECTS

When the subject follows its verb, the subject may be hard to find, which makes the process of agreeing subjects and verbs difficult. Subjects come after verbs in two particular situations—when the sentence begins with *here* or *there* and when a question begins with *Who, What, Where, When, Why,* or *How.* Here are some examples:

Verb Before Subject: Here **are** the **decorations** ~~for the party~~.

Verb Before Subject: There **is iced tea** ~~in the refrigerator~~.

In sentences that begin with *here* or *there*, the verb always comes before the subject. Don't forget to cross out prepositional phrases to help you identify the subject. One of the words that's left will be the subject, and then you can check that the verb agrees with it.

                                         V   S

Verb Before Subject: Who **is** that **woman** ~~in red~~?

                                        V   S

Verb Before Subject: Where **are** the application **forms**?

                                        V   S   V

Verb Before Subject: What time **are you leaving** ~~for school~~?

In questions that begin with *Who, What, When, Where, Why,* and *How,* the verb comes before the subject, as in the first two examples, or is split by the subject, as in the last example.

REVIEWING VERBS BEFORE SUBJECTS

Where will you find the verb in sentences that begin with here *or* there?

_____

Where will you find the verb in questions that begin with Who, What, Where, When, Why, *and* How?

_____

◈ *P r a c t i c e 1 0* **Identifying** Underline the subject once and the verb twice in each of the following sentences. Cross out the prepositional phrases first.

1. Where is the speaker for tonight's program?
2. There are scholarships available for next year.
3. Who was the winner of the Penn State–Purdue game?
4. Here comes the judge with his briefcase.
5. Where is the best place to pitch my tent?

Practice 11 **Completing** Fill in each blank in the following sentences with a verb that agrees with its subject. Cross out the prepositional phrases first.

1. What _____ that strange noise in the basement?

2. There _____ several reasons for staying in school.

3. Why _____ Michelle so quiet?

4. Here _____ the tree I planted on Mother's Day.

5. When _____ he _____ smoking?

Practice 12 **Writing Your Own** Write a sentence of your own for each of the following words and phrases. Make sure that your subjects and verbs agree.

1. Here is _____

2. There are _____

3. Who made _____

4. How did you _____

5. When were _____

COLLECTIVE NOUNS

Collective nouns name a group of people or things. Examples include such nouns as *army, audience, band, class, committee, crew, crowd, family, flock, gang, jury, majority, minority, orchestra, senate, team,* and *troop.* Collective nouns can be singular or plural. They are singular when they refer to a group as a single unit. They are plural when they refer to the individual actions or feelings of the group members.

                      s   v

Singular: The marching **band plays** at all home games.

Band refers to the entire unit or group. Therefore, it requires the singular verb *plays.*

                     s   v

Plural: The marching **band get** their new uniforms today.

Here *band* refers to the individual members, who will each get a new uniform, so the plural verb *get* is used.

REVIEWING COLLECTIVE NOUNS
....

When is a collective noun singular?

_____

When is a collective noun plural?

_____

◆ **Practice 13** **Identifying** Underline the correct verb in each of the following sentences. Cross out the prepositional phrases first.

1. The crew (is, are) talking to their loved ones on the phone.
2. The minority (is, are) still a vocal group.
3. The family (was, were) watching TV, eating, and sleeping when the fire alarm began screaming.
4. The class (feels, feel) proud of raising enough money for a field trip.
5. The carnival troupe (performs, perform) in the spring.

◆ **Practice 14** **Completing** Fill in each blank in the following sentences with a present-tense verb that agrees with its subject. Cross out the prepositional phrases first.

1. The audience always _____ their seats when the show starts.
2. The school band _____ old favorites when they perform on Saturday.
3. Our team _____ wearing their letter sweaters.
4. Our committee _____ people who take action immediately.
5. A group of tourists _____ arriving at noon.

◆ *P r a c t i c e 1 5* **Writing Your Own** Write a sentence of your own using each of the following words as a plural subject. Make sure that your subjects and verbs agree.

1. committee _____

2. team _____

3. family _____

4. jury _____

5. audience _____

INDEFINITE PRONOUNS

Indefinite pronouns do not refer to anyone or anything specific. Some indefinite pronouns are always singular, and some are always plural. A few can be either singular or plural, depending on the other words in the sentence. When an indefinite pronoun is the subject of a sentence, the verb must agree with the pronoun. Here is a list of indefinite pronouns.

Indefinite Pronouns

ALWAYS SINGULAR		ALWAYS PLURAL	EITHER SINGULAR OR PLURAL
another	*neither*	*both*	*all*
anybody	*nobody*	*few*	*any*
anyone	*none*	*many*	*more*
anything	*no one*	*others*	*most*
each	*nothing*	*several*	*some*
either	*one*		
everybody	*other*		
everyone	*somebody*		
everything	*someone*		
little	*something*		
much			

Singular: **No one answers** the phone when a customer calls.

Everybody simply **listens** to the ringing phone.

Plural: **Many get** up and **walk** away.

Others remain seated, tired, and unmotivated.

The pronouns that can be either singular or plural are singular when they refer to singular words and plural when they refer to plural words.

Singular: **Some** of Lamar's time **was** spent daydreaming.

Some is singular because it refers to *time*, which is singular. The singular verb *was* agrees with the singular subject *some*.

Plural: **Some** of Lamar's friends **were** late.

Some is plural because it refers to *friends*, which is plural. The plural verb *were* agrees with the plural subject *some*.

REVIEWING INDEFINITE PRONOUNS

What is an indefinite pronoun?

_____

When are all, any, more, most, and some singular or plural?

_____

_____

◆ *P r a c t i c e 1 6* **Identifying** Underline the verb that agrees with its subject in each of the following sentences. Cross out the prepositional phrases first.

1. Of all the guests, none (was, were) dressed appropriately.

2. Someone (sneak, sneaks) into my room while I am gone.

3. Some never (seem, seems) to learn from their own mistakes.

4 In reference to the candidates, any who wish to apply for the job (need, needs) to fill out an application.

5. Somebody always (take, takes) Tabitha to lunch on Wednesdays.

◆ *P r a c t i c e   1 7*   **Completing** Fill in each blank in the following sentences with a present-tense verb that agrees with its subject. Cross out the prepositional phrases first.

1. No one _____ he's innocent of the crime.

2. Each of the oranges _____ spoiled.

3. None of the cars _____ power windows or a rear window defroster.

4. Only a few of the senior employees _____ three weeks of vacation a year.

5. Most of my supply _____ gone.

◆ *P r a c t i c e   1 8*   **Writing Your Own** Write sentences of your own using each of the following words as a subject, combined with one of the following verbs: *is, are, was, were*. Make sure that your subjects and verbs agree.

1. another _____

2. both _____

3. others _____

4. each _____

5. none _____

CHAPTER REVIEW

You might want to review your answers to the questions in all the review boxes before you do the following exercises.

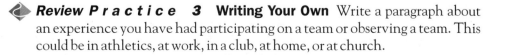

◆ *Review P r a c t i c e   1 A*   **Identifying** Underline the subject once and the verb twice in each of the following sentences. Cross out the prepositional phrases first. Then put an X to the left of each sentence in which the subject and verb do not agree.

1. _____ The orchestra with new instruments gets paid every Tuesday.

2. _____ Here are all the pieces to the puzzle.

3. _____ Neither the cheese nor the vegetables was fresh.

4. _____ The class down the hall is studying math.

5. _____ Anyone with questions can speak to the manager.

6. _____ Why have that team of dancers left the show early?

7. _____ Peanut butter and honey, when mixed together, are wonderful on crackers.

8. _____ The cat and the duck on my uncle's farm makes an unlikely pair.

9. _____ What is that flock of birds doing on our tree?

10. _____ There are most of the water from the flood.

◆ *Review P r a c t i c e   1 B*   **Correcting** Correct the subjects and verbs that don't agree in Review Practice 1A by rewriting the incorrect sentences.

◆ *Review P r a c t i c e   2*   **Completing** Fill in each blank in the following sentences with a present-tense verb that agrees with its subject.

1. Despite their ages, Angelica and Cindy _____ playing with each other at school.

2. The family with the most children _____ always seated first.

3. How _____ the levers and pulleys work?

4. Some of your apples _____ ripe.

5. Neither the curtains nor the comforter _____ the paint in the room.

◆ *Review P r a c t i c e   3*   **Writing Your Own** Write a paragraph about an experience you have had participating on a team or observing a team. This could be in athletics, at work, in a club, at home, or at church.

◆ *Review Practice 4* **Editing Through Collaboration** Exchange paragraphs from Review Practice 3 with another student, and do the following:

1. Underline the subject once in each sentence.
2. Underline the verbs twice.
3. Put an X by any verbs that do not agree with their subjects.

Then return the paper to its writer, and use the information in this chapter to correct any subject-verb agreement errors in your own paragraph. Record your errors on the Error Log in Appendix 6.

CHAPTER 36

MORE ON VERBS

☑ CHECKLIST for Correcting Tense and Voice Problems

> ✔ Are verb tenses consistent?
> ✔ Are sentences written in the active voice?

Test Yourself

Label each sentence I if the verb tenses are inconsistent or P if it uses the passive voice.

- _____ When my brother won the gold medal, my father looks very proud.
- _____ All new employees are trained by a professional.
- _____ The child was saved by the firefighters.
- _____ My friend got home early, so we go to the movies.
- _____ The student was given the answers in advance.

(Answers are in Appendix 4.)

Verbs communicate the action and time of each sentence. So it is important that you use verb tense consistently. Also, you should strive to write in the active, not the passive, voice. This chapter provides help with both of these sentence skills.

CONSISTENT VERB TENSE

Verb tense refers to the time an action takes place—in the present, the past, or the future. The verb tenses in a sentence should be consistent. That is, if you start out using one tense, you should not switch tenses unless absolutely necessary. Switching tenses can be confusing. Here are some examples:

NOT
Present
When the sun **sits** high in the sky, and the cloud

Present   Past
cover **is** just right, we **saw** the water glistening.

CORRECT
Present
When the sun **sits** high in the sky and the cloud

Present   Present
cover **is** just right, we **see** the water glistening.

NOT
Past
They **climbed** Mt. Shasta last week when the

Present
snowfall **is** heavy.

CORRECT
Past
They **climbed** Mt. Shasta last week when the

Past
snowfall **was** heavy.

NOT
Future
The astronauts **will finish** training this week, and

Present
then they **lead** the first mission to Saturn.

CORRECT
Future
The astronauts **will finish** training this week, and

Future
then they **will lead** the first mission to Saturn.

REVIEWING CONSISTENT VERB TENSES

Why should verb tenses be consistent?

_____

> *What problem do inconsistent verb tenses create?*
>
> _____

◆ **Practice 1A** **Identifying** In the following sentences, write C if the verb tense is consistent or I if it is inconsistent.

1. _____ The explorers will be leaving early in the morning and returned late at night.

2. _____ My dogs, Zak and Apollo, enjoy a day at the park and will love to play on the beach.

3. _____ Explaining the assignments to my sick roommate was hard, and it tried my patience.

4. _____ The summer movies looked interesting but will be big disappointments.

5. _____ The game was won with brute strength and is fun to watch.

◆ **Practice 1B** **Correcting** Correct the verb-tense errors in Practice 1A by rewriting the inconsistent sentences.

◆ **Practice 2** **Completing** Fill in each blank in the following sentences with consistent verbs.

1. The stores _____ many sales and _____ a lot of money.

2. Most people _____ comedies and _____ tragedies.

3. Most people _____ forward to vacations because they _____ to rest.

4. Students _____ hard before they _____ final exams.

5. Samantha _____ her bike and _____ a scooter.

◆ **Practice 3** **Writing Your Own** Write five sentences of your own with at least two verbs in each. Make sure your tenses are consistent.

_____

_____

_____

_____

_____

USING THE ACTIVE VOICE

In the **active voice,** the subject performs the action. In the **passive voice,** the subject receives the action. Compare the following two examples:

Passive Voice: The employees **were charged** with disturbing the peace **by the police.**

Active Voice: The **police charged** the employees with disturbing the peace.

The active voice adds energy to your writing. Here is another example. Notice the difference between active and passive.

Passive Voice: The water **was boiled** for the pasta **by Carmen.**

Active Voice: **Carmen boiled** the water for the pasta.

REVIEWING ACTIVE AND PASSIVE VOICE

What is the difference between the active and passive voice?

_____

_____

Why is the active voice usually better than the passive?

_____

◆ *P r a c t i c e* **4 A Identifying** Write A if the sentence is in the active voice and P if it is in the passive voice.

1. _____ The mail was opened by Sarah.

2. _____ Albert and Walter are sending flowers to their girlfriends.

3. _____ My purse was stolen by someone!

4. _____ The judge sentenced the criminals to serve five years.

5. _____ I would like to walk on the beach with you.

◆ *P r a c t i c e*   *4 B*   **Correcting** Rewrite the passive sentences in Practice 4A in the active voice.

◆ *P r a c t i c e*   *5*   **Completing** Complete the following sentences in the active voice.

1. Many styles of jeans _____.

2. A can of Coke _____.

3. A bowl of beans _____.

4. A vacation _____.

5. The baseball _____.

◆ *P r a c t i c e*   *6*   **Writing Your Own** Write five sentences in the passive voice. Then rewrite them in the active voice.

_____

_____

_____

_____

_____

CHAPTER REVIEW

You might want to reread your answers to the questions in all the review boxes before you do the following exercises.

◆ *Review P r a c t i c e*   *1*   **Identifying** Label each sentence I if the verb tenses are inconsistent, P if it is in the passive voice, or C if it is correct. Then correct the inconsistent and passive sentences by rewriting them.

1. _____ All of the chocolate doughnuts have been eaten by José.

2. _____ Mr. Johnson walks five miles every day, but has eaten whatever he likes.

3. _____ The children were read to by Grandma Ginny.

4. _____ The lawns and gardens have always been groomed by Mr. Shultz, our gardener.

5. _____ The blue team raced down the hill, jumped the hurdles in their path, and then will cross the finish line.

6. _____ I love anything made with chocolate, but I will dislike the taste of mocha.

7. _____ Paul listens to classical music, particularly Beethoven.

8. _____ We quickly called home to see if we had any messages, and then were rushing back to the meeting.

9. _____ My dad bought a new car with the money he won on a TV game show.

10. _____ In her spare time, my Aunt Juaquita volunteers at the local animal shelter and also helped cook meals for the homeless shelter.

◈ *Review **P r a c t i c e** 2* **Completing** Fill in each blank with consistent, active verbs.

1. Cheyenne always _____ the heat in summer and _____ the cold in winter.

2. The Key Club at our school _____ a bake sale and _____ all the money to charity.

3. The award-winning racehorse _____ through its routine.

4. Evan _____ to visit Tony in Las Vegas, but he _____ after only two days.

5. The soup for our dinner _____ on the stove.

◈ *Review **P r a c t i c e** 3* **Writing Your Own** Write a paragraph about your favorite college course. What do you like most about it? Why is it your favorite? Stay in the present tense, and use the active voice.

◈ *Review **P r a c t i c e** 4* **Editing Through Collaboration** Exchange paragraphs from Review Practice 3 with another student, and do the following:

1. Circle all verbs that are not consistent in tense.

2. Underline any verbs in the passive voice.

Then return the paper to its writer, and use the information in this chapter to correct any verb consistency or voice errors in your own paragraph. Record your errors on the Error Log in Appendix 6.

UNIT TESTS

Here are some exercises that test your understanding of all the material in this unit: Regular and Irregular Verbs, Verb Tense, Subject-Verb Agreement, and More on Verbs (Consistent/Inconsistent and Active/Passive).

Unit Test I

A. Underline all the verb errors in the following sentences.

1. Yesterday he laid in the sun too long and got burned.
2. Raymond's invitation was turned down by Sally.
3. She jump on the couch and turn up the volume.
4. Mr. Wilson said he has spoke to them.
5. I been working the early shift, but now I be working the late shift.
6. Amy said that you was going to bring the charcoal and grill.
7. The coach ain't going to let you skip practice.
8. Yesterday I sit my alarm clock for 7:00 a.m.
9. The runner who won last year have come in first again.
10. He don't have his driver's license with him.
11. Last week, Justin join the Marines.
12. Britta need to declare a major.
13. Some workers at the plant expects to go on strike.
14. The police and FBI often works on cases together.
15. We have both fell behind in our reading assignments.
16. When is the fireworks starting?
17. The cheerleading squad dance wildly every time the basketball team make a shot.
18. No one really think that he will run for re-election.
19. Robin and Jack expected to arrive early, so they drive quickly to get there.
20. Jordan was asked his name by the hotel clerk.

B. Correct the verb errors in Part A by rewriting each incorrect sentence.

Unit Test II

A. Underline the verb errors in the following paragraph.

People in small towns often has few choices when deciding how to spend their Friday and Saturday nights. Many small towns in America still had an old movie theater. The movie theater usually have only one screen. Also, the theater rarely got movies until they are out for at least two or three weeks. In big cities, theaters like this are put out of business by newer, flashier, multiscreen theaters. However, in a small town, the old theater be providing one of the few sources of entertainment and be full most weekends. Without the theater, many people ain't got nothing to do except set around.

B. Correct the verb errors in Part A by rewriting the paragraph.

CHAPTER 37

PRONOUN PROBLEMS

✔ CHECKLIST for Using Pronouns

✔ Are all subject pronouns used correctly?

✔ Are all object pronouns used correctly?

✔ Are all possessive pronouns used correctly?

✔ Are pronouns used in *than* or *as* comparisons in the correct form?

✔ Are the pronouns *this, that, these,* and *those* used correctly?

Test Yourself

Correct the pronoun errors in the following sentences.

• The toy was hers' to begin with.

• Diego told Megan and I the funniest story.

• He can run a lot faster than me.

• Those there ballet shoes are Laura's.

• Ted and me are going to the game tonight.

(Answers are in Appendix 4.)

Pronouns are words that take the place of nouns. They help us avoid repeating nouns. In this chapter, we'll discuss five types of pronoun problems: (1) using the wrong pronoun as a subject, (2) using the wrong pronoun as an object, (3) using an apostrophe with a possessive pronoun, (4) misusing pronouns in comparisons, and (5) misusing demonstrative pronouns.

PRONOUNS AS SUBJECTS

Single pronouns as subjects usually don't cause problems.

Subject Pronoun: I went to the movies with Jamie.

Subject Pronoun: **They** moved to San Francisco.

You wouldn't say "*Me* went to the movies" or "*Them* moved to San Francisco." But an error often occurs when a sentence has a compound subject and one or more of the subjects is a pronoun.

NOT   The Cardinals and **us** tied for first place.

CORRECT   The Cardinals and **we** tied for first place.

NOT   **Him** and **me** will wait on the porch.

CORRECT   **He** and I will wait on the porch.

To test whether you have used the correct form of the pronoun in a compound subject, try each subject alone:

Subject Pronoun?   **The Cardinals** and **us** tied for first place.

Test: **The Cardinals** tied for first place. **YES**

Test: **Us** tied for first place. **NO**

Test: **We** tied for first place. **YES**

Correction: **The Cardinals** and **we** tied for first place.

Here is a list of subject pronouns.

Subject Pronouns

Singular	Plural
I	*we*
you	*you*
he, she, it	*they*

REVIEWING PRONOUNS AS SUBJECTS

Name two subject pronouns.

_____

> *How can you test whether you are using the correct pronoun as the sub-ject of a sentence?*
>
> _____

 **P r a c t i c e   1   Identifying** Underline the pronouns used as subjects in each of the following sentences.

1. Her favorite china pattern was no longer made because it was over 50 years old.
2. Paul got his feet massaged since he had worked hard all week.
3. We figured that the machinery had a crack in it.
4. They played a game of baseball just for a charitable organization.
5. "Some days are better than others for them," he said.

P r a c t i c e   2   Completing Fill in each blank in the following para-graph with a subject pronoun.

Ron and Selma love to ride their bikes early in the morning. Selma bikes for pleasure, so _____ rides in the countryside. On the other hand, Ron plans to race in competitions, so _____ often bikes at the local university's track. Sometimes, however, _____ bike together in the city. _____ gives them a chance to visit each other. Personally, _____ think it's wonderful that they have an interest in common.

P r a c t i c e   3   Writing Your Own Write a sentence of your own for each of the following subject pronouns.

1. I _____

2. you _____

3. we _____

4. it _____

5. he _____

PRONOUNS AS OBJECTS

One of the most frequent pronoun errors is using a subject pronoun when the sentence calls for an object pronoun. The sentence may require an object after a verb, showing that someone or something receives the action of the verb. Or it may be an object of a preposition that is required (see page 370 for a list of prepositions).

NOT	She invited Bob and **I** to dinner.
CORRECT	She invited Bob and **me** to dinner.

NOT	This is between you and **I**.
CORRECT	This is between you and **me**.

Like the subject pronoun error, the object pronoun error usually occurs with compound objects. Also like the subject pronoun error, you can test whether you are using the correct pronoun by using each object separately.

Object Pronoun?	She invited **Bob and I** to dinner.
Test:	She invited **Bob** to dinner. **YES**
Test:	She invited **I** to dinner. **NO**
Test:	She invited **me** to dinner. **YES**
Correction:	She invited **Bob and me** to dinner.

Here is a list of object pronouns:

Object Pronouns

Singular	Plural
me	*us*
you	*you*
him, her, it	*them*

REVIEWING PRONOUNS AS OBJECTS

In what two places are pronouns used as objects?

_____

> *How can you test whether you have used the correct pronoun as the object in a sentence?*
>
> _____
>
> _____

◆ **P r a c t i c e   4**   **Identifying** Underline the correct object pronoun in each of the following sentences.

1. Crystal accidentally hit (he, him) with the ping-pong ball.
2. She played the violin for (us, we).
3. The mischievous child spilled milk all over Dana and (I, me).
4. Her grandmother took (she, her) shopping for a prom dress.
5. Mary picked a bouquet of flowers for (them, they).

◆ **P r a c t i c e   5**   **Completing** Fill in each blank in the following sentences with an object pronoun.

1. Alyssa gave _____ a Valentine's Day card.
2. Beau, my dog, bit Tina on the leg, but he didn't hurt _____.
3. I bought something for _____.
4. Mickey Mouse gave _____ a tour of Disneyland.
5. My grandmother lent _____ the family pearls for the wedding.

◆ **P r a c t i c e   6**   **Writing Your Own** Write a sentence of your own for each of the following object pronouns.

1. me _____

2. him _____

3. us _____

4. them _____

5. her _____

POSSESSIVE PRONOUNS

Possessive pronouns show ownership (*my* wallet, *his* suitcase, *our* trip). (See pages 364–365 for a list of pronouns.) An apostrophe is used with nouns to show ownership (*Tara's* car, the *clock's* hands, the *children's* toys). But an apostrophe is never used with possessive pronouns.

Possessive Pronouns

Singular	Plural
my, mine	*our, ours*
your, yours	*you, yours*
his, her, hers	*their, theirs*

NOT   That hairbrush is **hers'**.

CORRECT   That hairbrush is **hers**.

NOT   The umbrella by the door is **your's**.

CORRECT   The umbrella by the door is **yours**.

NOT   The puppy wanted **its'** tummy scratched.

CORRECT   The puppy wanted **its** tummy scratched.

REVIEWING POSSESSIVE PRONOUNS

When do you use an apostrophe with a noun?

_____

Do possessive pronouns take apostrophes?

_____

◆ *P r a c t i c e 7* **Identifying** Underline the correct possessive pronoun in each of the following sentences.

1. Krista gave her hair and clothes a quick pat.
2. The Corvette needs its windshield fixed.

3. I believe that book on the dresser is yours.

4. Their bikes were left unattended, so they were stolen.

5. That dog should have its nails trimmed.

◆ *P r a c t i c e* **8** **Completing** Fill in each blank in the following sentences with a possessive pronoun.

1. _____ vacation to Mexico was fun and exciting, but not so relaxing.

2. The games are _____.

3. The grandfather clock is broken, but _____ face is still in good condition.

4. _____ sister makes the best chocolate fudge cake.

5. The dogs performing in the circus are _____.

◆ *P r a c t i c e* **9** **Writing Your Own** Write a sentence of your own for each of the following possessive pronouns.

1. mine _____

2. her _____

3. its _____

4. our _____

5. theirs _____

PRONOUNS IN COMPARISONS

Sometimes pronoun problems occur in comparisons with *than* or *as*. An object pronoun may be mistakenly used instead of a subject pronoun. To find out if you are using the right pronoun, you should finish the sentence as shown here.

| **NOT** | She can run a mile much faster than **me.** |
| CORRECT | She can run a mile much faster than **I** [can run a mile]. |

| **NOT** | Paula is not as good a cook as **him.** |
| CORRECT | Paula is not as good a cook as **he** [is]. |

Hint: Sometimes an object pronoun is required in a *than* or *as* comparison. But errors rarely occur in this case because the subject pronoun sounds so unnatural.

NOT   Susan likes him more than she likes **I**.

CORRECT   Susan likes him more than she likes **me**.

REVIEWING PRONOUNS IN COMPARISONS

What causes pronoun problems in comparisons?

_____

_____

How can you test whether to use a subject pronoun or an object pronoun in a than *or* as *comparison?*

_____

_____

◆ *P r a c t i c e   1 0* **Identifying** Underline the correct pronoun in each of the following comparisons.

1. Brenda can sew better than (she, her).
2. The kittens are much friskier than (they, them).
3. Martha isn't as outspoken as (she, her).
4. She is nicer to her friends than to (I, me).
5. My husband can fix a car as well as (him, he).

◆ *P r a c t i c e   1 1* **Completing** Fill in each blank in the following sentences with an appropriate pronoun for comparison.

1. Because Lupe grew up on a ranch, she is more relaxed around horses than _____.

2. She is a more accurate proofreader than _____.

3. Robert is just as smart as _____.

4. He makes you just as crazy as he makes _____.

5. Those girls ate more food than _____ did.

◆ *P r a c t i c e   1 2*   **Writing Your Own** Write a sentence of your own using each of the following pronouns in *than* or *as* comparisons.

1. I _____

2. we _____

3. he _____

4. she _____

5. they _____

DEMONSTRATIVE PRONOUNS

There are four demonstrative pronouns: *this, that, these,* and *those.* **Demonstrative pronouns** point to specific people or objects. Use *this* and *these* to refer to items that are near and *that* and *those* to refer to items farther away. Look at the following examples.

Demonstrative (near):	**This** tastes great.
Demonstrative (near):	**These** are delicious peaches.
Demonstrative (farther):	**That** will be decided later.
Demonstrative (farther):	**Those** are the clothes she brought with her.

Sometimes demonstrative pronouns are not used correctly.

	Incorrect	Correct
NOT	this here, that there	this, that
NOT	these here, these ones	these
NOT	them, those there, those ones	those

NOT	**Them** are the boots she wants.
CORRECT	**Those** are the boots she wants.

NOT	I'd like to order **these here** pictures.
CORRECT	I'd like to order **these** pictures.

NOT	I made **those ones** by hand.
CORRECT	I made **those** by hand.

NOT	**Those there** are the ones I ordered.
CORRECT	**Those** are the ones I ordered.

When demonstrative pronouns are used with nouns, they become adjectives.

Pronoun:	**This** is his.
Adjective:	**This notebook** is his.

Pronoun:	**Those** are words you may regret.
Adjective:	You may regret **those words.**

The problems that occur with demonstrative pronouns can also occur when these pronouns act as adjectives.

NOT	Please hand me **that there** hammer.
CORRECT	Please hand me **that** hammer.

REVIEWING DEMONSTRATIVE PRONOUNS

Name the four demonstrative pronouns.

_____   _____ · _____   _____

Give two examples of errors with demonstrative pronouns.

_____

_____

◆ *P r a c t i c e   1 3 A*   **Identifying** Underline the demonstrative pronoun errors in each of the following sentences.

1. These here dishes are dirty and those need to be put away.
2. Yes, these ones can be taken back to the warehouse.
3. Them classes are the hardest I have ever taken.
4. I decided those ones will do nicely for the game.
5. That there belongs to the girl waiting in line.

◆ *P r a c t i c e 1 3 B* **Correcting** Correct the demonstrative pronoun errors in Practice 13A by rewriting the incorrect sentences.

◆ *P r a c t i c e 1 4* **Completing** Fill in each blank in the following sentences with a logical demonstrative pronoun.

1. Later on today, _____ will be answered.
2. When seen from up close, _____ looks quite large.
3. _____ are the best seats in the house.
4. _____ should be displayed in the window.
5. Mary had never seen any of _____ before.

◆ *P r a c t i c e 1 5* **Writing Your Own** Write four sentences of your own, one using each demonstrative pronoun. Be sure you don't use these pronouns as adjectives in your sentences.

_____

_____

_____

_____

_____

CHAPTER REVIEW

You might want to reread your answers to the questions in all the review boxes before you do the following exercises.

 ◆ *Review P r a c t i c e 1* **Identifying** Underline the pronoun errors in each of the following sentences.

1. The ring is hers'.
2. Ours' is the best short story out of those.
3. He is a better singer than me.
4. These here are our cars which are expected to sell.
5. The children and us went for a Sunday drive in his new convertible.
6. Those ones may be out of fashion, but she still wears them.
7. Her brother can play ball better than him.
8. Geoffrey used all of your art supplies when he drew a picture for she.
9. My little brother begged to go to the mall with Sarah and I.
10. This here is the car Mary thinks he should buy.

◀ *Review P r a c t i c e 2* **Completing** Correct the pronoun errors in Review Practice 1 by rewriting the incorrect sentences.

◀ *Review P r a c t i c e 3* **Writing Your Own** Write a paragraph about the town you grew up in. What is one vivid memory you have of this place?

◀ *Review P r a c t i c e 4* **Editing Through Collaboration** Exchange paragraphs from Review Practice 3 with another student, and do the following:

1. Circle all pronouns.
2. Put an X through any that are not in the correct form. Check that all the subject and object pronouns are used correctly. Also check that possessive pronouns, pronouns used in comparisons, and demonstrative pronouns are used correctly.

Then return the paper to its writer, and use the information in this chapter to correct the pronoun errors in your own paragraph. Record your errors on the Error Log in Appendix 6.

CHAPTER 38

PRONOUN REFERENCE AND POINT OF VIEW

✓ CHECKLIST for Correcting Problems with Pronoun Reference and Point of View

> ✔ Does every pronoun have a clear antecedent?
> ✔ Are pronouns as close as possible to the words they refer to?
> ✔ Do you maintain a single point of view?

Test Yourself

Underline the pronouns in these sentences. Then put an X over any pronouns that are confusing or unclear.

- Emily and Grace decided that she would try out for the team.
- They say you should drink eight glasses of water a day.
- I take the bus because you can save a lot of money that way.
- The reporter did not check her facts or talk to the main witness, which she regretted.
- It says to notify the dean if you are dropping a class.

(Answers are in Appendix 4.)

Any time you use a pronoun, it must clearly refer to a specific word. The word it refers to is called its **antecedent.** Two kinds of problems occur with pronoun references: The antecedent may be unclear, or the antecedent may be missing altogether. You should also be careful to stick to the same point of view in your writing. If, for example, you start out talking about "I," you should not shift to "you" in the middle of the sentence.

PRONOUN REFERENCE

Sometimes a sentence is confusing because the reader can't tell what a pronoun is referring to. The confusion may occur because the pronoun's antecedent is unclear or is completely missing.

Unclear Antecedents

In the following examples, the word each pronoun is referring to is unclear.

Unclear: On the shelf, a camera sat next to a small tape recorder. As Mr. Crutcher reached for **it,** the shelf began to tip.
(Was Mr. Crutcher reaching for the camera or the tape recorder? Only Mr. Crutcher knows for sure.)

Clear: On the shelf, a camera sat next to a small tape recorder. As Mr. Crutcher reached for **the camera,** the shelf began to tip.

Clear: On the shelf, a camera sat next to a small tape recorder. As Mr. Crutcher reached for **the tape recorder,** the shelf began to tip.

Unclear: Sarah agreed with April that **she** shouldn't get involved.
(Does *she* refer to Sarah or April? Only the writer knows.)

Clear: Sarah agreed with April that **Sarah** shouldn't get involved.

Clear: Agreeing with April, **Sarah** vowed that **she** wouldn't get involved.

How can you be sure that every pronoun you use has a clear antecedent? First, you can proofread carefully. Probably an even better test, though, is to ask a friend to read what you have written and tell you if your meaning is clear or not.

Missing Antecedents

Every pronoun should have a clear antecedent, the word it refers to. But what happens when there is no antecedent at all? The writer's message is not communicated. Two words in particular should alert you to the possibility of missing antecedents: *it* and *they*.

The following sentences have missing antecedents:

Missing Antecedent: In a recent study on teenage pregnancy, **it** says that counseling has a dramatically positive effect.
(What does *it* refer to? It has no antecedent.)

Clear: **A recent study on teenage pregnancy** says that counseling has a dramatically positive effect.

Missing Antecedent: **They** say that the early bird catches the worm.
(Who is *they*?)

Clear: **An old saying** claims that the early bird catches the worm.

REVIEWING PRONOUN REFERENCE

What is an antecedent?

_____

How can you be sure every pronoun you use has a clear antecedent?

_____

_____

What two words warn you that an antecedent may be missing?

_____   _____

◆ **P r a c t i c e   1 A   Identifying** Underline the pronouns in each of the following sentences. Then put an X next to any sentences with missing or unclear antecedents.

1. _____ Five hot dog vendors were on the same street, and they were each trying to outsell the others.

2. _____ The safety technician and the fire fighter gave her speech in the park.

3. _____ Barbara's birthday and Sam's anniversary are coming soon; it is the same day as Valentine's Day.

4. _____ In a recent study, it said, "Four times out of five, shoppers prefer Hallmark cards."

5. _____ They say that most students have some debts.

◆ *P r a c t i c e 1 B* **Correcting** Correct the sentences with pronoun errors in Practice 1A by rewriting them.

◆ *P r a c t i c e 2* **Completing** Correct the unclear or missing pronoun references in the following sentences by rewriting them. Pronouns that should be corrected are underlined.

1. <u>It</u> says in the paper that tickets go on sale tomorrow.
2. I put the letters in my bag. Then I peeled an apple and an orange for a snack before I realized I hadn't addressed <u>them</u>.
3. Trish told Diana that <u>she</u> was going to have to move.
4. Mario told Lendel that <u>he</u> should go on a diet.
5. Both Pat and Danielle went to Mills College together. Then <u>she</u> finished her degree at the University of Maryland.

◆ *P r a c t i c e 3* **Writing Your Own** Write five sentences of your own using pronouns with clear antecedents.

_____

_____

_____

_____

_____

SHIFTING POINT OF VIEW

Point of view refers to whether a statement is made in the first person, the second person, or the third person. Each person—or point of view— requires different pronouns. The following chart lists the pronouns for each point of view.

Point of View

First Person:	*I, we*
Second Person:	*you, you*
Third Person:	*he, she, it, they*

If you begin writing from one point of view, you should stay in that point of view. Do not shift to another point of view. For example, if you start out writing "I," you should continue with "I" and not shift to "you." Shifting point of view is a very common error in college writing.

Shift: If **a person** doesn't exercise regularly, **you** can lose flexibility and strength.

Correct: If **a person** doesn't exercise regularly, **he or she** can lose flexibility and strength.

Shift: I consulted a financial advisor because **you** can save money on interest payments.

Correct: I consulted a financial advisor because **I** can save money on interest payments.

REVIEWING POINT OF VIEW

What is point of view?

_____

_____

What does it mean to shift point of view?

_____

◆ *P r a c t i c e   4 A*   **Identifying**   Underline the pronouns that shift in point of view in the following sentences.

1. A person should avoid eating too much fat if you don't want to become overweight.

2. I think that the new tax laws should be revised because they are so complicated that you can't understand them.

3. Doctors must go to school for many years before they can practice medicine.

4. Since students have so little free time, you should always try to manage your time efficiently.

5. You should try to save money whenever you can because we never know when we might need it.

◆ *P r a c t i c e* **4 B** **Correcting** Correct the point-of-view errors in Practice 4A by rewriting the incorrect sentences.

◆ *P r a c t i c e* **5** **Completing** Complete the following sentences with pronouns that stay in the same point of view.

1. I went shopping at the mall because I heard that _____ could get some good bargains there.

2. A driver should always pay attention to others on the road if _____ wants to avoid being in an accident.

3. The show was sold out so they checked the Internet since _____ can usually find tickets for sale there.

4. If a person wants to make friends, _____ should try to smile at others.

5. I always cook more than enough food for the picnic, for _____ never know how many people will attend.

◆ *P r a c t i c e* **6** **Writing Your Own** Write a sentence of your own for each of the following pronouns. Be sure the pronouns have clear antecedents and do not shift point of view.

1. you _____

2. they _____

3. we _____

4. it _____

5. them _____

CHAPTER REVIEW

You might want to reread your answers to the questions in all the review boxes before you do the following exercises.

◆ *Review P r a c t i c e 1* **Identifying** Label the following sentences U if the antecedent is unclear, M if the antecedent is missing, or S if the sentence shifts point of view. Then correct the pronoun errors by rewriting the incorrect sentences.

1. _____ Alvin bought bananas, oranges, and apples at the store because you know fruit is healthy.

2. _____ They say a chef should train at home and abroad to be successful.

3. _____ You should hurry because we always need extra time.

4. _____ After my dog bit my neighbor's dog, he got sick.

5. _____ It is said that "every good dog deserves a bone."

6. _____ My mom often told my sister that she was a good dancer.

7. _____ Before Jan paints the garage and the house, she must clean it out.

8. _____ I drove to Cambria because you can really relax there.

9. _____ They tell me I should never walk down dark alleys alone.

10. _____ I watched a video on France since I have to write a report on it.

◆ *Review P r a c t i c e 2* **Completing** Correct the pronoun errors in the following sentences by rewriting each incorrect sentence.

1. Mary and Samantha are best friends, and she is my best friend too.

2. It is said that all people are created equal.

3. I am going to buy the most expensive dishwasher because you know that's the only way to get the best.

4. We have both chocolate and vanilla bon-bons, but it tastes better.

5. They believe that secondhand cigarette smoke can cause cancer.

6. I visited the animal shelter today since I believe you should always try to adopt a pet in need rather than one from a pet store.

7. Josephine and Yuki both went out tonight, but she didn't come home on time.

8. Shawn bought himself a hamburger, french fries, and a soda, but then left it sitting on the counter when he went to watch TV.

9. A person can always ask questions in this class, for how else are you going to learn the answers?

10. According to the statistics, it implies that a recession will soon hit our economy.

◀ *Review P r a c t i c e 3* **Writing Your Own** Using a variety of pronouns, write a paragraph about something you have learned from your friends this week.

◀ *Review P r a c t i c e 4* **Editing Through Collaboration** Exchange paragraphs from Review Practice 3 with another student, and do the following:

1. Underline all pronouns.

2. Draw arrows to the words they modify.

3. Put an X through any pronouns that do not refer to a clear antecedent or that shift point of view.

Then return the paper to its writer, and use the information in this chapter to correct any pronoun-reference and point-of-view errors in your own paragraph. Record your errors on the Error Log in Appendix 6.

CHAPTER 39

PRONOUN AGREEMENT

✅ CHECKLIST for Correcting Pronoun Agreement Problems

> ✔ Do all pronouns and their antecedents agree in number (singular or plural)?
>
> ✔ Do any pronouns that refer to indefinite pronouns agree in number?
>
> ✔ Are any pronouns used in a sexist way?

Test Yourself

Underline the pronoun in each sentence, and draw an arrow to its antecedent. Put an X over any pronouns that do not agree with their antecedents.

- Harriett and Maureen walked their dogs in the park.
- Each person is responsible for their own transportation.
- Although the pieces of furniture were used, it looked new.
- Someone left their dirty dishes in the sink.
- Everyone contributed his work to the assignment.

(Answers are in Appendix 4.)

As you learned in Chapter 30, subjects and verbs must agree for clear communication. If the subject is singular, the verb must be singular; if the subject is plural, the verb must be plural. The same holds true for pronouns and the words they refer to—their *antecedents*. They must agree in number—both singular or both plural. Usually, pronoun agreement is not a problem, as these sentences show:

Singular: Jacob told **his** client to buy more stock.

Plural: Rosalinda and Hugo did **their** laundry yesterday.

INDEFINITE PRONOUNS

Pronoun agreement may become a problem with indefinite pronouns. Indefinite pronouns that are always singular give writers the most trouble.

NOT	**One** of the students turned in **their** paper late. (How many students were late? Only one, so use a singular pronoun.)
CORRECT	**One** of the students turned in **her** paper late.
CORRECT	**One** of the students turned in **his** paper late.
NOT	**Somebody** left **their** keys on the table. (How many people left keys? One person, so use a singular pronoun.)
CORRECT	**Somebody** left **her** keys on the table.
CORRECT	**Somebody** left **his** keys on the table.

Here is a list of indefinite pronouns that are always singular.

Singular Indefinite Pronouns

another	*everybody*	*neither*	*one*
anybody	*everyone*	*nobody*	*other*
anyone	*everything*	*none*	*somebody*
anything	*little*	*no one*	*someone*
each	*much*	*nothing*	*something*
either			

Hint: A few indefinite pronouns can be either singular or plural, depending on their meaning in the sentence. These pronouns are *any*, *all*, *more*, *most*, and *some*.

Singular: **All** of the senior class had **its** picture taken.

Plural: **All** of the seniors had **their** pictures taken.

In the first sentence, *class* is considered a single body, so the singular pronoun *its* is used. In the second sentence, the *seniors* are individuals, so the plural pronoun *their* is used.

REVIEWING INDEFINITE PRONOUNS

Why should a pronoun agree with the word it refers to?

_____

Name five indefinite pronouns that are always singular.

_____ _____ _____ _____ _____

◆ **P r a c t i c e 1 Identifying** Underline the correct pronoun from the choices in parentheses, and be prepared to explain your choices.

1. Neither of the boys could give (his, their) opinion on the subject.
2. Before someone can appear on the program, (he or she, they) must audition.
3. Some of the bookstores put (its, their) books on sale for Father's Day.
4. Tom and Jack decided to hold (his, their) meetings on the first Thursday of each month.
5. Each of the dancers showed (his or her, their) dedication by practicing four hours a day.

◆ **P r a c t i c e 2 Completing** Fill in each blank in the following sentences with a pronoun that agrees with its antecedent.

1. Joshua and Timothy explained _____ method for cleaning chimneys.
2. Everyone should take the time to wash _____ clothes.
3. Each of the trees has lost _____ leaves.
4. Matthew asked _____ brother to fix the car.
5. Because of the cold weather, someone will have to share _____ warm clothes.

◆ **P r a c t i c e 3 Writing Your Own** Write a sentence of your own for each of the following pronouns.

1. nobody _____

2. one _____

3. everyone _____

4. each _____

5. nothing _____

AVOIDING SEXISM

In the first section of this chapter, you learned that you should use singular pronouns to refer to singular indefinite pronouns. For example, the indefinite pronoun *someone* requires a singular pronoun, *his* or *her*, not the plural *their*. But what if you don't know whether the person referred to is male or female? Then you have a choice: (1) You can say "he or she" or "his or her"; (2) you can make the sentence plural; or (3) you can rewrite the sentence to avoid the problem altogether. What you should not do is ignore half the population by referring to all humans as males.

NOT	If **anyone** wants to join us, then **they** can.
NOT	If **anyone** wants to join us, then **he** can.
CORRECT	If **anyone** wants to join us, then **he or she** can.
CORRECT	**People** who want to can join us.
NOT	**Everyone** paid **their** dues this month.
NOT	**Everyone** paid **his** dues this month.
CORRECT	**Everyone** paid **his or her** dues this month.
CORRECT	**All students** paid **their** dues this month.

Sexism in writing can also occur in ways other than with indefinite pronouns. We often assume that doctors, lawyers, and bank presidents are men and that nurses, schoolteachers, and secretaries are women. But that is not very accurate.

NOT	You should ask your **doctor** what **he** recommends. (Why automatically assume that the doctor is a male instead of a female?)
CORRECT	You should ask your **doctor** what **he or she** recommends.
NOT	The **policeman** gave me a warning but no ticket. (Since both men and women serve on police forces, the more correct term is *police officer* or *officer*.)
CORRECT	The **police officer** gave me a warning but no ticket.

NOT	**A nurse** cannot let **herself** become too emotionally involved in **her** work.
	(Why leave the men who are nurses out of this sentence?)
CORRECT	**A nurse** cannot let **him- or herself** become too emotionally involved in **his or her** work.
CORRECT	**Nurses** cannot let **themselves** become too emotionally involved in **their** work.

REVIEWING SEXISM IN WRITING

What is sexism in writing?

_____

What are two ways to get around the problem of using male pronouns to refer to both women and men?

_____   _____

Give two other examples of sexism in writing.

_____   _____

 P r a c t i c e   **4 A**   **Identifying** Underline the sexist references in the following sentences.

1. At least one student did not memorize his test material.
2. A judge will always give her verdict at the end of the trial.
3. A navy officer can wear his white uniform to weddings.
4. A mailman knows he must deliver the mail rain or shine.
5. A passenger usually can't fit all her luggage in the overhead bin.

 P r a c t i c e   **4 B**   **Correcting** Correct the sexist pronouns in Practice 4A by rewriting the incorrect sentences.

 P r a c t i c e   **5**   **Completing** Fill in each blank in the following sentences with an appropriate pronoun.

1. An athlete is always determined to overcome _____ injury.

2. The contestant who sells the most candy can choose _____ own prize.

3. An airplane pilot always has to make sure _____ remains alert and awake.

4. A teacher should always explain _____ assignments.

5. A truck driver can pull _____ truck over to sleep for a few hours.

◆ *P r a c t i c e   6*   **Writing Your Own** Write a sentence of your own for each of the following antecedents. Include at least one pronoun in each sentence.

1. doctor _____

2. professor _____

3. hair dresser _____

4. army recruit _____

5. senator _____

CHAPTER REVIEW

You might want to reread your answers to the questions in all the review boxes before you do the following exercises.

◆ *Review P r a c t i c e   1*   **Identifying** Underline and correct the pronoun errors in the following sentences.

1. Neither of the women went to their parents' house for Thanksgiving.

2. Each of the students picked up their test from the Psychology Department office.

3. A newspaper writer can work on his assignment for months.

4. Anyone can learn how to sew if they are patient.

5. A neat gardener always sweeps up after he mows the lawn.

6. Something in the files seemed like they were confidential.

7. A coach constantly yells for his team to play harder.

8. Someone in the crowd should stick up for their rights.

9. Nobody ever believes their driving is bad.

10. Everything in the sales bin has their price marked down.

◆ ***Review P r a c t i c e 2*** **Completing** Correct the following pronoun errors by rewriting the following sentences.

1. None of the fraternity brothers were open about their rituals.

_____

2. A doctor can choose his specialty from many different options.

_____

3. Every one of the nurses has had their uniform cleaned for inspection.

_____

4. Each of the people thought of their family as the story was being told.

_____

5. A sales clerk is never allowed to take her vacation in December.

_____

6. Everyone should have to watch her own performance on videotape.

_____

7. A janitor is not responsible for purchasing all of his cleaning supplies.

_____

8. Nobody wants their house robbed.

_____

9. A firefighter must cover his face with protective gear.

_____

10. Only one of the workers turned in their time sheet today.

_____

◆ *Review P r a c t i c e 3* **Writing Your Own** Write a paragraph explaining what you think the qualities of a good teacher are.

◆ *Review P r a c t i c e 4* **Editing Through Collaboration** Exchange paragraphs from Review Practice 3 with another student, and do the following:

1. Underline any pronouns.
2. Circle any pronouns that do not agree with the words they refer to.

Then return the paper to its writer, and use the information in this chapter to correct any pronoun agreement errors in your own paragraph. Record your errors on the Error Log in Appendix 6.

UNIT TESTS

Here are some exercises that test your understanding of all the material in this unit: Pronoun Problems, Pronoun Reference and Point of View, and Pronoun Agreement.

Unit Test I

A. Underline the pronoun errors in the following sentences.

1. The pilot was ready in the private plane to take he and she on the flight.
2. Kim cooked a delicious meal for we after the meeting.
3. Anybody can create their own painting.
4. Margaret didn't want to see Vivian because she didn't want to get involved.
5. That backpack is her's.
6. Jeremy is much more enthusiastic about our vacation than me.
7. I am going to take a walk on the beach since you can always benefit from a little fresh air.
8. A steel worker must always know he could go on strike.
9. The waiters gathered around she and sang "Happy Birthday."
10. The cat didn't want it's food.
11. A secretary must be able to identify her mistakes.
12. This here is just too hard for me to do.

13. We performed our dance routine just as well as them.

14. At the store, an ice chest was next to a lawn chair in a window display, but it was expensive.

15. In the summer, you and me should go swimming in the river.

16. I will give you these ones if you will give me those ones.

17. Something in the speakers sounded like they had broken.

18. I always carry an umbrella with me since you can never tell when it's going to rain in Louisiana.

19. Antonio is a much better painter than me.

20. The officer and the inmates want peace in his or her environment.

B. Correct the pronoun errors in Part A by rewriting each incorrect sentence.

Unit Test II

A. Underline the pronoun errors in the following paragraph.

In a recent study, it shows that a student involved in some sort of music program scores more highly on their standardized tests. It is not clear what about music education leads to this improvement in your skills. They now agree that music education is a valuable asset to all students. However, many school districts have cut all or most of it's music education programs. Them cite rising costs and plummeting resources as the cause for the elimination of these here programs. Because of pressures from their communities and state governments, the districts feel they need to focus on teaching the basics: reading, writing, and arithmetic. Unfortunately, in the long run, dumping music education to focus on the basics will do we a great disservice. Music is not less important than them. Anyone who is concerned about music education should write to their congressional representative to support it.

B. Correct the pronoun errors in Part A by rewriting the paragraph.

ADJECTIVES

✓ CHECKLIST for Using Adjectives Correctly

✔ Are all adjectives that show comparison used correctly?

✔ Are the forms of *good* and *bad* used correctly?

Test Yourself

Underline the adjectives in the following sentences. Then put an X over the adjectives that are used incorrectly.

- The gray stingrays were very beautiful.
- We were more happier when the rain cooled the hot day.
- This is the worstest cold I've ever had.
- This textbook is more better than that one.
- She is the oldest of the two sisters.

(Answers are in Appendix 4.)

Adjectives are modifiers. They help us communicate more clearly (I have a *red* sweater; I want a *blue* one) and vividly (her voice was *soft* and *gentle*). Without adjectives, our language would be drab and boring.

USING ADJECTIVES

Adjectives are words that modify—or describe—nouns or pronouns. Adjectives often tell how something or someone looks: *dark, light, tall, short, large, small*. Most adjectives come before the words they modify, but with linking verbs (such as *is, are, look, become,* and *feel*), adjectives follow the words they modify.

Adjectives Before a Noun: We ate the **moist, sweet** cake.

Adjectives After a Linking Verb: The cake was **moist** and **sweet**.

REVIEWING ADJECTIVES

What are adjectives?

_____

Where can you find adjectives in a sentence?

_____

◆ **P r a c t i c e 1 Identifying** In the following sentences, underline the adjectives, and circle the words they modify.

1. I could eat a large elephant for lunch.
2. My biology class is difficult but interesting.
3. The good news is that her older brother volunteers for the Boy Scouts.
4. She owns an antique store.
5. Our yard has both flowering trees and evergreen trees.

◆ **P r a c t i c e 2 Completing** Fill in each blank in the following sentences with logical adjectives.

When my (1) _____ brother Nathan was in high school, he became (2) _____ at math. The teacher wanted to teach concepts according to the textbook, but Nathan always seemed to find a (3) _____ way to solve the math problems. Though he would have the right answers, the teacher would often take off points because of the process he used. After having (4) _____ conversations with the teacher, Nathan convinced her that he was (5) _____. He got an A in the course and became a good friend of the teacher's.

◆ **P r a c t i c e   3   Writing Your Own** Write a sentence of your own for each of the following adjectives.

1. funny _____

2. seventeen _____

3. long-lasting _____

4. reliable _____

5. stressful _____

COMPARING WITH ADJECTIVES

Most adjectives have three forms: a **basic** form, a **comparative** form (used to compare two items or indicate a greater degree), and a **superlative** form (used to compare three or more items or indicate the greatest degree).

For positive comparisons, adjectives form the comparative and superlative in two different ways.

1. For one-syllable adjectives and some two-syllable adjectives, use *-er* to compare two items and *-est* to compare three or more items.

Basic	Comparative (used to compare two items)	Superlative (used to compare three or more items)
tall	taller	tallest
old	older	oldest
hot	hotter	hottest

2. For some two-syllable adjectives and all longer adjectives, use *more* to compare two items and *most* to compare three or more items.

Basic	Comparative (used to compare two items)	Superlative (used to compare three or more items)
careful	more careful	most careful
relaxed	more relaxed	most relaxed
content	more content	most content

For negative comparisons, use *less* to compare two items and *least* to compare three or more items.

Basic	Comparative (used to compare two items)	Superlative (used to compare three or more items)
beautiful	less beautiful	least beautiful
familiar	less familiar	least familiar

Hint: Some adjectives are not usually compared. For example, one task cannot be "more complete" or "more impossible" than another. Here are some more examples.

complete	*favorite*	*square*
dead	*horizontal*	*supreme*
empty	*impossible*	*unanimous*
equal	*pregnant*	*unique*

REVIEWING ADJECTIVE FORMS

When do you use the comparative form of an adjective?

_____

When do you use the superlative form of an adjective?

_____

How do one-syllable and some two-syllable adjectives form the comparative and superlative in positive comparisons?

_____

How do some two-syllable adjectives and all longer adjectives form the comparative and superlative in positive comparisons?

_____

How do you form negative comparisons?

_____

◆ *P r a c t i c e* **4** **Identifying** Underline the adjectives, and note whether they are basic (B), comparative (C), or superlative (S).

1. _____ The grass is always greener on the other side.

2. _____ Your car will look good if you wash it.

3. _____ Voters today are more educated.

4. _____ The longest mile of the marathon is the last one.

5. _____ My mother often asked my older brother to help her with the cooking.

◆ *P r a c t i c e* **5** **Completing** Fill in each blank in the following paragraph with the correct comparative or superlative form of the adjective in parentheses.

Yesterday was the (1) _____ (rainy) day of the entire

year. Consequently, my garden is looking (2) _____

(beautiful) today than it did two days ago. I have also seen the

(3) _____ (slimy) earthworms on the sidewalk, wiggling

faster than ever to get back into the dirt. Though I was pleased to see

my flowers starting to bloom, I became even (4) _____

(excited) when I saw the tulip bulbs breaking through the

ground. That means in a few weeks, my garden will be the (5)

_____ (spectacular) one on the block.

◆ *P r a c t i c e* **6** **Writing Your Own** Write a sentence of your own for each of the following adjectives.

1. a superlative form of *happy* _____

2. the basic form of *practical* _____

3. a comparative form of *tight* _____

4. a superlative form of *disgusting* _____

5. a comparative form of *responsible* _____

COMMON ADJECTIVE ERRORS

Two types of problems occur with adjectives used in comparisons.

1. Instead of using one method for forming the comparative or superlative, both are used. That is, both *-er* and *more* or *less* are used to compare two items, or both *-est* and *most* or *least* are used to compare three or more items.

   NOT   The top shelf is **more longer** than the bottom shelf.

   CORRECT   The top shelf is **longer** than the bottom shelf.

   NOT   That is the **most silliest** hat I've ever seen.

   CORRECT   That is the **silliest** hat I've ever seen.

2. The second type of error occurs when the comparative or superlative is used with the wrong number of items. The comparative form should be used for two items and the superlative for three or more items.

   NOT   Barb's chili recipe is the hott**est** of the **two.**

   CORRECT   Barb's chili recipe is the hott**er** of the **two.**

   NOT   Ross is the young**er** of the **three** brothers.

   CORRECT   Ross is the young**est** of the **three** brothers.

REVIEWING COMMON ADJECTIVE ERRORS

Can you ever use -er + more or -est + most?

_____

When do you use the comparative form of an adjective?

_____

When do you use the superlative form of an adjective?

_____

 P r a c t i c e   7 A   Identifying Underline the adjectives in the following sentences that are used incorrectly in comparisons. Mark sentences that are correct C.

1. _____ I always thought Lamar was more better at math than I was.

2. _____ Terry is the wildest of all her friends.

3. _____ Sean is the stronger of his five cousins.

4. _____ I've owned both a cat and a dog, and the cat was the cleanest of the two.

5. _____ The most happiest day of my life was the day I got married.

◆ *P r a c t i c e 7 B* **Correcting** Correct the adjective errors in Practice 7A by rewriting the incorrect sentences.

◆ *P r a c t i c e 8* **Completing** Choose the correct adjective forms in the following paragraph to complete the sentences.

     The (1) _____ (latest/most latest) fads in cars are hard to keep up with. The (2) _____ (more common/most common) of the many options now available is a car that uses both solar energy and natural gas for power. That way, if the solar cells are empty, the natural gas keeps the car running. What would be (3) _____ (sadder/more sadder) than running out of fuel while trying to meet a deadline or get to the hospital? Natural gas is (4) _____ (more cleaner/cleaner) than the gasoline used by most cars today. Between these two sources, natural gas is the (5) _____ (easier/easiest) on the environment.

◆ *P r a c t i c e 9* **Writing Your Own** Write a sentence of your own for each of the following adjectives.

1. most logical _____

2. happier _____

3. longest _____

4. more serious _____

5. scariest _____

USING *GOOD* AND *BAD* CORRECTLY

The adjectives *good* and *bad* are irregular. They do not form the comparative and superlative like most other adjectives. Here are the correct forms for these two irregular adjectives:

Basic	Comparative (used to compare two items)	Superlative (used to compare three or more items)
good	better	best
bad	worse	worst

Problems occur with *good* and *bad* when writers don't know how to form their comparative and superlative forms.

NOT   more better, more worse, worser, most best, most worst, bestest, worstest

CORRECT   better, worse, best, worst

These errors appear in sentences in the following ways:

NOT   That is the **bestest** play I have ever seen.

CORRECT   That is the **best** play I have ever seen.

NOT   His health is getting **more worse** as time goes by.

CORRECT   His health is getting **worse** as time goes by.

REVIEWING *Good* AND *Bad*

What are the three forms of good?

_____   _____   _____

What are the three forms of bad?

_____   _____   _____

 P r a c t i c e   1 0 A   Identifying In the following sentences, underline the forms of *good* and *bad* used correctly, and circle the forms of *good* and *bad* used incorrectly.

1. I got a C in chemistry, but did more better in Spanish.
2. The most best drawing is a bowl of fruit.
3. Even though he practiced, his soccer skills got more and more bad.
4. Going to work is better now that I am a manager.
5. I like my hair bestest when it is curly.

◆ *P r a c t i c e **10B** **Correcting** Correct the errors with *good* and *bad* in Practice 10A by rewriting the incorrect sentences.

◆ *P r a c t i c e **11** **Completing** Using the correct forms of *good* or *bad*, complete the following paragraph.

> Dusting is definitely the (1) _____ household chore. I can't think of anything (2) _____ than having to take everything off a shelf just to wipe a rag across it. It would be (3) _____ to buy those cans of compressed air and just spray the dust away instead of wiping the dust away. I can think of so many (4) _____ things to do with my time than dusting. But according to Dear Abby, the (5) _____ housekeepers have dust-free furniture.

◆ *P r a c t i c e **12** **Writing Your Own** Write a sentence of your own for each of the following forms of *good* and *bad*.

1. bad _____

2. better _____

3. worst _____

4. good _____

5. best _____

CHAPTER REVIEW

You might want to reread your answers to the questions in all the review boxes before you do the following exercises.

◆ **Review P r a c t i c e 1** **Identifying** Label the following adjectives basic (B), comparative (C), superlative (S), or not able to be compared (X).

1. _____ most lovable

2. _____ stickier

3. _____ final

4. _____ heavier

5. _____ more genuine

6. _____ new

7. _____ impossible

8. _____ delicious

9. _____ windy

10. _____ funniest

◆ **Review P r a c t i c e 2** **Completing** Supply the comparative and superlative forms (both positive and negative) for each of the following adjectives.

Basic	Comparative	Superlative
1. tight	_____	_____
2. crooked	_____	_____
3. long	_____	_____
4. smart	_____	_____
5. greasy	_____	_____
6. ignorant	_____	_____
7. great	_____	_____

8. friendly   _____   _____

9. cheap   _____   _____

10. happy   _____   _____

◆ *Review P r a c t i c e* **3** **Writing Your Own** Write a paragraph describing one of the most memorable people you have ever met. What did the person look like? How did he or she talk? What did he or she wear? Where did you meet this person? Why is this person so memorable?

◆ *Review P r a c t i c e* **4** **Editing Through Collaboration** Exchange paragraphs from Review Practice 3 with another student, and do the following:

1. Underline all the adjectives.
2. Circle those that are not in the correct form.

Then return the paper to its writer, and use the information in this chapter to correct any adjective errors in your own paragraph. Record your errors on the Error Log in Appendix 6.

CHAPTER 41

ADVERBS

✓ CHECKLIST for Using Adverbs

> ✔ Are all adverbs that show comparison used correctly?
> ✔ Are *good/well* and *bad/badly* used correctly?

Test Yourself

Underline the adverbs in the following sentences. Then put an X over the adverbs that are used incorrectly.

- We were led quickly out the back door.
- He hugged her tight when he saw her.
- Tina left early because she wasn't feeling good.
- She feels badly that she couldn't stay.
- I can't never meet on Tuesdays because I work that night.

(Answers are in Appendix 4.)

Like adjectives, adverbs help us communicate more clearly (she walked *quickly*) and more vividly (she stopped *suddenly*). They make their sentences more interesting.

USING ADVERBS

Adverbs modify verbs, adjectives, and other adverbs. They answer the questions *how? when? where? how often?* and *to what extent?* Look at the following examples.

How:	Zachary dusted the antiques **carefully.**
When:	The antique shop **always** opens on time.
Where:	The antique shop is **here.**
How often:	I shop there **regularly.**
To what extent:	The shop is **extremely** busy on Saturdays.

Some words are always adverbs, including *here, there, not, never, now, again, almost, often,* and *well.*

Other adverbs are formed by adding *-ly* to an adjective:

Adjective	Adverb
quiet	quietly
perfect	perfectly
strange	strangely

Hint: Not all words that end in *-ly* are adverbs. Some, such as *friendly, early, lonely, chilly,* and *lively,* are adjectives.

REVIEWING ADVERBS

What are adverbs?

_____

What five questions do adverbs answer?

_____ _____ _____ _____ _____

List four words that are always adverbs.

_____ _____ _____ _____

How do many adverbs end?

_____

◆ *P r a c t i c e 1* **Identifying** In the following sentences, underline the adverbs, and circle the words they modify.

1. The little boy cried loudly.
2. That was a very good movie.
3. Walk quickly to the car because it's raining.
4. We never miss our favorite TV show.
5. The dimly lit restaurant served horrible food.

◆ **P r a c t i c e   2   Completing** Fill in each blank in the following sentences with an adverb that makes sense.

Tom was (1) _____ tired after spending the day at Disneyland. He (2) _____ changed his clothes and (3) _____ crawled into bed. But before he closed his eyes, he heard a little fly (4) _____ buzzing around his head. Fortunately, his fatigue overpowered the buzzing, and he (5) _____ fell asleep.

◆ **P r a c t i c e   3   Writing Your Own** Write a sentence of your own for each of the following adverbs.

1. seemingly _____

2. almost _____

3. brightly _____

4. angrily _____

5. repeatedly _____

COMPARING WITH ADVERBS

Like adjectives, most adverbs have three forms: a **basic** form, a **comparative** form (used to compare two items), and a **superlative** form (used to compare three or more items).

For positive comparisons, adverbs form the comparative and superlative forms in two different ways:

1. For one-syllable adverbs, use *-er* and *-est* to form the comparative and superlative.

Basic	Comparative (used to compare two items)	Superlative (used to compare three or more items)
fast	faster	fastest
near	nearer	nearest
far	farther	farthest

2. For adverbs of two or more syllables, use *more* to compare two items and *most* to compare three or more items.

Basic	Comparative (used to compare two items)	Superlative (used to compare three or more items)
beautifully	more beautifully	most beautifully
awkwardly	more awkwardly	most awkwardly
loudly	more loudly	most loudly

For negative comparisons, adverbs, like adjectives, use *less* to compare two items and *least* to compare three or more items.

Basic	Comparative (used to compare two items)	Superlative (used to compare three or more items)
often	less often	least often
frequently	less frequently	least frequently
vividly	less vividly	least vividly

Hint: Like adjectives, certain adverbs are not usually compared. Something cannot last "more eternally" or work "more uniquely." The following adverbs cannot logically be compared.

endlessly	*eternally*	*infinitely*
equally	*impossibly*	*invisibly*

REVIEWING ADVERB FORMS

When do you use the comparative form of an adverb?

_____

When do you use the superlative form of an adverb?

_____

How do one-syllable adverbs form the comparative and superlative in positive comparisons?

_____

How do adverbs of two or more syllables form the comparative and superlative in positive comparisons?

_____

How do you form negative comparisons with adverbs?

_____

◆ *P r a c t i c e* **4** **Identifying** Underline the adverbs, and note whether they are basic (B), comparative (C), or superlative (S).

1. _____ Can you drive faster?

2. _____ This house is the most beautifully painted one in the neighborhood.

3. _____ My sister speaks more kindly to me when Mom is in the room.

4. _____ The crowd yelled loudly when the referee made a bad call.

5. _____ They completed the project most efficiently.

◆ *P r a c t i c e* **5** **Completing** Fill in each blank in the following paragraph with the correct comparative or superlative form of the adverb in parentheses.

　　Sasha gave the (1) _____ (creatively) presented oral report in the science class. Her visual aids were (2) _____ (colorfully) decorated than Paul's, and Paul is an art major. Sasha even spoke (3) _____ (clearly) than Odella, who is a speech major. But best of all, she approached the assignment (4) _____ (cleverly) than the best student in the class. She based her presentation on a popular TV game show. Everyone could identify with the information she presented, and (5) _____ (importantly), she kept our attention.

◆ *P r a c t i c e   6*   Writing Your Own Write a sentence of your own for each of the following adverbs.

1. the superlative form of *often* _____

2. the comparative form of *quickly* _____

3. the basic form of *selfishly* _____

4. the superlative form of *clearly* _____

5. the comparative form of *regularly* _____

ADJECTIVE OR ADVERB?

One of the most common errors with modifiers is using an adjective when an adverb is called for. Keep in mind that adjectives modify nouns and pronouns, whereas adverbs modify verbs, adjectives, and other adverbs. Adverbs *do not* modify nouns or pronouns. Here are some examples.

NOT	She spoke too **slow.** [adjective]
CORRECT	She spoke too **slowly.** [adverb]

NOT	He was **real** happy with the decision. [adjective]
CORRECT	He was **really** happy with the decision. [adverb]

REVIEWING THE DIFFERENCE BETWEEN ADJECTIVES
AND ADVERBS
....

How do you know whether to use an adjective or an adverb in a sentence?

_____

_____

Give an example of an adverb in a sentence.

_____

Give an example of an adjective in a sentence.

_____

◆ **P r a c t i c e   7 A**   **Identifying** Underline the adverbs in the following sentences. Write C next to the sentences that are correct.

1. _____ She talked too quick for me to understand.

2. _____ Your car engine runs so quiet.

3. _____ I patiently read the same picture book five times.

4. _____ This is a nice decorated dorm room.

5. _____ The ducks began to quack loud when they saw us.

◆ **P r a c t i c e   7 B**   **Correcting** Correct the adverb errors in Practice 7A by rewriting the incorrect sentences.

◆ **P r a c t i c e   8**   **Completing** Choose the correct adverb to complete the sentences in the following paragraph.

Last August, we drove to San Diego to visit a couple of friends that we hadn't seen in a (1) _____ (real/really) long time. She is a doctor at a San Diego area hospital, and he stays (2) _____ (incredible/incredibly) busy doing his artwork and taking care of their two kids. After we arrived, they took us to the beach, and we laughed (3) _____ (loudly/loud) at the kids playing in the water. When it was time for us to go, we (4) _____ (repeated/repeatedly) promised not to wait so long before the next visit. We hugged each other (5) _____ (tightly/tight) and said goodbye.

◆ *P r a c t i c e 9* **Writing Your Own** Write a sentence of your own for each of the following adverbs.

1. loosely _____

2. especially _____

3. cheaply _____

4. honestly _____

5. thankfully _____

DOUBLE NEGATIVES

Another problem that involves adverbs is the **double negative**—using two negative words in one clause. Examples of negative words include *no, not, never, none, nothing, neither, nowhere, nobody, barely,* and *hardly.* A double negative creates the opposite meaning of what is intended.

> **NOT**   We **never** had **no** break today.

The actual meaning of these double negatives is "we did have a break today."

> **CORRECT**   We had **no** break today.

> **NOT**   Jim does **not** owe me **nothing.**

The actual meaning of these double negatives is "Jim does owe me something."

> **CORRECT**   Jim does **not** owe me **anything.**

Double negatives often occur with contractions.

> **NOT**   My mom doesn't **hardly** get any time to herself.

The actual meaning of these double negatives is "My mom gets a lot of time to herself."

> **CORRECT**   My mom **doesn't** get much time to herself.

Using two negatives is confusing and grammatically wrong. Be on the lookout for negative words, and use only one per clause.

Rᴇᴠɪᴇᴡɪɴɢ Dᴏᴜʙʟᴇ Nᴇɢᴀᴛɪᴠᴇs

What is a double negative?

_____

List five negative words.

_____ _____ _____ _____ _____

Why should you avoid double negatives?

_____

◈ P r a c t i c e   1 0 A   **Identifying**   Mark each of the following sentences either correct (C) or incorrect (X).

1. _____ I don't think you owe me nothing.

2. _____ Michelle couldn't hardly wait to go to the Bahamas.

3. _____ Miguel can't barely fit in Tony's tennis shoes.

4. _____ The last one in is not really a rotten egg.

5. _____ Having a driver's license doesn't say nothing about your driving skills.

◈ P r a c t i c e   1 0 B   **Correcting**   Correct the double negatives in Practice 10A by rewriting the incorrect sentences.

◈ P r a c t i c e   1 1   **Completing**   Choose the correct negative modifiers to complete the following paragraph.

     The first time I went furniture shopping, I was (1) _____ (hardly/not hardly) concerned with the quality of the furniture. I just wanted things that looked good, and I (2) _____ (didn't/didn't never) think about how long they would last. I bought a plaid couch and was excited about decorating my living room around it, so I spent even more money on curtains, pillows, and wall hangings. Soon, I had a party at my house, and that couch was (3) _____ (not never/never) so abused. One of my friends, who must weigh (4) _____ (scarcely/ not scarcely) less than 300 pounds, plopped down on the couch, and it immediately broke. He apologized repeatedly, but no matter how he tried to fix it, there (5) _____ (wasn't nothing/was nothing) he could do. That's when I learned to buy things that last.

◆ *Practice 12* **Writing Your Own** Write a sentence of your own for each of the following negative words.

1. nowhere _____

2. barely _____

3. not _____

4. never _____

5. nobody _____

USING *GOOD/WELL* AND *BAD/BADLY* CORRECTLY

The pairs *good/well* and *bad/badly* are so frequently misused that they deserve special attention.

Good is an adjective; *well* is an adverb.

Use *good* with a noun (n) or after a linking verb (lv).

                                        n
Adjective: What a **good** dog.

                                        lv
Adjective: The soup tastes **good**.

Use *well* for someone's health or after an action verb (av).

                        lv
Adverb: I am **well**, thank you. [health]

                        av
Adverb: She plays **well** with others.

Bad is an adjective; *badly* is an adverb.

Use *bad* with a noun (n) or after a linking verb (lv). Always use *bad* after *feel* if you're talking about emotions.

                                  n

Adjective: That looks like a **bad** cut.

               lv

Adjective: I feel **bad** that I lost the tickets.

Use *badly* with an adjective (adj) or after an action verb (av).

                           adj

Adverb: The steak is **badly** burned.

                  av

Adverb: She drives **badly**.

REVIEWING *Good/Well* AND *Bad/Badly*

When should you use the adjective good?

_____

When should you use the adverb well?

_____

When should you use the adjective bad?

_____

When should you use the adverb badly?

_____

◆ *P r a c t i c e   1 3 A*   **Identifying** Label each of the following sentences either correct (C) or incorrect (X).

1. _____ Gwyneth said she felt good enough to travel.

2. _____ Don't talk so bad about Mike.

3. _____ That one bad play cost us the game.

4. _____ I want to do good in this class so my GPA improves.

5. _____ Tamika writes well.

◆ *Practice 13B* **Correcting** Correct the adverb errors in Practice 13A by rewriting the incorrect sentences.

◆ *Practice 14* **Completing** Choose the correct modifiers to complete the following paragraph.

Remember when you were in third grade and wanted so (1) _____ (bad/badly) to have lots of friends? The worst feeling in the world is to be teased and shunned by peers. And third graders are very (2) _____ (good/well) at creating nicknames that stay with a person for life. Nicknames often point out something unusual about your physical features or an activity you don't play very (3) _____ (good/well). Whatever kids find to tease you about, they repeat it and repeat it until you feel (4) _____ (bad/badly) about yourself—until you never want to return to school again. That is why parents should discourage name-calling and teasing. A child's self-image will affect how (5) _____ (good/well) he or she handles all aspects of life.

◆ *Practice 15* **Writing Your Own** Write a sentence of your own for each of the following modifiers.

1. bad _____

2. well _____

3. badly _____

4. good _____

5. well _____

CHAPTER REVIEW

You might want to reread your answers to the questions in all the review boxes before you do the following exercises.

◆ **Review P r a c t i c e 1 Identifying** Underline the correct word in each of the following sentences.

1. The committee was (real, very) tired by the end of the day.
2. Justin walked (most, more) slowly than Alec.
3. *The Simpsons* has been on TV (continued, continuously) for years.
4. We don't have (no, any) candy to offer the children.
5. The golden retriever ran more (quicklier, quickly) than the German shepherd.
6. Of all the kings, he ruled (most, more) fairly.
7. Her computer crashed (less, least) often than mine.
8. He danced with the (most, more) energy of them all.
9. They haven't (no, any) more to give you.
10. I will love you (eternally, more eternally).

◆ **Review P r a c t i c e 2 Completing** Fill in each blank in the following paragraph with an adverb that makes sense. Try not to use any adverb more than once.

Working as a telemarketer is much (1) _____ difficult than you might expect. It requires people to work (2) _____ long hours and to put up with rudeness. For instance, I've had to work for up to 13 hours without any more than a 10-minute break and a 30-minute lunch. The people that a telemarketer must call are not (3) _____ nice. Some are (4) _____ rude. Many people hang up (5) _____ when they learn I'm a telemarketer. They could at least say, "Thank you, but I'm (6) _____ not interested." With this job, I must (7) _____ remind myself to keep a positive attitude and

(8) _____ give up. I (9) _____ want to succeed at this job, but I don't know if I am (10) _____ strong enough.

◆ Review P r a c t i c e 3 Writing Your Own Write a paragraph explaining a favorite pastime of yours. What does the activity involve? Why do you like it? What does it do for you?

◆ Review P r a c t i c e 4 Editing Through Collaboration Exchange paragraphs from Review Practice 3 with another student, and do the following:

1. Underline all the adverbs.
2. Circle those that are not in the correct form.
3. Put an X above any double negatives.

Then return the paper to its writer, and use the information in this chapter to correct any adverb errors in your own paragraph. Record your errors on the Error Log in Appendix 6.

CHAPTER 42

MODIFIER ERRORS

✔ CHECKLIST for Identifying and Correcting Modifier Problems

> ✔ Are modifiers as close as possible to the words they modify?
>
> ✔ Are any sentences confusing because the words that the modifiers refer to are missing?

Test Yourself

Underline the modifier problem in each sentence.

- When we arrived at the concert, Sandy told her mother that she should call home.
- Before going to the store, the car needed gas.
- The teacher told the students their grades would be posted before she dismissed them.
- To enter the contest, the application must be submitted by Friday.
- We found the magazine and put it in a safe place that had an article about saving money.

(Answers are in Appendix 4.)

As you know, a modifier describes another word or group of words. Sometimes, however, a modifier is too far from the words it refers to (*misplaced modifier*), or the word it refers to is missing altogether (*dangling modifier*). As a result, the sentence is confusing.

MISPLACED MODIFIERS

A modifier should be placed as close as possible to the word or words it modifies, but this does not always happen. A **misplaced modifier** is too far from the word or words it refers to, making the meaning of the sentence unclear. Look at these examples.

NOT   Brad yelled at his roommate **in his underwear.**

(Who is wearing the underwear—Brad or Brad's roommate? The modifier *in his underwear* must be moved closer to the word it modifies.)

CORRECT   **In his underwear,** Brad yelled at his roommate.

CORRECT   Brad yelled at his roommate, who was **in his underwear.**

NOT   The students were told to turn in their papers **after the bell.**

(This sentence has two meanings. Were the students supposed to turn in their papers after the bell rang? Or after the bell rang, did someone tell them to turn in their papers?)

CORRECT   The teacher told the students to turn in their papers **after the bell.**

CORRECT   **After the bell,** the teacher told the students to turn in their papers.

Certain modifiers that limit meaning are often misplaced, causing problems. Look at how meaning changes by moving the limiting word *only* in the following sentences:

Only Laverne says that Shirley was at home in the evening.
(Laverne says this, but no one else does.)

Laverne **only** says that Shirley was at home in the evening.
(Laverne says this, but she doesn't really mean it.)

Laverne says that **only** Shirley was at home in the evening.
(Shirley—and no one else—was at home in the evening.)

Laverne says that Shirley was **only** at home in the evening.
(Shirley didn't leave the house in the evening.)

Laverne says that Shirley was at home **only** in the evening.
(Shirley was at home in the evening but out the rest of the day.)

Here is a list of common limiting words.

almost	hardly	merely	only
even just	just	nearly	scarcely

REVIEWING MISPLACED MODIFIERS

What is a misplaced modifier?

_____

How can you correct a misplaced modifier?

_____

◆ *P r a c t i c e   1 A* **Identifying** Underline the misplaced modifiers in the following sentences.

1. Stolen from his car, Henry saw his wallet at a pawn shop.
2. The flowers bloomed when the weather changed in the front yard.
3. Wearing her school colors, Javier went to the football game with Susan.
4. The officers quickly wanted to solve the crime.
5. I sold my old desk when I left college at a yard sale.
6. Bill told Tom when he was driving it that the car made a funny noise.
7. We make cookies after school on Fridays with lots of chocolate chips.
8. I went dancing with my boyfriend in my new Gap jeans.
9. Paul just bought the white house next to the supermarket with blue trim.
10. I want my goatee to grow as long as Fabian's with braids in it.

◆ *P r a c t i c e   1 B* **Correcting** Correct the misplaced modifiers in Practice 1A by rewriting the incorrect sentences.

◆ *P r a c t i c e   2* **Completing** Fill in each blank in the following paragraph with a modifier that makes sense.

In the (1) _____ town of Salem, Sam can see himself (2) _____ walking across the stage to receive his degree. This goal was (3) _____ but he thinks now that he will make it (4) _____. He always has doubts about himself, but he is slowly learning (5) _____.

◆ *P r a c t i c e 3* **Writing Your Own** Write a sentence of your own for each of the following modifiers.

1. since last fall _____

2. after running for 30 minutes _____

3. while taking a shower _____

4. though he was sleepy _____

5. before taking them to court (*end of sentence*) _____

DANGLING MODIFIERS

Modifiers are "dangling" when they have nothing to refer to in a sentence. **Dangling modifiers** (starting with an *-ing* word or with *to*) often appear at the beginning of a sentence. Here is an example.

NOT	**Having lived in Los Angeles for 20 years,** the traffic is horrible.

A modifier usually modifies the words closest to it. So the phrase *Having lived in Los Angeles* modifies *traffic*. But traffic doesn't live in Los Angeles. In fact, there is no logical word in the sentence that the phrase modifies. It is left dangling. You can correct a dangling modifier in one of two ways—by inserting the missing word that is being referred to or by rewriting the sentence.

CORRECT	**Having lived in Los Angeles for 20 years, Carrie** will tell you that the traffic is horrible.
CORRECT	**Carrie has lived in Los Angeles for 20 years,** and she will tell you that the traffic is horrible.
NOT	**To order more food,** the coupon must be presented in person.
CORRECT	**To order more food, you** must present the coupon in person.
CORRECT	You must present the coupon in person **to order more food.**

NOT	The refrigerator was full **after buying groceries.**
CORRECT	**After buying groceries, we** had a full refrigerator.
CORRECT	The refrigerator was full **after we bought more groceries.**
CORRECT	**After buying groceries, we** filled the refrigerator with them.

REVIEWING DANGLING MODIFIERS

What is a dangling modifier?

_____

How do you correct a dangling modifier?

_____

_____

Practice 4A **Identifying** Underline the dangling modifiers in the following sentences.

1. After price-checking for hours, the stereo at Costco was the best deal.
2. To register for the dance, the money must be paid a week in advance.
3. The restaurant was very busy waiting 10 minutes for a table.
4. Sitting on the blanket, the sun shone brightly during our family picnic.
5. To meet with your counselor, an appointment must be made.

Practice 4B **Correcting** Correct the dangling modifiers in Practice 4A by rewriting the incorrect sentences.

Practice 5 **Completing** Fill in the blanks with modifiers in the following paragraph.

(1) _____, Cheryl sets out to weed her garden and trim her bushes. Her yard has really been neglected (2) _____, because she was taking classes and had two part-time jobs. Her

evenings (3) _____ are her favorite times. She knows she
can rest then (4) _____. She can also dream about the
future during these times (5) _____.

♦ *P r a c t i c e* **6** **Writing Your Own** Write a sentence of your own for
each of the following phrases.

1. crunchy and chewy _____

2. sending an e-mail _____

3. hopping on one foot _____

4. to get up at dawn _____

5. having never been to Hawaii _____

CHAPTER REVIEW

You might want to reread your answers to the questions in all the review
boxes before you do the following exercises.

♦ *Review P r a c t i c e* **1** **Identifying** Underline the modifier errors in
the following sentences.

1. Singing and cheering, the van full of students pulled off.
2. Broken for almost two months, we finally bought a new flat screen
   television.
3. My parents tried as a young child to teach me right from wrong.
4. To build endurance and muscle tone, a health plan should be followed.
5. While talking on the telephone, my alarm clock went off.
6. Depressed about not getting the job he applied for, Deanna tried to
   cheer Sergio up with some ice cream.
7. Darlene said at the health club she would give Bert a free tennis lesson.
8. To be successful in the stock market, research is important.
9. An overnight success story, the papers followed the actor everywhere.
10. Upset about losing her wallet, the police officer talked to the tourist.

◆ *Review P r a c t i c e 2* **Completing** Rewrite the sentences in Review Practice 1 so that the phrases you underlined are as close as possible to the words they modify.

◆ *Review P r a c t i c e 3* **Writing Your Own** Write a paragraph about the career you hope to have after college and your plans to begin working in this field.

◆ *Review P r a c t i c e 4* **Editing Through Collaboration** Exchange paragraphs from Review Practice 3 with another student, and do the following:

1. Underline any misplaced modifiers.
2. Put brackets around any dangling modifiers.

Then return the paper to its writer, and use the information in this chapter to correct any modifier problems in your own paragraph. Record your errors on the Error Log in Appendix 6.

UNIT TESTS

Here are some exercises that test your understanding of all the material in this unit: Adjectives, Adverbs, and Modifier Errors.

Unit Test I

A. Underline the modifier errors in the following sentences.

1. The Dodge Neon is the more popular car in its class.
2. Sam didn't hardly go to class this term.
3. The little boys in the class were more good at reading than the little girls.
4. Helen touched the cactus very gentle.
5. He was never more busier than after he started that big project.
6. The snake was coiled up tight.
7. Sara was nervous and sang bad at the recital.
8. Dale Earnhardt died sudden during a race in February 2001.
9. I never get nothing good on my birthday.
10. To pass this class, no more than three absences are allowed.

11. The roller coaster turned sharp, and we held on for our lives.

12. A young person shouldn't never start smoking.

13. Using bleach made my shirts more whiter.

14. Nobody did none of the work but me.

15. Seeing my grandfather in the hospital is the most worst memory I have.

16. He wanted to go so bad.

17. You can really dress good if you want to.

18. Of my two uncles, the youngest one is the most fun.

19. The car must be driven for at least 100 miles to know if you bought a lemon.

20. Basketball is best to play than to watch.

B. Correct the modifier errors in Part A by rewriting each incorrect sentence.

Unit Test II

A. Underline the modifier errors in the following paragraph.

Family picnics do not seem like nothing to get excited about. However, as many Americans long for a more simpler time, they are becoming more popular. Spending a Saturday at the park, the grass is covered with families enjoying time away from their busy lives. Each family participating in this enjoyable activity has a more unique way of spending the afternoon. Some families like to play volleyball or other sports. Other families may simply spend the time daydreaming together while lounging on their blankets. For some families, eating good food is the better of all of these activities. The most important part of any family picnic is having fun, so planning the worse picnic is even more impossible than boiling water wrong. Family picnics are the more better way to spend a spring afternoon!

B. Correct the modifier errors in Part A by rewriting the paragraph.

43

END PUNCTUATION

✔ CHECKLIST for Using End Punctuation

> ✔ Does each sentence end with a period, a question mark, or an exclamation point?
>
> ✔ Are question marks used when asking questions?
>
> ✔ Do sentences that exclaim end with exclamation points?

Test Yourself

Add the appropriate end punctuation to the following sentences.

- That car almost hit us
- How can you say that
- She didn't want to go on the trip
- He asked if he could go
- I absolutely refuse to be a part of this

(Answers are in Appendix 4.)

End punctuation signals the end of a sentence in three ways: The period ends a statement, the question mark signals a question, and the exclamation point marks an exclamation.

PERIOD

1. A **period** is used with statements, mild commands, and indirect questions.

   Statement: Mason took his golden retriever down to the river.

Command:	Take this leash with you.
Indirect Question:	I forgot to ask him if he needed help.

2. A period is also used with abbreviations and numbers.

Abbreviations:	Dr. Finn lives at 123 Grammont St., next door to Ms. Margery Salisbury.
Numbers:	$4.35 1.5 $849.50 .033

REVIEWING PERIODS

What are the three main uses of a period?

_____

What are two other uses of a period?

_____

◆ *P r a c t i c e 1* **Identifying** In the following sentences, circle the periods used incorrectly, and add those that are missing.

1. Hers was the first house on Palm Ave south of Santa Barbara Street.
2. If you made more than $145.0 from one yard sale, you should consider it a success.
3. Mr Woo is a nice neighbor.
4. Now that Ed Johnson has finished medical school, we call him Dr Johnson.
5. Go with me to confront Sam

◆ *P r a c t i c e 2* **Completing** Add periods to the following paragraph where they are needed.

Driving a car with a stick shift is very easy once you can feel in your feet what the engine is doing When I learned to drive a stick shift, I practiced on an old farm road called Weedpatch Hwy. because I was too nervous to practice in traffic Mr Turner, my driving instructor, was quite impressed when I took my final driving test in my dad's five-speed Ford Escort

◆ **P r a c t i c e   3**   **Writing Your Own** Write a sentence of your own for each of the following descriptions.

1. a statement about drunk driving

_____

2. a statement including an address with an abbreviated street name

_____

3. an indirect question about directions

_____

4. a statement including a dollar amount

_____

5. a command to stop doing something

_____

QUESTION MARK

The **question mark** is used after a direct question.

Question Mark: Did you vote in the election today?

Question Mark: "Will Matthew turn his paper in on time?" her mother asked.

REVIEWING QUESTION MARKS

What is the main role of a question mark?

_____

Give an example of a question.

_____

◈ *P r a c t i c e*   **4**   **Identifying** In the following sentences, circle the question marks used incorrectly, and add those that are needed.

1. Is this the right way to George's house?
2. I think you have the right answer?
3. Is your grandfather Charles Curran.
4. Susie, what time is your appointment.
5. He asked his mother if she was still feeling ill?

◈ *P r a c t i c e*   **5**   **Completing** Add question marks to the following paragraph where they are needed.

What makes an ideal student. A good student is one who studies very hard, gets to class on time with homework in hand, doesn't work too many hours, and has a limited social life. Now what makes a realistic student. This is one who works hard to pay for school, studies as much as possible, goes to class with homework in hand (most of the time), and doesn't party too much, right. Now you might ask where an ideal student comes from. Most of us are really ideal students most of the time. It's just that sometimes we need a break and might not put school first every night. But isn't that what makes school fun.

◈ *P r a c t i c e*   **6**   **Writing Your Own** Write a sentence of your own for each of the following descriptions.

1. a direct question about college requirements

   _____

2. a direct question about one of your classes

   _____

3. a direct question about the weather

   _____

4. a direct question about car maintenance

   _____

5. a direct question about dinner

   _____

EXCLAMATION POINT

The **exclamation point** indicates strong feeling.

If it is used too often, it is not as effective as it could be. You shouldn't use more than one exclamation point at a time.

Exclamation Point:	No way!
Exclamation Point:	I can't believe it!
Exclamation Point:	Stop, or I'll scream!
Exclamation Point:	"You make me so mad!" he yelled.

REVIEWING EXCLAMATION POINTS

What is the main use of an exclamation point?

_____

Give an example of an exclamation.

_____

Practice 7 **Identifying** Circle the exclamation points used incorrectly, and add those that are needed.

1. I don't think that would be possible today!
2. Are you crazy!
3. I'm not sure what you mean by that!
4. "You must be joking!" Matt screamed.
5. If we win this, we're going to the playoffs,

Practice 8 **Completing** Add exclamation points to the following paragraph where they are appropriate.

"Shoot, Charlie. Shoot." I can hear my mom in the crowd. Hearing her voice always gives me that extra push I need. I know we're down by one point. I can hear the crowd. "Shoot." "Five more seconds." "Shoot." I slowly let the ball fly through the air. I watch as if time is in slow motion. *Swoosh.* Nothing but net. As my teammates run onto the floor, I glance at the stands to find my mom. I see her beaming face looking down on me. I scream for all to hear, "Thanks, mom."

◆ *P r a c t i c e* **9** **Writing Your Own** Write five sentences of your own using exclamation points correctly.

_____

_____

_____

_____

CHAPTER REVIEW

You might want to reread your answers to the questions in all the review boxes before you do the following exercises.

◆ *Review P r a c t i c e* **1** **Identifying** For each sentence, add the correct end punctuation. You may also have to capitalize some letters.

1. What do you think you're doing
2. Why you continue to smoke certainly confuses me
3. Oh my can you believe it
4. Take this piece of pie home with you
5. "Where are you going" she asked
6. No, wait
7. My brother wants to know who is taking us
8. Is there a reason we have to wait
9. You should do what you think is right
10. I wonder if there is a way out

◆ *Review P r a c t i c e* **2** **Completing** Turn sentences 1–5 into questions and sentences 6–10 into exclamations.

1. The aerobics class is canceled.
2. The Arkansas Razorbacks won.
3. You will marry me.
4. Caroline made the final cut.

5. You will save me a place.

6. Please don't drive on the grass.

7. The train is coming.

8. Did you hear me?

9. You will never find out.

10. No, I won't.

◆ *Review **P r a c t i c e** 3* **Writing Your Own** Write a paragraph about the house you grew up in. Try to include each type of end punctuation—the period, the question mark, and the exclamation point.

◆ *Review **P r a c t i c e** 4* **Editing Through Collaboration** Exchange paragraphs from Review Practice 3 with another student, and do the following:

1. Circle any errors in end punctuation.

2. Suggest the correct punctuation above your circle.

Then return the paragraph to its writer, and use the information in this chapter to correct any end punctuation errors in your own paragraph. Record your errors on the Error Log in Appendix 6.

Commas

CHAPTER 44

☑ CHECKLIST for Using Commas

> ✔ Are commas used to separate items in a series?
>
> ✔ Are commas used to set off introductory material?
>
> ✔ Is there a comma before *and, but, for, nor, or, so,* and *yet* when they are followed by an independent clause?
>
> ✔ Are commas used to set off interrupting material in a sentence?
>
> ✔ Are commas used to set off direct quotations?
>
> ✔ Are commas used correctly in numbers, dates, addresses, and letters?

Test Yourself

Add commas to the following sentences.

- We went to the plaza and we saw a great movie.
- When we get really tired we act really silly.
- "He's taking flying lessons" said Steven.
- The job market however is starting to look better.
- On Saturday we went hiking fishing and camping.
- He was born August 5 1985 in Duluth Minnesota.

(Answers are in Appendix 4.)

The **comma** is the most frequently used punctuation mark, but it is also the most often misused. Commas make reading sentences easier because they separate the parts of sentences. Following the rules in this chapter will help you write clear sentences that are easy to read.

COMMAS WITH ITEMS IN A SERIES

Use commas to separate items in a series.

This means that you should put a comma between all items in a series.

Series: I ordered a pizza with mushrooms, sausage, and green peppers.

Series: He washed the dishes, swept the floor, and took out the garbage.

Series: Susan plans to move out when her parents give her permission, when she has enough money, and when she learns how to cook.

Sometimes this rule applies to a series of adjectives in front of a noun, but sometimes it does not. Look at these two examples.

Adjectives with Commas: The **cool, sweet** plums were delicious.

Adjectives Without Commas: The **loose top** button fell off the TV.

Both of these examples are correct. So how do you know whether or not to use commas? You can use one of two tests. One test is to insert the word "and" between the adjectives. If the sentence makes sense, use a comma. Another test is to switch the order of the adjectives. If the sentence still reads clearly, use a comma between the two words.

Test 1:   The **cool and sweet** plums were delicious. **OK, so use a comma**

Test 2:   The **sweet, cool** plums were delicious. **OK, so use a comma**

Test 1:   The **loose and top** button fell off the TV. **NO comma**

Test 2:   The **top loose** button fell off the TV. **NO comma**

REVIEWING COMMAS WITH ITEMS IN A SERIES

Why use commas with items in a series?

_____

Where do these commas go?

_____

◆ *P r a c t i c e* **1** **Identifying** In the following sentences, circle the commas that are used incorrectly, and add any commas that are missing.

1. I need to go to the store for bread, milk, and, eggs.
2. My favorite teams are the Lakers, the Spurs and the Bulls.
3. The best things about a college education are the social aspects, the wide variety of instruction, and the career opportunities, college offers.
4. Love, peace and goodwill are my wish for you.
5. To complete this fun exciting course successfully, you must write four papers, take two tests and give one oral report.

◆ *P r a c t i c e* **2** **Completing** Add the missing commas to the following paragraph.

When I get to the coffee house, I'm going to find a big comfortable couch order a latte and read today's newspaper. I like to hang out at the coffeehouse because I see many of my friends. I usually meet Ron, Aldona and Jennifer there. We spend our time doing homework, gossiping, or just hanging out. We tend to laugh a lot. This usually draws a lot of attention to us because Ron has a loud hearty laugh. I love spending time with my friends at the coffeehouse. It's like spending time in a special secret club.

◆ *P r a c t i c e* **3** **Writing Your Own** Write a sentence of your own for each of the following sets of items.

1. three items on a grocery list

   _____

2. three of your favorite movies

   _____

3. three things to do at the beach

   _____

4. three kinds of sports cars

   _____

5. three cities you would like to visit

   _____

COMMAS WITH INTRODUCTORY WORDS

Use a comma to set off an introductory word, phrase, or clause from the rest of its sentence.

If you are unsure whether to add a comma, try reading the sentence with your reader in mind. If you want your reader to pause after the introductory word or phrase, you should insert a comma.

Introductory Word:	**Yes,** that would be great.
Introductory Word:	**Actually,** the plane wasn't as late as we thought it might be.
Introductory Phrase:	**In reality,** she's the best coach in town.
Introductory Phrase:	**To make the best of a bad situation,** we all went out for frozen yogurt.
Introductory Clause:	**When the band finished,** everyone clapped.
Introductory Clause:	**As the lights dimmed,** we all began screaming.

REVIEWING COMMAS WITH INTRODUCTORY WORDS

....

Why use commas with introductory words, phrases, and clauses?

_____

How can you tell if a comma is needed?

_____

_____

 P r a c t i c e   4   Identifying In the following sentences, circle the commas that are used incorrectly, and add any commas that are missing.

1. When, he was a young boy he lived in Texas.

2. The next time I go to the store, I will buy some snack foods.

3. Hoping to solve, the problem Katie wrote to the school president.

4. Truly that was the best home-cooked meal I've had in months.

5. As the band entered, the stadium everyone stood up.

◆ *P r a c t i c e* **5** **Completing** Add the missing commas to the following paragraph.

     This past weekend my sister and I took her 8-month-old daughter, Jamie, to the beach for the first time. At first Jamie was afraid of the ocean, but she soon learned to love it. When my sister would hold Jamie in the water Jamie would scream out loud and laugh uncontrollably. However Jamie was still frightened when my sister wasn't holding her. Overall we had a great time watching Jamie explore the water, sand, and seagulls for the first time. In two weeks we are going back, and I can't wait.

◆ *P r a c t i c e* **6** **Writing Your Own** Write a sentence of your own for each of the following introductory words, phrases, or clauses.

1. well

    _____

2. to make matters worse

    _____

3. when we got in the car

    _____

4. no

    _____

5. as he approached the house

    _____

COMMAS WITH INDEPENDENT CLAUSES

Use a comma before *and, but, for, nor, or, so,* and *yet* when they join two independent clauses. (Remember that an independent clause must have both a subject and a verb.)

Independent Clauses: Australia is a beautiful continent, **and** it holds many surprises for tourists.

Independent Clauses: Norman went to Europe, **but** he enjoyed Australia more.

Hint: Do not use a comma when a single subject has two verbs.

no
comma
↓
s   v   v
Australia is a beautiful country and **has** a large tourist trade.

Adding a comma when none is needed is one of the most common errors in college writing assignments. Only if the second verb has its own subject should you add a comma.

comma
↓
s   v   s   v
Australia is a beautiful country, and **it has** a large tourist trade.

REVIEWING COMMAS WITH INDEPENDENT CLAUSES

Name three coordinating conjunctions.

_____   _____   _____

When should you use a comma before a coordinating conjunction?

_____

Should you use a comma before a coordinating conjunction when a single subject has two verbs?

_____

 P r a c t i c e 7 **Identifying** Underline the subjects, and circle the coordinating conjunctions in the following sentences. Then cross out any commas used incorrectly, and add those that are missing.

1. I finished my paper tonight, so I will be ready for class tomorrow.
2. This gumbo smells good, and tastes even better.

3. Watching TV made Zack calm, and relaxed.

4. Mariah is going to the library today and then she will go home.

5. The gardener mowed the lawn, and pruned the hedge in the front yard.

◆ *P r a c t i c e* **8** **Completing** Add the missing commas to the following paragraph.

On Valentine's Day, my boyfriend told me we would have a special day. He would pick me up at 5:00 and he would take me to a very romantic place. He told me to dress up and look my best. I wore my new red dress and spent an hour on my hair and makeup. He picked me up promptly at 5:00. I had never been so disappointed for he took me to the movies. We watched an action flick. I tried not to get angry but I just couldn't help myself. After the movie, he said he needed to pick up something from his apartment and he made me come inside. Boy, was I surprised to see the entire apartment lit up with candles and to hear music playing all around me. His table was elegantly set and his two best friends were in tuxes waiting to serve us a five-course meal. Valentine's Day was exciting and special after all.

◆ *P r a c t i c e* **9** **Writing Your Own** Write a sentence of your own using each of the following coordinating conjunctions to separate two independent clauses.

1. or

_____

2. and

_____

3. so

_____

4. but

_____

5. yet

_____

COMMAS WITH INTERRUPTERS

Use a comma before and after a word or phrase that interrupts the flow of a sentence.

Most words that interrupt a sentence are not necessary for understanding the main point of a sentence. Setting them off makes it easier to recognize the main point.

Word:	She called her boyfriend, **Ramon,** to pick us up.
Word:	I didn't hear the buzzer, **however,** because the radio was on.
Phrase:	My favorite dessert, **banana cream pie,** is on the menu.
Phrase:	The governor, **running for a third term,** is very popular.
Phrase:	The state with the fastest growing population, **according to government figures,** is Florida.

A very common type of interrupter is a clause that begins with *who, whose, which, when,* or *where* and is not necessary for understanding the main point of the sentence:

Clause:	Rosemary Smith, **who is a travel agent,** was chosen jury foreman.

Because the information "who is a travel agent" is not necessary for understanding the main idea of the sentence, it is set off with commas.

Clause:	The YMCA, **which is on Central Street,** now offers daycare.

The main point here is that the YMCA offers daycare. Since the other information isn't necessary to understanding the sentence, it can be set off with commas.

Hint: Do not use commas with *who, whose, which, when,* or *where* if the information is necessary for understanding the main point of the sentence.

My friend **who is a travel agent** was chosen jury foreman.

Since I have more than one friend, we need the information after *who* to know which friend I am referring to. Do not use commas if you need this information.

Hint: Do not use commas to set off clauses beginning with *that*.

The YMCA **that is on Central Street** now offers daycare.

REVIEWING COMMAS WITH INTERRUPTERS

Why should you use commas to set off words and phrases in the middle of a sentence?

_____

When should you use commas with who, whose, which, when, *or* where?

_____

_____

When should you not *use commas before these words?*

_____

◆ *P r a c t i c e   1 0*   **Identifying** Label each sentence C if commas are used correctly with the underlined words and phrases or X if they are not.

1. _____ My brother, <u>trying to pass the class studied</u>, for an entire week.

2. _____ The dog, <u>with a bone in his mouth ran</u>, quickly down the street.

3. _____ The best, <u>shopping mall Fashion Plaza</u>, is not open on Sundays.

4. _____ The sister's baby, <u>who is asleep in the back room</u>, is my nephew.

5. _____ Stewart Cink, <u>a golfer played in</u>, the PGA tour.

◆ *P r a c t i c e   1 1*   **Completing** Insert commas around the interrupting words and phrases in the following paragraph.

A rocking chair worn by years of use sits in a corner of my room. My grandmother used it when she had my mom Sarah many years ago. My mom used it with me, and I'll use it of course when I have children. I like looking at the rocker which holds so many memories for so many people because it makes me think of home. I sometimes read in the chair however so I can quietly sit in the most peaceful place and let my mind rest. This rocking chair which is simply made of wood keeps me sane while I am so far away from home.

◆ *P r a c t i c e   1 2*   **Writing Your Own** Write a sentence of your own for each of the following phrases.

1. the basketball player _____

2. of course _____

3. who drives recklessly _____

4. giving us his approval _____

5. which is on the kitchen counter _____

COMMAS WITH DIRECT QUOTATIONS

Use commas to mark direct quotations.

   A direct quotation records a person's exact words. Commas set off the exact words from the rest of the sentence, making it easier to understand who said what.

Direct Quotation:	My friends often say, **"You are so lucky."**
Direct Quotation:	**"You are so lucky,"** my friends often say.
Direct Quotation:	**"You are so lucky,"** says my grandmother, **"to have good friends."**

Hint: If a quotation ends with a question mark or an exclamation point, do not use a comma. Only one punctuation mark is needed.

NOT	**"What did he say?,"** she asked.
CORRECT	**"What did he say?"** she asked.

REVIEWING COMMAS WITH DIRECT QUOTATIONS

Why should you use commas with a direct quotation?

_____

> *Should you use a comma if the quotation ends with a question mark or*
> *an exclamation point? Why or why not?*
>
> _____

Practice 13 Identifying In the following sentences, circle the commas that are used incorrectly, and add any commas that are missing.

1. She remarked ",My favorite food is Mexican."
2. "I don't know the answer," Mark confessed "but I'll keep trying to figure it out."
3. "Are you out of your mind?," he asked.
4. "I remember," Ruben said, "when we all went camping in Tahoe."
5. "Get here right now!," screamed the mother.

Practice 14 Completing Add the missing commas to the following passage.

Joey and Dawn decided to go to a movie. "What do you want to see?" he asked.

"Definitely the new *Harry Potter*" Dawn replied.

Joey was disappointed and responded "But I've already seen that one."

"If you see it again " she said "you might catch something you missed before."

"Well, I guess that's a good point" he admitted.

Practice 15 Writing Your Own Write five sentences of your own using commas to set off direct quotations.

_____

_____

_____

_____

_____

OTHER USES OF COMMAS

Other commas clarify information in everyday writing.

Numbers:	The answer to the third problem is **12,487.**
Dates:	My grandmother was born **July 12, 1942,** in Buffalo, New York.

Notice that there is a comma both before and after the year.

Addresses:	Bruce's new address is **2105 Peterson Rd., Arma, KS 66712.**

Notice that there is no comma between the state and the zip code.

States:	He lives in **Monroe, Michigan,** and she lives in **Monroe, Louisiana.**

Notice that there is a comma both before and after a state.

Letters:	**Dear John,** **Sincerely yours,**

REVIEWING OTHER USES OF COMMAS

Give one example of commas in each of the following situations:

Numbers: _____

Dates: _____

Addresses: _____

Letters: _____

Why are these commas important?

_____

◆ **P r a c t i c e 1 6   Identifying** In the following sentences, circle the commas that are used incorrectly, and add any commas that are missing.

1. I live at 4,801 Pine Street in Denver Colorado.
2. He threw 3,847 pitches in his baseball career.
3. I need to deliver 14,00 mailers before the big sale this weekend.
4. There are more than 5,000 people with the last name of Martinez in the city of, Los Angeles California.
5. I think he moved to Las, Vegas, Nevada.

◆ *Practice 17* **Completing** Add the missing commas to the following paragraph.

   The world record for jump-roping is 1200 hours. The jump-roper accomplished this feat on October 12 1961 at his home in Biloxi Mississippi. Another guy who was from Ontario Canada tried to break the record in 1973, but he could only jump rope for 1070 consecutive hours.

◆ *Practice 18* **Writing Your Own** Write a sentence of your own including each of the following items.

1. your date of birth

   _____

2. the city and state where you were born

   _____

3. your full address, including the ZIP code

   _____

4. the estimated number of miles between Santa Barbara, California, and New York City

   _____

5. the amount of money you would expect to pay for your dream house

   _____

CHAPTER REVIEW

You might want to reread your answers to the questions in all the review boxes before you do the following exercises.

◆ **Review Practice 1** **Identifying** Add the missing commas to the following sentences.

1. On the second Saturday of each month Sensei Allen holds a Karate tournament.
2. Victor and Lou took the truck in to be fixed but the automotive shop was closed.
3. Although Chesney had taken tap classes before she still couldn't remember what to do.
4. The boy however believed that his horse would win.
5. I stood in awe as Kelsey my beautiful golden retriever won first place in the state dog show.
6. "Take a left at the last street on the block " said the crossing guard.
7. Downhill skiing diving and swimming are my favorite Olympic events.
8. The tall lean good-looking motorcycle cop was ticketing a speeder.
9. When the clock strikes twelve meet me in the cemetery.
10. Saul Tom and Will are going to the town meeting if they get home in time.

◆ **Review Practice 2** **Completing** Add the missing commas to the following paragraph.

Sometimes when I walk into the library I am immediately overwhelmed. Books magazines and newspapers are everywhere and then I think to myself "This is only the first floor!" Last Friday evening I went to the library with Ophelia who is my science lab partner to join a study group. We never made it to the study group however because we got sidetracked by the popular magazines on the first floor. Later that evening we saw the tired depressed faces of our study group members and were glad we had stayed in the magazine section taking magazine quizzes and reading for pleasure.

◆ **Review Practice 3** **Writing Your Own** Write a paragraph about one of your neighbors. What are some identifying qualities of this person? Do you like him or her?

Review P r a c t i c e 4 **Editing Through Collaboration** Exchange paragraphs from Review Practice 3 with another student, and do the following:

1. Circle any misplaced commas.
2. Suggest corrections for the incorrect commas.

Then return the paper to its writer, and use the information in this chapter to correct any comma errors in your own paragraph. Record your errors on the Error Log in Appendix 6.

CHAPTER 45

APOSTROPHES

✔ CHECKLIST for Using Apostrophes

> ✔Are apostrophes used correctly in contractions?
> ✔Are apostrophes used correctly to show possession?

Test Yourself

Add an apostrophe or an apostrophe and *-s* to the following sentences.

- The followers went into their leaders home.
- Its not important that you understand its every function.
- Thats not a good enough reason to believe Tracys story.
- The childrens toys were scattered around the room.
- Charles party was a lot of fun.

(Answers are in Appendix 4.)

The **apostrophe** looks like a single quotation mark. Its two main purposes are to indicate where letters have been left out and to show ownership.

MARKING CONTRACTIONS

Use an apostrophe to show that letters have been omitted to form a contraction.

A **contraction** is the shortening of one or more words. Our everyday speech is filled with contractions.

I have	=	I've (*h* and *a* have been omitted)
you are	=	you're (*a* has been omitted)
let us	=	let's (*u* has been omitted)

Here is a list of commonly used contractions.

Some Common Contractions

I am	=	I'm	we have	=	we've
I would	=	I'd	we will	=	we'll
I will	=	I'll	they are	=	they're
you have	=	you've	they have	=	they've
you will	=	you'll	do not	=	don't
he is	=	he's	did not	=	didn't
she will	=	she'll	have not	=	haven't
it is	=	it's	could not	=	couldn't

Hint: Two words that are frequently misused are *it's* and *its*.

it's = contraction: it is (or it has)   **It's** too late to go to the movie.
its = pronoun: belonging to it   **Its** eyes are really large.

To see if you are using the correct word, say the sentence with the words *it is*. If that is what you want to say, add an apostrophe to the word.

?   I think **its** boiling.

Test: I think **it is** boiling.   **YES, add an apostrophe**

This sentence makes sense with *it is*, so you should write *it's*.

Correct: I think **it's** boiling.

?   The kitten drank **its** milk.

Test: The kitten drank **it is** milk.   **NO, so no apostrophe**

This sentence does not make sense with *it is*, so you should not use the apostrophe in *its*.

Correct: The kitten drank **its** milk.

REVIEWING CONTRACTIONS

What is the purpose of an apostrophe in a contraction?

_____

Write five contractions, and tell which letters have been omitted.

_____   _____

_____   _____

_____   _____

_____   _____

_____   _____

What is the difference between it's and its?

_____

◆ **P r a c t i c e   1   Identifying** In the following sentences, circle the apostrophes that are used incorrectly, and add any apostrophes that are missing.

1. It's about time to get out of bed.
2. I think Damian should'nt join us.
3. They ve got a lot of nerve saying that.
4. If you're happy about it, then Im happy for you.
5. This is the last time shell borrow my car.

◆ **P r a c t i c e   2   Completing** Write contractions for the following words.

1. we + would   =   _____

2. they + will   =   _____

3. would + not   =   _____

4. does + not　　=　_____

5. can + not　　=　_____

◆ *P r a c t i c e　3* **Writing Your Own** Write a sentence of your own for each of the contractions you wrote in Practice 2.

_____

_____

_____

_____

_____

SHOWING POSSESSION

Use an apostrophe to show **possession.**

1. For a singular word, use 's to indicate possession or ownership. You can always replace a possessive with *of* plus the noun or pronoun.

the dog**'s** collar	=	the collar **of the dog** (the dog owns the collar)
everyone**'s** opinion	=	the opinion **of everyone** (all the people possess a single opinion)
boss**'s** office	=	the office **of the boss** (the boss possesses the office)
today**'s** news	=	the news **of today** (today "owns" or "possesses" the news)

2. For plural nouns ending in *-s*, use only an apostrophe.

the dogs**'** collars	=	the collars **of the dogs**
the ladies**'** pearls	=	the pearls **of the ladies**
the owners**'** children	=	the children **of the owners**
the teachers**'** friends	=	the friends **of the teachers**
the friends**'** families	=	the families **of the friends**

3. For plural nouns that do not end in *-s*, add *'s*.

the men**'s** shirts   =   the shirts **of the men**

the children**'s** teachers =   the teachers **of the children**

the women**'s** savings   =   the savings **of the women**

REVIEWING POSSESSIVES

How do you mark possession or ownership for a singular word?

_____

How do you mark possession or ownership for a plural word that ends in -s?

_____

How do you mark possession or ownership for a plural word that doesn't end in -s?

_____

◆ *P r a c t i c e 4* **Identifying** In the following sentences, circle the apostrophes that are used incorrectly, and add any apostrophes that are missing.

1. The kids skateboards are in the garage.
2. Serenity had to get five shot's today in compliance with her doctor's order's.
3. The mens retreat is this weekend.
4. My boyfriend's attitude is very negative today.
5. All of the babies diaper's need to be changed.

◆ *P r a c t i c e 5* **Completing** Write a possessive for each of the following phrases.

1. the parrot of Mr. Brown _____

2. the shoes of Marcus _____

3. the meal of the prison inmates _____

4. the holiday celebration of the Smith families _____

_____

5. the water level of the lake _____

◆ *P r a c t i c e   6* **Writing Your Own** Write a sentence of your own for each of the possessives you wrote in Practice 5.

_____

_____

_____

_____

_____

COMMON APOSTROPHE ERRORS

Two common errors occur with apostrophes. The following guidelines will help you avoid these errors.

No Apostrophe with Possessive Pronouns

Do not use an apostrophe with a possessive pronoun.

Possessive pronouns already show ownership, so they do not need an apostrophe.

Incorrect	Correct
his'	his
her's or hers'	hers
it's or its'	its
your's or yours'	yours
our's or ours'	ours
their's or theirs'	theirs

No Apostrophe to Form the Plural

Do not use an apostrophe to form a plural word.

This error occurs most often with plural words ending in *-s*. An apostrophe indicates possession or contraction; it does *not* indicate the plural. Therefore, a plural word never takes an apostrophe unless it is possessive.

NOT	The **shirts'** are on the hangers.
CORRECT	The **shirts** are on the hangers.
NOT	She went to get the **groceries'** over an hour ago.
CORRECT	She went to get the **groceries** over an hour ago.
NOT	Watching old family **movies'** is a lot of fun.
CORRECT	Watching old family **movies** is a lot of fun.

REVIEWING APOSTROPHE ERRORS

List three possessive pronouns.

_____ _____ _____

Why don't possessive pronouns take apostrophes?

_____

What is wrong with the apostrophe in each of the following sentences?
The last float in the parade is ours'.

_____

There must be 100 floats' in the parade.

_____

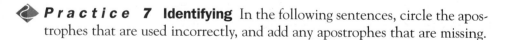 **Practice 7 Identifying** In the following sentences, circle the apostrophes that are used incorrectly, and add any apostrophes that are missing.

1. The cat licked it's paws for ten minutes after eating.
2. Why don't we go to the movie's?
3. If you join these two club's with me, we can take the members' pledge together.

4. I'm going to buy pant's just like your's.

5. That's my friend Dakota from my computer classes'.

◆ *P r a c t i c e*   *8*   **Completing**   Write a possessive for each of the following phrases.

1. the pen of him _____

2. the car of her _____

3. the shirts of them _____

4. the sound of it _____

5. a book of yours _____

◆ *P r a c t i c e*   *9*   **Writing Your Own**   Write a sentence of your own for each of the possessives you wrote in Practice 8.

_____

_____

_____

_____

_____

CHAPTER REVIEW

You might want to reread your answers to the questions in all the review boxes before you do the following exercises.

◆ *Review P r a c t i c e*   *1*   **Identifying**   In the following sentences, circle the apostrophes that are used incorrectly, and add any apostrophes that are missing.

1. Modern time's are difficult for many people to live in.

2. The Garners went on vacation this week.

3. Jame's dog's were jumping on the furniture.

4. I was'nt surprised that everyone admires Raymond.

5. I always have more fun on Tuesday's because Wednesday classe's are boring.

6. This pencil looks like its mine.

7. The biochemist's could'nt figure out the error in the two formula's.

8. Eleanor's grandmother's look a lot alike.

9. The car you see sitting outside is her's.

10. Tomorrow is my grandparent's anniversary.

◆ *Review P r a c t i c e* **2** **Completing** Add the missing apostrophes to the following sentences.

1. Everyones choice is pizza, but somebody has to call in the order.

2. Womens clothing has been marked down, but all childrens items are still regular price.

3. My father-in-laws job has been eliminated through downsizing.

4. The scouts admitted that the campfire was theirs.

5. There arent any more cookies in the cupboard.

6. Ronnys apartment is located just five minutes from the beach.

7. The purse was Danas, but the jacket belonged to someone else.

8. Dont tell me that there isnt enough; I know that the Joneses bought too much.

9. The head waiter is worried since sixteen people havent shown up yet.

10. Tanyas mother doesnt believe the handwriting is hers.

◆ *Review P r a c t i c e* **3** **Writing Your Own** Write a paragraph about your favorite birthday celebration in your life so far. Use at least six apostrophes correctly.

◆ *Review P r a c t i c e* **4** **Editing Through Collaboration** Exchange paragraphs from Review Practice 3 with another student, and do the following:

1. Circle any misplaced or missing apostrophes.

2. Indicate whether they mark possession (P) or contraction (C).

Then return the paper to its writer, and use the information in this chapter to correct any apostrophe errors in your own paragraph. Record your errors on the Error Log in Appendix 6.

Quotation Marks

✔ CHECKLIST for Using Quotation Marks

- ✔ Are quotation marks used to indicate someone's exact words?
- ✔ Are all periods and commas inside quotation marks?
- ✔ Are words capitalized correctly in quotations?
- ✔ Are quotation marks used to indicate the title of a short work, such as a short story or a poem?

Test Yourself

Add quotation marks where needed in the following sentences.

- Let's have a picnic, she said.
- My mom screamed, Tom! Get this spider!
- Put ice on the muscle, said Dr. Jansen, as soon as possible.
- I read three poems, including The Groundhog.
- Derek said I'll make dinner.

(Answers are in Appendix 4.)

Quotation marks are punctuation marks that work together in pairs. Their most common use is to indicate someone's exact words. They are also used to mark the title of a short piece of writing, such as a short story or a poem.

DIRECT QUOTATIONS

Use quotation marks to indicate a **direct quotation**—someone's exact words.

Here are some examples. They show the three basic forms of a direct quotation.

Direct Quotation: "I am not leaving without you," said the spy.

In this example, the quoted words come first.

Direct Quotation: The spy said, "I am not leaving without you."

In the example above, the quoted words come after the speaker is named.

Direct Quotation: "I am not," the spy said, "leaving without you."

In this example, the quoted words are interrupted, and the speaker is named in the middle. This form emphasizes the first few words.

INDIRECT QUOTATIONS

If you just talk about someone's words, an **indirect quotation,** you do not need quotation marks. Indirect quotations usually include the word *that*, as in *said that*. In questions, the wording is often *asked if*. Look at these examples of **indirect quotations**.

Direct Quotation: "I interviewed for a job at the Scott Corporation," said Bob.

These are Bob's exact words, so you must use quotation marks.

Indirect Quotation: Bob **said that** he interviewed for a job at the Scott Corporation.

This sentence explains what Bob said but does not use Bob's exact words. So quotation marks should not be used.

Direct Quotation: "We walked four miles," said Kira.
Indirect Quotation: Kira **said that** they walked four miles.

Direct Quotation: "Did you apply for a student loan?" Mom asked.
Indirect Quotation: Mom **asked if** I had applied for a student loan.

REVIEWING QUOTATION MARKS WITH QUOTATIONS

How do you show that you are repeating someone's exact words?

_____

What is an indirect quotation?

_____

◆ *P r a c t i c e* **1** **Identifying** In the following sentences, circle the quotation marks used incorrectly, and add any quotation marks that are missing.

1. "Watch out! screamed the police officer."
2. "I wish they'd stop throwing things" on the field, commented the football player.
3. He asked, How "much longer do we wait?"
4. "Go to your room, said the father, and clean it up."
5. Pablo said that "he enjoyed the game."

◆ *P r a c t i c e* **2** **Completing** Add the missing quotation marks to the following paragraph.

      Yesterday my manager stuck up for me when a customer came in saying, That young man sold me a defective computer. She was really mad. Ma'am, my manager patiently replied, he sold you our top-of-the-line computer. She said, But my computer still doesn't work. After a series of questions, my manager finally asked her what was wrong with her computer. The monitor is black, she replied. After another series of questions, my manager discovered her monitor was not plugged in, but he handled the customer as if her mistake was the most logical and frequent one ever made. The customer left happy that her system would now work. No matter what, my manager said, the customer is always right . . . and smart.

◆ *P r a c t i c e* **3** **Writing Your Own** Write a sentence of your own for each of the following expressions.

1. a question asked by Natasha

_____

2. a statement spoken by the plumber

_____

3. an exclamation spoken by Thomas

_____

4. an indirect question that Ricki asked

_____

5. a statement spoken by the chemist

_____

CAPITALIZING AND USING OTHER PUNCTUATION MARKS WITH QUOTATION MARKS

When you are quoting someone's complete sentences, begin with a capital letter and use appropriate end punctuation—a period, a question mark, or an exclamation point.

Capitalize the first letter of the first word being quoted, and put a period at the end of the sentence if it is a statement. Separate the spoken words from the rest of the sentence with a comma.

"**S**he doesn't really love me," he said.
She replied, "**T**ie your shoelaces."

If the quotation ends with a question mark or an exclamation point, use that punctuation instead of a comma or a period.

He yelled, "**T**urn off that music**!**"
"**W**hy do you want to know**?**" she asked.

In a quotation that is interrupted, capitalize the first word being quoted, but do not capitalize words in the middle of the sentence. Use a comma both before and after the interruption. End with a period if it is a statement.

"**N**o**,**" said the student, "this seat isn't taken."

You do not need to capitalize the first word of a quotation that is only part of a sentence.

I don't think that he will ever "**f**ind himself**.**"

Hint: Look at the examples again. Notice that periods and commas always go inside the quotation marks.

NOT	"Yes", she said, "please sit here".
CORRECT	"Yes," she said, "please sit here."

REVIEWING CAPITALIZATION AND PUNCTUATION
WITH QUOTATION MARKS

When you quote someone's exact words, why should you begin with a capital letter?

_____

Where do commas go in relation to quotation marks? Where do periods go?

_____

Practice 4 Identifying In the following sentences, circle the quotation marks, capital letters, and other punctuation marks that are used incorrectly, and add any missing quotation marks and punctuation.

1. "How are the Broncos doing this season"? she asked her boyfriend.
2. I need a new job" said Stan.
3. Victor wondered "How will they ever make it without me?"
4. "If you want to meet me", he said "just come to the concert tonight."
5. "I can't be there," Manny explained ", unless I get time off work.

Practice 5 Completing Add the missing quotation marks and punctuation to the following paragraph.

I have always said that I love the snow, but I hate the cold. I'm not sure how this works actually. My best friend asked How can you hate the cold so much when you are constantly out skiing or making a snowman I replied, I'm just weird that way, I guess I have always been like this. My mom never had to say Put on your jacket It was more like, Why are you wearing a jacket in 80-degree weather No one understands this weird quirk in me. I'll say Yes to skiing any day. Maybe someone will invent snow skiing in Jamaica. Then I'd be set.

◆ *P r a c t i c e   6* **Writing Your Own** Write a sentence of your own for each of the following direct quotations, and punctuate it correctly.

1. "I can't believe it!"

   _____

2. "What?"

   _____

3. "We need to clean the garage."

   _____

4. "No," . . . "you are not invited."

   _____

5. "I'm sorry," . . . "you didn't understand what I said."

   _____

QUOTATION MARKS AROUND TITLES

Put quotation marks around the titles of short works that are parts of larger works. The titles of longer works are put in italics (or underlined).

Quotation Marks	Italics/Underlining
"The Black Cat" (short story)	*Harry Potter and the Goblet of Fire* (book)
"The Emperor of Ice Cream" (poem)	*An Introduction to Literature* (book)
"Rainy Day Women" (song)	*Bob Dylan's Greatest Hits* (album)
"Florida Keys Beckon Tourists" (magazine article)	*Travel and Leisure* (magazine)
"Bush Elected President" (newspaper article)	*The Washington Post* (newspaper)
"The Wedding" (episode on TV series)	*Friends* (TV series)

REVIEWING QUOTATION MARKS WITH TITLES

When do you put quotation marks around a title?

_____

When do you italicize (or underline) a title?

_____

◆ **P r a c t i c e 7 Identifying** Put an X in front of each sentence with errors in quotation marks or italics/underlining. Add any missing quotation marks and italics or underlining.

1. _____ I really like the song I Will Survive by Gloria Gaynor.

2. _____ Did you read Keats's poem *Ode to a Nightingale?*

3. _____ My favorite short story is Faulkner's Barn Burning.

4. _____ The best entry in the poetry contest was "Trial" by Evelyn Main.

5. _____ If you want to come over, we're watching the *I Love Lucy* episode called Grape Smashing.

◆ **P r a c t i c e 8 Completing** Place quotation marks around the titles of short works, and underline the titles of long works in the following paragraph.

When Terrance was in high school, he was in a literature club. They read the short stories Araby, Young Goodman Brown, and A Dill Pickle. They also read several poems by Edward Taylor. Terrance's favorite poems were Huswifery, Upon Wedlock, and Death of Children. Every week the club wrote a book review for the school newspaper, The Northbrook News. One particular article was called Finding Bliss. It was about Edith Wharton's novel, The House of Mirth. These articles really encouraged other students to read for pleasure.

◆ **P r a c t i c e 9 Writing Your Own** Write a sentence of your own for each of the following items. Make up a title if you can't think of one.

1. a short story _____

2. a song title _____

3. a newspaper article _____

4. a poem _____

5. a magazine article _____

CHAPTER REVIEW

You might want to reread your answers to the questions in all the review boxes before you do the following exercises.

Review Practice 1 **Identifying** Add the missing quotation marks and punctuation to the following sentences.

1. Priscilla's favorite song is Smooth by Carlos Santana and Rob Thomas.
2. I, on the other hand, like loud songs.
3. The short story The Almond Tree is my son's favorite.
4. I hate to break the news to you Louis said but I've found someone new
5. Malik's keys are on the desk.
6. To be, or not to be, that is the question said Hamlet.
7. Did you see the old-fashioned car drive by our house asked Paula.
8. She said I'm still in love with you.
9. Did she ever answer her cell phone? I asked.
10. The news writer titled his article Somewhere in the Devil's Domain.

Review Practice 2 **Completing** Add the missing quotation marks, commas, and underlining for italics to the following dialogue.

Hey, Janalee I called let's go to Barnes and Noble.
We were just there she answered.
Well, let's go again. I have to get a novel for English I said.
Which novel do you need? asked Janalee.
It's called Waiting by Her Jinn I said.
Oh, I read that. It's great. You'll love it she said as she waved good bye.

◆ *Review P r a c t i c e 3* **Writing Your Own** In paragraph form, record a conversation from your day. What did you talk about? What was the point of this conversation? What were your exact words?

◆ *Review P r a c t i c e 4* **Editing Through Collaboration** Exchange paragraphs from Review Practice 3 with another student, and do the following:

1. Circle any incorrect or missing quotation marks.

2. Underline any faulty punctuation.

3. Put an X over any incorrect use of italics/underlining.

Then return the paper to its writer, and use the information in this chapter to correct any errors with quotation marks and italics/underlining in your own paragraph. Record your errors on the Error Log in Appendix 6.

CHAPTER 47

OTHER PUNCTUATION MARKS

✔ CHECKLIST for Using Semicolons, Colons, Dashes, and Parentheses

> ✔ Are semicolons used to join two closely related complete sentences?
>
> ✔ Are long items in a series that already contain commas separated by semicolons?
>
> ✔ Are colons used correctly to introduce a list?
>
> ✔ Are dashes used to emphasize or further explain a point?
>
> ✔ Are parentheses used to include additional, but not necessary, information?

Test Yourself

Add semicolons, colons, dashes, or parentheses to the following sentences.

- Matthew turned his paper in early Erica decided not to turn in a paper at all.

- Dave felt sorry for the defendant however, he had to vote for a conviction.

- Aaron needed several items for his dorm room a comforter, new sheets, a lamp, and a rug.

- Inez had only two words to say about bungee jumping "Never again."

- The recipe says to fold gently mix the berries into the batter.

(Answers are in Appendix 4.)

This chapter explains the uses of the **semicolon, colon, dash,** and **parentheses.** We'll look at these punctuation marks one by one.

SEMICOLONS

Semicolons are used to separate equal parts of a sentence. They are also used to avoid confusion when listing items in a series.

1. Use a semicolon to separate two closely related independent clauses.

   An independent clause is a group of words with a subject and a verb that can stand alone as a sentence. You might use a semicolon instead of a coordinating conjunction (*and, but, for, nor, or, so, yet*) or a period. Any one of the three options would be correct.

	Independent	Independent
Semicolon:	Henry never took a lunch break; he was too busy at his job.	
Conjunction:	Henry never took a lunch break, **for** he was too busy at his job.	
Period:	Henry never took a lunch break. **He** was too busy at his job.	

2. Use a semicolon to join two independent clauses that are connected by such words as *however, therefore, furthermore, moreover, for example,* or *consequently.* Put a comma after the connecting word.

	Independent	Independent
Semicolon:	Shrimp is expensive; **nevertheless,** it's always worth the money.	
Semicolon:	Juanita is very talented musically; **for example,** she can play the piano and the flute.	
Semicolon:	She has always worked hard; **in fact,** she put herself through college.	

3. Use a semicolon to separate items in a series when any of the items contain commas.

NOT	At the party, Lily drank some tasty red punch, ate some delicious chicken with garlic, herbs, and lemon, and danced with several old boyfriends.
CORRECT	At the party, Lily drank some tasty red punch; ate some delicious chicken with garlic, herbs, and lemon; and danced with several old boyfriends.

REVIEWING SEMICOLONS
....

How are semicolons used between two independent clauses?

_____

How are semicolons used with items in a series?

_____

◆ **P r a c t i c e   1   Identifying** In the following sentences, circle the semicolons that are used incorrectly, and add any commas and semicolons that are missing.

1. Baking homemade bread is very easy however; it's faster to use a bread maker.

2. I walked my dog to the park; ran into Mike; Zoe, and Christine; and invited them over for dinner.

3. She's allergic to chocolate and honey she rarely eats other sweets either.

4. I'm a horrible cook for example, I burned the toast at breakfast today.

5. This trip cost us a fortune we'll be paying off the credit card for a year.

◆ **P r a c t i c e   2   Completing** Add semicolons to the following paragraph.

One day I went fishing with Uncle Peter it was the last day I would spend with him before he left for college. When we arrived at the lake, we realized that we forgot the bait nevertheless, we knew where we could buy more nearby. Inside the store were racks and racks of things for sale, but we were interested in only three of them. One rack displayed bait, tackle, and fishing line one shelved candy and snack foods and the other held cigarettes and chewing tobacco. The bait gave us about fourteen fish, and the candy gave me a cavity however, that can of Copenhagen gave us grief from our moms every time they caught us chewing.

◆ **P r a c t i c e   3   Writing Your Own** Write five sentences of your own using semicolons correctly.

_____

_____

_____

_____

_____

COLONS

Colons introduce a list or idea that follows them.

1. The main use of the colon is to introduce a list or thought. Here are some examples:

   Colon: Bring the following supplies to class: sketch pad, India ink, pen tips, and a charcoal pencil.

   Colon: I noticed several fire hazards: old paint cans and rags, curtains near the stove, and lit candles with no one present.

   Colon: The decision was easy: return the favor.

   The most common error with colons is using one where it isn't needed.

2. Do not use a colon after the words *such as* or *including*. A complete sentence must come before a colon.

   NOT   Use good packing materials, **such as:** bubble wrap, styro pellets, and foam.

   CORRECT   Use good packing materials, **such as** bubble wrap, styro pellets, and foam.

   NOT   We saw many sights, **including:** the Grand Canyon, Yosemite, and Mount Ranier.

   CORRECT   We saw many sights, **including** the Grand Canyon, Yosemite, and Mount Ranier.

3. In addition, you should not use a colon after a verb or after a preposition. Remember that a complete sentence must come before a colon.

   NOT   The topics to be discussed **are:** memory, hard drive, and new software.

   CORRECT   The topics to be discussed **are** memory, hard drive, and software.

NOT	The program consisted **of:** a lecture, a Powerpoint presentation, and lunch.
CORRECT	The program consisted **of** a lecture, a Powerpoint presentation, and lunch.

REVIEWING COLONS

What is the main use of a colon?

_____

Why should you not use a colon after such words as is *or* of?

_____

 P r a c t i c e   4   Identifying In the following sentences, circle the colons that are used incorrectly, and add any colons that are missing.

1. You should take: hiking boots, cotton socks, and sunscreen.
2. Mark still has to take the following classes biology, chemistry, political science, and geometry.
3. I have a lot to do today wash the car, pick up Theo at the airport, and finish my English paper.
4. The aerobics class consisted of: step exercises, line dancing, and the stairmaster.
5. I like: the fireplace, the gardens, and the vaulted ceilings.
6. The presentation covered many topics, including: company goals, stock options, and 401K plans.

P r a c t i c e   5   Completing Add colons to the following paragraph.

   People can learn a lot from visiting museums they can learn about history, psychology, and sociology for numerous cultures. Many museums have enormous collections of various types of art ancient, Renaissance, Victorian, modern, and so on. I particularly like ancient art. Two museums have tremendous ancient art exhibits the J. Paul Getty Museum and the San Antonio Metropolitan Museum of Art. I can spend hours looking at all the statuary and pottery. Museums are just loaded with fabulous cultural information.

P r a c t i c e   6 **Writing Your Own** Write five sentences of your own using colons correctly.

_____

_____

_____

_____

_____

DASHES AND PARENTHESES

Dashes and parentheses set ideas off from the rest of their sentence.

Dashes

Dashes emphasize ideas.

1. Use dashes to emphasize or draw attention to a point.

   Dash: I know what I want out of life—happiness.

   In this example, the beginning of the sentence introduces an idea, and the dash then sets off the answer.

   Dash: Peace, love, and good health—these are my words for the new year.

   In this example, the key words are set off at the beginning, and the explanation follows. Beginning this way adds some suspense to the sentence.

   Dashes: I know what I want in a roommate—thoughtfulness—and I plan to get it.

   The dashes divide this sentence into three distinct parts, which makes the reader pause and think about each part.

Parentheses

Whereas dashes set off material that the writer wants to emphasize, **parentheses** do just the opposite.

2. Use parentheses to set off information that is interesting or helpful but not necessary for understanding the sentence.

Parentheses: Their oldest son left his family at age 18 **(never to return again)**.

Parentheses: The handbook put out by the MLA **(Modern Language Association)** is the best guideline.

3. Parentheses are also used to mark a person's life span and to number items in a sentence. They are always used in pairs. Here are some examples:

Parentheses: Emily Dickinson **(1830–1886)** is one of America's great poets.

Parentheses: Follow these steps in writing a paragraph: **(1)** brainstorm for ideas, **(2)** choose a topic, and **(3)** formulate a topic sentence.

REVIEWING DASHES AND PARENTHESES

What is the difference between dashes and parentheses?

_____

_____

When do you use dashes?

_____

When do you use parentheses?

_____

 ***Practice 7* Identifying** Use dashes or parentheses with the under-lined words in the following sentences.

1. I met the new neighbors   <u>the ones at the end of the block</u>   and brought them cookies.

2. My wife is going out with her friends tomorrow   <u>and taking the kids</u>   so I can watch the big fight on TV.

3. My neighbors   <u>the Parkers</u>   are nice people, but they're awful house-keepers.

4. There is one kind of food that everyone likes   <u>barbecue</u>.

5. While you are house-sitting for us, please don't forget to   <u>1</u>   feed the cats,   <u>2</u>   check the mail, and   <u>3</u>   water the houseplants.

◆ *P r a c t i c e 8* **Completing** Add dashes and parentheses to the following paragraph.

Stephano and I became best friends 10 years ago in college at UCLA. Our British literature teacher an enormously tall and bald man who enjoyed playing pranks on other faculty members made us senior seminar partners. Ever since then, we've been best friends. We've been through a lot together ex-wives, self-doubt, and other trying issues but we've never abandoned each other. I hope as I'm sure he does that we never lose contact with one another.

◆ *P r a c t i c e 9* **Writing Your Own** Write three sentences of your own using dashes and two using parentheses.

_____

_____

_____

_____

_____

CHAPTER REVIEW

You might want to reread your answers to the questions in all the review boxes before you do the following exercises.

◆ *Review P r a c t i c e 1* **Identifying** Add semicolons, colons, dashes, and parentheses to the following sentences.

1. She never lost her money she forgot to take the check out of her pocket.

2. Her competition was from three other girls Brittany, Marci, and Desiree.

3. She never listens she always asks questions that were already answered.

4. My favorite TV show is about to come on *NYPD Blue*.

5. Hand me a pencil the yellow one so I can make up a grocery list.

6. We could still win if we changed the lineup put Dave in front of Stuart.

7. There are several reasons I refuse to go out with you you tend to ignore what I say, you treat your girlfriends disrespectfully, and I am dating your brother.

8. I'm making chocolate cake for dessert your favorite.

9. Steve finally decided which college to attend the University of Maryland.

10. The impatient people in line at the bank the rude ones are usually the ones who take the longest at the counter.

◆ **Review Practice 2 Completing** Add semicolons, colons, dashes, and parentheses to the following paragraph.

Our house is affectionately known as the "Gibson Zoo." Outside we have two very large dogs inside we have a smaller dog and two cats. The bird population is also recognized in our house since we have two love birds Dorris and Pierre. All of our animals the ones we have purchased and the ones we found as strays have been given appropriate names. Our favorite names are from literature and Greek mythology Zeus, Apollo, Beowulf, Romeo, Juliet, and Macbeth. We're still thinking about adding one more pet it will be either an iguana or a hamster. And we have only one requirement for the new addition it must be able to get along with the rest of the family.

◈ *Review Practice 3* **Writing Your Own** Write a paragraph explaining to someone how to do something that you do well.

◈ *Review Practice 4* **Editing Through Collaboration** Exchange paragraphs from Review Practice 3 with another student, and do the following:

1. Circle any incorrect or missing semicolons.
2. Circle any incorrect or missing colons.
3. Circle any incorrect or missing dashes.
4. Circle any incorrect or missing parentheses.

Then return the paper to its writer, and use the information in this chapter to correct any punctuation errors in your own paragraph. Record your errors on the Error Log in Appendix 6.

UNIT TESTS

Here are some exercises that test your understanding of all the material in this unit: End Punctuation, Commas, Apostrophes, Quotation Marks, Semicolons, Colons, Dashes, and Parentheses.

Unit Test I

Correct the punctuation errors in the following sentences.

1. My girlfriend wants me to visit her in college, but I can't get off work.
2. Gabi's dentist has an office on 3rd.St by the drug store.
3. Don't you think you've studied hard enough.
4. Did you see the "Third Watch" episode last night, The Edge?
5. We left our two dog's toys all over the yard.
6. The test will be given on September 28 2005.
7. The Lincoln Memorial, the Washington Monument and, the Vietnam Veterans Memorial were surrounded by pushy irritable people this afternoon.
8. What I like best about Mike is what he's most shy about his beautiful poetry

9. "Don't waste my time!" he exclaimed.

10. Ted's flag was red, white, and blue, Millie's was orange, green, and gold. and Ivan's was just black and white.

11. The four things left in my refrigerator are: a can of Pepsi, a slice of left-over pizza, an ice cream sandwich, and a candy bar.

12. Mark Thomas is divorcing, his wife Martha, after several years of marriage.

13. If I wanted your advice I would ask for it?

14. Too much sun is coming through the front window's and I can't tell if his' computer screen is on.

15. Martina asked, "Have you read that book" yet.?

16. Yesterday s weather was very warm

17. "If you buy this today" the clerk said, "you can save 20 percent."

18. Quite frankly I always thought I was in over my head.

19. Could you imagine how awful being homeless would be.

20. I cant believe they won

Unit Test II

Correct the punctuation errors in the following paragraph.

Once when I was in high school my friends and I organized something together (a protest of Valentines' Day) Im pretty sure the idea started as a silly conversation at lunch but it became something much bigger than any of us imagined? The high school in my hometown of Slate Creek California was very small with a population of about 300 students (therefore, most ideas traveled very quickly) My friends and I started discussing our protest of Valentine's Day the last week of January. We had decided to dress in all black instead of the normal color combinations for Valentine's Day; red, white, and pink, all red, all pink, or pink and white. By February 14 2001, over 50 students' had joined our "crusade." In fact, we made the front page of the student newspaper the next week. The article, just Say no to Love, featured student quotes', such as: I hate this holiday! and "i was wondering why all those kids were dressed in black last week". Looking back on it now, I wonder, why so many of my fellow students wanted to join in our protest of this holiday? I think there were three reasons (1) most people like to be part of something bigger than themselves, 2 we were all looking for something to rally against, and (3) we were all single and a little bitter about romance. Whatever my classmates' reasons were, I know that I had fun that day

CHAPTER 48

CAPITALIZATION

☑ CHECKLIST for Editing Capitalization

> ✔ Are all proper nouns capitalized?
> ✔ Are all words in titles capitalized correctly?
> ✔ Have you followed the other rules for capitalizing correctly?

Test Yourself

Correct the capitalization errors in the following sentences.

- The smith family lives on washington street.
- we fly into newark airport and then get a taxi to seton hall university.
- This term I'm taking spanish, biology 200, history, and english.
- In june, I drove to california in my dodge durango.
- We read several plays by shakespeare, including *hamlet*.

(Answers are in Appendix 4.)

Because every sentence begins with a capital letter, **capitalization** is the best place to start discussing the mechanics of good writing. Capital letters signal where sentences begin. They also call attention to certain kinds of words, making sentences easier to read and understand.

Correct capitalization coupled with correct punctuation adds up to good, clear writing. Here are some guidelines to help you capitalize correctly.

1. Capitalize the first word of every sentence, including the first word of a quotation that forms a sentence.

The best route is down Alpine Street.
"The best route is down Alpine Street," he said.
He said, "The best route is down Alpine Street."

Do not capitalize the second part of a quotation that is split.

"The best route," he said, "is down Alpine Street."

2. Capitalize all proper nouns. Do not capitalize common nouns.

Common Nouns	Proper Nouns
person	John Doe
city	Topeka
building	Sears Tower
lake	Lake Michigan
spacecraft	*Apollo 11*

Here are some examples of proper nouns.

People:	Susan, Michael Jordan, Vanna White
Groups:	Americans, Navajos, African Americans, Puerto Ricans, Japanese
Languages:	English, Spanish, French
Religions, Religious Books, Holy Days:	Protestantism, Buddhism, Koran, Bible, Passover
Organizations:	New York Yankees, Republican Party, National Rifle Association, the Kiwanis Club, Alpha Kappa Delta
Places:	Yellowstone National Park, Rocky Mountains, Africa, Louisiana, Union County, Pennsylvania Avenue, Route 66, Golden Gate Bridge, La Guardia Airport
Institutions, Agencies, Businesses:	Xavier High School, Eugene Public Library, United Nations, Cook County Hospital, Ford Motor Company
Brand Names, Ships, Aircraft:	Chevy Blazer, Tide, Snickers, **U.S.S.** *Constitution*, Goodyear Blimp

3. Capitalize titles used with people's names or in place of their names.

>   **Mr.** John W. Cooper, **Ms.** Gladys Reynolds, **Dr.** Kayla Robinson
>   **Aunt** Judy, **Grandpa** John, **Cousin** Larry

Do not capitalize words that identify family relationships.

NOT	I will ask my Mother.
CORRECT	I will ask my mother.
CORRECT	I will ask Mother.

4. Capitalize the titles of creative works.

Books:	*I Know Why the Caged Bird Sings*
Short Stories:	"The Lottery"
Plays:	*Our Town*
Poems:	"Song of Myself"
Articles:	"The Best Small Colleges in America"
Magazines:	*Sports Illustrated*
Songs:	"Jailhouse Rock"
Albums or CDs:	*Metallica Live*
Films:	*What Lies Beneath*
TV Series:	*Friends*
Works of Art:	*The Scream*
Computer Programs:	*Microsoft Word*

Do not capitalize *a, an, the,* or short prepositions unless they are the first or last word in a title.

5. Capitalize days of the week, months, holidays, and special events.

>   Friday, August, Memorial Day, Thanksgiving, Kwanzaa,
>   Mardi Gras

Do not capitalize the names of seasons: *summer, fall, winter, spring.*

6. Capitalize the names of historical events, periods, and documents.

>   American Revolution, Stone Age, Renaissance Period, Seventies,
>   Declaration of Independence, Battle of Hastings

7. Capitalize specific course titles and the names of language courses.

>   History 201, Psychology 101, English 200

Do not capitalize a course or subject you are referring to in a general way unless the course is a language.

> my economics course, my philosophy course, my Spanish course, my history course

8. Capitalize references to regions of the country but not words that merely indicate direction.

> If you travel due south from Ohio, eventually you will end up in the South, probably in Kentucky or Tennessee.

9. Capitalize the opening of a letter and the first word of the closing.

> Dear Liza, Dear Sir,
> Best wishes, Sincerely,

Notice that a comma comes after the opening and closing.

REVIEWING CAPITALIZATION

Why is capitalization important in your writing?

_____

_____

What is the difference between a proper noun and a common noun?

_____

_____

◆ **P r a c t i c e 1 Identifying** Correct the capitalization errors in the following sentences.

1. My Dad bought a new ford bronco last saturday.
2. Lake street is where the pastor of the local Church resides.
3. Jim Morrison's Song "the End" was used as the opening music for *Apocalypse Now,* a Movie by Francis ford Copolla.
4. The national association of building contractors will sponsor a trade show at the astrodome in houston, texas, next january.

5. My family—all my brothers, sisters, cousins, Aunts, and Uncles—love to watch the macy's Thanksgiving day parade.

◆ *P r a c t i c e 2* **Completing** Fill in each blank with words that complete the sentence. Be sure to capitalize words correctly. (You can make up titles if necessary.)

1. Last week I went to see _____ in concert.

2. Shelley will graduate from _____ University.

3. I signed up to take _____ because _____ is such a popular teacher.

4. My favorite holiday is _____ because I get to see my favorite relative, _____.

5. The _____ is sponsoring a barbecue this weekend.

◆ *P r a c t i c e 3* **Writing Your Own** Write five sentences of your own that cover at least five of the capitalization rules.

_____

_____

_____

_____

_____

CHAPTER REVIEW

You might want to reread your answers to the questions in all the review boxes before you do the following exercises.

◆ *R e v i e w P r a c t i c e 1* **Identifying** Correct the capitalization errors in the following sentences.

1. Even though my zenith television has only a 13-inch screen, I still enjoy watching *american idol.*

2. According to dr. phillips, many Americans felt their loyalties were torn during the american revolution.

3. Diane Glancy's *pushing the bear* is a retelling of the Trail of Tears.

4. Didn't Hamlet say, "to be or not to be"?

5. If you turn South at lover's lane, you'll run directly into my Sister's Ranch, affectionately named lovers' ranch.

6. My Uncle Conrad would like to hire mrs. Chandra Smith for the Department of english and communications.

7. My favorite Novel by Jane Austin is *emma*.

8. many people believe that the south is holding on to a dying concept.

9. I suppose I can always move in with mother while I attend loyola university.

10. During Rush Week, I had tea with pi phi beta, played tennis with kappa delta, and listened to poetry with gamma phi.

◆ **Review P r a c t i c e 2 Completing** Fill in each blank with words that complete the sentence. Be sure to capitalize words correctly.

1. Over the weekend, I stayed home and reread one of my favorite books, _____.

2. Katherine hopes to obtain a degree in _____.

3. My mother joined _____, and the work she does helps save lives.

4. My friend _____ is from _____; another friend is from _____.

5. It's possible to climb Mt. _____, but not Mt. _____.

6. My relative, _____, lives in _____.

7. We have to read _____ for my _____ literature class.

8. Travel _____ to get to _____, and _____ to get to _____.

9. The letter opened with these words, "_____."

10. The injured man was taken to _____, where he received treatment from _____.

◆ *Review P r a c t i c e 3* **Writing Your Own** Write a paragraph about a state, famous person, or course you find particularly interesting.

◆ *Review P r a c t i c e 4* **Editing Through Collaboration** Exchange paragraphs from Review Practice 3 with another student, and do the following tasks:

1. Circle any capital letters that don't follow the capitalization rules.
2. Write the rule number next to the error for the writer to refer to.

Then return the paper to its writer, and use the information in this chapter to correct any capitalization errors in your own paragraph. Record your errors on the Error Log in Appendix 6.

ABBREVIATIONS AND NUMBERS

✔ CHECKLIST for Using Abbreviations and Numbers

> ✔ Are titles before and after proper names abbreviated correctly?
>
> ✔ Are government agencies and other organizations abbreviated correctly?
>
> ✔ Are numbers *zero* through *nine* spelled out?
>
> ✔ Are numbers 10 and over written as figures (10, 25, 1–20, 324)?

Test Yourself

Correct the abbreviation and number errors in these sentences.

- Gov. Schwartzeneger is trying to protect water in this state.
- My dog had 4 puppies.
- Over one thousand two hundred and twelve people attended.
- After college, I hope to join the Cent Int Agency.
- Crystal just moved to the U.S. from Spain.

(Answers are in Appendix 4.)

Like capitalization, abbreviations and numbers are also mechanical features of writing that help us communicate what we want to say. Following the rules that govern their use will make your writing as precise as possible.

ABBREVIATIONS

Abbreviations help us move communication along. They follow a set of rules when used in writing.

1. Abbreviate titles before proper names.

    Mr.   Mrs.   Ms.   Dr.   Rev.   Sen.   Sgt.

    Abbreviate religious, governmental, and military titles when used with an entire name. Do not abbreviate them when used only with a last name.

NOT	We thought that **Sen.** Matthews would speak first.
CORRECT	We thought that **Senator** Matthews would speak first.
CORRECT	We thought that **Sen.** Dorothy Matthews would speak first.

    Professor is not usually abbreviated: Professor Sandra Cole is here.

2. Abbreviate academic degrees.

    B.S. (Bachelor of Science)
    R.N. (Registered Nurse)
    D.V.M. (Doctor of Veterinary Medicine)

3. Use the following abbreviations with numbers.

    A.M. *or* **a.m.** (ante meridiem)
    P.M. *or* **p.m.** (post meridiem)
    mph (miles per hour)

4. Abbreviate *United States* only when it is used as an adjective.

NOT	The **U.S.** is a democracy.
CORRECT	The **United States** is a democracy.
CORRECT	The **U.S.** Supreme Court will give their ruling today.

5. Abbreviate the names of certain government agencies, businesses, and educational institutions by using their initials without periods.

    CIA (Central Intelligence Agency)
    IRS (Internal Revenue Service)
    CBS (Columbia Broadcasting System)
    UCLA (University of California, Los Angeles)
    IBM (International Business Machines)

6. Abbreviate state names when addressing mail or writing out the postal address. Otherwise, spell out the names of states.

> Tamara's new address is 451 Kingston St., Phoenix, **AZ** 85072.
> Tamara has moved to Phoenix, **Arizona.**

REVIEWING ABBREVIATIONS

When you write, are you free to abbreviate any words you want?

_____

P r a c t i c e 1 Identifying Correct the underlined words in each of the following sentences.

1. The <u>Rev.</u> Jackson gave a wonderful sermon.
2. The letter was addressed to <u>Mister</u> Clark Reynolds, 758 First Avenue, Sioux Falls, <u>South Dakota</u> 57116.
3. Former <u>TX</u> Governor George W. Bush became a <u>United States</u> president.
4. When the police clocked Beth on Ridgeland Highway, she was going 76 <u>miles per hour.</u>
5. My favorite show has been picked up by <u>C.B.S.</u>

P r a c t i c e 2 Completing In each sentence, write either an abbreviation or the complete word, whichever is correct.

1. The _____ (U.S./United States) will send two representatives to Paris.
2. I have _____ (Prof./Professor) Perry for English this term.
3. For years, J. Edgar Hoover was head of the _____ (FBI/F.B.I./ Federal Bureau of Investigation).
4. She was introduced to _____ (Rev./Reverend) Barbara Shaw.
5. Matt has lived in _____ (NJ/New Jersey) and _____ (NH/New Hampshire).

◆ *P r a c t i c e 3* **Writing Your Own** Write a sentence of your own for each of the following abbreviations.

1. Mr. _____

2. mph _____

3. U.S. _____

4. CA _____

5. B.A. _____

NUMBERS

Most writers ask the same question about using **numbers:** When should a number be spelled out, and when is it all right to use numerals? The following simple rules will help you make this decision.

1. Spell out numbers from *zero* to *nine*. Use figures for numbers 10 and over.

> I have **four** brothers.
>
> My mom has **12** nieces and nephews and **43** cousins.

Do not mix spelled-out numbers and figures in a sentence if they refer to the same types of items. Use numerals for all numbers in that case.

NOT	I have **four** brothers, **12** nieces and nephews, and **43** cousins.
CORRECT	I have **4** brothers, **12** nieces and nephews, and **43** cousins.

2. For very large numbers, use a combination of figures and words.

> The athletic department's yearly budget is **$4.6 million.**
>
> Sales last year totaled approximately **$1.2 billion.**

3. Always spell out a number that begins a sentence. If this becomes awkward, reword the sentence.

> **Twenty-two** people were injured in the train accident.
>
> Approximately **250,000** people live in Jackson.

4. Use figures for dates, addresses, zip codes, telephone numbers, identi-fication numbers, and time.

> On June **1, 1985,** my parents moved to **4250** Oak St., El Dorado, AR **71730.**
> My new telephone number is **(555) 877-1420.**
> My Social Security number is **123-45-6789.**
> My alarm went off at **6:37** a.m.

5. Use figures for fractions, decimals, and percentages.

> The recipe calls for **3/4** cup of milk and **1/2** cup of sugar.
> He registered **.03** on the Breathalyzer test.
> Almost **15** percent of the city's inhabitants are Asian American.

Notice that *percent* is written out and is all one word.

6. Use figures for exact measurements, including amounts of money. Use a dollar sign for amounts over $1.

> The room is **16** feet wide and **20** feet, **4** inches long.
> I made **$34.60** in tips today.

7. Use figures for the parts of a book.

> Chapter **10**   page **20**   Exercise **5**   questions **4** and **6**

Notice that *Chapter* and *Exercise* are capitalized.

REVIEWING NUMBERS
....

What is the general rule for spelling out numbers as opposed to using numerals?

_____

♦ *P r a c t i c e* **4** **Identifying** Correct any errors with numbers in each of the following sentences.

1. The school's 2005 budget is approximately $75,000,000.

2. The committee will choose 6 finalists for the thousand-dollar scholarship.

3. Nearly half of a cup of chocolate went into this recipe.

4. The hotel manager agreed to give us a twenty % discount since we had fourteen people in our group.

5. 292 people voted in the school election; there were fifteen candidates.

◆ P r a c t i c e 5 Completing Fill in each blank in the following sentences with numbers in the proper form.

1. With _____ billion dollars in the bank, he is the richest man I know.

2. _____ fireworks were set off for our annual charity drive.

3. Five minus two is _____.

4. To review the comma rules, do Exercise _____ on page _____.

5. You will need _____ cups of flour, _____ cup of water, and _____ eggs to make fried bread.

◆ P r a c t i c e 6 Write Your Own Write a sentence demonstrating each of the following rules for numbers.

1. Spell out numbers from *zero* to *nine*. Use figures for number 10 and higher.

_____

2. Always spell out a number that begins a sentence.

_____

3. Use figures for amounts of money preceded by a dollar sign.

_____

4. Use figures for fractions, decimals, percentages, and amounts of money.

_____

5. For very large numbers, use a combination of figures and words.

_____

CHAPTER REVIEW

You might want to reread your answers to the questions in all the review boxes before you do the following exercises.

◆ ***Review P r a c t i c e 1* Identifying** Circle the abbreviation errors and underline the number errors in each of the following sentences. Some sentences contain more than one error.

1. We must leave at ten a.m., or we will miss Sen. Breven's speech.
2. 25 candidates showed up for the one job opening.
3. My address is four hundred two Park Lane Avenue, Bakersfield, California 93313.
4. The U.S. is a powerful nation.
5. I am going to college to receive a Registered Nurse degree.
6. I'll need to add one-half cup of sea salt to the fish tank.
7. Last week, Christy earned fifty-five dollars babysitting.
8. Joanna reported the three-thousand-dollar gift to the Internal Revenue Service.
9. If you had 7 puppies, and you gave away 3, then you would have 4 puppies.
10. The U.S. has a consumer economy.

◆ ***Review P r a c t i c e 2* Completing** Correct the errors in Review Practice 1 by rewriting the sentences.

◆ ***Review P r a c t i c e 3* Writing Your Own** Write a paragraph giving directions to a place near your college. Use numbers and abbreviations in your paragraph.

◆ ***Review P r a c t i c e 4* Editing Through Collaboration** Exchange paragraphs from Review Practice 3 with another student, and do the following:

1. Underline all abbreviations, numbers, and figures.
2. Circle any abbreviations, numbers, or figures that are not in their correct form.

Then return the paper to its writer, and use the information in this chapter to correct any abbreviation and number errors in your own paragraph. Record your errors on the Error Log in Appendix 6.

UNIT TESTS

Here are some exercises that test your understanding of all the material in this unit: Capitalization, Abbreviations, and Numbers.

Unit Test I

A. Underline the errors in capitalization, abbreviations, and numbers in the following sentences.

1. I gave you 6 tulips, and you gave me 3 roses; then we had a bouquet of 9 flowers.

2. I love paintings from the renaissance period.

3. My Mom bought a new chevy trailblazer last saturday.

4. A copy of the defendant's phone bill shows that at six fifteen ante meridiem he called 601-555-4251 and talked for ten minutes.

5. Joe Namath was an all-american quarterback for the Alabama crimson tide, one of College Football's top teams.

6. The shopping mall will be one hundred seventy-five thousand square feet and cost two point three billion dollars.

7. Have you signed up for humanities 201, or have you decided to take a psychology or Sociology course instead?

8. Last month, Cesar earned three hundred dollars in his student assistant job.

9. Terry was born on August tenth, 1976.

10. We got up at 5:30 ante meridiem to watch the sun rise on the lake, and then had cheese and wine at 7:30 post meridiem on the same lake, so we could watch the sun set.

11. Did you say that Doctor Reynolds told you to lose 20 pounds?

12. In Chapter ten, Exercise five, do questions 4 through 7.

13. The store manager gave us a twenty % discount since we bought sixteen items.

14. my good friend is going south for the summer, staying with relatives in the Southern parts of arkansas.

15. Prof. Turner gave a very enlightening lecture on the writing process today.

16. Most geologists estimate that the world is between 4 and 5,000,000,000 years old.

17. Having lived in many countries, I prefer the U.S.

18. In order to join the Central Intelligence Agency, I had to first get my Bachelor of Science degree.

19. My 1998 zenith tv still works great, and i've never had to get it serviced.

20. In *the merchant of venice* by william shakespeare, portia says, "the quality of mercy is not strained."

B. Correct the errors in capitalization, abbreviations, and numbers in Part A by rewriting each incorrect sentence.

Unit Test II

A. Underline the errors in capitalization, abbreviations, and numbers in the following paragraph.

When I graduated from High School last year, I moved from ashe, Oklahoma, to stockville, kansas. I was a little nervous about moving out on my own right after high school, but I was excited to start my new life as a Psychology Major at midwestern College of the social sciences. Since I could not afford more than two hundred dollars per month for rent, I decided to rent a room instead of an entire apartment. My College is a small private school, so my psychology 101 professor, Dr. smith, was able to spend time helping me find a room to rent. We met in may to discuss my big move on august twentieth two thousand two. He recommended misses Berry, a registered nurse with a basement room to rent on Franklin Boulevard. I was so nervous the first time I arrived at thirty-five Grey way, but it only took me 5 minutes to feel at home. Mrs. berry is a wonderful land-lady, and she treats me more like her granddaughter than a tenant. Renting a room for one hundred fifty dollars per month has helped me save a lot of money. Living with misses berry has also made the transition to college easier. Sometimes having less money to spend at age Eighteen is better!

B. Correct the errors in capitalization, abbreviations, and numbers in Part A by rewriting the paragraph.

CHAPTER 50

VARYING SENTENCE STRUCTURE

☑ CHECKLIST for Varying Sentence Patterns

> ✔ Do you add introductory material to vary your sentence patterns?
>
> ✔ Do you occasionally reverse the order of some subjects and verbs?
>
> ✔ Do you move sentence parts to add variety to your sentences?
>
> ✔ Do you sometimes use questions and exclamations to vary your sentence structure?

Test Yourself

Turn each of the following pairs of sentences into one sentence that is more interesting.

- I live in an old house. I have lived here my whole life.
- I am too busy. I need to work less.
- I love cheeseburgers and fries. I love fast-food places.
- My dog sleeps 14 hours every day. She is overweight.
- I enjoy writing. I keep a notebook for jotting down my thoughts.

(Answers are in Appendix 4.)

Reading the same sentence pattern sentence after sentence can become very monotonous for your readers. This chapter will help you solve this problem in your writing. Look at the following example.

> I have never lived away from home. I am about to start my second year of college. I think I am ready to be on my own. I am excited about this new phase of my life. I have student loans and a part-time job. I can't wait to feel true independence.

This paragraph has some terrific ideas, but they are expressed in such a monotonous way that the readers might doze off. What this paragraph needs is variety in its sentence structure. Here are some ideas for keeping your readers awake and ready to hear your good thoughts.

ADD INTRODUCTORY WORDS

Add some introductory words to your sentences so that they don't all start the same way.

> **In my lifetime,** I have never lived away from home. **Now** I am about to start my second year of college. I think I am ready to be on my own. I am excited about this new phase of my life. **To pay for life away from home,** I have student loans and a part-time job. I can't wait to feel true independence.

◈ *P r a c t i c e* **1** **Identifying** Underline the sentence in each pair that could be turned into an introductory word, phrase, or clause.

1. It was early morning. Jay had a throbbing headache.
2. We stripped the paper from the walls. We started in the kitchen.
3. I'm shocked. The Flying Zombies Show sold out in one day.
4. We want fast delivery. We must place our order this week.
5. We got center row tickets for the concert. I can't believe it.

◈ *P r a c t i c e* **2** **Completing** Rewrite the sentences in Practice 1 by turning each sentence you underlined into an introductory word, phrase, or clause.

◈ *P r a c t i c e* **3** **Writing Your Own** Write five sentences of your own with introductory elements.

_____

_____

_____

_____

_____

REVERSE WORDS

Reverse the order of some subjects and verbs. For example, instead of *I am so excited*, try *Am I ever excited*. You can also add or drop words and change punctuation to make the sentence read smoothly.

In my lifetime, I have never lived away from home. Now I am about to start my second year of college. I think I am ready to be on my own. **Am I ever** excited about this new phase in my life. To pay for life away from home, I have student loans and a part-time job. I can't wait to feel true independence.

 P r a c t i c e 4 **Identifying** Underline the words you could reverse in each of the following sentences.

1. I am glad to see you!
2. She is so excited about the trip.
3. He was very scared.
4. I am glad I studied.
5. Sue was nervous about her speech.

 P r a c t i c e 5 **Completing** Rewrite the sentences in Practice 4 by reversing the words you underlined.

 P r a c t i c e 6 **Writing Your Own** Write five sentences of your own with subjects and verbs reversed.

_____

_____

_____

_____

_____

MOVE SENTENCE PARTS

Move some parts of the sentence around. Experiment to see which order works best.

In my lifetime, I have never lived away from home. Now I am about to start my second year of college. I think I am ready to be on my own. Am I ever excited about this new phase in my life. **Student loans and a part-time job can pay for a life away from home.** I can't wait to feel true independence.

◆ *P r a c t i c e* **7** **Identifying** Underline any parts of the following sentences that can be moved around.

1. I was incredibly hungry after breakfast.
2. Some experts say that computers increase isolation among people.
3. Your outfit is lovely today.
4. There is a great deal we don't know about the common cold.
5. I absolutely love chocolate, not surprisingly.

◆ *P r a c t i c e* **8** **Completing** Rewrite the sentences in Practice 7, moving the words you underlined.

◆ *P r a c t i c e* **9** **Writing Your Own** Write two sentences of your own. Then rewrite each sentence two different ways.

_____

_____

_____

_____

_____

VARY SENTENCE TYPE

Use a question, a command, or an exclamation occasionally.

In my lifetime, I have never lived away from home. **Have you?** Now I am about to start my second year of college. I think I am ready to be on my own. **Boy, am I ever excited about this new phase in** my life! Student loans and a part-time job can pay for a life away from home. I can't wait to feel true independence.

Practice 10 Identifying Identify each of the following sentences as a statement (S), a question (Q), a command (C), or an exclamation (E).

1. _____ Look over there at the elephant

2. _____ How does she do that

3. _____ My mom always asked herself why she never finished graduate school

4. _____ Whatever you decide is fine with me

5. _____ Look out for that falling rock

Practice 11 Completing Complete the following sentences, making them into questions, commands, or exclamations. Then supply the correct punctuation.

1. Will there ever _____

2. You should not have taken _____

3. Do you know if _____

4. At the first stop light _____

5. Don't you ever _____

Practice 12 Writing Your Own Write two statements, two questions, two commands, and two exclamations of your own.

_____

_____

_____

_____

_____

REVIEWING WAYS TO VARY SENTENCE PATTERNS

Why is varying sentence patterns important in your writing?

_____

Name four ways to vary your sentence patterns.

_____

_____

_____

_____

What other kinds of sentences besides statements can you use for variety?

_____   _____   _____

CHAPTER REVIEW

You might want to reread your answers to the questions in the review box before you do the following exercises.

Review P r a c t i c e 1 **Identifying** Underline the words or groups of words that have been added or moved in each revised sentence. Then use the following key to tell which rule was applied to the sentence:

1. Add introductory words.
2. Reverse the order of subject and verb.
3. Move parts of the sentence around.
4. Use a question, a command, or an exclamation occasionally.

1. She does that very well.

    _____ How does she do that so well?

2. I must call Jarrett in an emergency. Can anyone tell me Jarrett's phone number?

    _____ In case of an emergency, can anyone tell me Jarrett's phone number?

3. Please buy some brown sugar for chocolate chip cookies at the store around the corner.

_____ At the store around the corner, please buy some brown sugar for chocolate chip cookies.

4. I started to dance because I was so excited!

_____ I was so excited that I started to dance!

5. I am grateful to you!

_____ Am I ever grateful to you!

6. You can't play now. Finish your homework first.

_____ Before you can play, you must finish your homework.

7. Do it quickly. Catch Dustin before he leaves.

_____ Quickly, catch Dustin before he leaves.

8. He is an optimist. He always believes everything will turn out all right.

_____ An optimist, he always believes everything will turn out all right.

9. Call our store, send a fax, or visit our Web site to order.

_____ To order, call our store, send a fax, or visit our Web site.

10. I don't believe it. Did you really say that?

_____ Oh no, did you really say that?

 **Review P r a c t i c e 2 Completing** Vary the structure of the following sentences with at least three of the four ideas you just learned.

    The local teen center has a problem. It cannot afford to stay open, so it might be shut down this weekend. It can't make its monthly dues any higher because most of its members cannot afford increased fees. Government funding and donations aren't enough to keep the center open. A solution has to exist.

Review P r a c t i c e 3 Writing Your Own Write a paragraph about a historical event. Try to use each of the four ways you have learned to make sentences interesting.

◆ *Review P r a c t i c e 4* **Editing Through Collaboration** Exchange paragraphs from Review Practice 3 with another student, and do the following:

1. Put brackets around any sentences that sound monotonous.

2. Suggest a way to vary each of these sentences.

Then return the paper to its writer, and use the information in this chapter to vary the sentence structure in your own paragraph. Record your errors on the Error Log in Appendix 6.

CHAPTER 51

PARALLELISM

☑ CHECKLIST for Using Parallelism

> ✔ Can you use parallelism to add coherence to your sentences and paragraphs?
>
> ✔ Are all items in a series grammatically balanced?

Test Yourself

Underline the parts in each of the following sentences that seem awkward or unbalanced.

- We decided to forget about the lawsuit and then moving on with our lives.

- Last year, I graduated from college, moved from Texas to California, and have been married.

- My sister and brother raise money to feed the homeless and for building a new shelter.

- Exercising, eating right, and water will improve a person's health.

- Jack went back to school because he wanted to get a better job and because of the girls on campus.

(Answers are in Appendix 4.)

When sentences are **parallel,** they are balanced. That is, words, phrases, or clauses in a series start with the same grammatical form. Parallel structures make your sentences interesting and clear.

Following is a paragraph that could be greatly improved with parallel structures.

My teen-aged sister, Amanda, was not thrilled when she learned the family was going to drive to San Antonio, Texas, for a spring break. She has been looking forward to her time at home. She was planning on reading romance novels, to hang out with her friends, and was going to organize her schoolwork. Instead, she will be touring the Alamo, seeing the Riverwalk, and will visit many missions.

Words and phrases in a series should be parallel, which means they should start with the same type of word. Parallelism makes your sentence structure smoother and more interesting. Look at this sentence, for example.

NOT   She was planning on **reading** romance novels,

                                      to hang out with her friends, and

                                      was going to organize her schoolwork.

CORRECT   She was planning on **reading** romance novels,

                                      hanging out with her friends, and

                                      organizing her schoolwork.

CORRECT   She was planning to **read** romance novels,

                                      hang out with her friends, and

                                      organize her schoolwork.

Here is another sentence that would read better if the parts were parallel:

NOT   Instead, she will be **touring** the Alamo,

                                      seeing the Riverwalk, and

                                      will visit many missions.

CORRECT   Instead, she will be **touring** the Alamo,

                                      seeing the Riverwalk, and

                                      visiting many missions.

CORRECT   Instead, she will tour **the Alamo,**

                                      the Riverwalk, and

                                      many missions.

Now read the paragraph with these two sentences made parallel or balanced.

My teen-aged sister, Amanda, was not thrilled when she learned the family was going to drive to San Antonio, Texas, for a spring break. She has been looking forward to her time at home. She was planning on reading romance novels, hanging out with her friends, and organizing her schoolwork. Instead, she will be touring the Alamo, seeing the Riverwalk, and visiting many missions.

REVIEWING PARALLELISM

What is parallelism?

_____

_____

Why should you use parallelism in your writing?

_____

Practice 1 Identifying Underline the parallel structures in each of the following sentences.

1. We never expected the girls to start buying alcohol and bringing it into the dorms.
2. She often prepares recipes that she finds in her fancy cooking magazines or that she sees on the Food Network.
3. He would start skipping class and sleeping late.
4. One day when I was 10 years old, my dad revealed that there was no Santa Claus and that babies did not come from storks.
5. I baked cookies, cleaned the house, and paid the bills.

Practice 2 Completing Make the underlined elements parallel in each of the following sentences.

1. Jessica likes <u>skiing</u>, <u>cooking</u>, and <u>to do crossword puzzles</u> in her spare time.

_____

2. On our trip to New York City, we have many <u>things to do</u>, <u>people to visit</u>, and <u>sights that should be seen</u>.

_____

3. Carmella went to the picnic <u>because she wanted to support her co-workers</u> and <u>because of the massive fireworks show</u>.

_____

4. In 1950, my mom and dad <u>moved out of the city</u>, <u>bought land in the high country</u>, and <u>have become self-sufficient</u>.

_____

5. <u>Fighting</u>, <u>cheating</u>, and <u>to use drugs</u> will get you kicked out immediately.

_____

◆ *P r a c t i c e   3* **Writing Your Own** Write five sentences of your own using parallel structures in each.

_____

_____

_____

_____

_____

CHAPTER REVIEW

You might want to reread your answers to the questions in the review box before you do the following exercises.

◆ *Review P r a c t i c e   1* **Identifying** Underline the parallel structures in each of the following sentences.

1. Kristi will make deviled eggs, bring baked beans, and order the cake.
2. In Las Vegas, you should see Celine Dion, play blackjack, and ride a roller-coaster.
3. The house needs to be painted, and the grass needs to be cut.
4. To stay healthy, do not smoke, stay out of the sun, and don't abuse alcohol.

5. Students should learn to manage their time, to study efficiently, and to have a social life.

6. She bought the gift, she wrapped the gift, and she delivered the gift.

7. Biking, swimming, and hiking are all good sports to build endurance, stamina, and flexibility.

8. He can run faster than a speeding bullet, leap tall buildings in a single bound, and see through solid materials.

9. Please wake up the baby, give her a bath, and feed her.

10. Mr. Wattenbarger invests in stocks, contributes to a retirement fund, and saves a small percentage of his yearly income.

◆ **Review P r a c t i c e 2 Completing** Complete each of the following sentences with parallel structures.

1. My favorite hobbies are _____, _____, and _____.

2. Because _____ and because _____, I decided to stay home.

3. You will need to _____, _____, and _____ before going to your appointment.

4. Brandon _____ and _____, but he still can't fix the problem.

5. He always planned _____, _____, and _____.

6. I'm so tired of _____, _____, and _____.

7. You could have _____, _____, and _____ if you had truly wanted to pass that test.

8. _____, _____, and _____ are essential items at the beach.

9. I've already told you that _____ and that _____.

10. Sam and Tabitha enjoy _____, _____, and _____.

◆ *Review P r a c t i c e 3* **Writing Your Own** Write a paragraph about your favorite movie. What is the movie? Why is it your favorite? Use two examples of parallelism in your paragraph.

◆ *Review P r a c t i c e 4* **Editing Through Collaboration** Exchange paragraphs from Review Practice 3 with another student, and do the following:

1. Underline any items in a series.
2. Put brackets around any of these items that are not grammatically parallel.

Then return the paper to its writer, and use the information in this chapter to correct any parallelism errors in your own paragraph. Record your errors on the Error Log in Appendix 6.

CHAPTER 52

COMBINING SENTENCES

✔ CHECKLIST for Combining Sentences

> ✔ Do you combine sentences to avoid too many short, choppy sentences in a row?
>
> ✔ Do you use different types of sentences?

Test Yourself

Combine each set of sentences into one sentence.

- My mother is taking ballet lessons. She takes her lessons at the YWCA.
- We love to swim. It's just too hot to be outside.
- Robin lives in Fort Lauderdale. Jack lives in Houston.
- We lived on the beach. We were there for two weeks.
- I am going to study hard. I want to get a good grade on my final.
- I love to travel. I love the strange animals in Australia. I want to go to Australia.

(Answers are in Appendix 4.)

Still another way to add variety to your writing is to combine short, choppy sentences into longer sentences. You can combine simple sentences to make compound or complex sentences. You can also combine compound and complex sentences.

SIMPLE SENTENCES

A **simple sentence** consists of one independent clause. Remember that a clause has a subject and a main verb.

In the following examples, notice that a simple sentence can have more than one subject and more than one verb. (For more on compound subjects and compound verbs, see Chapter 30.)

s   v

I have several very good friends.

s   s   v

Martin and Louis are good friends.

s   s v   v

Martin and I do interesting things and go to interesting places.

REVIEWING SIMPLE SENTENCES

What does a simple sentence consist of?

_____

Write a simple sentence.

_____

◆ *P r a c t i c e 1* **Identifying** Underline the subjects once and the verbs twice in each of the following sentences. Then label the simple sentences SS.

1. _____ Every day I went to the bagel shop and bought a newspaper.

2. _____ Sinya and I knew the answer.

3. _____ Before the last show begins, I'll get some popcorn.

4. _____ They're flying to Denver on Thursday.

5. _____ Going to the movies alone is peaceful.

◆ *P r a c t i c e 2* **Completing** Make simple sentences out of the sentences in Practice 1 that are not simple.

◆ *P r a c t i c e 3* **Writing Your Own** Write a simple sentence of your own for each of the following subjects and verbs.

1. Carlos and Linda _____

2. routinely eats and sleeps _____

3. reading for long periods of time _____

4. Many people _____

5. The fish in the tank _____

COMPOUND SENTENCES

A **compound sentence** consists of two or more independent clauses joined by a coordinating conjunction (*and, but, for, nor, or, so,* or *yet*). In other words, you can create a compound sentence from two (or more) simple sentences.

Simple:	I can add quickly in my head.
Simple:	I am very good at math.

                    s   v   s   v

Compound: I can add quickly in my head, **and** I am very good at math.

Simple:	He leads a very busy life.
Simple:	His family always comes first.

                 s   v   s

Compound: He leads a very busy life, **but** his family always

                          v

comes first.

Simple:	Bonita and Tamara are running a 5K on Saturday.
Simple:	They will not go with us Friday night.

                 s   s   v

Compound: Bonita and Tamara are running a 5K Saturday, **so**

                 s   v   v

they will not be going with us Friday night.

Hint: As the examples show, a comma comes before the coordinating conjunction in a compound sentence.

REVIEWING COMPOUND SENTENCES
....

What does a compound sentence consist of?

_____

Write a compound sentence.

_____

◆ *P r a c t i c e* **4** **Identifying** Underline the independent clauses in the following sentences, and circle the coordinating conjunctions.

1. I hate to repeat myself, but I will.
2. Just beyond that sign is a motorcycle cop waiting to ticket someone, yet he won't catch me.
3. Harry began the race, and he never looked back.
4. She's been in these kinds of predicaments before, yet each time she's come out ahead.
5. You are not allowed to bring food or drinks into this room, nor are you allowed to move the desks.

◆ *P r a c t i c e* **5** **Completing** Combine each pair of simple sentences into a compound sentence.

1. Mom and Dad love to play golf.   They never seem to have enough time for it.
2. Our backyard faces the highway.   It's always noisy.
3. My Uncle Simon and Aunt Jean always take a month-long vacation. They are always relieved to return home.
4. Our phone rings day and night.   It is very annoying.
5. My favorite meal is chicken and sausage gumbo.   My favorite dessert is peach cobbler.

◆ *P r a c t i c e* **6** **Writing Your Own** Write five compound sentences of your own.

_____

_____

_____

_____

_____

COMPLEX SENTENCES

A **complex sentence** is composed of one independent clause and at least one dependent clause. A **dependent clause** begins with either a subordinating conjunction or a relative pronoun.

Subordinating Conjunctions

after	because	since	until
although	before	so	when
as	even if	so that	whenever
as if	even though	than	where
as long as	how	that	wherever
as soon as	if	though	whether
as though	in order that	unless	while

Relative Pronouns

who	whom	whose	which	that

You can use subordinating conjunctions and relative pronouns to make a simple sentence (an independent clause) into a dependent clause. Then you can add the new dependent clause to an independent clause to produce a complex sentence that adds interest and variety to your writing.

How do you know which simple sentence should be independent and which should be dependent? The idea that you think is more important should be the independent clause. The less important idea will then be the dependent clause.

Following are some examples of how to combine simple sentences to make a complex sentence.

Simple: Shawna has a big collection of video games.

Simple: Shawna plays the same games over and over.

                                                Dep
Complex: **Even though** Shawna has a big collection of video

                                    Ind
games, she plays the same ones over and over.

This complex sentence stresses that Shawna plays the same games over and over. The size of her collection is of secondary importance.

                                    Ind
Complex: Shawna has a big collection of video games, **though**

                                        Dep
she plays the same ones over and over.

In this complex sentence, the size of the collection is most important, so it is the independent clause.

Simple: The winner of the 5K race was Torrie.

Simple: Torrie is my roommate.

                            Ind   Dep
Complex: The winner of the 5K race was Torrie, **who** is my
           roommate.

This complex sentence answers the question "Who won the 5K race?" The information about Torrie being the roommate is secondary in importance.

                        Ind   Dep
Complex: My roommate is Torrie, **who** won the 5K race.

This complex sentence answers the question "Who is your roommate?" The information that she won the race is secondary.

REVIEWING COMPLEX SENTENCES

What does a complex sentence consist of?

_____

Write a complex sentence.

_____

◈ *P r a c t i c e   7*   **Identifying** Label the underlined part of each sentence as either an independent (I) or a dependent (D) clause.

1. _____ <u>Although I was exhausted</u>, I still went to work.
2. _____ If someone scores 50, <u>the game is over</u>.
3. _____ Trisha is majoring in marine biology <u>since she loves working with sea life</u>.
4. _____ Brittany, <u>whom I've known for years</u>, decided to move to Alaska.
5. _____ While people in third world countries starve, <u>people in the United States eat too much and waste food</u>.

◈ *P r a c t i c e   8*   **Completing** Finish each sentence, and label the new clause either dependent (D) or independent (I).

1. _____ _____, call your mother.
2. _____ When you signed up for this class, _____?
3. _____ Mrs. Benson, _____, won the lottery and moved to Florida.
4. _____ Whenever Diane's face turns red, _____.
5. _____ If Mark is cold, _____.

◈ *P r a c t i c e   9*   **Writing Your Own** Write five complex sentences, making sure you have one independent clause and at least one dependent clause in each.

_____

_____

_____

_____

_____

COMPOUND-COMPLEX SENTENCES

If you combine a compound sentence with a complex sentence, you produce a **compound-complex sentence.** That means your sentence has at least two independent clauses (to make it compound) and at least one dependent clause (to make it complex). Here are some examples.

Simple: We both love warm weather.

Simple: We will go to Jamaica for our honeymoon.

Simple: We plan to have a good time.

                                          Ind

Compound-Complex: We will go to Jamaica for our honeymoon,

                                          Ind

and we plan to have a good time **since**

                                          Dep

we both love warm weather.

Simple: She bought a used car.

Simple: It has 50,000 miles on it.

Simple: It runs like a dream.

                                          Ind

Compound-Complex: She bought a used car, **which** has

                          Dep   Ind

50,000 miles on it, **but** it runs like a dream.

Simple: Rush-hour traffic is very bad.

Simple: You could miss your flight.

Simple: You should leave soon.

                                          Ind

Compound-Complex: Rush-hour traffic is very bad, **and** you could

                          Ind   Dep

miss your flight **if** you don't leave soon.

Hint: Notice in these examples that we occasionally had to change words
in the combined sentences so they make sense.

REVIEWING COMPOUND-COMPLEX SENTENCES

What does a compound-complex sentence consist of?

Write a compound-complex sentence.

_____

◆ *P r a c t i c e **1 0** **Identifying** Underline the clauses in each of the following compound-complex sentences. Then identify each clause as either independent (I) or dependent (D).

1. We cannot host the meeting, nor can we attend because we will be out of town.

2. Professor Shilling said that I couldn't turn in my essay late because I had three months to write it, so I decided to turn it in on time.

3. Because we were out of money, we begged our guide to take us to the bank, yet our guide said that he didn't have enough gas in the bus.

4. Even though Marcy doesn't like the water and even though she can't swim, she should go fishing with us, for she will have a good time.

5. After all the fuss died down, the boys decided to shake hands and let bygones be bygones; then, they took each other out for pizza.

◆ *P r a c t i c e **1 1** **Completing** Make each sentence below into a compound-complex sentence. You may have to change some of the wording.

1. Gina believes in ghosts.

_____

2. Edward collects rare books.

_____

3. The contestants were nervous.

_____

4. Motorcycles can be dangerous.

_____

5. Jack says that he will eat liver and onions "when pigs fly."

_____

◆ *P r a c t i c e   1 2*   **Writing Your Own** Write five compound-complex sentences of your own.

_____

_____

_____

_____

_____

CHAPTER REVIEW

You might want to reread your answers to the questions in all the review boxes before you do the following exercises.

◆ *Review P r a c t i c e   1*   **Identifying** Underline the independent clauses in each sentence. Then label the sentence simple (SS), compound (C), complex (X), or compound-complex (CX). The following definitions might help you.

Simple	=	one independent clause
Compound	=	two or more independent clauses joined by *and, but, for, nor, or, so,* or *yet*
Complex	=	one independent clause and at least one dependent clause
Compound-complex	=	at least two independent clauses and one or more dependent clauses

1. _____ DVD players are becoming more popular than VCRs.

2. _____ Bananas are a nutritious part of Leo's breakfast each morning.

3. _____ The grandparents' house, which sits at the edge of the woods, was built around the turn of the century.

4. _____ Sheila says that music is her passion, but she has little time to pursue her interests since she took on a part-time job.

5. _____ I like the feel of sand between my toes when I walk along the beach.

6. _____ We watched the MTV awards, and then we went out for a late-night snack.

7. _____ Last year, we scraped and saved every penny, and we took a trip during spring break.

8. _____ Whistling, screaming, and clapping, the fans showed their approval.

9. _____ Will you please help me find the top to this jar?

10. _____ He sat and stared at the stars, and he decided to travel to Mexico while he wondered what adventures were ahead of him.

♦ **Review P r a c t i c e 2 Completing** Combine each set of sentences to make the sentence pattern indicated in parentheses. You may need to change some wording in the sentences so they make sense. The list of sentence types in Review Practice 1 may help you with this exercise.

1. Please turn down the television.   I can't sleep. (compound)

2. My best friend, Tina, and I always have a great time together.   We share all of our secrets. (compound)

3. I have so much energy.   I'm going to clean my closet. (complex)

4. You should never leave an iron on unattended.   You should never use an iron on clothes you are wearing.   You may be injured. (compound-complex)

5. Bob has been running marathons for many years.   He trains all year.   He hopes to win a marathon. (compound-complex)

6. _____ I know you don't like pears. Try some of this pastry anyway. (complex)

7. Please take these boxes out to the curb.   Don't take the boxes sitting on the stairs. (compound)

8. I'm sorry.   I can't lend you any money.   I am broke. (compound-complex)

9. Billy-Bob is in charge of the artwork.   He is a master with colors and light. (compound)

10. The fly is annoying me.   It is buzzing around my head. (complex)

◆ *Review P r a c t i c e* **3** **Writing Your Own** Write a paragraph about your fondest teenage memory. What are the details of this memory? Why do you remember this event?

◆ *Review P r a c t i c e* **4** **Editing Through Collaboration** Exchange paragraphs from Review Practice 3 with another student, and do the following:

1. Put brackets around any sentences that you think should be combined.

2. Underline sentences that are incorrectly combined (for example, ones that have a weak connecting word or no connecting word).

Then return the paper to its writer, and use the information in this chapter to combine sentences in your own paragraph. Record your errors on the Error Log in Appendix 6.

UNIT TESTS

Here are some exercises that test your understanding of all the material in this unit: Varying Sentence Structure, Parallelism, and Combining Sentences.

Unit Test I

A. Underline and label the errors in each of the following sentences in variety, parallelism, and sentence combining.

1. The turn-off will be hard to see. I will be driving at night.

2. She lived like a queen and to enjoy her lifestyle.

3. We stopped to get lunch, fill up on gas, and stretching our legs.

4. Martha and George always invite my brother and me to swim in their pool. They never invite our neighbors. Our neighbors really want to come.

5. I listen to the radio in the car. I listen to station WGAC.

6. We took Yolanda to Pismo Beach. We let Yolanda feed the seals.

7. We had a family reunion. Josh fell out of a tree there and broke his wrist.

8. We decided to scuba dive for five days, explore the jungle for three days, and climbed the Mayan ruins for two days.

9. They had been building this database. They collected it for over three years.

10. Tuesday is today. My paper is due on Tuesday.

11. Working for the FBI comes with many perks. I take advantage of them all.

12. Being my friend will make you happy. You will never have to be alone.

13. His birthday is on Thursday. We're celebrating it on Friday.

14. Training for the marathon means eating right, running hard, and will be getting plenty of sleep.

15. The martial arts instructor is a professional. The martial arts instructor said that Cole could compete as long as he practiced hard.

16. Trimming, weeding, and to plant flowers always make a yard look better.

17. It's best to wait for my mom. My mom will be home soon.

18. The mouse chewed through the wire. I had to pay to replace it.

19. I used to dance in puddles. I used to squish my toes in the mud. Now I am an adult with a job and family. I don't have time for these simple pleasures.

20. Skydiving is great. You need to know what you are doing when you skydive. Skydiving can be a very dangerous sport.

B. Correct the errors you identified in Part A by rewriting each incorrect sentence.

Unit Test II

A. Underline and label the errors in the following paragraph in variety, parallelism, and sentence combining.

Entering high school is scary at first. Entering high school is fun once students get used to their new environment. Entering high school and to deal with all the stress of being a teenager is the first step to adulthood. In high school, students have to learn to manage their time to get good grades, a social life, and get involved in hobbies. Some students are really afraid of high school. They just want to stay kids forever. They need to give high school a chance. They will see that it is a lot of fun. They will see that growing up is exciting.

B. Correct the errors you identified in Part A by rewriting the paragraph.

STANDARD AND NONSTANDARD ENGLISH

CHAPTER **53**

✔ CHECKLIST for Standard and Nonstandard English

> ✔ Do you consistently use standard English in your paper?
>
> ✔ Is your paper free of nonstandard, ungrammatical words?
>
> ✔ Have you changed any slang to standard English?

Test Yourself

Label the following sentences as correct, incorrect, or slang.

- So she goes, can't I meet you at the theater? _____
- Julie be planning the farewell party. _____
- We were totally grossed out. _____
- They changed the tire theirselves. _____
- We're jamming in the morning. _____

(Answers are in Appendix 4.)

Choosing the right words for what you want to say is an important part of effective communication. This chapter will help you find the right words and phrases for the audience you are trying to reach.

Look, for example, at the following sentences. They all have a similar message, expressed in different words.

I want to do good in college, the reason being that I can get a good job.

I be studying hard in college, so I can get a good job.

I'm going to hit the books so I can rake in the bucks.

I want to go to college, graduate, and get a good job.

Which of these sentences would you probably say to a friend or to someone in your family? Which would you most likely say in a job interview? Which would be good for a college paper?

The first three sentences are nonstandard English. They might be said or written to a friend or family member, but they would not be appropriate in an academic setting or in a job situation. Only the fourth sentence would be appropriate in an academic paper or in a job interview.

STANDARD AND NONSTANDARD ENGLISH

Most of the English language falls into one of two categories—either *standard* or *nonstandard*. **Standard English** is the language of college, business, and the media. It is used by reporters on television, by newspapers, in most magazines, and on Web sites created by schools, government, business, and organizations. Standard English is always grammatically correct and free of slang.

Nonstandard English does not follow all the rules of grammar and often includes slang. Nonstandard English is not necessarily wrong, but it is more appropriate in some settings (with friends and family) than others. It is not appropriate in college or business writing. To understand the difference between standard and nonstandard English, compare the following paragraphs.

Nonstandard English

My man, Max, don't understand why people go to college. He believes that college is a waste of time and the long green. He goes, my parents never gone to college, and what they be making ain't exactly chump change. But lotsa people go to college for other reasons than raising up their earning power. Irregardless of whether college be preparing you for a career or not, it helps a person find hisself and meet others who are sorta like you I definitely be believing that a college education is worth the money and time.

Standard English

My friend, Max, can't understand why people go to college. He believes that in terms of money and time, higher education is wasteful. He likes to point out that both of his parents have high-paying jobs and never went to college. However, he doesn't realize that many people go to college for other reasons than increasing their earning power. They also hope to discover what they would enjoy doing for the rest of their lives. College not only prepares people for a career, it helps them learn more about themselves and meet others with similar interests. I strongly believe that the money and time invested in a college education are justified.

In the rest of this chapter, you will learn how to recognize and correct ungrammatical English and how to avoid slang in your writing.

REVIEWING STANDARD AND NONSTANDARD ENGLISH

Where do you hear standard English in your daily life?

_____

What is nonstandard English?

_____

Give two examples of nonstandard English.

_____   _____

NONSTANDARD ENGLISH

Nonstandard English is ungrammatical. It does not follow the rules of standard English that are required in college writing. The academic and business worlds expect you to be able to recognize and avoid nonstandard English. This is not always easy because some nonstandard terms are used so often in speech that many people think they are acceptable in writing. The following list might help you choose the correct words in your own writing.

ain't

NOT	Ricardo **ain't** going to school today.
CORRECT	Ricardo **is not** going to school today.

anywheres

NOT	Jake makes himself at home **anywheres** he goes.
CORRECT	Jakes makes himself at home **anywhere** he goes.

be

NOT	I **be** so tired.
CORRECT	I **am** so tired.

(For additional help with *be*, see Chapter 34, "Verb Tense.")

being as, being that

NOT	**Being as** Rhonda is late, we can't start the party.
CORRECT	**Because** Rhonda is late, we can't start the party.

coulda/could of, shoulda/should of

NOT	My brother **could of** played basketball in college. He **should of** stuck with it.
CORRECT	My brother **could have** (or **could've**) played basketball in college. He **should have** (or **should've**) stuck with it.

different than

NOT	I am no **different than** all your other friends.
CORRECT	I am no **different from** all your other friends.

drug

NOT	I couldn't lift the box, so I **drug** it across the room.
CORRECT	I couldn't lift the box, so I **dragged** it across the room.

enthused

NOT	Jay was **enthused** about his trip to Hawaii.
CORRECT	Jay was **enthusiastic** about his trip to Hawaii.

everywheres

NOT	My little sister follows me **everywheres** I go.
CORRECT	My little sister follows me **everywhere** I go.

goes

NOT	Then he **goes,** I'll wait for you downstairs.
CORRECT	Then he **says,** "I'll wait for you downstairs."
CORRECT	Then he **said** he would wait for me downstairs.

hisself

NOT	Marshall made **hisself** a budget for the next month.
CORRECT	Marshall made **himself** a budget for the next month.

in regards to

NOT   In regards to your proposal, we have decided to consider it.

CORRECT In regard to your proposal, we have decided to consider it.

irregardless

NOT   Irregardless of how much time you spent on your paper, it still needs work.

CORRECT Regardless of the time you spent on your paper, it still needs work.

kinda/kind of, sorta/sort of

NOT   Abby's perfume smells kinda sweet, sorta like vanilla.

CORRECT Abby's perfume smells rather sweet, much like vanilla.

most

NOT   Most everyone we invited will come to the party.

CORRECT Almost everyone we invited will come to the party.

must of

NOT   I must of left my gloves in the car.

CORRECT I must have left my gloves in the car.

off of

NOT   Jim accidentally knocked the vase off of the coffee table.

CORRECT Jim accidentally knocked the vase off the coffee table.

oughta

NOT   Sometimes I think I oughta try out for the swim team.

CORRECT Sometimes I think I ought to try out for the swim team.

real

NOT   My mom was real upset when I came in at 4 a.m.

CORRECT My mom was really upset when I came in at 4 a.m.

somewheres

NOT   You must have left your notebook somewheres at school.

CORRECT You must have left your notebook somewhere at school.

suppose to

NOT	Marc was **suppose to** meet me at the library.
CORRECT	Marc was **supposed to** meet me at the library.

theirselves

NOT	My grandfather thinks people should help **theirselves** instead of waiting for a handout.
CORRECT	My grandfather thinks people should help **themselves** instead of waiting for a handout.

use to

NOT	Nassar **use to** live in Egypt.
CORRECT	Nassar **used to** live in Egypt.

ways

NOT	Both sides say they are a long **ways** from agreement.
CORRECT	Both sides say they are a long **way** from agreement.

where . . . at

NOT	Do you know **where** your keys are **at?**
CORRECT	Do you know **where** your keys **are?**

REVIEWING NONSTANDARD ENGLISH
....

What is one reason using nonstandard English in written work is easy to do?

_____

Give four examples of nonstandard English; then correct them.

_____   _____

_____   _____

_____   _____

_____   _____

◆ *P r a c t i c e   1 A* **Identifying** Underline the ungrammatical words or phrases in each of the following sentences.

1. I ain't going to eat these turnips.
2. I was real excited to see my new baby brother.
3. Sometimes people should keep their thoughts to theirselves.
4. Being as my brother has more money than I, he should pay for dinner.
5. We use to go to the lake every summer.

◆ *P r a c t i c e   1 B* **Correcting** Correct the ungrammatical words and expressions in Practice 1A by rewriting the incorrect sentences.

◆ *P r a c t i c e   2* **Completing** Change the underlined ungrammatical words and phrases to standard English.

1. where am I at   _____

2. Because I drug   _____

3. She goes, "Sure."   _____

4. kinda   _____

5. I be   _____

◆ *P r a c t i c e   3* **Writing Your Own** Write five sentences of your own using the grammatical words and phrases you chose in Practice 2.

_____

_____

_____

_____

_____

SLANG

Another example of nonstandard English is **slang,** popular words and expressions that come and go, much like the latest fashions. For example, in the 1950s, someone might call his or her special someone a *dreamboat.* In the 1960s, you might hear a boyfriend or girlfriend described as *groovy*, and in the 1990s, *sweet* was the popular slang term. Today your significant other might be *hot* or *dope*.

These expressions are slang because they are part of the spoken language that changes from generation to generation and from place to place. As you might suspect, slang communicates to a limited audience who share common interests and experiences. Some slang words, such as *cool* and *neat*, have become part of our language, but most slang is temporary. What's in today may be out tomorrow, so the best advice is to avoid slang in your writing.

REVIEWING SLANG

What is slang?

_____

Give two examples of slang terms that were popular but aren't any longer.

_____   _____

Give two examples of slang terms that you and your friends use today.

_____   _____

◆ *P r a c t i c e 4* **Identifying** Underline the slang words and expressions in each of the following sentences.

1. Just because she's pretty doesn't mean she's all that.
2. We were just hangin with our homies.
3. My sister and I are tight.
4. That guy is hot.
5. Give it up for Dave Matthews.

◆ *P r a c t i c e 5* **Completing** Translate the following slang expressions into standard English.

1. That rocks. _____

2. Say what? _____

3. Keep it real, man. _____

4. What up? _____

5. We're just kickin' it. _____

◆ *P r a c t i c e   6* **Writing Your Own** List five slang words or expressions, and use them in sentences of your own. Then rewrite each sentence using standard English to replace the slang expressions.

_____

_____

_____

_____

_____

CHAPTER REVIEW

You might want to reread your answers to the questions in all the review boxes before you do the following exercises.

◆ *Review P r a c t i c e   1* **Identifying** Underline the ungrammatical or slang words in the following sentences.

1. In regards to your recent request we are not able to give you an answer.
2. I have a shirt somewheres that looks just like that.
3. The music got louder and faster, and then we were really rolling.
4. Hey, that's real cool.
5. Do you know where my sunglasses are at?
6. Don't be tellin' me what to do.
7. My bro John likes to roller-blade on the boardwalk.
8. Everywheres I go, that dog follows.
9. She's very enthused about the trip.
10. Despite the snow, most all of the employees came to work today.

◆ *Review P r a c t i c e 2* **Completing** Correct any nonstandard English in each of the following sentences by rewriting the sentences.

1. The girl in my economics class is phat.
2. You really need to chill out.
3. Wow, I really like your new leather jacket; it's bad.
4. Weren't you suppose to go to the movie with Eddie today?
5. Timmy's brother done it now.
6. I'm so sorry that I knocked your picture off of the wall.
7. Hey man, do you think you can make room for one more person?
8. Today, I be feelin' fine.
9. You could of always asked for help.
10. Whatcha doin' in the basement?

◆ *Review P r a c t i c e 3* **Writing Your Own** Write a paragraph on a community problem. What are the details? What is the problem? What solution do you propose?

◆ *Review P r a c t i c e 4* **Editing Through Collaboration** Exchange paragraphs from Review Practice 3 with another student, and do the following:

1. Underline any ungrammatical language.
2. Circle any slang.

Then return the paper to its writer, and use the information in this chapter to correct any nonstandard or slang expressions in your own paragraph. Record your errors on the Error Log in Appendix 6.

54 EASILY CONFUSED WORDS

✓ CHECKLIST for Easily Confused Words

✔ Is the correct word chosen from the easily confused words?
✔ Are the following words used correctly: *its/it's, their/there/they're, to/too/two, who's/whose, your/you're?*

Test Yourself

Choose the correct word in parentheses.

- I have to (accept, except) that I won't be graduating this spring.
- (Who's, Whose) bike is this?
- I'm not saying (it's, its) Johnny's fault.
- We are going to need (their, there, they're) help.
- (Wear, where, were) did you say your parents lived?

(Answers are in Appendix 4.)

Some words are easily confused. They may look alike, sound alike, or have similar meanings. But they all play different roles in the English language. This chapter will help you choose the right words for your sentences.

EASILY CONFUSED WORDS, PART I

a/an: Use *a* before words that begin with a consonant. Use *an* before words that begin with a *vowel* (*a, e, i, o, u*).

a party, **a** dollar, **a** car
an apple, **an** elephant, **an** opportunity

accept/except: *Accept* means "receive." *Except* means "other than."

Yolanda says she will not **accept** my apology.

I answered every question **except** the last one.

advice/advise: *Advice* means "helpful information." *Advise* means "give advice or help."

Whenever I need **advice,** I call my older brother Greg.

Greg usually **advises** me to make a list before taking action.

affect/effect: *Affect* (verb) means "influence." *Effect* means "bring about" (verb) or "a result" (noun).

Omar hopes his new job won't **affect** his study time.

The governor believes higher taxes will **effect** positive economic changes.

The pill produced a calming **effect.**

already/all ready: *Already* means "in the past." *All ready* means "completely prepared."

Hope has **already** registered for the spring semester.

We were **all ready** to go when the phone rang.

among/between: Use *among* when referring to three or more people or things. Use *between* when referring to only two people or things.

Among all the students in our class, Shonda is the most mature.

I can't decide **between** cheesecake and apple pie for dessert.

bad/badly: *Bad* means "not good." *Badly* means "not well."

That milk is **bad,** so don't drink it.

The team played **badly** in the first half but came back to win.

Kiki felt **bad** that she could not go.

beside/besides: *Beside* means "next to." *Besides* means "in addition (to)."

Burt stood **beside** Kevin in the team photo.

She's a very calm person. **Besides,** she has nothing to worry about.

brake/break: *Brake* means "stop" or "the parts that stop a moving vehicle." *Break* means "shatter, come apart" or "a rest between work periods."

My car needs new **brakes.**

Esther wants to **break** up with Stan.

breath/breathe: *Breath* means "air." **Breathe** means "taking in air."

Take several big **breaths** as you cool down.
To cure hiccups, **breathe** into a paper bag.

choose/chose: *Choose* means "select." **Chose** is the past tense of *choose*.

Please **choose** something from the menu.
Andy **chose** the trip to Paris as his prize.

REVIEWING WORDS THAT ARE EASILY CONFUSED, PART I

Do you understand the differences in the sets of words in Part I of the list?

_____

Have you ever confused any of these words? If so, which ones?

_____

Practice 1 Identifying Underline the correct word in each of the following sentences.

1. You should try to (choose, chose) a computer that will meet your needs.
2. When I mixed vinegar with baking soda, the (affect, effect) was astounding.
3. (Beside, Besides) being cold, I was also hungry.
4. I'll call you when I'm on my (brake, break) at work.
5. Your car keys are (among, between) the two books on the fireplace mantel.

Practice 2 Completing Complete the following sentences with a correct word from Part I of this list.

1. I was so shocked I couldn't catch my _____.
2. I decided to take your _____.
3. Elaine will _____ your invitation to the prom if you will only ask her.

4. I feel _____ that I arrived late.

5. Thank you for the invitation to lunch, but I have _____ eaten.

P r a c t i c e 3 Writing Your Own Use each pair of words correctly in a sentence of your own.

1. bad/badly _____

2. beside/besides _____

3. brake/break _____

4. choose/chose _____

5. accept/except _____

EASILY CONFUSED WORDS, PART II

coarse/course: *Coarse* refers to something that is rough. *Course* refers to a class.

> Sandpaper can be very fine or very **coarse.**
> My computer science **course** is really interesting.

desert/dessert: *Desert* refers to dry, sandy land or means "abandon." *Dessert* refers to the last course of a meal.

> Las Vegas was once nothing but a **desert.**
> The main character in the short story **deserted** his family.
> We had strawberry shortcake for **dessert.**

Hint: You can remember that *dessert* has two *s*'s if you think of *strawberry shortcake*.

does/dose: *Does* means "performs." *Dose* refers to a specific portion of medicine.

> Karla **does** whatever she wants to on the weekends.
> The doctor gave the child a small **dose** of penicillin.

fewer/less: *Fewer* refers to things that can be counted. *Less* refers to things that cannot be counted.

There are **fewer** cookies in the jar since Joey has been home.

Because my mom is working another job, she has **less** time to spend with us.

good/well: *Good* modifies nouns. *Well* modifies verbs, adjectives, and adverbs. *Well* also refers to a state of health.

Barbie looks **good** in her new outfit.

Dave looks as if he doesn't feel **well.**

Karen didn't do **well** on the typing test because she was nervous.

hear/here: *Hear* refers to the act of listening. *Here* means "in this place."

I can't **hear** you because the music is too loud.

You dropped some food **here** on the carpet.

it's/its: *It's* is the contraction for *it is* or *it has*. *Its* is a possessive pronoun.

The forecasters say **it's** going to snow this afternoon.

The cat ate breakfast and then washed **its** face.

knew/new: *Knew* is the past tense of *know. New* means "recent."

I thought you **knew** I had a **new** car.

know/no: *Know* means "understand." *No* means "not any" or is the opposite of *yes*.

We all **know** that Bart has **no** conscience.

lay/lie: *Lay* means "set down." (Its principal parts are *lay, laid, laid.*) *Lie* means "recline." (Its principal parts are *lie, lay, lain.*)

The train crew **lays** about a mile of track a day.

He **laid** down his burden.

Morrie **lies** down and takes a short nap every afternoon.

I **lay** on the beach until the sun set.

(For additional help with *lie* and *lay*, see Chapter 33, "Regular and Irregular Verbs.")

loose/lose: *Loose* means "free" or "unattached." *Lose* means "misplace" or "not win."

> I tightened the **loose** screws on the door hinge.
> If the Tigers **lose** this game, they will be out of the playoffs.

passed/past: *Passed* is the past tense of *pass*. *Past* refers to an earlier time or means "beyond."

> Mei **passed** the exam with an "A."
> Having survived the Civil War, the mansion has an interesting **past.**
> He ran **past** Ginger and into Reba's outstretched arms.

REVIEWING WORDS THAT ARE EASILY CONFUSED, PART II

Do you understand the differences in the sets of words in Part II of the list?

_____

Have you ever confused any of these words? If so, which ones?

_____

◆ *P r a c t i c e 4* **Identifying** Underline the correct word in each of the following sentences.

1. Sandy, will you please come (hear, here) so I can show you how to set the VCR?
2. Now that I have eaten dinner, I feel (good, well).
3. The outdoor shutters came (loose, lose) during the storm.
4. (It's, Its) going to be a very long day.
5. My go-cart blew a tire, and so Jed (passed, past) me on the third lap.

◆ *P r a c t i c e 5* **Completing** Complete the following sentences with a correct word from Part II of this list.

1. I need to take only one more _____ to complete my degree.
2. Would you please _____ those clean clothes on the bed?

3. The doctor told my dad that he could _____ longer eat salt.

4. Camels can live in the _____ because they store water in their humps.

5. Since Janelle has _____ cookies, you should share with her.

◆ *P r a c t i c e* **6** **Writing Your Own** Use each pair of words correctly in a sentence of your own.

1. loose/lose _____

2. passed/past _____

3. hear/here _____

4. good/well _____

5. knew/new _____

EASILY CONFUSED WORDS, PART III

principal/principle: *Principal* means "main, most important," "a school official," or "a sum of money." A *principle* is a rule. (Think of *principle* and *rule*—both end in *-le*.)

My **principal** reason for moving is to be nearer my family.
Mr. Kobler is the **principal** at Westside Elementary School.
He lives by certain **principles,** including honesty and fairness.

quiet/quite: *Quiet* means "without noise." *Quite* means "very."

It was a warm, **quiet** night.
Vanessa said she was **quite** satisfied with her grade.

raise/rise: *Raise* means "increase" or "lift up." *Rise* means "get up from a sitting or reclining position."

The governor does not plan to **raise** taxes.
Ernie **rises** at 5 a.m. every morning to go to the health club.

set/sit: *Set* means "put down." *Sit* means "take a seated position."

Mohammed, you can **set** the packages over there.
If I **sit** for a long period of time, my back starts hurting.

(For additional help with *sit* and *set*, see Chapter 33, "Regular and Irregular Verbs.")

than/then: *Than* is used in making comparisons. *Then* means "next."

Louise is younger **than** her sister Linda.
The ball rolled around the hoop, **then** dropped through the net.

their/there/they're: *Their* is possessive. *There* indicates location. *They're* is the contraction of *they are*.

Their car broke down in the middle of the freeway.
Too much trash is over **there** by the riverbank.
They're not coming to the party because **they're** tired.

threw/through: *Threw*, the past tense of *throw*, means "tossed." *Through* means "finished" or "passing from one point to another."

Beth **threw** the ball to Wes, who easily caught it.
Allen is **through** with his lunch, so he will leave soon.
Rico went **through** his closet searching for his G.I. Joes.

to/too/two: *To* means "toward" or is used with a verb. *Too* means "also" or "very." *Two* is a number.

Tori went **to** Johnny's house **to** return his ring.
Tori returned Johnny's photo albums, **too.**
Mariel thinks **two** is her lucky number.

wear/were/where: *Wear* means "have on one's body." *Were* is the past tense of *be*. *Where* refers to a place.

Where were you going when I saw you?
Can you **wear** jeans to that restaurant?

weather/whether: *Weather* refers to outdoor conditions. *Whether* expresses possibility.

Whether the **weather** will improve or not is a good question.

who's/whose: *Who's* is a contraction of *who is* or *who has*. *Whose* is a possessive pronoun.

We wonder **who's** going to decide **whose** opinion is correct.

your/you're: *Your* means "belonging to you." *You're* is the contraction of *you are.*

Your appointment will be canceled if **you're** not on time.

REVIEWING WORDS THAT ARE EASILY CONFUSED, PART III

Do you understand the differences in the sets of words in Part III of this list?

_____

Have you ever confused any of these words? If so, which ones?

_____

◆ **P r a c t i c e   7   Identifying** Underline the correct word in each of the following sentences.

1. There are (to, too, two) many swimmers in the pool.
2. (Were, Wear, Where) were you going in such a hurry?
3. For extra income, we (raise, rise) hamsters and sell them on the Internet.
4. If you don't mow the lawn, (your, you're) mom is going to get upset.
5. (Who's, Whose) that girl with Bob?

◆ **P r a c t i c e   8   Completing** Complete the following sentences with a correct word from Part III of this list.

1. Pedro has a better sense of humor _____ his sister.
2. If the firefighters can't put out the blaze, _____ going to call for reinforcements.
3. Much to our surprise, the bird flew _____ our car window.
4. The _____ of our school is very strict.
5. Could you please be _____ so I can hear the speaker?

◆ **P r a c t i c e   9   Writing Your Own** Use each set of words correctly in a sentence of your own.

1. set/sit _____

2. weather/whether _____

3. threw/through _____

4. then/than _____

5. raise/rise _____

CHAPTER REVIEW

You might want to reread your answers to the questions in all the review boxes before you do the following exercises.

◆ **Review P r a c t i c e   1   Identifying** Underline the correct word in each of the following sentences.

1. Simone had (fewer, less) mistakes on her quiz this time.
2. Could you please (were, wear, where) something nice for tonight's banquet?
3. I got all the answers right (accept, except) two.
4. You performed that dance very (good, well).
5. Every time Mel goes (to, too, two) the beach, he gets sunburned.
6. He scraped his knee (bad, badly) on the sidewalk.
7. The doctor recommended a small (does, dose) of the experimental medicine.
8. Sharla has (already, all ready) had her turn on the computer.
9. (Their, There, They're) are too many people in this room to be comfortable.
10. That smell (affects, effects) me in strange ways.

◆ **Review P r a c t i c e   2   Completing** Complete the following sentences with a correct word from all three parts of the list.

1. The nurse told Wilbur to _____ down and try to relax.
2. The _____ should be just fine for our picnic today.
3. _____ all those thorns, I found a rose.

4. I am sure that I don't _____ all the answers to life's questions.

5. If you need help, I can give you my _____.

6. The proudest day of Ricky's life was when he _____ the big test.

7. Whenever you get anxious, _____ deeply.

8. The group had _____ picture taken.

9. If you have a choice, _____ the solution that has the fewest obstacles.

10. Yoshi should _____ those books down before he hurts himself.

◆ *Review P r a c t i c e 3*   **Writing Your Own** Write a paragraph about a recent decision you had to make, explaining what the problem was and why you made the decision you did. Try to use some of the easily confused words from this chapter.

◆ *Review P r a c t i c e 4*   **Editing Through Collaboration** Exchange paragraphs from Review Practice 3 with another student, and do the following:

1. Circle any words used incorrectly.

2. Write the correct form of the word above the error.

Then return the paper to its writer, and use the information in this chapter to correct any confused words in your own paragraph. Record your errors on the Error Log in Appendix 6.

SPELLING

✓ CHECKLIST for Identifying Misspelled Words

> ✔ Do you follow the basic spelling rules?
> ✔ Are all words spelled correctly?

Test Yourself

Correct the misspelled words in the following sentences.

- My cousin just moved to a forign country.
- Your grandmother makes delishous chicken and dumplings.
- Dennis is trying to persuaid me to join his fraternity.
- Winning two years in a row is quite an achievment.
- Eat your vegtables.

(Answers are in Appendix 4.)

If you think back over your education, you will realize that teachers believe spelling is important. There is a good reason they feel that way: Spelling errors send negative messages. Misspellings seem to leap out at readers, creating serious doubts about the writer's abilities in general. Because you will not always have access to spell-checkers—and because spell-checkers do not catch all spelling errors—improving your spelling skills is important.

SPELLING HINTS

The spelling rules in this chapter will help you become a better speller. But first, here are some practical hints that will also help you improve your spelling.

1. Start a personal spelling list of your own. Use the list of commonly misspelled words on pages 654–658 as your starting point.

2. Study the lists of easily confused words in Chapter 54.

3. Avoid all nonstandard expressions (see Chapter 53).

4. Use a dictionary when you run across words you don't know.

5. Run the spell-check program if you are writing on a computer. Keep in mind, however, that spell-check cannot tell if you have incorrectly used one word in place of another (such as *to, too,* or *two*).

REVIEWING HINTS FOR BECOMING A BETTER SPELLER

Name two things you can do immediately to become a better speller.

_____

Why can't you depend on a spell-check program to find every misspelled word?

_____

Practice 1A Identifying Underline the misspelled words in each of the following sentences. Refer to the list of easily confused words in Chapter 54 and to the spelling list in this chapter as necessary.

1. Maria is a beatiful person.

2. Hugo is familar with these math formulas.

3. My mother says there are many different kinds of intelligance.

4. Would you please acompany me to the store?

5. This is a new developement.

Practice 1B Correcting Correct the spelling errors in Practice 1A by rewriting the incorrect sentences.

Practice 2 Completing Fill in each blank in the following sentences with hints that help with spelling.

1. Use a _____ to look up words you don't know.

2. Start a _____ to help you remember words you commonly misspell.

3. You can always use the _____ on your computer, but you should remember that it cannot correct easily confused words, only misspelled words.

4. Try to avoid all _____ English.

5. Study the list of _____ in Chapter _____.

◆ **P r a c t i c e   3   Writing Your Own** Choose the correctly spelled word in each pair, and write a sentence using it. Refer to the spelling list on pages 654–658 if necessary.

1. vaccum/vacuum _____

2. neccessary/necessary _____

3. weird/wicrd _____

4. separate/seperate _____

5. tomorrow/tommorow _____

SPELLING RULES

Four basic spelling rules can help you avoid many misspellings. It pays to spend a little time learning them now.

1. **Words that end in -e:** When adding a suffix beginning with a vowel (*a, e, i, o, u*), drop the final *-e*.

   believe + -ing   =   believing
   include + -ed   =   included (*-e* is from the *-ed*)
   value + -able   =   valuable

   When adding a suffix beginning with a consonant, keep the final *-e*.

   aware + -ness   =   awareness
   improve + -ment   =   improvement
   leisure + -ly   =   leisurely

2. **Words with *ie* and *ei*:** Put *i* before *e* except after *c* or when sounded like *ay* as in *neighbor* and *weigh*.

c + ei	*(no c) + ie*	Exceptions
receive	grieve	height
conceive	niece	leisure

| deceive | friend | foreign |
| neighbor | relief | science |

3. **Words that end in -y:** When adding a suffix to a word that ends in a consonant plus -y, change the y to i.

funny + -er	=	funnier
try + -ed	=	tried
easy + -er	=	easier

4. **Words that double the final consonant:** When adding a suffix starting with a vowel to a one-syllable word, double the final consonant.

big + -est	=	biggest
quit + -er	=	quitter
get + -ing	=	getting

With words of more than one syllable, double the final consonant if (1) the final syllable is stressed and (2) the word ends in a single vowel plus a single consonant.

begin + -ing	=	beginning
admit + -ed	=	admitted
rebel + -ious	=	rebellious

The word *travel* has more than one syllable. Should you double the final consonant? No, you should not, because the stress is on the first syllable (**tra´vel**). The word ends in a vowel and a consonant, but that is not enough. Both parts of the rule must be met.

REVIEWING FOUR BASIC SPELLING RULES

What is the rule for adding a suffix to words ending in -e (such as date + -ing*)?*

_____

_____

What is the rule for spelling ie *and* ei *words (such as* receive, neighbor, *and* friend*)?*

When do you change -y to i before a suffix (such as sunny + *-est)?*

When do you double the final consonant of a word before adding a suffix (such as cut, begin, *or* travel + *-ing)?*

◆ *P r a c t i c e* **4 A** **Identifying** Underline the spelling errors in each of the following sentences.

1. The secretarys went out to lunch together.
2. Your encouragment helped me get through a tough time.
3. Sarah percieved that Fernando was upset.
4. The reason should have occured to you.
5. In winter, Frances likes going on sliegh rides.

◆ *P r a c t i c e* **4 B** **Correcting** Correct the spelling errors in Practice 4A by rewriting the incorrect sentences.

◆ *P r a c t i c e* **5** **Completing** Complete the following spelling rules.

1. With words that end with -*e*, _____ when adding a suffix beginning with a vowel.

2. -*I* comes before -*e* except after _____ or when sounded as _____ as in _____ .

3. With words that end in -*y*, change the _____ to an _____ when adding a suffix to a word that end in a consonant plus -*y*.

4. When adding a suffix that begins with a _____ to a one syllable word, _____ the final consonant.

5. With words that are more than one syllable, _____ the final consonant if (1) the last syllable is stressed, and (2) the word ends in a single vowel plus a single consonant.

◆ ***P r a c t i c e   6*   Writing Your Own** Make a list of words you commonly misspell. Then choose five of the words, and use each correctly in a sentence.

_____

_____

_____

_____

_____

COMMONLY MISSPELLED WORDS

Use the following list of commonly misspelled words to check your spelling when you write.

abbreviate	ache	aisle
absence	achievement	although
accelerate	acknowledgment	aluminum
accessible	acre	amateur
accidentally	actual	ambulance
accommodate	address	ancient
accompany	adequate	anonymous
accomplish	advertisement	anxiety
accumulate	afraid	anxious
accurate	aggravate	appreciate

appropriate	business	competent
approximate	cabbage	competition
architect	cafeteria	complexion
arithmetic	calendar	conceive
artificial	campaign	concession
assassin	canoe	concrete
athletic	canyon	condemn
attach	captain	conference
audience	career	congratulate
authority	carriage	conscience
autumn	cashier	consensus
auxiliary	catastrophe	continuous
avenue	caterpillar	convenience
awkward	ceiling	cooperate
baggage	cemetery	corporation
balloon	census	correspond
banana	certain	cough
bankrupt	certificate	counterfeit
banquet	challenge	courageous
beautiful	champion	courteous
beggar	character	cozy
beginning	chief	criticize
behavior	children	curiosity
benefited	chimney	curious
bicycle	coffee	curriculum
biscuit	collar	cylinder
bought	college	dairy
boundary	column	dangerous
brilliant	commit	dealt
brought	committee	deceive
buoyant	communicate	decision
bureau	community	definition
burglar	comparison	delicious

descend
describe
description
deteriorate
determine
development
dictionary
difficulty
diploma
disappear
disastrous
discipline
disease
dissatisfied
divisional
dormitory
economy
efficiency
eighth
elaborate
electricity
eligible
embarrass
emphasize
employee
encourage
enormous
enough
enthusiastic
envelope
environment
equipment
equivalent

especially
essential
establish
exaggerate
excellent
exceptionally
excessive
exhaust
exhilarating
existence
explanation
extinct
extraordinary
familiar
famous
fascinate
fashion
fatigue
faucet
February
fiery
financial
foreign
forfeit
fortunate
forty
freight
friend
fundamental
gauge
genius
genuine
geography

gnaw
government
graduation
grammar
grief
grocery
gruesome
guarantee
guess
guidance
handkerchief
handsome
haphazard
happiness
harass
height
hesitate
hoping
humorous
hygiene
hymn
icicle
illustrate
imaginary
immediately
immortal
impossible
incidentally
incredible
independence
indispensable
individual
inferior

infinite	lieutenant	niece
influential	lightning	nineteen
initial	likable	ninety
initiation	liquid	noticeable
innocence	listen	nuisance
installation	literature	obedience
intelligence	machinery	obstacle
interfere	magazine	occasion
interrupt	magnificent	occurred
invitation	majority	official
irrelevant	manufacture	omission
irrigate	marriage	omitted
issue	material	opponent
jealous	mathematics	opportunity
jewelry	maximum	opposite
journalism	mayor	original
judgment	meant	outrageous
kindergarten	medicine	pamphlet
knife	message	paragraph
knowledge	mileage	parallel
knuckles	miniature	parentheses
laboratory	minimum	partial
laborious	minute	particular
language	mirror	pastime
laugh	miscellaneous	patience
laundry	mischievous	peculiar
league	miserable	permanent
legible	misspell	persistent
legislature	monotonous	personnel
leisure	mortgage	persuade
length	mysterious	physician
library	necessary	pitcher
license	neighborhood	pneumonia

politician	science	tournament
possess	scissors	tragedy
prairie	secretary	truly
precede	seize	unanimous
precious	separate	undoubtedly
preferred	significant	unique
prejudice	similar	university
previous	skiing	usable
privilege	soldier	usually
procedure	souvenir	vacuum
proceed	sovereign	valuable
pronounce	spaghetti	various
psychology	squirrel	vegetable
publicly	statue	vehicle
questionnaire	stomach	vicinity
quotient	strength	villain
realize	subtle	visible
receipt	succeed	volunteer
recipe	success	weather
recommend	sufficient	Wednesday
reign	surprise	weigh
religious	syllable	weird
representative	symptom	whose
reservoir	technique	width
responsibility	temperature	worst
restaurant	temporary	wreckage
rhyme	terrible	writing
rhythm	theater	yacht
salary	thief	yearn
satisfactory	thorough	yield
scarcity	tobacco	zealous
scenery	tomorrow	zoology
schedule	tongue	

REVIEWING COMMONLY MISSPELLED WORDS

Why is spelling important in your writing?

_____

Start a personal spelling log of your most commonly misspelled words.

_____   _____   _____

_____   _____   _____

_____   _____   _____

Practice   7 A   Identifying Underline any words that are misspelled in the following sentences.

1. My best freind has a tendency to exagerate.
2. If Justin stays on scheduele, he'll be a sophomore next year.
3. My third-grader gets perfect arithmatic scores.
4. She is a very sucessful lawyer.
5. The restarant is undoutedly the finest in town.

Practice   7 B   Correcting Correct any spelling errors that you identified in Practice 7A by rewriting the incorrect sentences.

Practice   8   Completing Correct the spelling errors in the following paragraph.

This past Febuary, an anonimous tip was called into the police station. Apparently, a local politition was having severe finantial difficulties, so he started making counterfit money. There was really no noticible difference between his funny money and real money. He passed the money through his wife's retail company. It was only when the politition became overly enthusiastick about his scam that he got caught. He revealed his scam to another politition, one who did not want the whole goverment to take the fall for one man. So, he called the police and left the anonimous tip. Now the only londry the dirty politition is doing is in jail.

◆ *P r a c t i c e 9* **Writing Your Own** Write a complete sentence for each word listed here.

1. laboratory _____

2. embarrass _____

3. familiar _____

4. hoping _____

5. manufacture _____

CHAPTER REVIEW

You might want to reread your answers to the questions in all the review boxes before you do the following exercises.

◆ *Review P r a c t i c e 1* **Identifying** Underline the misspelled words in each of the following sentences.

1. I always mispel the word "mischeivous."
2. I don't think Chris used good sense in leting his lisence expire.
3. My parents have truely had a good marriege.
4. The new restraunt will offer incredably delishious deserts.
5. In my psichology class, one guy always interupts the profeser.
6. The rhime in that song sounds ridiculous.
7. The recommended salery for a professer is not what it should be these days.
8. I met two curagous war heroes who were interesting to talk to.
9. Professor Barton is an extrordinary teacher.
10. Rafael's parents perfered that he pursue a career in psycology.

◆ *Review P r a c t i c e 2* **Completing** Correct the spelling errors in Review Practice 1 by rewriting the incorrect sentences.

⬥ *Review P r a c t i c e* **3** **Writing Your Own** Write a paragraph explaining how you might go about becoming a better speller. Can you learn how to spell in college? Before college?

⬥ *Review P r a c t i c e* **4** **Editing Through Collaboration** Exchange paragraphs from Review Practice 3 with another student, and do the following:

1. Underline any words that are used incorrectly.

2. Circle any misspelled words.

Then return the paper to its writer, and use the information in this chapter to correct any spelling errors in your own paragraph. Record your errors on the Spelling Log in Appendix 7.

UNIT TESTS

Here are some exercises that test your understanding of all the material in this unit: Standard and Nonstandard English, Easily Confused Words, and Spelling.

Unit Test I

A. Underline the word choice and spelling errors in the following sentences.

1. You shoulda seen the show; it was fantastic.
2. This coat is so big that it feels akward.
3. Dean was embarased by her rude behavior.
4. Many of us live by our principals.
5. Incidentaly, I met someone who says she works with you.
6. I gave the fern fewer water since its soil is still moist.
7. I would love some desert after dinner.
8. Marco felt badly that he'd broken the dish.
9. He prefered to eat at the coffee shop on campus.
10. Could you please advice me on the best course of action?
11. The sackcloth we had to wear in the play was course and itchy.
12. Billy Joel is playing at the arena tommorow night.
13. My mom freaked out when I came in at 5 a.m.

14. Finish your homework, and than you can go to the movies.
15. No exchanges will be made without a reciept.
16. Let's cut class and go catch some rays.
17. My 1968 Corvette is very different than your 1968 Mustang.
18. The children are already to go to the park.
19. Irregardless of the time change, I slept late and was tardy to work.
20. I believe you've had quiet enough cake for today.

B. Correct the errors in Part A by rewriting each incorrect sentence.

Unit Test II

A. Underline the word choice and spelling errors in the following paragraph.

   The number of teenagers and young adults suffering from depression is growing each year. The medical and sikological communities have worked together to try to determine the cause of depresion and to develop treatment options. So far, it is unclear as to weather deppression is caused by genetics or enviurnment or both. Whatever. Irregardless of these dissagreements, most profesionals now beleive that the best treatment option is a combination of therapy and medication. Most people who suffer from depression are able to live healthy, productive lives with litle or no medisin and some kinda therapy. Even so, they're are some people who are a risk to theirselves or others. These folks oughta be hospitlized for a spell. No matter how severe there problems are, people should not be embarrassed about getting help. Anybody who says differently is messed up.

B. Correct the word choice and spelling errors in Part A by rewriting the paragraph.

APPENDIX 1 Critical Thinking Log

Circle the critical thinking questions that you missed after each essay you read. Have your instructor explain the pattern of errors.

Reading	Content	Purpose and Audience	Paragraphs	Number Correct
Describing				
Amy Tan	1 2 3	4 5 6	7 8 9 10	
Alice Walker	1 2 3	4 5 6	7 8 9 10	
Narrating				
Sandra Cisneros	1 2 3	4 5 6	7 8 9 10	
Michael Arredondo	1 2 3	4 5 6	7 8 9 10	
Illustrating				
"Diane"	1 2 3	4 5 6	7 8 9 10	
Brent Staples	1 2 3	4 5 6	7 8 9 10	
Analyzing a Process				
Julia Bourland	1 2 3	4 5 6	7 8 9 10	
Russell Freedman	1 2 3	4 5 6	7 8 9 10	
Comparing and Contrasting				
Ernesto Galarza	1 2 3	4 5 6	7 8 9 10	
Rachel Carson	1 2 3	4 5 6	7 8 9 10	
Dividing and Classifying				
Camille Lavington	1 2 3	4 5 6	7 8 9 10	
Edwin Bliss	1 2 3	4 5 6	7 8 9 10	
Defining				
Richard Rodriguez	1 2 3	4 5 6	7 8 9 10	
Jo Goodwin Parker	1 2 3	4 5 6	7 8 9 10	
Analyzing Causes and Effects				
Linda Lee Andujar	1 2 3	4 5 6	7 8 9 10	
Corky Clifton	1 2 3	4 5 6	7 8 9 10	
Arguing				
Dwight van Avery	1 2 3	4 5 6	7 8 9 10	
Hate Crimes	1 2 3	4 5 6	7 8 9 10	

The legend on the next page will help you identify your strengths and weaknesses in critical thinking.

Legend for Critical Thinking Log

Questions	Skill
1–2	Literal and interpretive understanding
3–6	Critical thinking and analysis
7–9	Analyzing sentences
10	Writing paragraphs

APPENDIX 2A

Revising
Describing
Peer Evaluation Form

Use the following questions to evaluate your partner's paragraph. Direct your comments to your partner.

Writer: _____ **Peer:** _____

Describing

1. Is the dominant impression clearly communicated? If not, how can the writer make it clearer?

2. Does the paragraph *show* rather than *tell?* Explain your answer.

Topic Sentence

3. Does the topic sentence convey the paragraph's controlling idea? Explain your answer.

Development

4. Does the paragraph contain enough specific details to develop the topic sentence? Explain your answer.

Unity

5. Do all the sentences in the paragraph support the topic sentence? Explain your answer.

Organization

6. Is the paragraph organized so that readers can easily follow it? Explain your answer.

Coherence

7. Do the sentences move smoothly and logically from one to the next? Explain your answer.

APPENDIX 2B

Use the following questions to help you find editing errors in your partner's paragraph. Mark the errors directly on your partner's paper using the Editing Symbols on the inside back cover.

Writer: _____ **Peer:** _____

Sentences

1. Does each sentence have a subject and verb?

   Mark any fragments you find with *frag.*

   Put a slash (/) between any fused sentences and comma splices.

2. Do all subjects and verbs agree?

   Mark any subject-verb agreement errors you find with *sv.*

3. Do all pronouns agree with their nouns?

   Mark any pronoun errors you find with *pro agr.*

4. Are all modifiers as close as possible to the words they modify?

   Mark any modifier errors you find with *ad* (adjective or adverb problem), *mm* (misplaced modifier), or *dm* (dangling modifier).

Punctuation and Mechanics

5. Are sentences punctuated correctly?

   Mark any punctuation errors you find with the appropriate symbol under Unit 5 of the Editing Symbols (inside back cover).

6. Are words capitalized properly?

   Mark any capitalization errors you find with *lc* (lowercase) or *cap* (capital).

Word Choice and Spelling

7. Are words used correctly?

   Mark any words that are used incorrectly with *wc* (word choice) or *ww* (wrong word).

8. Are words spelled correctly?

   Mark any misspelled words you find with *sp.*

APPENDIX 2C

Use the following questions to evaluate your partner's paragraph. Direct your comments to your partner.

Writer: _____   **Peer:** _____

Illustrating

1. What is the paragraph's main point? If you're not sure, show the writer how he or she can make the main point clearer.

2. Did the writer choose examples that focus on the main point? If not, which examples need to be changed?

3. Does the writer use a sufficient number of examples to make his or her point? Where can more examples be added?

Topic Sentence

4. Does the topic sentence convey the paragraph's controlling idea? Explain your answer.

Development

5. Does the paragraph contain enough specific details to develop the topic sentence? Explain your answer.

Unity

6. Do all the sentences in the paragraph support the topic sentence? Explain your answer.

Organization

7. Is the paragraph organized so that readers can easily follow it? Explain your answer.

Coherence

8. Do the sentences move smoothly and logically from one to the next? Explain your answer.

APPENDIX 2C

Editing
Illustrating
Peer Evaluation Form

Use the following questions to help you find editing errors in your partner's paragraph. Mark the errors directly on your partner's paper using the Editing Symbols on the inside back cover.

Writer: _____ **Peer:** _____

Sentences

1. Does each sentence have a subject and verb?

   Mark any fragments you find with *frag.*

   Put a slash (/) between any fused sentences and comma splices.

2. Do all subjects and verbs agree?

   Mark any subject-verb agreement errors you find with *sv.*

3. Do all pronouns agree with their nouns?

   Mark any pronoun errors you find with *pro agr.*

4. Are all modifiers as close as possible to the words they modify?

   Mark any modifier errors you find with *ad* (adjective or adverb problem), *mm* (misplaced modifier), or *dm* (dangling modifier).

Punctuation and Mechanics

5. Are sentences punctuated correctly?

   Mark any punctuation errors you find with the appropriate symbol under Unit 5 of the Editing Symbols (inside back cover).

6. Are words capitalized properly?

   Mark any capitalization errors you find with *lc* (lowercase) or *cap* (capital).

Word Choice and Spelling

7. Are words used correctly?

   Mark any words that are used incorrectly with *wc* (word choice) or *ww* (wrong word).

8. Are words spelled correctly?

   Mark any misspelled words you find with *sp.*

Use the following questions to evaluate your partner's paragraph. Direct your comments to your partner.

Writer: _____ _____ **Peer:** _____

Analyzing a Process

1. Does the writer state in the topic sentence what the reader should be able to do or understand by the end of the paragraph? If not, what information does the topic sentence need to be clearer?

2. Does the remainder of the paragraph explain the rest of the process? If not, what seems to be missing?

Topic Sentence

3. Does the topic sentence convey the paragraph's controlling idea? Explain your answer.

Development

4. Does the paragraph contain enough specific details to develop the topic sentence? Explain your answer.

Unity

5. Do all the sentences in the paragraph support the topic sentence? Explain your answer.

Organization

6. Is the paragraph organized in chronological order? Explain your answer.

Coherence

7. Do the sentences move smoothly and logically from one to the next? Explain your answer.

APPENDIX 2D

Editing
Analyzing a Process
Peer Evaluation Form

Use the following questions to help you find editing errors in your partner's paragraph. Mark the errors directly on your partner's paper using the Editing Symbols on the inside back cover.

Writer: _____ **Peer:** _____

Sentences

1. Does each sentence have a subject and verb?

   Mark any fragments you find with *frag.*

   Put a slash (/) between any fused sentences and comma splices.

2. Do all subjects and verbs agree?

   Mark any subject-verb agreement errors you find with *sv.*

3. Do all pronouns agree with their nouns?

   Mark any pronoun errors you find with *pro agr.*

4. Are all modifiers as close as possible to the words they modify?

   Mark any modifier errors you find with *ad* (adjective or adverb problem), *mm* (misplaced modifier), or *dm* (dangling modifier).

Punctuation and Mechanics

5. Are sentences punctuated correctly?

   Mark any punctuation errors you find with the appropriate symbol under Unit 5 of the Editing Symbols (inside back cover).

6. Are words capitalized properly?

   Mark any capitalization errors you find with *lc* (lowercase) or *cap* (capital).

Word Choice and Spelling

7. Are words used correctly?

   Mark any words that are used incorrectly with *wc* (word choice) or *ww* (wrong word).

8. Are words spelled correctly?

   Mark any misspelled words you find with *sp.*

APPENDIX 2E

Use the following questions to evaluate your partner's paragraph. Direct your comments to your partner.

Writer: _____ **Peer:** _____

Comparing and Contrasting

1. Does the paragraph state the point the writer is trying to make with a comparison in the topic sentence? If not, what part of the comparison does the writer need to focus on?

2. Does the writer choose items to compare and contrast that will make his or her point most effectively? What details need to be added to make the comparison more effective?

Topic Sentence

3. Does the topic sentence convey the paragraph's controlling idea? Explain your answer.

Development

4. Does the paragraph contain enough specific details to develop the topic sentence? Explain your answer.

Unity

5. Do all the sentences in the paragraph support the topic sentence? Explain your answer.

Organization

6. Is the paragraph organized either by topics or by points of comparison? Explain your answer.

Coherence

7. Do the sentences move smoothly and logically from one to the next? Explain your answer.

APPENDIX 2E

Editing
Comparing and Contrasting
Peer Evaluation Form

Use the following questions to help you find editing errors in your partner's paragraph. Mark the errors directly on your partner's paper using the Editing Symbols on the inside back cover.

Writer: _____ **Peer:** _____

Sentences

1. Does each sentence have a subject and verb?

   Mark any fragments you find with *frag.*

   Put a slash (/) between any fused sentences and comma splices.

2. Do all subjects and verbs agree?

   Mark any subject-verb agreement errors you find with *sv.*

3. Do all pronouns agree with their nouns?

   Mark any pronoun errors you find with *pro agr.*

4. Are all modifiers as close as possible to the words they modify?

   Mark any modifier errors you find with *ad* (adjective or adverb problem), *mm* (misplaced modifier), or *dm* (dangling modifier).

Punctuation and Mechanics

5. Are sentences punctuated correctly?

   Mark any punctuation errors you find with the appropriate symbol under Unit 5 of the Editing Symbols (inside back cover).

6. Are words capitalized properly?

   Mark any capitalization errors you find with *lc* (lowercase) or *cap* (capital).

Word Choice and Spelling

7. Are words used correctly?

   Mark any words that are used incorrectly with *wc* (word choice) or *ww* (wrong word).

8. Are words spelled correctly?

   Mark any misspelled words you find with *sp.*

APPENDIX 2F

Use the following questions to evaluate your partner's paragraph. Direct your comments to your partner.

Writer: _____   **Peer:** _____

Dividing and Classifying

1. What is the overall purpose for the paragraph, and is it stated in the topic sentence? If not, where does the paragraph need clarification?

2. Does the writer divide the topic into categories (division) and explain each category with details and examples (classification)? If not, where is more division or classification needed?

Topic Sentence

3. Does the topic sentence convey the paragraph's controlling idea? Explain your answer.

Development

4. Does the paragraph contain enough specific details to develop the topic sentence? Explain your answer.

Unity

5. Do all the sentences in the paragraph support the topic sentence? Explain your answer.

Organization

6. Is the paragraph organized so that the categories communicate the meaning clearly? Explain your answer.

Coherence

7. Do the sentences move smoothly and logically from one to the next? Explain your answer.

APPENDIX 2F

Use the following questions to help you find editing errors in your partner's paragraph. Mark the errors directly on your partner's paper using the Editing Symbols on the inside back cover.

Writer: _____ **Peer:** _____

Sentences

1. Does each sentence have a subject and verb?

   Mark any fragments you find with *frag.*

   Put a slash (/) between any fused sentences and comma splices.

2. Do all subjects and verbs agree?

   Mark any subject-verb agreement errors you find with *sv.*

3. Do all pronouns agree with their nouns?

   Mark any pronoun errors you find with *pro agr.*

4. Are all modifiers as close as possible to the words they modify?

   Mark any modifier errors you find with *ad* (adjective or adverb problem), *mm* (misplaced modifier), or *dm* (dangling modifier).

Punctuation and Mechanics

5. Are sentences punctuated correctly?

   Mark any punctuation errors you find with the appropriate symbol under Unit 5 of the Editing Symbols (inside back cover).

6. Are words capitalized properly?

   Mark any capitalization errors you find with *lc* (lowercase) or *cap* (capital).

Word Choice and Spelling

7. Are words used correctly?

   Mark any words that are used incorrectly with *wc* (word choice) or *ww* (wrong word).

8. Are words spelled correctly?

   Mark any misspelled words you find with *sp.*

APPENDIX 2G

Use the following questions to evaluate your partner's paragraph. Direct your comments to your partner.

Writer: _____ _____ **Peer:** _____

Defining

1. Does the paragraph have a clear audience and purpose? What are they? If you are not sure, how can the writer make them clearer?

2. Does the writer define his or her term or idea by synonym, category, or negation? Is this approach effective? Why or why not?

3. Does the writer use examples to expand on his or her definition of the term or idea? Where does the definition need more information?

Topic Sentence

4. Does the topic sentence convey the paragraph's controlling idea? Explain your answer.

Development

5. Does the paragraph contain enough specific details to develop the topic sentence? Explain your answer.

Unity

6. Do all the sentences in the paragraph support the topic sentence? Explain your answer.

Organization

7. Is the paragraph organized so that it communicates the definition as clearly as possible? Explain your answer.

Coherence

8. Do the sentences move smoothly and logically from one to the next? Explain your answer.

APPENDIX 2G

Editing
Defining
Peer Evaluation Form

Use the following questions to help you find editing errors in your partner's paragraph. Mark the errors directly on your partner's paper using the Editing Symbols on the inside back cover.

Writer: _____   **Peer:** _____

Sentences

1. Does each sentence have a subject and verb?

   Mark any fragments you find with *frag.*

   Put a slash (/) between any fused sentences and comma splices.

2. Do all subjects and verbs agree?

   Mark any subject-verb agreement errors you find with *sv.*

3. Do all pronouns agree with their nouns?

   Mark any pronoun errors you find with *pro agr.*

4. Are all modifiers as close as possible to the words they modify?

   Mark any modifier errors you find with *ad* (adjective or adverb problem), *mm* (misplaced modifier), or *dm* (dangling modifier).

Punctuation and Mechanics

5. Are sentences punctuated correctly?

   Mark any punctuation errors you find with the appropriate symbol under Unit 5 of the Editing Symbols (inside back cover).

6. Are words capitalized properly?

   Mark any capitalization errors you find with *lc* (lowercase) or *cap* (capital).

Word Choice and Spelling

7. Are words used correctly?

   Mark any words that are used incorrectly with *wc* (word choice) or *ww* (wrong word).

8. Are words spelled correctly?

   Mark any misspelled words you find with *sp.*

Use the following questions to evaluate your partner's paragraph. Direct your comments to your partner.

Writer: _____ _____ **Peer:** _____

Analyzing Causes and Effects

1. Does the topic sentence make a clear statement about what is being analyzed? If not, what information does it need to be clearer?

2. Does the writer use facts and details to support the topic sentence? What details need to be added?

3. Does the writer include the *real* causes and effects for his or her topic? What details are unnecessary?

Topic Sentence

4. Does the topic sentence convey the paragraph's controlling idea? Explain your answer.

Development

5. Does the paragraph contain enough specific details to develop the topic sentence? Explain your answer.

Unity

6. Do all the sentences in the paragraph support the topic sentence? Explain your answer.

Organization

7. Is the paragraph organized so that it communicates the message as clearly as possible? Explain your answer.

Coherence

8. Do the sentences move smoothly and logically from one to the next? Explain your answer.

APPENDIX 2H

Use the following questions to help you find editing errors in your partner's paragraph. Mark the errors directly on your partner's paper using the Editing Symbols on the inside back cover.

Writer: _____ **Peer:** _____

Sentences

1. Does each sentence have a subject and verb?

   Mark any fragments you find with *frag.*

   Put a slash (/) between any fused sentences and comma splices.

2. Do all subjects and verbs agree?

   Mark any subject-verb agreement errors you find with *sv.*

3. Do all pronouns agree with their nouns?

   Mark any pronoun errors you find with *pro agr.*

4. Are all modifiers as close as possible to the words they modify?

   Mark any modifier errors you find with *ad* (adjective or adverb problem), *mm* (misplaced modifier), or *dm* (dangling modifier).

Punctuation and Mechanics

5. Are sentences punctuated correctly?

   Mark any punctuation errors you find with the appropriate symbol under Unit 5 of the Editing Symbols (inside back cover).

6. Are words capitalized properly?

   Mark any capitalization errors you find with *lc* (lowercase) or *cap* (capital).

Word Choice and Spelling

7. Are words used correctly?

   Mark any words that are used incorrectly with *wc* (word choice) or *ww* (wrong word).

8. Are words spelled correctly?

   Mark any misspelled words you find with *sp.*

APPENDIX 21

Use the following questions to evaluate your partner's paragraph. Direct your comments to your partner.

Writer: _____ **Peer:** _____

Arguing

1. Does the writer state his or her opinion on the subject matter in the topic sentence? What information is missing?

2. Who is the intended audience for this paragraph? Does the writer adequately persuade this audience? Why or why not?

3. Does the writer choose appropriate evidence to support the topic sentence? What evidence is needed? What evidence is unnecessary?

Topic Sentence

4. Does the topic sentence convey the paragraph's controlling idea? Explain your answer.

Development

5. Does the paragraph contain enough specific details to develop the topic sentence? Explain your answer.

Unity

6. Do all the sentences in the paragraph support the topic sentence? Explain your answer.

Organization

7. Is the paragraph organized so that the evidence supports the argument as effectively as possible? Explain your answer.

Coherence

8. Do the sentences move smoothly and logically from one to the next? Explain your answer.

APPENDIX 21

Editing
Arguing
Peer Evaluation Form

Use the following questions to help you find editing errors in your partner's paragraph. Mark the errors directly on your partner's paper using the Editing Symbols on the inside back cover.

Writer: _____ **Peer:** _____

Sentences

1. Does each sentence have a subject and verb?

   Mark any fragments you find with *frag.*

   Put a slash (/) between any fused sentences and comma splices.

2. Do all subjects and verbs agree?

   Mark any subject-verb agreement errors you find with *sv.*

3. Do all pronouns agree with their nouns?

   Mark any pronoun errors you find with *pro agr.*

4. Are all modifiers as close as possible to the words they modify?

   Mark any modifier errors you find with *ad* (adjective or adverb problem), *mm* (misplaced modifier), or *dm* (dangling modifier).

Punctuation and Mechanics

5. Are sentences punctuated correctly?

   Mark any punctuation errors you find with the appropriate symbol under Unit 5 of the Editing Symbols (inside back cover).

6. Are words capitalized properly?

   Mark any capitalization errors you find with *lc* (lowercase) or *cap* (capital).

Word Choice and Spelling

7. Are words used correctly?

   Mark any words that are used incorrectly with *wc* (word choice) or *ww* (wrong word).

8. Are words spelled correctly?

   Mark any misspelled words you find with *sp.*

APPENDIX 3A

Use the following questions to evaluate your partner's essay. Direct your comments to your partner.

Writer: _____ **Peer:** _____

Thesis Statement

1. Does the thesis statement contain the paragraph's controlling idea and appear as the first or last sentence in the introduction? Explain your answer.

Basic Elements

2. Does the writer include effective basic elements (title, introduction, single-topic paragraphs, conclusion)? Explain your answer.

Development

3. Is the essay adequately developed (thesis, specific and enough details)? Explain your answer.

Unity

4. Is the essay unified (topics relate to thesis and sentences in paragraphs relate to topic sentences)? Explain your answer.

Organization

5. Is the essay organized logically (including the paragraphs within the essay)? Explain your answer.

Coherence

6. Do the paragraphs and sentences move smoothly and logically from one to the next? Explain your answer.

APPENDIX 3A

Use the following questions to help you find editing errors in your partner's essay. Mark the errors directly on your partner's paper using the Editing Symbols on the inside back cover.

Writer: _____ **Peer:** _____

Sentences

1. Does each sentence have a subject and verb?

    Mark any fragments you find with *frag.*

    Put a slash (/) between any fused sentences or comma splices.

2. Do all subjects and verbs agree?

    Mark any subject-verb agreement errors you find with *sv.*

3. Do all pronouns agree with their nouns?

    Mark any pronoun errors you find with *pro agr.*

4. Are all modifiers as close as possible to the words they modify?

    Mark any modifier errors you find with *ad* (adjective or adverb problem), *mm* (misplaced modifier), or *dm* (dangling modifier).

Punctuation and Mechanics

5. Are sentences punctuated correctly?

    Mark any punctuation errors you find with the appropriate symbol under Unit 5 of the Editing Symbols (inside back cover).

6. Are words capitalized properly?

    Mark any capitalization errors you find with *lc* (lowercase) or *cap* (capital).

Word Choice and Spelling

7. Are words used correctly?

    Mark any words that are used incorrectly with *wc* (word choice) or *ww* (wrong word).

8. Are words spelled correctly?

    Mark any misspelled words you find with *sp.*

APPENDIX 4

Here are the answers to the Test Yourself questions from the beginning of each chapter in the Handbook (Part V). Where are your strengths? Where are your weaknesses?

Introduction: Parts of Speech (p. 359)

The personality trait that I like best about myself is my healthy sense of humor. No matter how bad a situation is, I can usually say something funny to everyone. When Toby's ancient car was stolen, I told him it was a piece of junk anyway and I felt sorry for the foolish person who stole it. Man, we laughed so hard, imagining the thief stalled on the side of the road somewhere in town. Oh, there are some things that I don't ever joke about, like death and diseases. A person would be extremely insensitive to joke about those situations.

Introduction: Phrases (p. 376)

After the concert, to get some food

To get a good grade on the test to study

in the brick house at the end of the block behind the park

am going to get a job this year

Do want to see a movie with us

Introduction: Clauses (p. 378)

Mallory will get what she wants out of life because she is assertive

Since you don't have time to go to dinner I'll bring you some food

If Rachel is going to leave first she needs a map

We finished painting then we celebrated

I enjoyed the book the most when Harry Potter got the sorcerer's stone

Chapter 30: Subjects and Verbs (p. 383)

(We) really **liked** the movie.

(Melissa) and **Tracy** **left** early.

(She) **is** in class.

Clean your room. (implied (You))

The (Masons) **have** never **remodeled** their kitchen.

(She) **checked** the oil and **put** air in the tires.

Chapter 31: Fragments (p. 392)

_____   We were hoping that the test would be easy.

___X___   Which he did not see at first.

_____   She wanted to become a musician.

___X___   Running to catch the plane, with her suitcase flying.

___X___   Since the newspaper had reported it.

Chapter 32: Fused Sentences and Comma Splices (p. 408)

Jennifer was elected Academic President, / I voted for her.

The beach is a great getaway / we're fortunate it's only 45 minutes away.

He wanted to participate, but he wasn't sure of the rules.

Casey is hard to get to know / she hides her thoughts and feelings well.

I hope I get into Dr. Jones's class, / I hear he's the best teacher to get.

Chapter 33: Regular and Irregular Verbs (p. 419)

___X___   We **brang** our new neighbor a pizza for dinner.

_____   My brother **married** on February 14—Valentine's Day.

   X   He **drug** the heavy suitcase down the street.

   X   This CD **costed** $15.

   X   My roommate's water bed **has sprang** a leak.

Chapter 34: Verb Tense (p. 431)

   X   We **be planning** on leaving in the morning.

          The team **chose** an alligator as its mascot.

   X   My sister **practice** the flute every day.

   X   He **don't** look old enough to drive.

   X   Over 1,000 students **apply** to my college this year.

Chapter 35: Subject-Verb Agreement (p. 447)

   X   **Ben** and **Tess has** become great friends.

   X   **Each** of the nurses **are** with a patient.

   X   **Macaroni and cheese are** my favorite food.

          There **are** two **trains** to Baltimore in the morning.

   X   **Everyone are** ready to leave.

Chapter 36: More on Verbs (p. 462)

   I   When my brother won the gold medal, my father looks very proud.

   P   All new employees are trained by a professional.

   P   The child was saved by the firefighters.

   I   My friend got home early, so we go to the movies.

   P   The student was given the answers in advance.

Chapter 37: Pronoun Problems (p. 470)

The toy was ~~hers'~~ hers to begin with.

Diego told Megan and ~~I~~ me the funniest story.

He can run a lot faster than ~~me~~ I.

Those ~~there~~ ballet shoes are Laura's.

Ted and ~~me~~ I are going to the game tonight.

Chapter 38: Pronoun Reference and Point of View (p. 482)

Emily and Grace decided that <u>she</u> would try out for the team.

<u>They</u> say <u>you</u> should drink eight glasses of water a day.

I take the bus because <u>you</u> can save a lot of money that way.

The reporter did not check <u>her</u> facts or talk to the main witness, which <u>she</u> regretted.

<u>It</u> says to notify the dean if <u>you</u> are dropping a class.

Chapter 39: Pronoun Agreement (p. 490)

Harriett and Maureen walked <u>their</u> dogs in the park.

Each person is responsible for <u>their</u> own transportation.

Although the pieces of furniture were used, <u>it</u> looked new.

Someone left <u>their</u> dirty dishes in the sink.

Everyone contributed <u>his</u> work to the assignment.

Chapter 40: Adjectives (p. 499)

The <u>gray</u> stingrays were very <u>beautiful</u>.

We were <u>more happier</u> when the rain cooled the <u>hot</u> day.

This is the **worstest** cold I've ever had.

This textbook is **more better** than **that** one.

She is the **oldest** of the **two** sisters.

Chapter 41: Adverbs (p. 510)

We were led **quickly** out the back door.

He hugged her **tight** when he saw her.

Tina left **early** because she was**n't** feeling **good.**

She feels **badly** that she could**n't** stay.

I ca**n't never** meet on Tuesdays because I work that night.

Chapter 42: Modifier Errors (p. 524)

When we arrived at the concert, Sandy told her mother **that she should call home**.

Before going to the store, the car needed gas.

The teacher told the students their grades would be posted **before she dismissed them**.

To enter the contest, the application must be submitted by Friday.

We found the magazine and put it in a safe place **that had an article about saving money**.

Chapter 43: End Punctuation (p. 532)

That car almost hit us!

How can you say that?

She didn't want to go on the trip.

He asked if he could go.

I absolutely refuse to be a part of this!

Chapter 44: Commas (p. 539)

We went to the plaza, and we saw a great movie.

When we get really tired, we act really silly.

"He's taking flying lessons," said Steven.

The job market, however, is starting to look better.

On Saturday, we went hiking, fishing, and camping.

He was born August 5, 1985, in Duluth, Minnesota.

Chapter 45: Apostrophes (p. 554)

The followers went into their leader's home.

It's not important that you understand its every function.

That's not a good enough reason to believe Tracy's story.

The children's toys were scattered around the room.

Charles's party was a lot of fun.

Chapter 46: Quotation Marks (p. 563)

"Let's have a picnic," she said.

My mom screamed, "Tom! Get this spider!"

"Put ice on the muscle," said Dr. Jansen, "as soon as possible."

I read three poems, including "The Groundhog."

Derek said, "I'll make dinner."

Chapter 47: Other Punctuation Marks (p. 572)

Matthew turned his paper in early; Erica decided not to turn in a paper at all.

Dave felt sorry for the defendant; however, he had to vote for a conviction.

Aaron needed several items for his dorm room: a comforter, new sheets, a lamp, and a rug.

Inez had only two words to say about bungee jumping— "Never again."

The recipe says to fold (gently mix) the berries into the batter.

Chapter 48: Capitalization (p. 584)

The Smith family lives on Washington Street.

We fly into Newark Airport and then get a taxi to Seton Hall University.

This term I'm taking Spanish, Biology 200, history, and English.

In June, I drove to California in my Dodge Durango.

We read several plays by Shakespeare, including *Hamlet.*

Chapter 49: Abbreviations and Numbers (p. 591)

Governor Davis is trying to protect water in this state.

My dog had **four** puppies.

Over **1,212** people attended.

After college, I hope to join the **CIA.**

Crystal just moved to the **United States** from Spain.

Chapter 50: Varying Sentence Structure (p. 600)

Answers will vary.

Chapter 51: Parallelism (p. 608)

We decided **to forget about the lawsuit** and then **moving on with our lives**.

Last year, I **graduated from college**, **moved from Texas to California**, and **have been married**.

My sister and brother raise money **to feed the homeless** and **for building a new shelter**.

Exercising, **eating right**, and **water** will improve a person's health.

Jack went back to school **because he wanted to get a better job** and **because of the girls on campus**.

Chapter 52: Combining Sentences (p. 614)

Answers will vary.

Chapter 53: Standard and Nonstandard English (p. 628)

So she **goes**, can't I meet you at the theater? **(slang)**

Julie **be planning** the farewell party. **(incorrect)**

We were totally **grossed out**. **(slang)**

They changed the tire **theirselves**. **(incorrect)**

We're **jamming** in the morning. **(slang)**

Chapter 54: Easily Confused Words (p. 638)

I have to **accept** that I won't be graduating this spring.

Whose bike is this?

I'm not saying **it's** Johnny's fault.

We are going to need **their** help.

Where did you say your parents lived?

Chapter 55: Spelling (p. 649)

My cousin just moved to a ~~forign~~ foreign country.

Your grandmother makes ~~delishous~~ delicious chicken and dumplings.

Dennis is trying to ~~persuaid~~ persuade me to join his fraternity.

Winning two years in a row is quite an ~~achievment~~ achievement.

Eat your ~~vegtables~~ vegetables.

APPENDIX **5** Editing Quotient Error Chart

Put an X in the square that corresponds to each question that you missed.

	a	b	c	d	e	f
1						
2						
3						
4						
5						
6						
7						
8						
9						
10						

Then record your errors in the categories below to find out where you might need help.

Fragments

1a _____ 1b _____ 2c _____ 2e _____ 3d _____

4a _____ 6b _____ 7e _____ 8b _____ 9e _____

10a _____ 10c _____

Run-togethers

1c _____ 1d _____ 2a _____ 3b _____ 4f _____

5a _____ 5d _____ 6d _____ 7b _____ 7c _____

8d _____ 9b _____ 10b _____

Subject-verb agreement   2b _____ 2d _____ 9d _____

Verb forms   3a _____ 3e _____

Pronoun agreement   4b _____ 4c _____ 4d _____ 4e _____ 10f _____

Modifiers	5b _____	5c _____	
End punctuation	6e _____		
Commas	6c _____	9f _____	10e _____
Capitalization	6a _____	9a _____	
Abbreviations	7d _____		
Numbers	3c _____	7a _____	
Confused words	8e _____	9c _____	
Spelling	8a _____	8c _____	10d _____

APPENDIX 6 Error Log

List any grammar, punctuation, and mechanics errors you make in your writing on the following chart. Then, to the right of this label, record (1) the actual error from your writing, (2) the rule for correcting this error, and (3) your correction.

Error	**Example** I went to the new seafood restaurant and I ordered the lobster.
Comma	**Rule** Always use a comma before a coordinating conjunction when joining two independent clauses.
	Correction I went to the new seafood restaurant, and I ordered the lobster.
Error	**Example**
	Rule
	Correction
Error	**Example**
	Rule
	Correction
Error	**Example**
	Rule
	Correction
Error	**Example**
	Rule
	Correction
Error	**Example**
	Rule
	Correction
Error	**Example**
	Rule
	Correction
Error	**Example**
	Rule
	Correction

Error	Example
	Rule
	Correction
Error	Example
	Rule
	Correction
Error	Example
	Rule
	Correction
Error	Example
	Rule
	Correction
Error	Example
	Rule
	Correction
Error	Example
	Rule
	Correction
Error	Example
	Rule
	Correction
Error	Example
	Rule
	Correction

APPENDIX 7 Spelling Log

On this chart, record any words you misspell, and write the correct spelling in the space next to the misspelled word. In the right column, write a note to yourself to help you remember the correct spelling. (See the first line for an example.) Refer to this chart as often as necessary to avoid misspelling the same words again.

Misspelled Word	Correct Spelling	Definition/Notes
there	their	there = place; their = pronoun; they're = "they are"

CREDITS ❖

INDEX ❖